P9-DCO-695

Node.js in Action

MIKE CANTELON
MARC HARTER
T.J. HOLOWAYCHUK
NATHAN RAJLICH

MANNING
SHELTER ISLAND

For online information and ordering of this and other Manning books, please visit www.manning.com. The publisher offers discounts on this book when ordered in quantity. For more information, please contact

Special Sales Department
Manning Publications Co.
20 Baldwin Road
PO Box 261
Shelter Island, NY 11964
Email: orders@manning.com

©2014 by Manning Publications Co. All rights reserved.

No part of this publication may be reproduced, stored in a retrieval system, or transmitted, in any form or by means electronic, mechanical, photocopying, or otherwise, without prior written permission of the publisher.

Many of the designations used by manufacturers and sellers to distinguish their products are claimed as trademarks. Where those designations appear in the book, and Manning Publications was aware of a trademark claim, the designations have been printed in initial caps or all caps.

♾ Recognizing the importance of preserving what has been written, it is Manning's policy to have the books we publish printed on acid-free paper, and we exert our best efforts to that end. Recognizing also our responsibility to conserve the resources of our planet, Manning books are printed on paper that is at least 15 percent recycled and processed without the use of elemental chlorine.

Manning Publications Co.
20 Baldwin Road
PO Box 261
Shelter Island, NY 11964

Development editor: Renae Gregoire
Copyeditor: Andy Carroll
Proofreader: Katie Tennant
Typesetter: Dottie Marsico
Cover designer: Marija Tudor

ISBN 9781617290572
Printed in the United States of America
1 2 3 4 5 6 7 8 9 10 – MAL – 18 17 16 15 14 13

brief contents

contents

foreword

Writing a book about Node.js is a challenging endeavor. It's a relatively new platform, just now attaining stability. The Node.js core continues to evolve, and the community of user-created modules is exploding at a pace that no one can hope to keep track of. The community is still finding its voice. The only way to catch such a moving target in print is to get at the essence of what Node is, and why it has been succeeding as it has. These Node.js veterans have done just that. Mike Cantelon is extremely active in the Node community, experimenting with and speaking about Node. He has an excellent grasp on what Node is good for, and perhaps more importantly, what it isn't good for. T.J. Holowaychuk is one of the most prolific authors of Node.js modules, including the massively popular Express web framework. Nathan Rajlich, better known to many as TooTallNate, has been a Node.js core committer for some time now and is an active part of the development of the platform as it has matured into its current state.

This book draws on their considerable experience, taking you from the very first steps of installing Node.js on your computer all the way to creating, debugging, and deploying production applications. You'll learn what makes Node interesting and get a glimpse into the authors' combined understanding, so that the future directions the Node project takes will make sense. Most importantly, the content ramps up nicely from basic to advanced, building on prior learning at each stage.

Node is an ascending rocket, and the authors have done a great job of bringing you along for the ride. Think of *Node.js in Action* as the launching pad from which to explore your own horizons.

ISAAC Z. SCHLUETER
NPM AUTHOR
NODE.JS PROJECT LEAD

preface

In early 2011, when Manning approached us with the idea of writing a book on Node.js, the state of the Node community was much different than it is now. The community was small and, despite the fact that Node was starting to attract a great deal of interest, Node was still considered a bleeding-edge technology by the mainstream development community. No books had yet been written about it, and although the idea of writing a book was daunting, we decided to go for it.

Given our respective development inclinations, we wanted to create a book that not only focused on the use of Node for web application development, but also explored other interesting potential uses. We wanted to provide a way for web application developers using conventional technologies to harness Node's vision of bringing asynchronous development to the server.

We've worked for more than two years on the book, and during its writing the technology has evolved, so we've updated the book accordingly. In addition to the technology changing, the community has also evolved. It is now much larger, and many established companies have embraced Node.

For web application developers looking to try something different, this is a great time to learn Node, and we hope our book helps you learn the technology quickly and have fun doing so.

acknowledgments

Thanks are due to the great people at Manning for their role in the creation of this book. Renae Gregoire played a major role, pushing us toward eloquence, clarity, and quality. Bert Bates helped define the book's visual feel, working with us to design graphics expressing various concepts presented in the book. Marjan Bace and Michael Stephens believed in us enough to entrust us with the creation of the book and helped keep the project moving. And Manning's editorial, production, and technical staff were amazing to work with.

Many people reviewed the manuscript in various stages of its development, and we would like to thank them for their feedback. This includes our MEAP readers who posted comments and corrections in the book's online forum, and the following reviewers who read the manuscript multiple times and whose insights and comments helped make this a much better book: Àlex Madurell, Bert Thomas, Bradley Meck, Braj Panda, Brian L. Cooley, Brian Del Vecchio, Brian Dillard, Brian Ehmann, Brian Falk, Daniel Bretoi, Gary Ewan Park, Jeremy Martin, Jeroen Nouws, Jeroen Trappers, Kassandra Perch, Kevin Baister, Michael Piscatello, Patrick Steger, Paul Stack, and Scott Banachowski.

Thanks also to Valentin Crettaz and Michael Levin for their careful technical proofread of the final manuscript, shortly before it went into production. Last but not least, we'd like to thank Isaac Schlueter, Node Project Lead, for contributing the foreword to our book.

MIKE CANTELON

I'd like to thank my friend Joshua Paul for giving me my first break in the tech industry, introducing me to the world of open source, and encouraging me to write a book.

I'd also like to thank my partner Malcolm for encouraging me during the book's creation and for her patience during the times when writing kept me constantly cooped up at home. A big thanks, as well, to my parents for bringing me up with a passion for creativity and exploration, and for putting up with my less-than-balanced childhood obsession with 8-bit machines. I'd also like to thank my grandparents for gifting me with the machine that got me hooked, for life, on programming: the Commodore 64.

During the process of writing the book, T.J. and Nathan's expertise was invaluable and their good humor much appreciated. I thank them for taking a leap of faith and agreeing to collaborate. Marc Harter was also a huge help, chipping in on the Herculean task of editing, proofing, and writing content that tied everything together.

MARC HARTER

Thanks to Ryan Dahl, who inspired me to take a serious look at server-side JavaScript programming nearly four years ago. Thanks to Ben Noordhuis, an invaluable resource on the inner workings of Node. Thanks to Bert Bates, who believed in me, challenged me, and was always willing to help during the writing process. Thanks to Mike, Nate, and T.J. for welcoming me in at the 11th hour. It was an honor working with them. Thanks especially to my wife and friend Hannah, whose courage and kindness carried me into and through this new venture.

NATHAN RAJLICH

I would like to start by thanking Guillermo Rauch for taking me in and helping me find my place in the Node.js community. I would also like to thank David Blickstein for encouraging me to take on this book project. I thank Ryan Dahl for starting the Node.js movement, and Isaac Schlueter for doing an excellent job of stewarding this ship for the last couple for years. Thanks also to my family, my friends, and my girlfriend for putting up with the sleepless nights and wide range of emotions exhibited during the process. And of course a huge thanks to my parents for supporting me throughout the years in my computing endeavors. I wouldn't be where I am today without them at my side.

about this book

Node.js in Action's primary purpose is to teach you to how to create and deploy Node applications, with a focus on web applications. A considerable part of the book focuses on the Express web application framework and the Connect middleware framework because of their usefulness and community support. You'll also learn how to create automated tests for, and how to deploy, your applications.

This book is targeted toward experienced web application developers who are interested in creating responsive, scalable applications using Node.js.

Because Node.js applications are written using JavaScript, a working knowledge of the language is a prerequisite. Familiarity with the Windows, OS X, or Linux command line is also recommended.

Roadmap

This book is organized into three parts.

Part 1 provides an introduction to Node.js, teaching the fundamental techniques needed to develop with it. Chapter 1 explains the characteristics of Node and steps through some example code. Chapter 2 guides the reader through the creation of an example application. Chapter 3 explains the challenges of Node.js development, provides techniques for overcoming them, and teaches ways to organize application code.

Part 2 is the largest in the book and focuses on web application development. Chapter 4 teaches the basics of creating Node-driven web applications, and chapter 5 talks about how to store application data using Node.

Part 2 then continues into the world of web-related frameworks. Chapter 6 introduces the Connect framework, explaining its benefits and how it works. Chapter 7 teaches how various built-in Connect framework components can be used to add functionality to web applications. Chapters 8 provides an introduction to the Express framework, and chapter 9 guides the reader through advanced Express usage.

With the basics of web development covered, part 2 concludes after exploring two more related topics. Chapter 10 guides the reader through the use of various Node testing frameworks. Chapter 11 then teaches how templating can be used in Node web applications to separate presentation of data from logic.

Part 3 moves on to look at things beyond web development that can be done with Node. Chapter 12 talks about how Node applications can be deployed to production servers, how uptime can be maintained, and how performance can be maximized. Chapter 13 explains how non-HTTP applications can be created, how to use the Socket.io framework to create real-time applications, and the use of a number of handy build-in Node APIs. Chapter 14, the final chapter, discusses how the Node community works and how Node creations can be published using the Node Package Manager.

Code conventions and downloads

The code in this book follows common JavaScript conventions. Spaces, rather than tabs, are used for indentation. Lines longer than 80 characters are avoided. In many listings, the code is annotated to point out key concepts.

A single statement per line is used and semicolons are added at the end of simple statements. For blocks of code, where one or more statements are enclosed in curly braces, the left curly brace is placed at the end of the opening line of the block. The right curly brace is indented so it's vertically aligned with the opening line of the block.

Source code for the examples in this book is available for download from the publisher's website at www.manning.com/Node.jsinAction.

Author Online

Purchase of *Node.js in Action* includes free access to a private web forum run by Manning Publications where you can make comments about the book, ask technical questions, and receive help from the authors and from other users. To access the forum and subscribe to it, point your web browser to www.manning.com/Node.jsinAction. This page provides information on how to get on the forum once you're registered, what kind of help is available, and the rules of conduct on the forum.

Manning's commitment to our readers is to provide a venue where a meaningful dialog between individual readers and between readers and the authors can take place. It's not a commitment to any specific amount of participation on the part of the authors, whose contribution to the forum remains voluntary (and unpaid). We suggest you try asking the authors some challenging questions lest their interest stray!

The Author Online forum and the archives of previous discussions will be accessible from the publisher's website as long as the book is in print.

about the cover illustration

The figure on the cover of *Node.js in Action* is captioned "Man about Town." The illustration is taken from a nineteenth-century edition of Sylvain Maréchal's four-volume compendium of regional dress customs published in France. Each illustration is finely drawn and colored by hand. The rich variety of Maréchal's collection reminds us vividly of how culturally apart the world's towns and regions were just 200 years ago. Isolated from each other, people spoke different dialects and languages. Whether on city streets, in small towns, or in the countryside, it was easy to identify where they lived and what their trade or station in life was just by their dress.

Dress codes have changed since then and the diversity by region and class, so rich at the time, has faded away. It is now hard to tell apart the inhabitants of different continents, let alone different towns or regions. Perhaps we have traded cultural diversity for a more varied personal life—certainly for a more varied and fast-paced technological life.

At a time when it is hard to tell one computer book from another, Manning celebrates the inventiveness and initiative of the computer business with book covers based on the rich diversity of regional life of two centuries ago, brought back to life by Maréchal's pictures.

Part 1

Node fundamentals

When learning a programming language or framework, you'll often encounter new concepts that require you to think about things in a new way. Node is no exception, as it takes a new approach to a number of aspects of application development.

The first part of this book will outline exactly how Node is different from other platforms and will teach the basics of its use. You'll learn what applications created in Node look like, how they're organized, and how to deal with development challenges specific to Node. What you learn in part 1 will give you the foundation needed to learn how to create web applications in Node, detailed in part 2, and how to create nonweb applications, discussed in part 3.

1 Welcome to Node.js

> ***This chapter covers***
> - What Node.js is
> - JavaScript on the server
> - The asynchronous and evented nature of Node
> - Types of applications Node is designed for
> - Sample Node programs

So what is Node.js? It's likely you've heard the term. Maybe you already use Node. Maybe you're curious about it. At this point in time, Node is very popular and young (it debuted in 2009). It's the second-most-watched project on GitHub (https://github.com/joyent/node), it has quite a following in its Google group (http://groups.google.com/group/nodejs) and IRC channel (http://webchat.freenode.net/?channels=node.js), and it has more than 15,000 community modules published in NPM, the package manager (http://npmjs.org). All this to say, *there's considerable traction behind this platform.*

> **RYAN DAHL ON NODE** You can watch the first presentation on Node by creator Ryan Dahl on the JSCONF Berlin 2009 website: http://jsconf.eu/2009/video_nodejs_by_ryan_dahl.html.

The official website (http://www.nodejs.org) defines Node as "a platform built on Chrome's JavaScript runtime for easily building fast, scalable network applications. Node.js uses an event-driven, non-blocking I/O model that makes it lightweight and efficient, perfect for data-intensive real-time applications that run across distributed devices."

In this chapter, we'll look at these concepts:

- Why JavaScript matters for server-side development
- How the browser handles I/O using JavaScript
- How Node handles I/O on the server
- What's meant by *DIRTy* applications, and why they're a good fit for Node
- A sampling of a few basic Node programs

Let's first turn our attention to JavaScript...

1.1 Built on JavaScript

For better or worse, JavaScript is the world's most popular programming language.[1] If you've done any programming for the web, it's unavoidable. JavaScript, because of the sheer reach of the web, has fulfilled the "write once, run anywhere" dream that Java had back in the 1990s.

Around the time of the Ajax revolution in 2005, JavaScript went from being a "toy" language to something people wrote real and significant programs with. Some of the notable firsts were Google Maps and Gmail, but today there are a host of web applications from Twitter to Facebook to GitHub.

Since the release of Google Chrome in late 2008, JavaScript performance has improved at an incredibly fast rate due to heavy competition between browser vendors (Mozilla, Microsoft, Apple, Opera, and Google). The performance of these modern JavaScript virtual machines is literally changing the types of applications you can build on the web.[2] A compelling, and frankly mind-blowing, example of this is jslinux,[3] a PC emulator running in JavaScript where you can load a Linux kernel, interact with the terminal session, and compile a C program, all in your browser.

Node uses V8, the virtual machine that powers Google Chrome, for server-side programming. V8 gives Node a huge boost in performance because it cuts out the middleman, preferring straight compilation into native machine code over executing bytecode or using an interpreter. Because Node uses JavaScript on the server, there are also other benefits:

- Developers can write web applications in one language, which helps by reducing the context switch between client and server development, and allowing for code sharing between client and server, such as reusing the same code for form validation or game logic.
- JSON is a very popular data interchange format today and is native to JavaScript.

---

1 See "JavaScript: Your New Overlord" on YouTube: www.youtube.com/watch?v=Trurfqh_6fQ.

2 See the "Chrome Experiments" page for some examples: www.chromeexperiments.com/.

3 Jslinux, a JavaScript PC emulator: http://bellard.org/jslinux/.

- JavaScript is the language used in various NoSQL databases (such as CouchDB and MongoDB), so interfacing with them is a natural fit (for example, MongoDB's shell and query language is JavaScript; CouchDB's map/reduce is JavaScript).
- JavaScript is a compilation target, and there are a number of languages that compile to it already.[4]
- Node uses one virtual machine (V8) that keeps up with the ECMAScript standard.[5] In other words, you don't have to wait for all the browsers to catch up to use new JavaScript language features in Node.

Who knew JavaScript would end up being a compelling language for writing server-side applications? Yet, due to its sheer reach, performance, and other characteristics mentioned previously, Node has gained a lot of traction. JavaScript is only one piece of the puzzle though; the *way* Node uses JavaScript is even more compelling. To understand the Node environment, let's dive into the JavaScript environment you're most familiar with: the browser.

1.2 Asynchronous and evented: the browser

Node provides an event-driven and asynchronous platform for server-side JavaScript. It brings JavaScript to the server in much the same way a browser brings JavaScript to the client. It's important to understand how the browser works in order to understand how Node works. Both are event-driven (they use an event loop) and non-blocking when handling I/O (they use asynchronous I/O). Let's look an example to explain what that means.

> **EVENT LOOPS AND ASYNCHRONOUS I/O** For more about event loops and asynchronous I/O, see the relevant Wikipedia articles at http://en.wikipedia.org/wiki/Event_loop and http://en.wikipedia.org/wiki/Asynchronous_I/O.

Take this common snippet of jQuery performing an Ajax request using XMLHttpRequest (XHR):

```
$.post('/resource.json', function (data) {     <- I/O doesn't block execution
  console.log(data);
  });
  // script execution continues
```

This program performs an HTTP request for resource.json. When the response comes back, an anonymous function is called (the "callback" in this context) containing the argument `data`, which is the data received from that request.

Notice that the code was *not* written like this:

```
var data = $.post('/resource.json');     <- I/O blocks execution until finished
  console.log(data);
```

[4] See the "List of languages that compile to JS": https://github.com/jashkenas/coffee-script/wiki/List-of-languages-that-compile-to-JS.

[5] For more about the ECMAScript standard, see Wikipedia: http://en.wikipedia.org/wiki/ECMAScript.

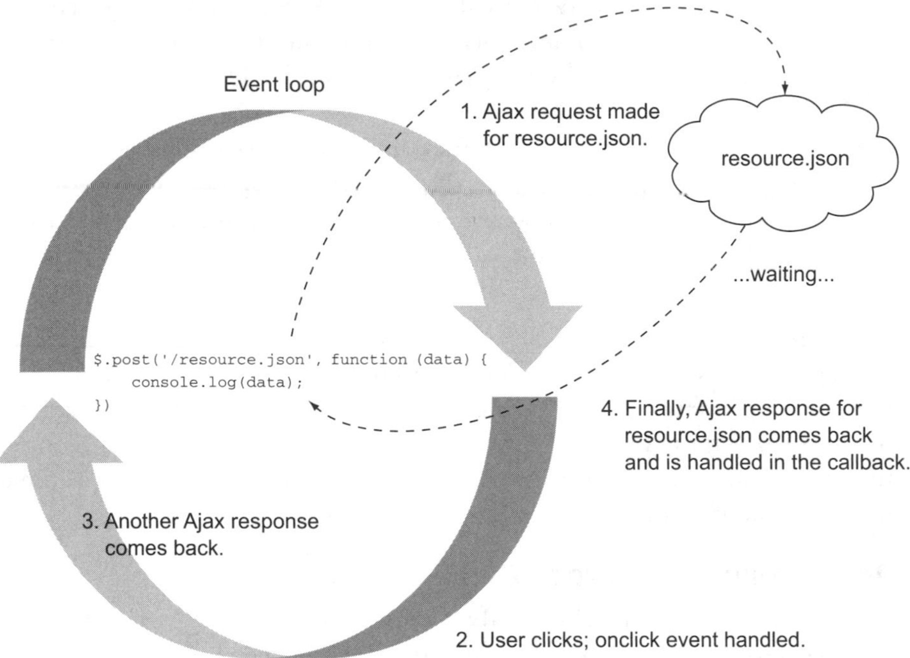

Figure 1.1 An example of non-blocking I/O in the browser

In this example, the assumption is that the response for resource.json would be stored in the `data` variable *when it is ready* and that the `console.log` function *will not execute until then.* The I/O operation (the Ajax request) would "block" script execution from continuing until ready. Because the browser is single-threaded, if this request took 400 ms to return, any other events happening on that page would wait until then before execution. You can imagine the poor user experience if an animation was paused or the user was trying to interact with the page somehow.

Thankfully, that's not the case. When I/O happens in the browser, it happens outside of the event loop (outside the main script execution) and then an "event" is emitted when the I/O is finished,[6] which is handled by a function (often called the "callback") as shown in figure 1.1.

The I/O happens asynchronously and doesn't "block" the script execution, allowing the event loop to respond to whatever other interactions or requests are being performed on the page. This enables the browser to be responsive to the client and to handle a lot of interactivity on the page.

Make a note of that, and let's switch over to the server.

[6] Note that there are a few exceptions that "block" execution in the browser, and their use is typically discouraged: alert, prompt, confirm, and synchronous XHR.

1.3 Asynchronous and evented: the server

For the most part, you're likely to be familiar with a conventional I/O model for server-side programming, like the "blocking" jQuery example in section 1.2. Here's an example of how it looks in PHP:

```
$result = mysql_query('SELECT * FROM myTable');
  print_r($result);
```

Execution stops until DB query completes

This code does some I/O, and the process is blocked from continuing until all the data has come back. For many applications this model is fine and is easy to follow. What may not be apparent is that the process has state, or memory, and is essentially doing nothing until the I/O is completed. That could take anywhere from 10 ms to minutes depending on the latency of the I/O operation. Latency can also result from unexpected causes:

- The disk is performing a maintenance operation, pausing reads/writes.
- A database query is slower because of increased load.
- Pulling a resource from sitexyz.com is sluggish today for some reason.

If a program blocks on I/O, what does the server do when there are more requests to handle? Typically you'd use a multithreaded approach in this context. A common implementation is to use one thread per connection and set up a thread pool for those connections. You can think of threads as computational workspaces in which the processor works on one task. In many cases, a thread is contained inside a process and maintains its own working memory. Each thread handles one or more server connections. Although this may sound like a natural way to delegate server labor—at least to developers who've been doing this a long time—managing threads within an application can be complex. Also, when a large number of threads is needed to handle many concurrent server connections, threading can tax operating system resources. Threads require CPU to perform context switches, as well as additional RAM.

To illustrate this, let's look at a benchmark (shown in figure 1.2, from http://mng.bz/eaZT) comparing NGINX and Apache. NGINX (http://nginx.com/), if you aren't familiar with it, is an HTTP server like Apache, but instead of using the multithreaded approach with blocking I/O, it uses an event loop with asynchronous I/O (like the browser and Node). Because of these design choices, NGINX is often able to handle more requests and connected clients, making it a more responsive solution.[7]

In Node, I/O is almost always performed outside of the main event loop, allowing the server to stay efficient and responsive, like NGINX. This makes it much harder for a process to become I/O-bound because I/O latency isn't going to crash your server or use the resources it would if you were blocking. It allows the server to be lightweight on what are typically the slowest operations a server performs.[8]

---

[7] If you're interested in learning more about this problem, see "The C10K problem": www.kegel.com/c10k.html.

[8] Node's "About" page has more details about this: http://nodejs.org/about/.

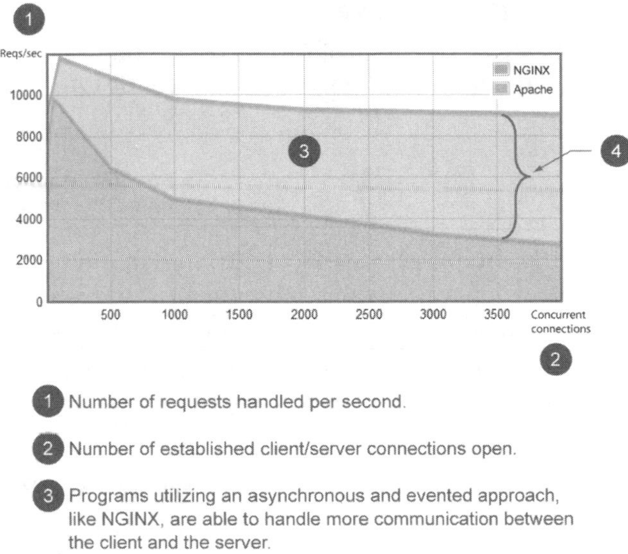
1
Reqs/sec
10000
8000
6000
4000
2000
0
500
1000
1500
2000
2500
3000
3500
Concurrent connections
2
NGINX
Apache
3
4
1 Number of requests handled per second.
2 Number of established client/server connections open.
3 Programs utilizing an asynchronous and evented approach, like NGINX, are able to handle more communication between the client and the server.

4 Such programs are also more responsive; in this example, at 3500 connections, each NGINX request is serviced roughly three times faster.

Figure 1.2 WebFaction Apache/NGINX benchmark

This mix of event-driven and asynchronous models and the widely accessible JavaScript language helps open up an exciting world of data-intensive real-time applications.

1.4 DIRTy applications

There actually is an acronym for the types of applications Node is designed for: *DIRT*. It stands for *data-intensive real-time* applications. Because Node itself is very lightweight on I/O, it's good at shuffling or proxying data from one pipe to another. It allows a server to hold a number of connections open while handling many requests and keeping a small memory footprint. It's designed to be responsive, like the browser.

Real-time applications are a new use case of the web. Many web applications now provide information virtually instantly, implementing things like online whiteboard collaboration, real-time pinpointing of approaching public transit buses, and multiplayer games. Whether it's existing applications being enhanced with real-time components or completely new types of applications, the web is moving toward more responsive and collaborative environments. These new types of web applications, however, call for a platform that can respond almost instantly to a large number of concurrent users. Node is good at this, and not just for web applications, but also for other I/O-heavy applications.

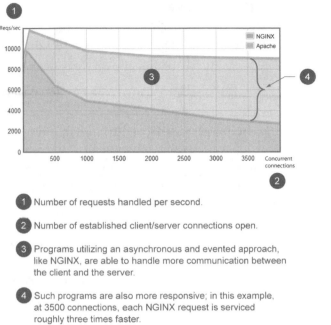

A good example of a DIRTy application written with Node is Browserling (browserling.com, shown in figure 1.3). The site allows in-browser use of other browsers. This is extremely useful to front-end web developers because it frees them from having to install numerous browsers and operating systems solely for testing. Browserling

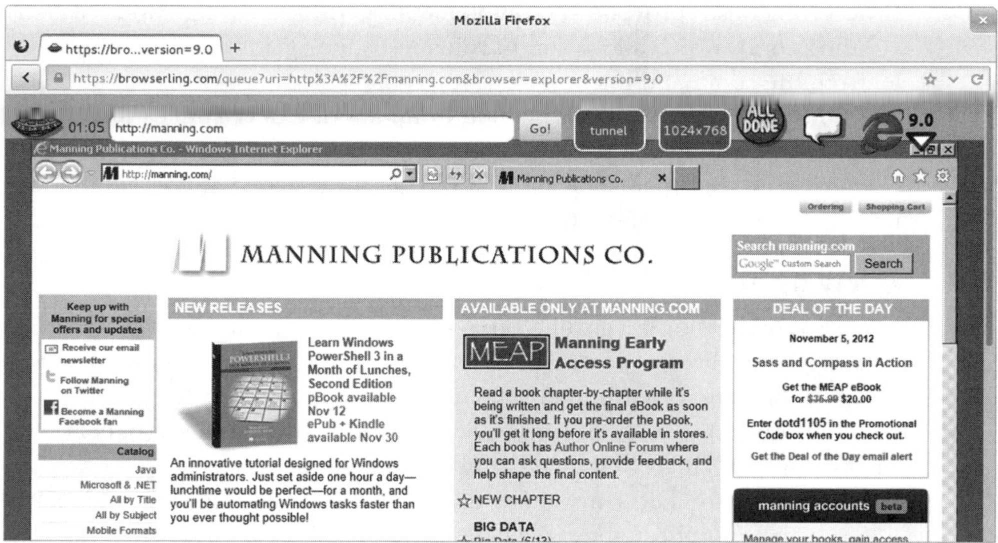

Figure 1.3 Browserling: interactive cross-browser testing using Node.js

leverages a Node-driven project called StackVM, which manages virtual machines (VMs) created using the QEMU (Quick Emulator) emulator. QEMU emulates the CPU and peripherals needed to run the browser.

Browserling has VMs run test browsers and then relays the keyboard and mouse input data from the user's browser to the emulated browser which, in turn, streams the repainted regions of the emulated browser and redraws them on the canvas of the user's browser. This is illustrated in figure 1.4.

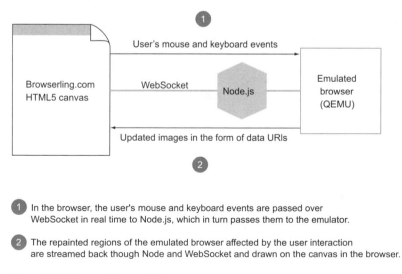

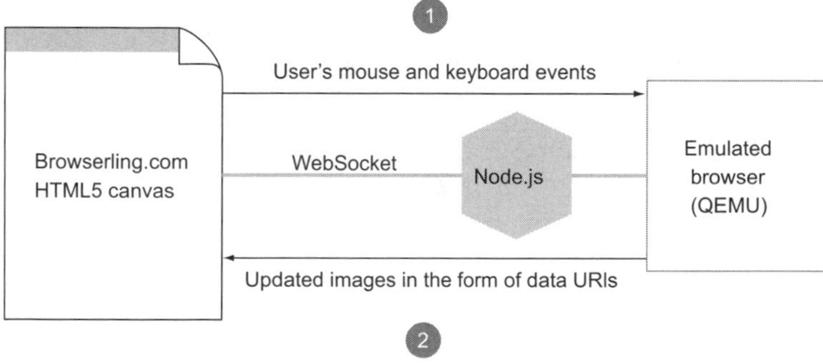

1. In the browser, the user's mouse and keyboard events are passed over WebSocket in real time to Node.js, which in turn passes them to the emulator.
2. The repainted regions of the emulated browser affected by the user interaction are streamed back though Node and WebSocket and drawn on the canvas in the browser.

Figure 1.4 Browserling workflow

Browserling also provides a complementary project using Node called Testling (testling.com), which allows you to run a test suite against multiple browsers in parallel from the command line.

Browserling and Testling are good examples of DIRTy applications, and the infrastructure for building scalable network applications like them is at play when you sit down to write your first Node application. Let's take a look at how Node's API provides this tooling right out of the box.

1.5 DIRTy by default

Node was built from the ground up to have an event-driven and asynchronous model. JavaScript has never had standard I/O libraries, which are common to server-side languages. The "host" environment has always determined this for JavaScript. The most common host environment for JavaScript—the one most developers are used to—is the browser, which is event-driven and asynchronous.

Node tries to keep consistency between the browser and the server by reimplementing common host objects, such as these:

- Timer API (for example, `setTimeout`)
- Console API (for example, `console.log`)

Node also includes a core set of modules for many types of network and file I/O. These include modules for HTTP, TLS, HTTPS, filesystem (POSIX), Datagram (UDP), and NET (TCP). The core is intentionally small, low-level, and uncomplicated, including just the building blocks for I/O-based applications. Third-party modules build upon these blocks to offer greater abstractions for common problems.

> **Platform vs. framework**
>
> Node is a *platform* for JavaScript applications, and it's not to be confused with a *framework*. It's a common misconception to think of Node as *Rails* or *Django for JavaScript*, whereas it's much lower level.
>
> But if you're interested in frameworks for web applications, we'll talk about a popular one for Node called Express later on in this book.

After all this discussion, you're probably wondering what Node code looks like. Let's cover a few simple examples:

- A simple asynchronous example
- A Hello World web server
- An example of streams

Let's look at a simple asynchronous application first.

1.5.1 Simple async example

In section 1.2, we looked at this Ajax example using jQuery:

```
$.post('/resource.json', function (data) {
  console.log(data);
});
```

Let's do something similar in Node, but instead we'll use the filesystem (`fs`) module to load resource.json from disk. Notice how similar the program is to the previous jQuery example:

```
var fs = require('fs');
fs.readFile('./resource.json', function (er, data) {
  console.log(data);
})
```

In this program, we read the resource.json file from disk. When all the data is read, an anonymous function is called (a.k.a. the "callback") containing the arguments `er`, if any error occurred, and `data`, which is the file data.

The process loops behind the scenes, able to handle any other operations that may come its way until the data is ready. All the evented and async benefits we talked about earlier are in play automatically. The difference here is that instead of making an Ajax request from the browser using jQuery, we're accessing the filesystem in Node to grab resource.json. This latter action is illustrated in figure 1.5.

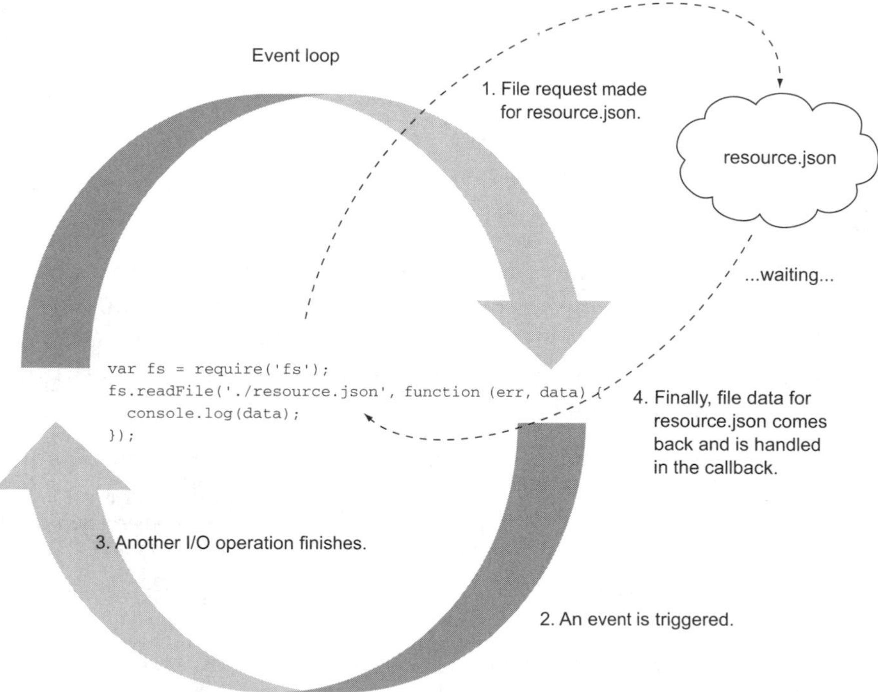

Figure 1.5 An example of non-blocking I/O in Node

1.5.2 Hello World HTTP server

A very common use case for Node is building servers. Node makes it very simple to create different types of servers. This can feel odd if you're used to having a server host your application (such as a PHP application hosted on an Apache HTTP server). In Node, the server and the application *are the same.*

Here's an example of an HTTP server that simply responds to any request with "Hello World":

```
var http = require('http');
http.createServer(function (req, res) {
  res.writeHead(200, {'Content-Type': 'text/plain'});
  res.end('Hello World\n');
}).listen(3000);
console.log('Server running at http://localhost:3000/');
```

Whenever a request happens, the `function (req, res)` callback is fired and "Hello World" is written out as the response. This event model is akin to listening to an `onclick` event in the browser. A click could happen at any point, so you set up a function to perform some logic to handle that. Here, Node provides a function that responds whenever a request happens.

Here's another way to write this same server to make the `request` event even more explicit:

```
var http = require('http');
var server = http.createServer();
server.on('request', function (req, res) {     <- Setting up an event listener for request
  res.writeHead(200, {'Content-Type': 'text/plain'});
  res.end('Hello World\n');
})
server.listen(3000);
console.log('Server running at http://localhost:3000/');
```

1.5.3 Streaming data

Node is also huge on streams and streaming. You can think of streams as being like arrays, but instead of having data distributed over space, streams can be thought of as data distributed *over time.* By bringing data in chunk by chunk, the developer is given the ability to handle that data as it comes in instead of waiting for it all to arrive before acting. Here's how you would stream resource.json:

```
var stream = fs.createReadStream('./resource.json')
stream.on('data', function (chunk) {     <- Data event fires when a new chunk is ready
  console.log(chunk)
})
stream.on('end', function () {
  console.log('finished')
})
```

A `data` event is fired whenever a new chunk of data is ready, and an `end` event is fired when all the chunks have been loaded. A chunk can vary in size, depending on the type of data. This low-level access to the read stream allows you to efficiently deal with data as it's read instead of waiting for it all to buffer in memory.

Node also provides writable streams that you can write chunks of data to. One of those is the response (`res`) object when a request happens on an HTTP server.

Readable and writable streams can be connected to make pipes, much like you can do with the | (pipe) operator in shell scripting. This provides an efficient way to write out data as soon as it's ready, without waiting for the complete resource to be read and then written out.

Let's use our previous HTTP server to illustrate streaming an image to a client:

```
var http = require('http');
var fs = require('fs');
http.createServer(function (req, res) {
  res.writeHead(200, {'Content-Type': 'image/png'});
  fs.createReadStream('./image.png').pipe(res);
}).listen(3000);
console.log('Server running at http://localhost:3000/');
```

Piping from a readable stream to a writable stream

In this one-liner, the data is read in from the file (`fs.createReadStream`) and is sent out (`.pipe`) to the client (`res`) as it comes in. The event loop is able to handle other events while the data is being streamed.

Node provides this DIRTy-by-default approach across multiple platforms, including various UNIXes and Windows. The underlying asynchronous I/O library (`libuv`) was built specifically to provide a unified experience regardless of the parent operating system, which allows programs to be more easily ported across devices and to run on multiple devices if needed.

1.6 Summary

Like any technology, Node is not a silver bullet. It just helps you tackle certain problems and opens new possibilities. One of the interesting things about Node is that it brings people from all aspects of the system together. Many come to Node as JavaScript client-side programmers; others are server-side programmers; and others are systems-level programmers. Wherever you fit, we hope you have an understanding of where Node may fit in your stack.

To review, Node is

- Built on JavaScript
- Evented and asynchronous
- Designed for data-intensive real-time applications

In chapter 2, we'll build a simple DIRTy web application so you can see how a Node application works.

2 Building a multiroom chat application

This chapter covers

- A first look at various Node components
- A sample real-time application using Node
- Server and client-side interaction

In chapter 1, you learned how asynchronous development using Node differs from conventional synchronous development. In this chapter, we'll take a practical look at Node by creating a small event-driven chat application. Don't worry if the details in this chapter seem over your head; our intent is to demystify Node development and give you a preview of what you'll be able to do when you've completed the book.

This chapter assumes you have experience with web application development, have a basic understanding of HTTP, and are familiar with jQuery. As you move through the chapter, you'll

- Tour the application to see how it will work
- Review technology requirements and perform the initial application setup
- Serve the application's HTML, CSS, and client-side JavaScript
- Handle chat-related messaging using Socket.IO
- Use client-side JavaScript for the application's UI

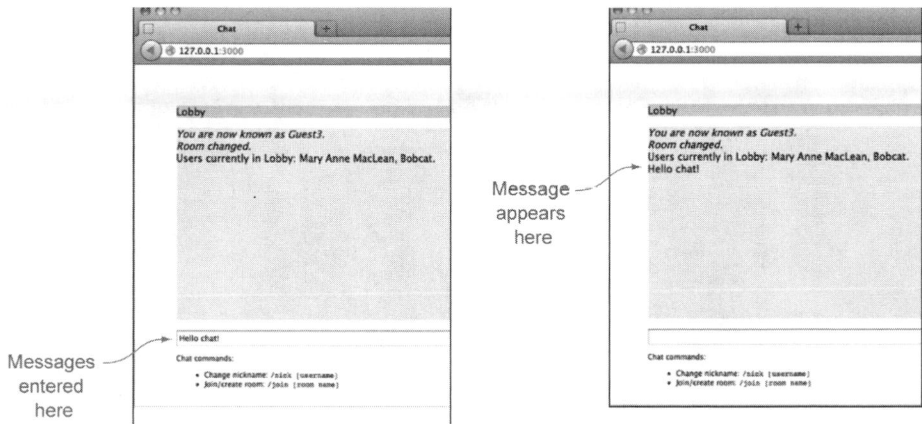

Figure 2.1 Entering a message into the chat application

Let's start with an application overview—you'll see what the application will look like and how it'll behave when it's completed.

2.1 Application overview

The application you'll build in this chapter allows users to chat online with each other by entering messages into a simple form, as shown in figure 2.1. A message, once entered, is sent to all other users in the same chat room.

When starting the application, a user is automatically assigned a guest name, but they can change it by entering a command, as shown in figure 2.2. Chat commands are prefaced with a slash (/).

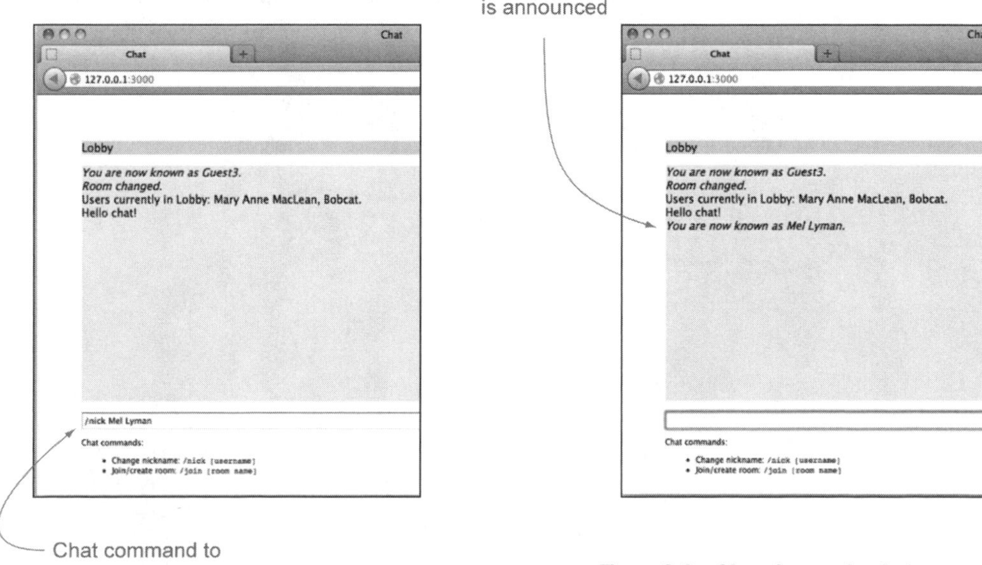

Figure 2.2 Changing one's chat name

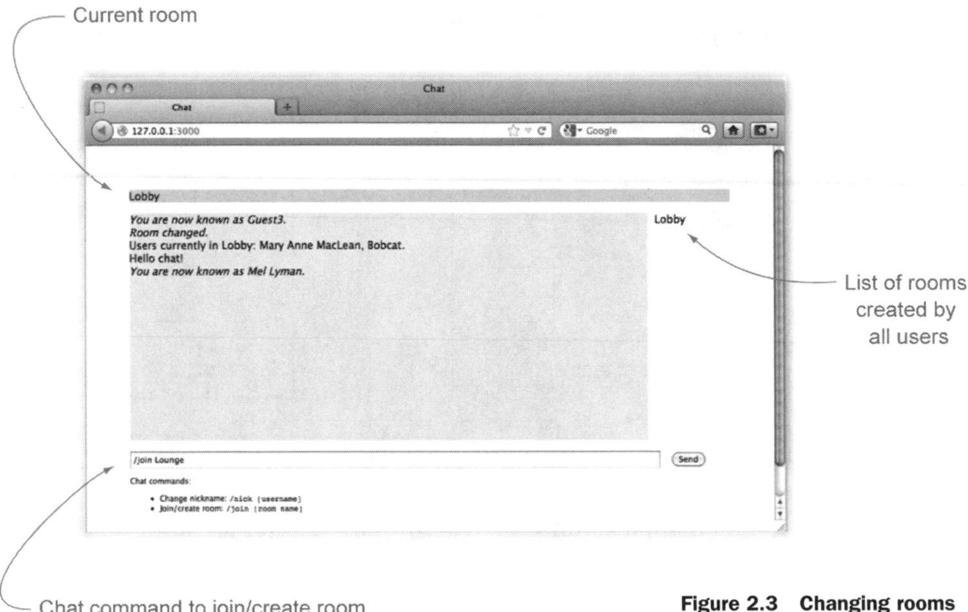

Figure 2.3 Changing rooms

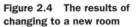

Similarly, a user can enter a command to create a new chat room (or join it if it already exists), as shown in figure 2.3. When joining or creating a room, the new room name will be shown in the horizontal bar at the top of the chat application. The room will also be included in the list of available rooms to the right of the chat message area.

After the user changes to a new room, the system will confirm the change, as shown in figure 2.4.

While the functionality of this application is deliberately bare-bones, it showcases important components and fundamental techniques needed to create a real-time web

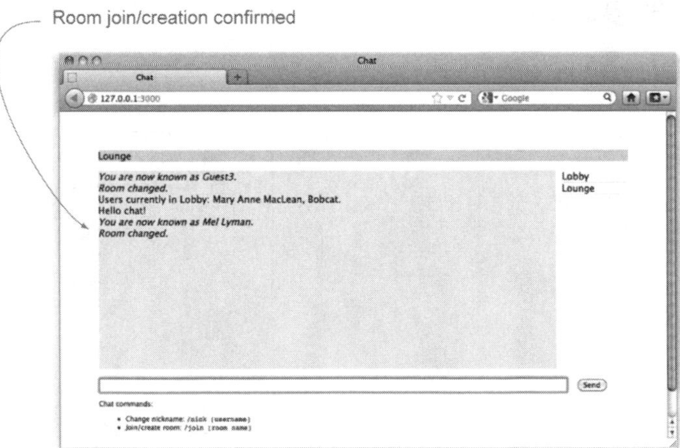

Figure 2.4 The results of changing to a new room

application. The application shows how Node can simultaneously serve conventional HTTP data (like static files) and real-time data (chat messages). It also shows how Node applications are organized and how dependencies are managed.

Let's now look at the technologies needed to implement this application.

2.2 Application requirements and initial setup

The chat application you'll create needs to do the following:

- Serve static files (such as HTML, CSS, and client-side JavaScript)
- Handle chat-related messaging on the server
- Handle chat-related messaging in the user's web browser

To serve static files, you'll use Node's built-in http module. But when serving files via HTTP, it's usually not enough to just send the contents of a file; you also should include the type of file being sent. This is done by setting the `Content-Type` HTTP header with the proper MIME type for the file. To look up these MIME types, you'll use a third-party module called *mime*.

MIME TYPES MIME types are discussed in detail in the Wikipedia article: http://en.wikipedia.org/wiki/MIME.

To handle chat-related messaging, you could poll the server with Ajax. But to make this application as responsive as possible, you'll avoid using traditional Ajax as a means to send messages. Ajax uses HTTP as a transport mechanism, and HTTP wasn't designed for real-time communication. When a message is sent using HTTP, a new TCP/IP connection must be used. Opening and closing connections takes time, and the size of the data transfer is larger because HTTP headers are sent on every request. Instead of employing a solution reliant on HTTP, this application will prefer WebSocket (http://en.wikipedia.org/wiki/WebSocket), which was designed as a bidirectional lightweight communications protocol to support real-time communication.

Since only HTML5-compliant browsers, for the most part, support WebSocket, the application will leverage the popular Socket.IO library (http://socket.io/), which provides a number of fallbacks, including the use of Flash, should using WebSocket not be possible. Socket.IO handles fallback functionality transparently, requiring no additional code or configuration. Socket.IO is covered more deeply in chapter 13.

Before we plunge in and actually do the preliminary work of setting up the application's file structure and dependencies, let's talk more about how Node lets you simultaneously handle HTTP and WebSocket—one of the reasons why it's such a good choice for real-time applications.

2.2.1 Serving HTTP and WebSocket

Although this application will avoid the use of Ajax for sending and receiving chat messages, it will still use HTTP to deliver the HTML, CSS, and client-side JavaScript needed to set things up in the user's browser.

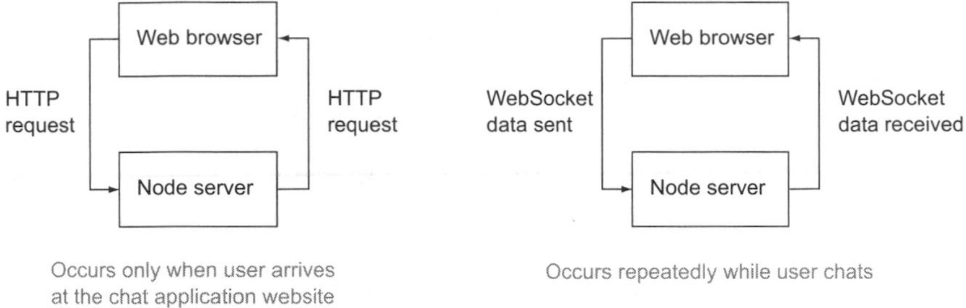

Figure 2.5 Handling HTTP and WebSocket within a single application

Node can easily handle simultaneously serving HTTP and WebSocket using a single TCP/IP port, as figure 2.5 depicts. Node comes with a module that provides HTTP serving functionality. There are a number of third-party Node modules, such as *Express*, that build upon Node's built-in functionality to make web serving even easier. We'll go into depth about how to use Express to build web applications in chapter 8. In this chapter's application, however, we'll stick to the basics.

Now that you have a rough idea of the core technologies the application will use, let's start fleshing it out.

> **Need to install Node?**
> If you haven't already installed Node, please head to appendix A now for instructions for doing so.

2.2.2 *Creating the application file structure*

To start constructing the tutorial application, create a project directory for it. The main application file will go directly in this directory. You'll need to add a *lib* subdirectory, within which some server-side logic will be placed. You'll need to create a *public* subdirectory where client-side files will be placed. Within the public subdirectory, create a *javascripts* subdirectory and a *stylesheets* directory.

Your directory structure should now look like figure 2.6. Note that while we've chosen to organize the files in this particular way in this chapter, Node doesn't require you to maintain any particular directory structure; application files can be organized in any way that makes sense to you.

Figure 2.6 The skeletal project directory for the chat application

Now that you've established a directory structure, you'll want to specify the application's dependencies.

An *application dependency*, in this context, is a module that needs to be installed to provide functionality needed by the application. Let's say, for example, that you were creating an application that needed to access data stored using a MySQL database. Node doesn't come with a built-in module that allows access to MySQL, so you'd have to install a third-party module, and this would be considered a dependency.

2.2.3 Specifying dependencies

Although you can create Node applications without formally specifying dependencies, it's a good habit to take the time to specify them. That way, if you want others to use your application, or you plan on running it in more than one place, it becomes more straightforward to set up.

Application dependencies are specified using a package.json file. This file is always placed in an application's root directory. A package.json file consists of a JSON expression that follows the CommonJS package descriptor standard (http://wiki.commonjs.org/wiki/Packages/1.0) and describes your application. In a package.json file you can specify many things, but the most important are the name of your application, the version, a description of what the application does, and the application's dependencies.

Listing 2.1 shows a package descriptor file that describes the functionality and dependencies of the tutorial application. Save this file as package.json in the root directory of the tutorial application.

Listing 2.1 A package descriptor file

```
{
  "name": "chatrooms",                                <— Name of package
  "version": "0.0.1",
  "description": "Minimalist multiroom chat server",
  "dependencies": {                                       <— Package dependencies
    "socket.io": "~0.9.6",
    "mime": "~1.2.7"
  }
}
```

If the content of this file seems a bit confusing, don't worry...you'll learn more about package.json files in the next chapter and, in depth, in chapter 14.

2.2.4 Installing dependencies

With a package.json file defined, installing your application's dependencies becomes trivial. The Node Package Manager (npm; https://github.com/isaacs/npm) is a utility that comes bundled with Node. It offers a great deal of functionality, allowing you to easily install third-party Node modules and globally publish any Node modules you yourself create. Another thing it can do is read dependencies from package.json files and install each of them with a single command.

Enter the following command in the root of your tutorial directory:

```
npm install
```

If you look in the tutorial directory now, there should be a newly created node_modules directory, as shown in figure 2.7. This directory contains your application's dependencies.

With the directory structure established and dependencies installed, you're ready to start fleshing out the application logic.

Figure 2.7 When npm is used to install dependencies, a node_modules directory is created.

2.3 Serving the application's HTML, CSS, and client-side JavaScript

As outlined earlier, the chat application needs to be capable of doing three basic things:

- Serving static files to the user's web browser
- Handling chat-related messaging on the server
- Handling chat-related messaging in the user's web browser

Application logic will be handled by a number of files, some run on the server and some run on the client, as shown in figure 2.8. The JavaScript files run on the client need to be served as static assets, rather than being executed by Node.

In this section, we'll tackle the first of those requirements: we'll define the logic needed to serve static files. We'll then add the static HTML and CSS files themselves.

2.3.1 Creating a basic static file server

To create a static file server, we'll leverage some of Node's built-in functionality as well as the third-party *mime* add-on for determining a file MIME type.

To start the main application file, create a file named server.js in the root of your project directory and put variable declarations from listing 2.2 in it. These declarations will give you access to Node's HTTP-related functionality, the ability to interact with the filesystem, functionality related to file paths, and the ability to determine a file's MIME type. The `cache` variable will be used to cache file data.

Listing 2.2 Variable declarations

```
var http  = require('http');
var fs    = require('fs');
var path  = require('path');
var mime  = require('mime');
var cache = {};
```

- Built-in http module provides HTTP server and client functionality
- Built-in fs module provides filesystem-related functionality
- Built-in path module provides filesystem path–related functionality
- Add-on mime module provides ability to derive a MIME type based on a filename extension
- cache object is where the contents of cached files are stored

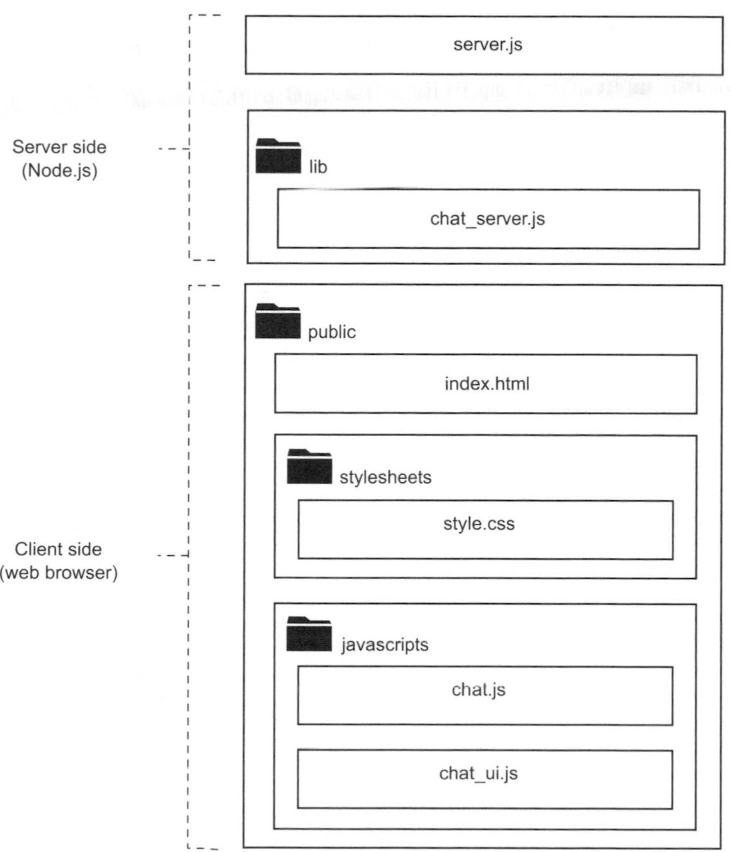

Figure 2.8 In this chat application, there's both client-side and server-side JavaScript logic.

SENDING FILE DATA AND ERROR RESPONSES

Next you need to add three helper functions used for serving static HTTP files. The first will handle the sending of 404 errors when a file is requested that doesn't exist. Add the following helper function to server.js:

```
function send404(response) {
  response.writeHead(404, {'Content-Type': 'text/plain'});
  response.write('Error 404: resource not found.');
  response.end();
}
```

The second helper function serves file data. The function first writes the appropriate HTTP headers and then sends the contents of the file. Add the following code to server.js:

```
function sendFile(response, filePath, fileContents) {
  response.writeHead(
    200,
    {"content-type": mime.lookup(path.basename(filePath))}
  );
  response.end(fileContents);
}
```

Accessing memory storage (RAM) is faster than accessing the filesystem. Because of this, it's common for Node applications to cache frequently used data in memory. Our chat application will cache static files to memory, only reading them from disk the first time they're accessed. The next helper determines whether or not a file is cached and, if so, serves it. If a file isn't cached, it's read from disk and served. If the file doesn't exist, an HTTP 404 error is returned as a response. Add this helper function to server.js.

Listing 2.3 Serving static files

```
function serveStatic(response, cache, absPath) {
  if (cache[absPath]) {                                    // Check if file is cached in memory
    sendFile(response, absPath, cache[absPath]);           // Serve file from memory
  } else {
    fs.exists(absPath, function(exists) {                  // Check if file exists
      if (exists) {
        fs.readFile(absPath, function(err, data) {         // Read file from disk
          if (err) {
            send404(response);
          } else {
            cache[absPath] = data;
            sendFile(response, absPath, data);             // Serve file read from disk
          }
        });
      } else {
        send404(response);                                 // Send HTTP 404 response
      }
    });
  }
}
```

CREATING THE HTTP SERVER

For the HTTP server, an anonymous function is provided as an argument to `createServer`, acting as a callback that defines how each HTTP request should be handled. The callback function accepts two arguments: `request` and `response`. When the callback executes, the HTTP server will populate these arguments with objects that, respectively, allow you to work out the details of the request and send back a response. You'll learn about Node's http module in detail in chapter 4.

Add the logic in the following listing to server.js to create the HTTP server.

Listing 2.4 Logic to create an HTTP server

```
var server = http.createServer(function(request, response) {   // Create HTTP server, using anonymous function to define per-request behavior
  var filePath = false;

  if (request.url == '/') {
    filePath = 'public/index.html';                       // Determine HTML file to be served by default
  } else {
    filePath = 'public' + request.url;                    // Translate URL path to relative file path
  }
```

```
  var absPath = './' + filePath;
  serveStatic(response, cache, absPath);           <- Serve static file
});
```

STARTING THE HTTP SERVER

You've created the HTTP server in the code, but you haven't added the logic needed to start it. Add the following lines, which start the server, requesting that it listen on TCP/IP port 3000. Port 3000 is an arbitrary choice; any unused port above 1024 would work (a port under 1024 might also work if you're running Windows or, if in Linux or OS X, you start your application using a privileged user such as "root").

```
server.listen(3000, function() {
  console.log("Server listening on port 3000.");
});
```

If you'd like to see what the application can do at this point, you can start the server by entering the following into your command-line prompt:

```
node server.js
```

With the server running, visiting http://127.0.0.1:3000 in your web browser will result in the triggering of the 404 error helper, and the "Error 404: resource not found" message will be displayed. Although you've added the static file–handling logic, you haven't added the static files themselves. A point to remember is that a running server can be stopped by using Ctrl-C on the command line.

Next, let's move on to adding the static files necessary to get the chat application more functional.

2.3.2 *Adding the HTML and CSS files*

The first static file you'll add is the base HTML. Create a file in the public directory named index.html and place the HTML in listing 2.5 in it. The HTML will include a CSS file, set up some HTML `div` elements in which application content will be displayed, and load a number of client-side JavaScript files. The JavaScript files provide client-side Socket.IO functionality, jQuery (for easy DOM manipulation), and a couple of application-specific files providing chat functionality.

Listing 2.5 The HTML for the chat application

```
<!doctype html>
<html lang='en'>

<head>
  <title>Chat</title>
  <link rel='stylesheet' href='/stylesheets/style.css'></link>
</head>

<body>                                         div in which the
<div id='content'>                             current room name
  <div id='room'></div>                     <- will be displayed
```

```
    <div id='room-list'></div>
    <div id='messages'></div>

  <form id='send-form'>
    <input id='send-message' />
    <input id='send-button' type='submit' value='Send'/>

    <div id='help'>
      Chat commands:
      <ul>
        <li>Change nickname: <code>/nick [username]</code></li>
        <li>Join/create room: <code>/join [room name]</code></li>
      </ul>
    </div>
  </form>
  </div>

  <script src='/socket.io/socket.io.js' type='text/javascript'></script>
  <script src='http://code.jquery.com/jquery-1.8.0.min.js'
  ➥type='text/javascript'></script>
  <script src='/javascripts/chat.js' type='text/javascript'></script>
  <script src='/javascripts/chat_ui.js' type='text/javascript'></script>
  </body>
  </html>
```

- div in which a list of available rooms will be displayed
- div in which chat messages will be displayed
- Form input element in which user will enter commands and messages

The next file you need to add defines the application's CSS styling. In the public/ stylesheets directory, create a file named style.css and put the following CSS code in it.

Listing 2.6 Application CSS

```
body {
  padding: 50px;
  font: 14px "Lucida Grande", Helvetica, Arial, sans-serif;
}

a {
  color: #00B7FF;
}

#content {
  width: 800px;
  margin-left: auto;
  margin-right: auto;
}

#room {
  background-color: #ddd;
  margin-bottom: 1em;
}

#messages {
  width: 690px;
  height: 300px;
  overflow: auto;
  background-color: #eee;
  margin-bottom: 1em;
  margin-right: 10px;
}
```

- Application will be 800 pixels wide and horizontally centered
- CSS rules for area in which current room name is displayed
- Message display area will be 690 pixels wide and 300 pixels high
- Allows div in which messages are displayed to scroll when it's filled up with content

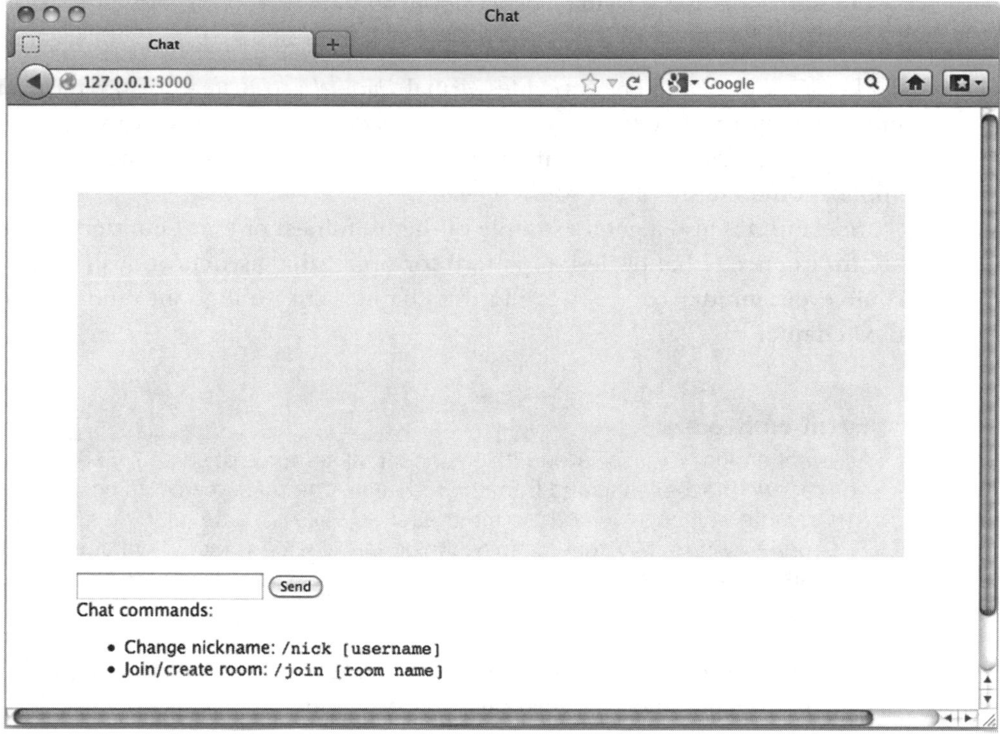

Figure 2.9 The application in progress

With the HTML and CSS roughed out, run the application and take a look using your web browser. The application should look like figure 2.9.

The application isn't yet functional, but static files are being served and the basic visual layout is established. With that taken care of, let's move on to defining the server-side chat message dispatching.

2.4 Handling chat-related messaging using Socket.IO

Of the three things we said the app had to do, we've already covered the first one, serving static files, and now we'll tackle the second—handling communication between the browser and server. Modern browsers are capable of using WebSocket to handle communication between the browser and the server. (See the Socket.IO browser support page for details on supported browsers: http://socket.io/#browser-support.)

Socket.IO provides a layer of abstraction over WebSocket and other transports for both Node and client-side JavaScript. Socket.IO will fall back transparently to other WebSocket alternatives if WebSocket isn't implemented in a web browser while keeping the same API. In this section, we'll

- Briefly introduce you to Socket.IO and define the Socket.IO functionality you'll need on the server side

- Add code that sets up a Socket.IO server
- Add code to handle various chat application events

Socket.IO, out of the box, provides virtual *channels*, so instead of broadcasting every message to every connected user, you can broadcast only to those who have subscribed to a specific channel. This functionality makes implementing chat rooms in your application quite simple, as you'll see later.

Socket.IO is also a good example of the usefulness of event emitters. *Event emitters* are, in essence, a handy design pattern for organizing asynchronous logic. You'll see some event emitter code at work in this chapter, but we'll go into more detail in the next chapter.

> **Event emitters**
>
> An event emitter is associated with a conceptual resource of some kind and can send and receive messages to and from the resource. The resource could be a connection to a remote server or something more abstract, like a game character. The Johnny-Five project (https://github.com/rwldrn/johnny-five), in fact, leverages Node for robotics applications, using event emitters to control Arduino microcontrollers.

First, we'll start the server functionality and establish the connection logic. Then we'll define the functionality you need on the server side.

2.4.1 Setting up the Socket.IO server

To begin, append the following two lines to server.js. The first line loads functionality from a custom Node module that supplies logic to handle Socket.IO-based server-side chat functionality. We'll define that module next. The next line starts the Socket.IO server functionality, providing it with an already defined HTTP server so it can share the same TCP/IP port:

```
var chatServer = require('./lib/chat_server');
chatServer.listen(server);
```

You now need to create a new file, chat_server.js, inside the lib directory. Start this file by adding the following variable declarations. These declarations allow the use of Socket.IO and initialize a number of variables that define chat state:

```
var socketio = require('socket.io');
var io;
var guestNumber = 1;
var nickNames = {};
var namesUsed = [];
var currentRoom = {};
```

ESTABLISHING CONNECTION LOGIC

Next, add the logic in listing 2.7 to define the chat server function `listen`. This function is invoked in server.js. It starts the Socket.IO server, limits the verbosity of

Socket.IO's logging to the console, and establishes how each incoming connection should be handled.

The connection-handling logic, you'll notice, calls a number of helper functions that you can now add to chat_server.js.

Listing 2.7 Starting up a Socket.IO server

```
exports.listen = function(server) {
  io = socketio.listen(server);
  io.set('log level', 1);

  io.sockets.on('connection', function (socket) {
    guestNumber = assignGuestName(socket, guestNumber,
      ➥nickNames, namesUsed);
    joinRoom(socket, 'Lobby');

    handleMessageBroadcasting(socket, nickNames);
    handleNameChangeAttempts(socket, nickNames, namesUsed);
    handleRoomJoining(socket);

    socket.on('rooms', function() {
      socket.emit('rooms', io.sockets.manager.rooms);
    });

    handleClientDisconnection(socket, nickNames, namesUsed);
  });
};
```

Start Socket.IO server, allowing it to piggyback on existing HTTP server

Define how each user connection will be handled

Assign user a guest name when they connect

Place user in Lobby room when they connect

Handle user messages, name-change attempts, and room creation/changes

Provide user with list of occupied rooms on request

Define cleanup logic for when user disconnects

With the connection handling established, you now need to add the individual helper functions that will handle the application's needs.

2.4.2 Handling application scenarios and events

The chat application needs to handle the following types of scenarios and events:

- Guest name assignment
- Room-change requests
- Name-change requests
- Sending chat messages
- Room creation
- User disconnection

To handle these you'll add a number of helper functions.

ASSIGNING GUEST NAMES

The first helper function you need to add is assignGuestName, which handles the naming of new users. When a user first connects to the chat server, the user is placed in a chat room named Lobby, and assignGuestName is called to assign them a name to distinguish them from other users.

Each guest name is essentially the word *Guest* followed by a number that increments each time a new user connects. The guest name is stored in the nickNames variable for reference, associated with the internal socket ID. The guest name is also added to namesUsed, a variable in which names that are being used are stored. Add the code in the following listing to lib/chat_server.js to implement this functionality.

Listing 2.8 Assigning a guest name

```
function assignGuestName(socket, guestNumber, nickNames, namesUsed) {
  var name = 'Guest' + guestNumber;                    // Generate new guest name
  nickNames[socket.id] = name;                         // Associate guest name with client connection ID
  socket.emit('nameResult', {                          // Let user know their guest name
    success: true,
    name: name
  });
  namesUsed.push(name);                                // Note that guest name is now used
  return guestNumber + 1;                              // Increment counter used to generate guest names
}
```

JOINING ROOMS

The second helper function you'll need to add to chat_server.js is joinRoom. This function, shown in listing 2.9, handles logic related to a user joining a chat room.

Having a user join a Socket.IO room is simple, requiring only a call to the join method of a socket object. The application then communicates related details to the user and other users in the same room. The application lets the user know what other users are in the room and lets these other users know that the user is now present.

Listing 2.9 Logic related to joining a room

```
function joinRoom(socket, room) {
  socket.join(room);                                   // Make user join room
  currentRoom[socket.id] = room;                       // Note that user is now in this room
  socket.emit('joinResult', {room: room});             // Let user know they're now in new room
  socket.broadcast.to(room).emit('message', {          // Let other users in room know that user has joined
    text: nickNames[socket.id] + ' has joined ' + room + '.'
  });

  var usersInRoom = io.sockets.clients(room);          // Determine what other users are in same room as user
  if (usersInRoom.length > 1) {                        // If other users exist, summarize who they are
    var usersInRoomSummary = 'Users currently in ' + room + ': ';
    for (var index in usersInRoom) {
      var userSocketId = usersInRoom[index].id;
      if (userSocketId != socket.id) {
        if (index > 0) {
          usersInRoomSummary += ', ';
        }
```

```
        usersInRoomSummary += nickNames[userSocketId];
      }
    }
    usersInRoomSummary += '.';
    socket.emit('message', {text: usersInRoomSummary});
  }
}
```

Send summary of other users in the room to the user

HANDLING NAME-CHANGE REQUESTS

If every user just kept their guest name, it would be hard to remember who's who. For this reason, the chat application allows the user to request a name change. As figure 2.10 shows, a name change involves the user's web browser making a request via Socket.IO and then receiving a response indicating success or failure.

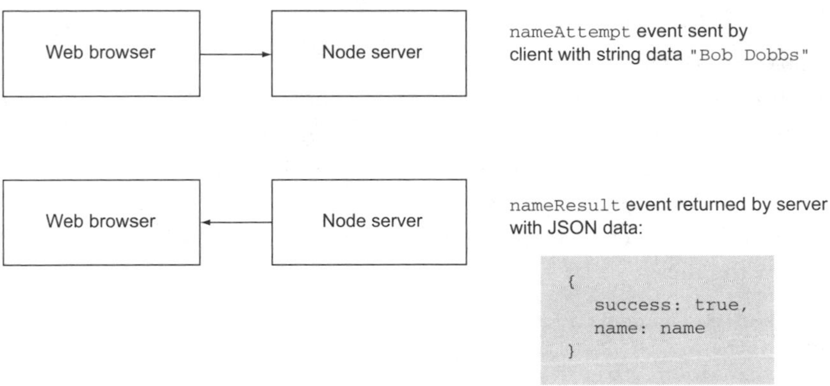

Figure 2.10 A name-change request and response

Add the code in the following listing to lib/chat_server.js to define a function that handles requests by users to change their names. From the application's perspective, the users aren't allowed to change their names to anything beginning with *Guest* or to use a name that's already in use.

Listing 2.10 Logic to handle name-request attempts

```
function handleNameChangeAttempts(socket, nickNames, namesUsed) {
  socket.on('nameAttempt', function(name) {
    if (name.indexOf('Guest') == 0) {
      socket.emit('nameResult', {
        success: false,
        message: 'Names cannot begin with "Guest".'
      });
    } else {
      if (namesUsed.indexOf(name) == -1) {
        var previousName = nickNames[socket.id];
        var previousNameIndex = namesUsed.indexOf(previousName);
        namesUsed.push(name);
        nickNames[socket.id] = name;
        delete namesUsed[previousNameIndex];
```

Add listener for nameAttempt events

Don't allow nicknames to begin with *Guest*

If name isn't already registered, register it

Remove previous name to make available to other clients

```
        socket.emit('nameResult', {
          success: true,
          name: name
        });
        socket.broadcast.to(currentRoom[socket.id]).emit('message', {
          text: previousName + ' is now known as ' + name + '.'
        });
      } else {
        socket.emit('nameResult', {                      <-- Send error to client
          success: false,                                    if name is already
          message: 'That name is already in use.'            registered
        });
      }
    }
  });
}
```

SENDING CHAT MESSAGES

Now that user nicknames are taken care of, you need to add a function that defines how a chat message sent from a user is handled. Figure 2.11 shows the basic process: the user emits an event indicating the room where the message is to be sent and the message text. The server then relays the message to all other users in the same room.

Add the following code to lib/chat_server.js. Socket.IO's `broadcast` function is used to relay the message:

```
function handleMessageBroadcasting(socket) {
  socket.on('message', function (message) {
    socket.broadcast.to(message.room).emit('message', {
      text: nickNames[socket.id] + ': ' + message.text
    });
  });
}
```

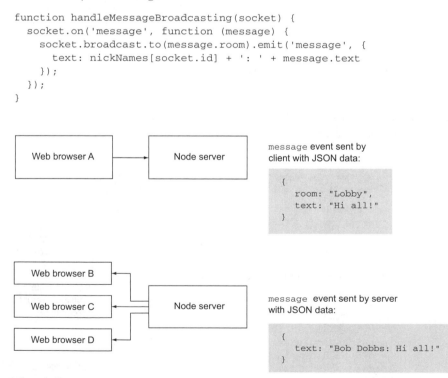

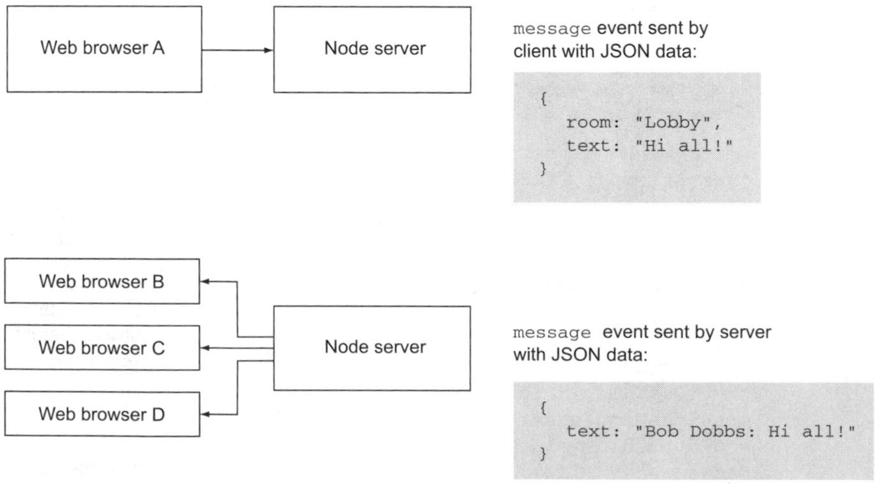

Figure 2.11 Sending a chat message

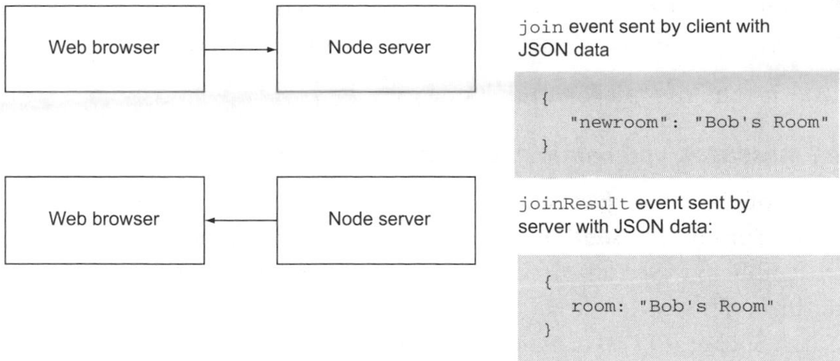

Figure 2.12 Changing to a different chat room

CREATING ROOMS

Next, you need to add functionality that allows a user to join an existing room or, if it doesn't yet exist, to create it. Figure 2.12 shows the interaction between the user and the server.

Add the following code to lib/chat_server.js to enable room changing. Note the use of Socket.IO's `leave` method:

```
function handleRoomJoining(socket) {
  socket.on('join', function(room) {
    socket.leave(currentRoom[socket.id]);
    joinRoom(socket, room.newRoom);
  });
}
```

HANDLING USER DISCONNECTIONS

Finally, you need to add the following logic to lib/chat_server.js to remove a user's nickname from `nickNames` and `namesUsed` when the user leaves the chat application:

```
function handleClientDisconnection(socket) {
  socket.on('disconnect', function() {
    var nameIndex = namesUsed.indexOf(nickNames[socket.id]);
    delete namesUsed[nameIndex];
    delete nickNames[socket.id];
  });
}
```

With the server-side components fully defined, you're now ready to further develop the client-side logic.

2.5 Using client-side JavaScript for the application's user interface

Now that you've added server-side Socket.IO logic to dispatch messages sent from the browser, it's time to add the client-side JavaScript needed to communicate with the server. Client-side JavaScript is needed to handle the following functionality:

- Sending a user's messages and name/room change requests to the server
- Displaying other users' messages and the list of available rooms

Let's start with the first piece of functionality.

2.5.1 Relaying messages and name/room changes to the server

The first bit of client-side JavaScript you'll add is a JavaScript prototype object that will process chat commands, send messages, and request room and nickname changes.

In the public/javascripts directory, create a file named chat.js and put the following code in it. This code starts JavaScript's equivalent of a "class" that takes a single argument, a Socket.IO socket, when instantiated:

```
var Chat = function(socket) {
  this.socket = socket;
};
```

Next, add the following function to send chat messages:

```
Chat.prototype.sendMessage = function(room, text) {
  var message = {
    room: room,
    text: text
  };
  this.socket.emit('message', message);
};
```

Add the following function to change rooms:

```
Chat.prototype.changeRoom = function(room) {
  this.socket.emit('join', {
    newRoom: room
  });
};
```

Finally, add the function defined in the following listing for processing a chat command. Two chat commands are recognized: `join` for joining or creating a room and `nick` for changing one's nickname.

Listing 2.11 Processing chat commands

```
Chat.prototype.processCommand = function(command) {
  var words = command.split(' ');
  var command = words[0]
                  .substring(1, words[0].length)
                  .toLowerCase();                    <-- Parse command from first word
  var message = false;

  switch(command) {
    case 'join':
      words.shift();
      var room = words.join(' ');
      this.changeRoom(room);                   <-- Handle room changing/creating
      break;
```

```
    case 'nick':
      words.shift();
      var name = words.join(' ');
      this.socket.emit('nameAttempt', name);
      break;

    default:
      message = 'Unrecognized command.';
      break;
  }

  return message;
};
```

Handle name-change attempts

Return error message if command isn't recognized

2.5.2 *Showing messages and available rooms in the user interface*

Now it's time to start adding logic that interacts directly with the browser-based user interface using jQuery. The first functionality you'll add will be to display text data.

In web applications there are, from a security perspective, two types of text data. There's *trusted* text data, which consists of text supplied by the application, and there's *untrusted* text data, which is text created by or derived from text created by users of the application. Text data from users is considered untrusted because malicious users may intentionally submit text data that includes JavaScript logic in `<script>` tags. This text data, if displayed unaltered to other users, could cause nasty things to happen, such as redirecting users to another web page. This method of hijacking a web application is called a cross-site scripting (XSS) attack.

The chat application will use two helper functions to display text data. One function will display untrusted text data, and the other function will display trusted text data.

The function `divEscapedContentElement` will display untrusted text. It will sanitize text by transforming special characters into HTML entities, as shown in figure 2.13, so the browser knows to display them as entered rather than attempting to interpret them as part of an HTML tag.

The function `divSystemContentElement` will display trusted content created by the system rather than by other users.

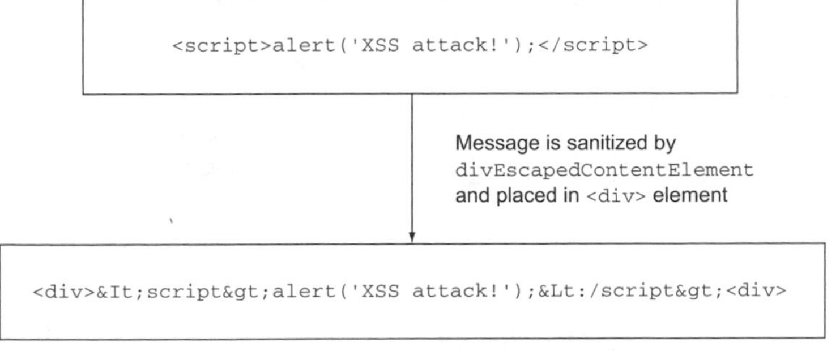

<script>alert('XSS attack!');</script>
Message is sanitized by
divEscapedContentElement
and placed in <div> element
<div>&It;script>alert('XSS attack!');&Lt:/script><div>

Figure 2.13 Escaping untrusted content

In the public/javascripts directory, add a file named chat_ui.js and put the following two helper functions in it:

```
function divEscapedContentElement(message) {
  return $('<div></div>').text(message);
}

function divSystemContentElement(message) {
  return $('<div></div>').html('<i>' + message + '</i>');
}
```

The next function you'll append to chat_ui.js is for processing user input; it's detailed in the following listing. If user input begins with the slash (/) character, it's treated as a chat command. If not, it's sent to the server as a chat message to be broadcast to other users, and it's added to the chat room text of the room the user's currently in.

Listing 2.12 Processing raw user input

```
function processUserInput(chatApp, socket) {
  var message = $('#send-message').val();
  var systemMessage;

  if (message.charAt(0) == '/') {
    systemMessage = chatApp.processCommand(message);
    if (systemMessage) {
      $('#messages').append(divSystemContentElement(systemMessage));
    }
  } else {
    chatApp.sendMessage($('#room').text(), message);
    $('#messages').append(divEscapedContentElement(message));
    $('#messages').scrollTop($('#messages').prop('scrollHeight'));
  }

  $('#send-message').val('');
}
```

If user input begins with slash, treat it as command

Broadcast noncommand input to other users

Now that you've got some helper functions defined, you need to add the logic in the following listing, which is meant to execute when the web page has fully loaded in the user's browser. This code handles client-side initiation of Socket.IO event handling.

Listing 2.13 Client-side application initialization logic

```
var socket = io.connect();

$(document).ready(function() {
  var chatApp = new Chat(socket);

  socket.on('nameResult', function(result) {
    var message;

    if (result.success) {
      message = 'You are now known as ' + result.name + '.';
    } else {
      message = result.message;
    }
    $('#messages').append(divSystemContentElement(message));
  });
```

Display results of a name-change attempt

```
  socket.on('joinResult', function(result) {              <-- Display results of a room change
    $('#room').text(result.room);
    $('#messages').append(divSystemContentElement('Room changed.'));
  });

  socket.on('message', function (message) {               <-- Display received messages
    var newElement = $('<div></div>').text(message.text);
    $('#messages').append(newElement);
  });

  socket.on('rooms', function(rooms) {                    <-- Display list of rooms available
    $('#room-list').empty();

    for(var room in rooms) {
      room = room.substring(1, room.length);
      if (room != '') {
        $('#room-list').append(divEscapedContentElement(room));
      }
    }

    $('#room-list div').click(function() {                <-- Allow click of a room name to change to that room
      chatApp.processCommand('/join ' + $(this).text());
      $('#send-message').focus();
    });
  });

  setInterval(function() {                                <-- Request list of rooms available intermittently
    socket.emit('rooms');
  }, 1000);

  $('#send-message').focus();

  $('#send-form').submit(function() {                     <-- Allow submitting the form to send a chat message
    processUserInput(chatApp, socket);
    return false;
  });
});
```

To finish the application off, add the final CSS styling code in the following listing to the public/stylesheets/style.css file.

Listing 2.14 Final additions to style.css

```
#room-list {
  float: right;
  width: 100px;
  height: 300px;
  overflow: auto;
}

#room-list div {
  border-bottom: 1px solid #eee;
}

#room-list div:hover {
  background-color: #ddd;
}
```

```
#send-message {
  width: 700px;
  margin-bottom: 1em;
  margin-right: 1em;
}

#help {
  font: 10px "Lucida Grande", Helvetica, Arial, sans-serif;
}
```

With the final code added, try running the application (using `node server.js`). Your results should look like figure 2.14.

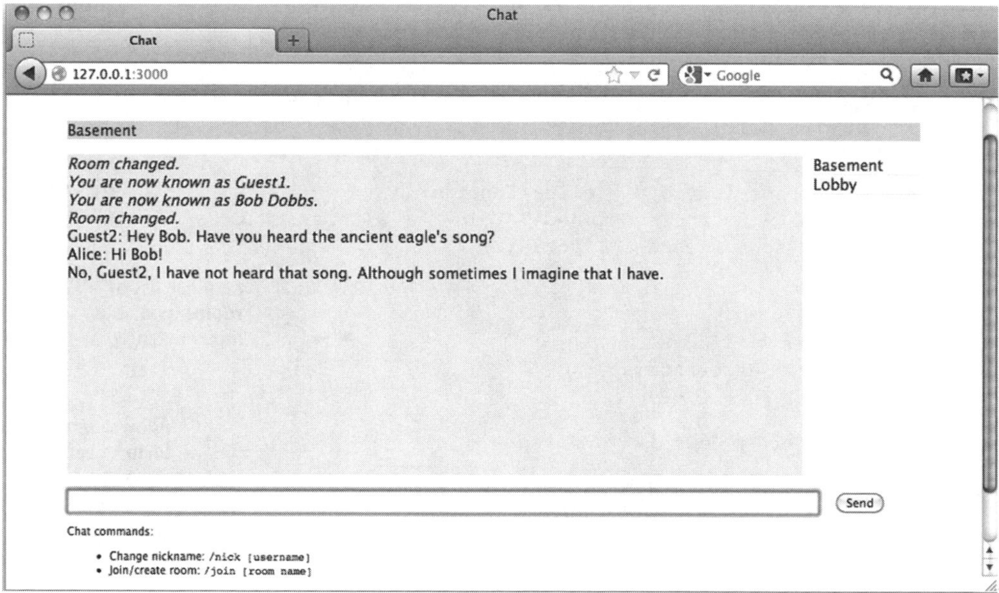

Figure 2.14 The completed chat application

2.6 Summary

You've now completed a small real-time web application using Node.js!

You should have a sense of how the application is constructed and what the code is like. If aspects of this example application are still unclear, don't worry: in the following chapters we'll go into depth on the techniques and technologies used in this example.

Before you delve into the specifics of Node development, however, you'll want to learn how to deal with the unique challenges of asynchronous development. The next chapter will teach you essential techniques and tricks that will save you a lot of time and frustration.

3 Node programming fundamentals

This chapter covers

- Organizing your code into modules
- Coding conventions
- Handling one-off events with callbacks
- Handling repeating events with event emitters
- Implementing serial and parallel flow control
- Leveraging flow-control tools

Node, unlike many open source platforms, is easy to set up and doesn't require much in terms of memory and disk space. No complex integrated development environments or build systems are required. Some fundamental knowledge will, however, help you a lot when starting out. In this chapter we'll address two challenges that new Node developers face:

- How to organize your code
- How asynchronous programming works

The problem of organizing code is familiar to most experienced programmers. Logic is organized conceptually into classes and functions. Files containing the classes and functions are organized into directories within the source tree. In the end, code is organized into applications and libraries. Node's module system provides a powerful mechanism for organizing your code, and you'll learn how to harness it in this chapter.

Asynchronous programming will likely take some time to grasp and master; it requires a paradigm shift in terms of thinking about how application logic should execute. With synchronous programming, you can write a line of code knowing that all the lines of code that came before it will have already executed. With asynchronous development, however, application logic can initially seem like a Rube Goldberg machine. It's worth taking the time, before beginning development of a large project, to learn how you can elegantly control your application's behavior.

In this chapter, you'll learn a number of important asynchronous programming techniques that will allow you to keep a tight rein on how your application executes. You'll learn

- How to respond to one-time events
- How to handle repeating events
- How to sequence asynchronous logic

We'll start, however, with how you can tackle the problem of code organization through the use of *modules*, which are Node's way of keeping code organized and packaged for easy reuse.

3.1 Organizing and reusing Node functionality

When creating an application, Node or otherwise, you often reach a point where putting all of your code in a single file becomes unwieldy. When this happens, the conventional approach, as represented visually in figure 3.1, is to take a file containing a lot of code and try to organize it by grouping related logic and moving it into separate files.

In some language implementations, such as PHP and Ruby, incorporating the logic from another file (we'll call this the "included" file) can mean all the logic executed

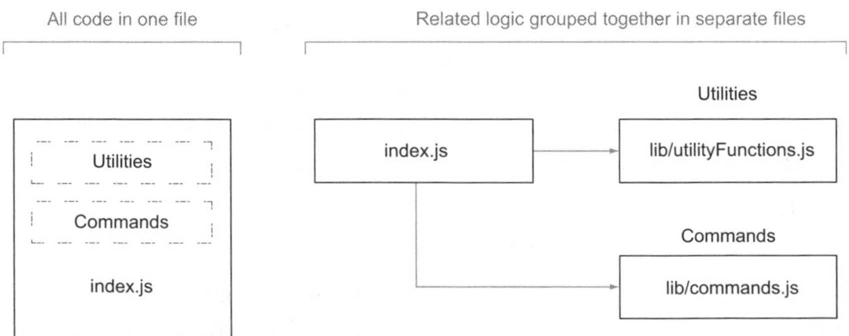

Figure 3.1 It's easier to navigate your code if you organize it using directories and separate files rather than keeping your application in one long file.

in the included file affects the global scope. This means that any variables created and functions declared in the included file risk overwriting those created and declared by the application.

Say you were programming in PHP; your application might contain the following logic:

```
function uppercase_trim($text) {
  return trim(strtoupper($text));
}

include('string_handlers.php');
```

If your string_handlers.php file also attempted to define an `uppercase_trim` function, you'd receive the following error:

```
Fatal error: Cannot redeclare uppercase_trim()
```

In PHP you can avoid this by using *namespaces*, and Ruby offers similar functionality through *modules*. Node, however, avoids this potential problem by not offering an easy way to accidentally pollute the global namespace.

> **PHP NAMESPACES, RUBY MODULES** PHP namespaces are discussed in the manual at http://php.net/manual/en/language.namespaces.php. Ruby modules are explained in the Ruby documentation: www.ruby-doc.org/core-1.9.3/Module.html.

Node modules bundle up code for reuse, but they don't alter global scope. Suppose, for example, you were developing an open source content management system (CMS) application using PHP, and you wanted to use a third-party API library that doesn't use namespaces. This library could contain a class with the same name as one in your application, which would break your application unless you changed the class name either in your application or the library. Changing the class name in your application, however, could cause problems for other developers using your CMS as the basis of their own projects. Changing the class name in the library would require you to remember to repeat this hack each time you update the library in your application's source tree. Naming collisions are a problem best avoided altogether.

Node modules allow you to select what functions and variables from the included file are exposed to the application. If the module is returning more than one function or variable, the module can specify these by setting the properties of an object called `exports`. If the module is returning a single function or variable, the property `module.exports` can instead be set. Figure 3.2 shows how this works.

If this seems a bit confusing, don't worry; we'll run through a number of examples in this chapter.

By avoiding pollution of the global scope, Node's module system avoids naming conflicts and simplifies code reuse. Modules can then be published to the npm (Node Package Manager) repository, an online collection of ready-to-use Node modules, and shared with the Node community without those using the modules having to worry

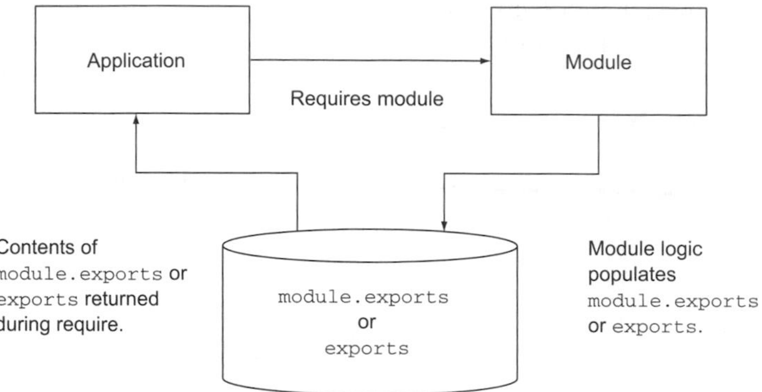

Figure 3.2 The population of the `module.exports` property or the `exports` object allows a module to select what should be shared with the application.

about one module overwriting the variables and functions of another. We'll talk about how to publish to the npm repository in chapter 14.

To help you organize your logic into modules, we'll cover the following topics:

- How you can create modules
- Where modules are stored in the filesystem
- Things to be aware of when creating and using modules

Let's dive into learning the Node module system by creating our first simple module.

3.1.1 *Creating modules*

Modules can either be single files or directories containing one or more files, as can be seen in figure 3.3. If a module is a directory, the file in the module directory that will be evaluated is normally named index.js (although this can be overridden: see section 3.1.4).

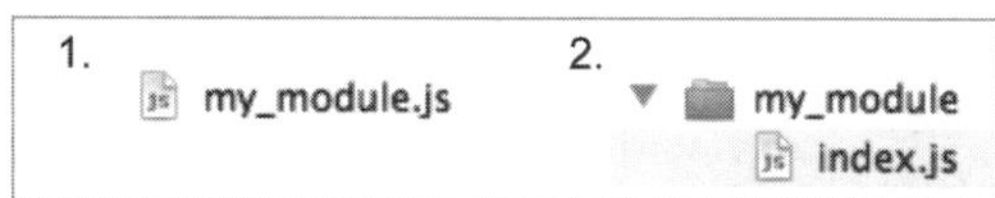

Figure 3.3 Node modules can be created by using either files (example 1) or directories (example 2).

To create a typical module, you create a file that defines properties on the `exports` object with any kind of data, such as strings, objects, and functions.

To show how a basic module is created, let's add some currency conversion functionality to a file named currency.js. This file, shown in the following listing, will contain two functions that will convert Canadian dollars to US dollars, and vice versa.

Listing 3.1 Defining a Node module

```
var canadianDollar = 0.91;

function roundTwoDecimals(amount) {
  return Math.round(amount * 100) / 100;
}
exports.canadianToUS = function(canadian) {
```

canadianToUS function is set in exports module so it can be used by code requiring this module

```
  return roundTwoDecimals(canadian * canadianDollar);
}
exports.USToCanadian = function(us) {
  return roundTwoDecimals(us / canadianDollar);
}
```

USToCanadian function is also set in exports module

Note that only two properties of the `exports` object are set. This means only the two functions, `canadianToUS` and `USToCanadian`, can be accessed by the application including the module. The variable `canadianDollar` acts as a private variable that affects the logic in `canadianToUS` and `USToCanadian` but can't be directly accessed by the application.

To utilize your new module, use Node's `require` function, which takes a path to the module you wish to use as an argument. Node performs a synchronous lookup in order to locate the module and loads the file's contents.

> **A note about require and synchronous I/O**
>
> `require` is one of the few synchronous I/O operations available in Node. Because modules are used often and are typically included at the top of a file, having `require` be synchronous helps keep code clean, ordered, and readable.
>
> But avoid using `require` in I/O-intensive parts of your application. Any synchronous call will block Node from doing anything until the call has finished. For example, if you're running an HTTP server, you would take a performance hit if you used `require` on each incoming request. This is typically why `require` and other synchronous operations are used only when the application initially loads.

In the next listing, which shows test-currency.js, you `require` the currency.js module.

Listing 3.2 Requiring a module

```
var currency = require('./currency');

console.log('50 Canadian dollars equals this amount of US dollars:');
console.log(currency.canadianToUS(50));

console.log('30 US dollars equals this amount of Canadian dollars:');
console.log(currency.USToCanadian(30));
```

Path uses ./ to indicate that module exists within same directory as application script

Use currency module's canadianToUS function

Use currency module's USToCanadian function

Requiring a module that begins with ./ means that if you were to create your application script named test-currency.js in a directory named currency_app, then your currency.js module file, as represented visually in figure 3.4, would also need to exist in the currency_app directory. When requiring, the .js extension is assumed, so you can omit it if desired.

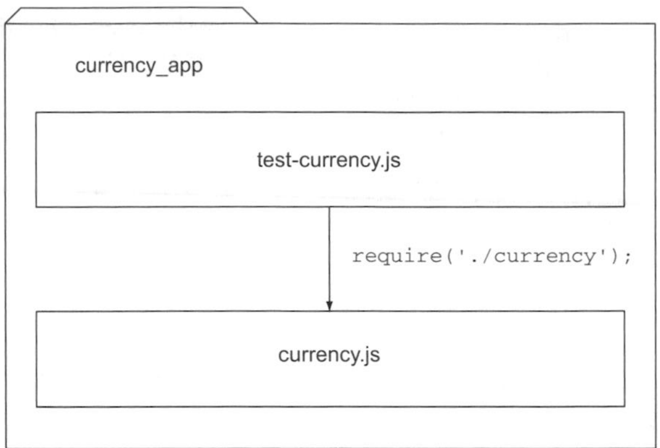

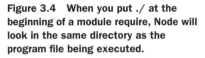

Figure 3.4 When you put ./ at the beginning of a module require, Node will look in the same directory as the program file being executed.

After Node has located and evaluated your module, the `require` function returns the contents of the `exports` object defined in the module. You're then able to use the two functions returned by the module to do currency conversion.

If you wanted to put the module into a subdirectory, such as lib, you could do so by simply changing the line containing the `require` logic to the following:

```
var currency = require('./lib/currency');
```

Populating the `exports` object of a module gives you a simple way to group reusable code in separate files.

3.1.2 Fine-tuning module creation using module.exports

Although populating the `exports` object with functions and variables is suitable for most module-creation needs, there will be times when you want a module to deviate from this model.

The currency converter module created earlier in this section, for example, could be redone to return a single `Currency` constructor function rather than an object containing functions. An object-oriented implementation could behave something like the following:

```
var Currency = require('./currency');
var canadianDollar = 0.91;

var currency = new Currency(canadianDollar);
console.log(currency.canadianToUS(50));
```

Returning a function from `require`, rather than an object, will make your code more elegant if it's the only thing you need from the module.

To create a module that returns a single variable or function, you might guess that you simply need to set `exports` to whatever you want to return. But this won't work, because Node expects `exports` to not be reassigned to any other object, function, or variable. The module code in the next listing attempts to set `exports` to a function.

Listing 3.3 This module won't work as expected

```
var Currency = function(canadianDollar) {
  this.canadianDollar = canadianDollar;
}

Currency.prototype.roundTwoDecimals = function(amount) {
  return Math.round(amount * 100) / 100;
}

Currency.prototype.canadianToUS = function(canadian) {
  return this.roundTwoDecimals(canadian * this.canadianDollar);
}

Currency.prototype.USToCanadian = function(us) {
  return this.roundTwoDecimals(us / this.canadianDollar);
}

exports = Currency;
```

Incorrect; Node doesn't allow exports to be overwritten

In order to get the previous module code to work as expected, you'd need to replace `exports` with `module.exports`. The `module.exports` mechanism enables you to export a single variable, function, or object. If you create a module that populates both `exports` and `module.exports`, `module.exports` will be returned and `exports` will be ignored.

What really gets exported

What ultimately gets exported in your application is `module.exports`. `exports` is set up simply as a global reference to `module.exports`, which initially is defined as an empty object that you can add properties to. So `exports.myFunc` is just shorthand for `module.exports.myFunc`.

As a result, if `exports` is set to anything else, it breaks the *reference* between `module.exports` and `exports`. Because `module.exports` is what really gets exported, `exports` will no longer work as expected—it doesn't reference `module.exports` anymore. If you want to maintain that link, you can make `module.exports` reference `exports` again as follows:

```
module.exports = exports = Currency;
```

By using either `exports` or `module.exports`, depending on your needs, you can organize functionality into modules and avoid the pitfall of ever-growing application scripts.

3.1.3 Reusing modules using the node_modules folder

Requiring modules in the filesystem to exist relative to an application is useful for organizing application-specific code, but isn't as useful for code you'd like to reuse between applications or share with others. Node includes a unique mechanism for

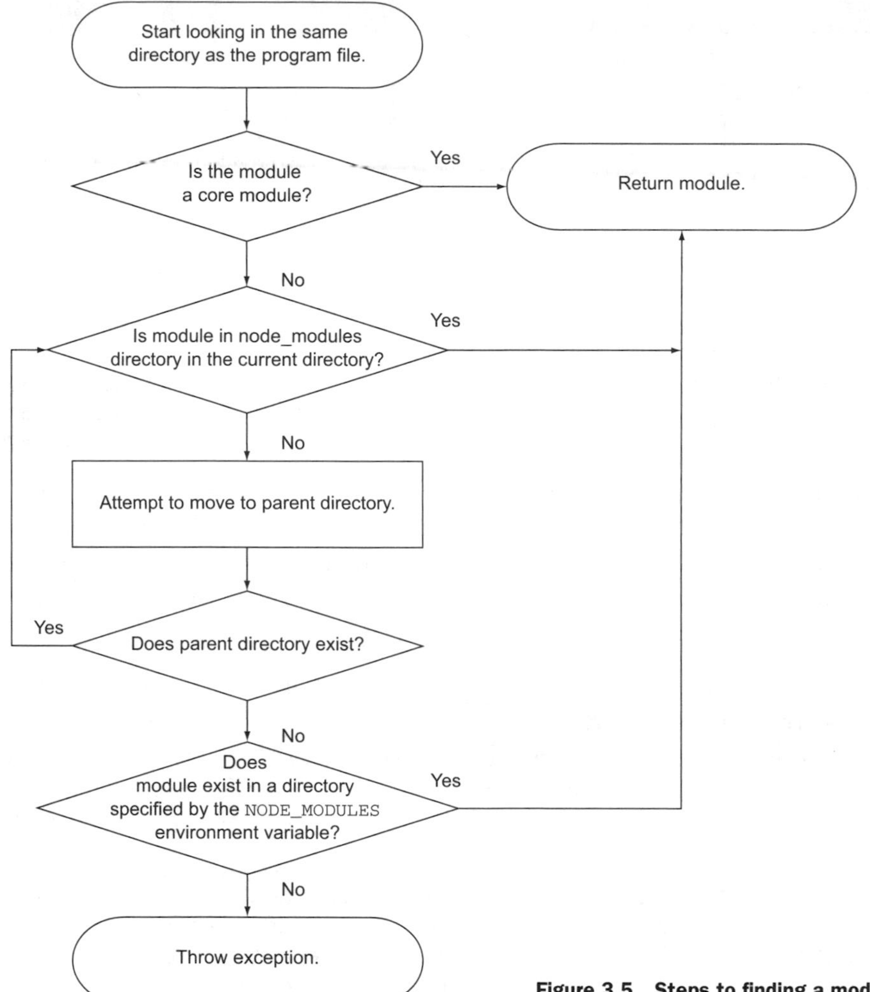

Figure 3.5 Steps to finding a module

code reuse that allows modules to be required without knowing their location in the filesystem. This mechanism is the use of node_modules directories.

In the earlier module example, you required ./currency. If you omit the ./ and simply require currency, Node will follow a number of rules, as specified in figure 3.5, to search for this module.

The `NODE_PATH` environmental variable provides a way to specify alternative locations for Node modules. If used, `NODE_PATH` should be set to a list of directories separated by semicolons in Windows or colons in other operating systems.

3.1.4 Caveats

While the essence of Node's module system is straightforward, there are two things to be aware of.

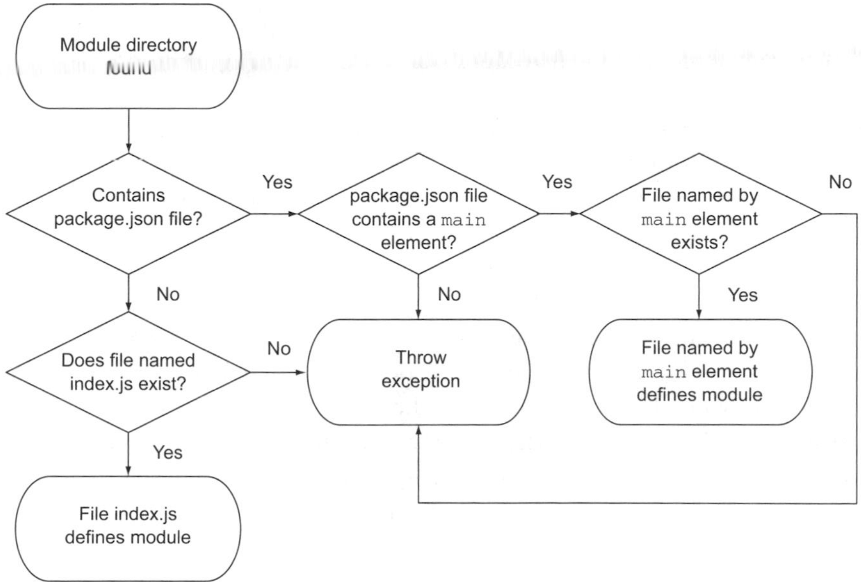

Figure 3.6 The package.json file, when placed in a module directory, allows you to define your module using a file other than index.js.

First, if a module is a directory, the file in the module directory that will be evaluated must be named index.js, unless specified otherwise by a file in the module directory named package.json. To specify an alternative to index.js, the package.json file must contain JavaScript Object Notation (JSON) data defining an object with a key named `main` that specifies the path, within the module directory, to the main file. Figure 3.6 shows a flowchart summarizing these rules.

Here's an example of a package.json file specifying that currency.js is the main file:

```
{
  "main": "./currency.js"
}
```

The other thing to be aware of is Node's ability to cache modules as objects. If two files in an application require the same module, the first require will store the data returned in application memory so the second require won't need to access and evaluate the module's source files. The second require will, in fact, have the opportunity to alter the cached data. This "monkey patching" capability allows one module to modify the behavior of another, freeing the developer from having to create a new version of it.

The best way to get comfortable with Node's module system is to play with it, verifying the behavior described in this section yourself.

Now that you have a basic understanding of how modules work, let's move on to asynchronous programming techniques.

3.2 Asynchronous programming techniques

If you've done front-end web programming in which interface events (such as mouse clicks) trigger logic, then you've done asynchronous programming. Server-side asynchronous programming is no different: events occur that trigger response logic. There are two popular models in the Node world for managing response logic: callbacks and event listeners.

Callbacks generally define logic for one-off responses. If you perform a database query, for example, you can specify a callback to determine what to do with the query results. The callback may display the database results, do a calculation based on the results, or execute another callback using the query results as an argument.

Event listeners, on the other hand, are essentially callbacks that are associated with a conceptual entity (an *event*). For comparison, a mouse click is an event you would handle in the browser when someone clicks the mouse. As an example, in Node an HTTP server emits a `request` event when an HTTP request is made. You can listen for that `request` event to occur and add some response logic. In the following example, the function `handleRequest` will be called whenever a `request` event is emitted:

```
server.on('request', handleRequest)
```

A Node HTTP server instance is an example of an *event emitter*, a class (`EventEmitter`) that can be inherited and that adds the ability to emit and handle events. Many aspects of Node's core functionality inherit from `EventEmitter`, and you can also create your own.

Now that we've established that response logic is generally organized in one of two ways in Node, let's jump into how it all works by learning about the following:

- How to handle one-off events with callbacks
- How to respond to repeating events using event listeners
- Some of the challenges of asynchronous programming

Let's look first at one of the most common ways asynchronous code is handled: the use of callbacks.

3.2.1 Handling one-off events with callbacks

A *callback* is a function, passed as an argument to an asynchronous function, that describes what to do after the asynchronous operation has completed. Callbacks are used frequently in Node development, more so than event emitters, and they're simple to use.

To demonstrate the use of callbacks in an application, let's make a simple HTTP server that does the following:

- Pulls the titles of recent posts stored as a JSON file asynchronously
- Pulls a basic HTML template asynchronously
- Assembles an HTML page containing the titles
- Sends the HTML page to the user

The results will be similar to figure 3.7.

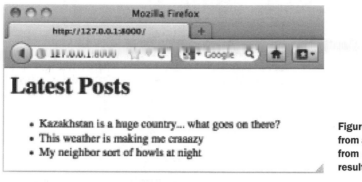

Figure 3.7 An HTML response from a web server that pulls titles from a JSON file and returns results as a web page

The JSON file (titles.json), shown in the following listing, will be formatted as an array of strings containing titles of posts.

Listing 3.4 A list of post titles

```
[
  "Kazakhstan is a huge country... what goes on there?",
  "This weather is making me craaazy",
  "My neighbor sort of howls at night"
]
```

The HTML template file (template.html), shown next, will include just a basic structure to insert the titles of the blog posts.

Listing 3.5 A basic HTML template to render the blog titles

```
<!doctype html>
<html>
  <head></head>
  <body>
    <h1>Latest Posts</h1>
    <ul><li>%</li></ul>          <-- % will be replaced with title data
  </body>
</html>
```

The code that pulls in the JSON file and renders the web page is shown next (blog_recent.js). The callback functions are displayed in bold.

Listing 3.6 An example of the use of callbacks in a simple application

```
var http = require('http');
var fs = require('fs');

http.createServer(function(req, res) {          <-- Create HTTP server and use callback to define response logic
  if (req.url == '/') {
    fs.readFile('./titles.json', function(err, data) {          <-- Read JSON file and use callback to define what to do with its contents
      if (err) {          <-- If error occurs, log error and return "Server Error" to client
        console.error(err);
        res.end('Server Error');
      }
```

```
      else {
        var titles = JSON.parse(data.toString());

        fs.readFile('./template.html', function(err, data) {
          if (err) {
            console.error(err);
            res.end('Server Error');
          }
          else {
            var tmpl = data.toString();

            var html = tmpl.replace('%', titles.join('</li><li>'));
            res.writeHead(200, {'Content-Type': 'text/html'});
            res.end(html);
          }
        });
      }
    });
  }
}).listen(8000, "127.0.0.1");
```

Parse data from JSON text

Read HTML template and use callback when it's loaded

Assemble HTML page showing blog titles

Send HTML page to user

This example nests three levels of callbacks:

```
http.createServer(function(req, res) { ...
  fs.readFile('./titles.json', function (err, data) { ...
    fs.readFile('./template.html', function (err, data) { ...
```

Three levels isn't bad, but the more levels of callbacks you use, the more cluttered your code looks, and the harder it is to refactor and test, so it's good to limit callback nesting. By creating named functions that handle the individual levels of callback nesting, you can express the same logic in a way that requires more lines of code, but that could be easier to maintain, test, and refactor. The following listing is functionally equivalent to listing 3.6.

Listing 3.7 An example of reducing nesting by creating intermediary functions

```
var http = require('http');
var fs = require('fs');

var server = http.createServer(function (req, res) {
  getTitles(res);
}).listen(8000, "127.0.0.1");

function getTitles(res) {
  fs.readFile('./titles.json', function (err, data) {
    if (err) {
      hadError(err, res);
    }
    else {
      getTemplate(JSON.parse(data.toString()), res);
    }
  })
}

function getTemplate(titles, res) {
  fs.readFile('./template.html', function (err, data) {
```

Client request initially comes in here

Control is passed to getTitles

getTitles pulls titles and passes control to getTemplate

getTemplate reads template file and passes control to formatHtml

```
    if (err) {
      hadError(err, res);
    }
    else {
      formatHtml(titles, data.toString(), res);
    }
  })
}

function formatHtml(titles, tmpl, res) {
  var html = tmpl.replace('%', titles.join('</li><li>'));
  res.writeHead(200, {'Content-Type': 'text/html'});
  res.end(html);
}

function hadError(err, res) {
  console.error(err);
  res.end('Server Error');
}
```

formatHtml takes titles and template, and renders a response back to client

If an error occurs along the way, hadError logs error to console and responds to client with "Server Error"

You can also reduce the nesting caused by `if/else` blocks with another common idiom in Node development: returning early from a function. The following listing is functionally the same but avoids further nesting by returning early. It also makes it explicit that the function should not continue executing.

Listing 3.8 An example of reducing nesting by returning early

```
var http = require('http');
var fs = require('fs');

var server = http.createServer(function (req, res)
  getTitles(res);
}).listen(8000, "127.0.0.1");

function getTitles(res) {
  fs.readFile('./titles.json', function (err, data) {
    if (err) return hadError(err, res)
    getTemplate(JSON.parse(data.toString()), res)
  })
}

function getTemplate(titles, res) {
  fs.readFile('./template.html', function (err, data) {
    if (err) return hadError(err, res)
    formatHtml(titles, data.toString(), res)
  })
}

function formatHtml(titles, tmpl, res) {
  var html = tmpl.replace('%', titles.join('</li><li>'));
  res.writeHead(200, {'Content-Type': 'text/html'});
  res.end(html);
}

function hadError(err, res) {
  console.error(err)
  res.end('Server Error')
}
```

Instead of creating an else branch, you return, because if an error occurred you don't need to continue executing this function.

Now that you've learned how to use callbacks to handle one-off events for such tasks as defining responses when reading files and web server requests, let's move on to organizing events using event emitters.

The Node convention for asynchronous callbacks

Most Node built-in modules use callbacks with two arguments: the first argument is for an error, should one occur, and the second argument is for the results. The error argument is often abbreviated as `er` or `err`.

Here's a typical example of this common function signature:

```
var fs = require('fs');
fs.readFile('./titles.json', function(er, data) {
  if (er) throw er;
  // do something with data if no error has occurred
});
```

3.2.2 Handling repeating events with event emitters

Event emitters fire events and include the ability to handle those events when triggered. Some important Node API components, such as HTTP servers, TCP servers, and streams, are implemented as event emitters. You can also create your own.

As we mentioned earlier, events are handled through the use of listeners. A *listener* is the association of an event with a callback function that gets triggered each time the event occurs. For example, a TCP socket in Node has an event called `data` that's triggered whenever new data is available on the socket:

```
socket.on('data', handleData);
```

Let's look at using `data` events to create an echo server.

AN EXAMPLE EVENT EMITTER

A simple example where repeated events could occur is an echo server, which, when you send data to it, will echo the data back, as shown in figure 3.8.

The following listing shows the code needed to implement an echo server. Whenever a client connects, a socket is created. The socket is an event emitter to which you

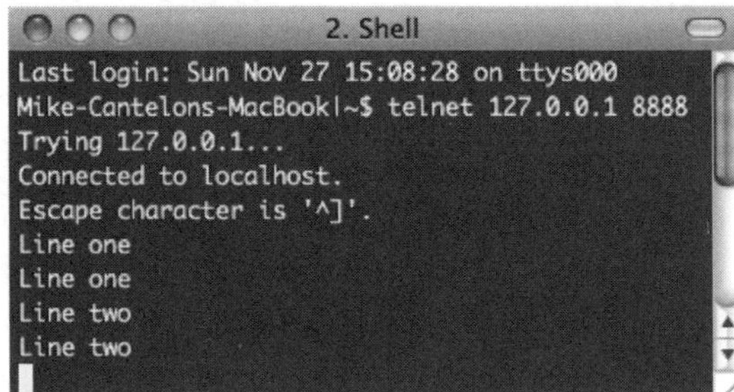

Figure 3.8 An echo server repeating the data sent to it

can then add a listener, using the on method, to respond to data events. These data events are emitted whenever new data is available on the socket.

Listing 3.9 Using the on method to respond to events

```
var net = require('net');

var server = net.createServer(function(socket) {
  socket.on('data', function(data) {
    socket.write(data);
  });
});

server.listen(8888);
```

data events handled whenever new data has been read

Data is written (echoed back) to client

You run this echo server by entering the following command:

```
node echo_server.js
```

After the echo server is running, you can connect to it by entering the following command:

```
telnet 127.0.0.1 8888
```

Every time data is sent from your connected telnet session to the server, it will be echoed back into the telnet session.

> **TELNET ON WINDOWS** If you're using the Microsoft Windows operating system, telnet may not be installed by default, and you'll have to install it yourself. TechNet has instructions for the various versions of Windows: http://mng.bz/egzr.

RESPONDING TO AN EVENT THAT SHOULD ONLY OCCUR ONCE

Listeners can be defined to repeatedly respond to events, as the previous example showed, or listeners can be defined to respond only once. The code in the following listing, using the once method, modifies the previous echo server example to only echo the first chunk of data sent to it.

Listing 3.10 Using the once method to respond to a single event

```
var net = require('net');

var server = net.createServer(function(socket) {
  socket.once ('data', function(data) {
    socket.write(data);
  });
});

server.listen(8888);
```

data event will only be handled once

CREATING EVENT EMITTERS: A PUB/SUB EXAMPLE

In the previous example, we used a built-in Node API that leverages event emitters. Node's built-in events module, however, allows you to create your own event emitters.

The following code defines a `channel` event emitter with a single listener that responds to someone joining the channel. Note that you use `on` (or, alternatively, the longer form `addListener`) to add a listener to an event emitter:

```
var EventEmitter = require('events').EventEmitter;
var channel = new EventEmitter();
channel.on('join', function() {
  console.log("Welcome!");
});
```

This `join` callback, however, won't ever be called, because you haven't emitted any events yet. You could add a line to the listing that would trigger an event using the `emit` function:

```
channel.emit('join');
```

> **EVENT NAMES** Events are simply keys and can have any string value: `data`, `join`, or `some crazy long event name`. There's only one special event, called `error`, that we'll look at soon.

In chapter 2 you built a chat application that leverages the Socket.io module for publish/subscribe capabilities. Let's look at how you could implement your own publish/subscribe logic.

If you run the script in listing 3.11, you'll have a simple chat server. A chat server channel is implemented as an event emitter that responds to `join` events emitted by clients. When a client joins the channel, the join listener logic, in turn, adds an additional client-specific listener to the channel for the `broadcast` event that will write any message broadcast to the client socket. The names of the event types, such as `join` and `broadcast`, are completely arbitrary. You could use other names for these event types if you wished.

Listing 3.11 A simple publish/subscribe system using an event emitter

```
var events = require('events');
var net = require('net');

var channel = new events.EventEmitter();
channel.clients = {};
channel.subscriptions = {};

channel.on('join', function(id, client) {
  this.clients[id] = client;
  this.subscriptions[id] = function(senderId, message) {
    if (id != senderId) {
      this.clients[id].write(message);
    }
  }
  this.on('broadcast', this.subscriptions[id]);
});

var server = net.createServer(function (client) {
  var id = client.remoteAddress + ':' + client.remotePort;
```

Add a listener for the join event that stores a user's client object, allowing the application to send data back to the user.

Ignore data if it's been directly broadcast by the user.

Add a listener, specific to the current user, for the broadcast event.

```
  client.on('connect', function() {
    channel.emit('join', id, client);
  });
  client.on('data', function(data) {
    data = data.toString();
    channel.emit('broadcast', id, data);
  });
});
server.listen(8888);
```

Emit a join event when a user connects to the server, specifying the user ID and client object.

Emit a channel broadcast event, specifying the user ID and message, when any user sends data.

After you have the chat server running, open a new command line and enter the following code to enter the chat:

```
telnet 127.0.0.1 8888
```

If you open up a few command lines, you'll see that anything typed in one command line is echoed to the others.

The problem with this chat server is that when users close their connection and leave the chat room, they leave behind a listener that will attempt to write to a client that's no longer connected. This will, of course, generate an error. To fix this issue, you need to add the listener in the following listing to the `channel` event emitter, and add logic to the server's `close` event listener to emit the channel's `leave` event. The `leave` event essentially removes the `broadcast` listener originally added for the client.

Listing 3.12 Creating a listener to clean up when clients disconnect

```
...
channel.on('leave', function(id) {
  channel.removeListener(
    'broadcast', this.subscriptions[id]);
  channel.emit('broadcast', id, id + " has left the chat.\n");
});

var server = net.createServer(function (client) {
  ...
  client.on('close', function() {
    channel.emit('leave', id);
  });
});
server.listen(8888);
```

Create listener for leave event

Remove broadcast listener for specific client

Emit leave event when client disconnects

If you want to prevent a chat for some reason, but don't want to shut down the server, you could use the `removeAllListeners` event emitter method to remove all listeners of a given type. The following code shows how this could be implemented for our chat server example:

```
channel.on('shutdown', function() {
  channel.emit('broadcast', '', "Chat has shut down.\n");
  channel.removeAllListeners('broadcast');
});
```

You could then add support for a chat command that would trigger the shutdown. To do so, change the listener for the `data` event to the following code:

```
client.on('data', function(data) {
  data = data.toString();
  if (data == "shutdown\r\n") {
    channel.emit('shutdown');
  }
  channel.emit('broadcast', id, data);
});
```

Now when any chat participant enters `shutdown` into the chat, it'll cause all chat participants to be kicked off.

Error handling

A convention you can use when creating event emitters is to emit an `error` type event instead of directly throwing an error. This allows you to define custom event response logic by setting one or more listeners for this event type.

The following code shows how an error listener handles an emitted error by logging into the console:

```
var events = require('events');
var myEmitter = new events.EventEmitter();
myEmitter.on('error', function(err) {
  console.log('ERROR: ' + err.message);
});
myEmitter.emit('error', new Error('Something is wrong.'));
```

If no listener for this event type is defined when the `error` event type is emitted, the event emitter will output a stack trace (a list of program instructions that had executed up to the point when the error occurred) and halt execution. The stack trace will indicate an error of the type specified by the `emit` call's second argument. This behavior is unique to `error` type events; when other event types are emitted, and they have no listeners, nothing happens.

If an `error` type event is emitted without an `error` object supplied as the second argument, a stack trace will indicate an "Uncaught, unspecified 'error' event" error, and your application will halt. There is a deprecated method you can use to deal with this error—you can define your own response by defining a global handler using the following code:

```
process.on('uncaughtException', function(err){
  console.error(err.stack);
  process.exit(1);
});
```

Alternatives to this, such as domains (http://nodejs.org/api/domain.html), are being developed, but they're considered experimental.

If you want to provide users connecting to chat with a count of currently connected users, you could use the following `listeners` method, which returns an array of listeners for a given event type:

```
channel.on('join', function(id, client) {
  var welcome = "Welcome!\n"
              + 'Guests online: ' + this.listeners('broadcast').length;
  client.write(welcome + "\n");
  ...
```

To increase the number of listeners an event emitter has, and to avoid the warnings Node displays when there are more than ten listeners, you could use the `setMaxListeners` method. Using your channel event emitter as an example, you'd use the following code to increase the number of allowed listeners:

```
channel.setMaxListeners(50);
```

EXTENDING THE EVENT EMITTER: A FILE WATCHER EXAMPLE

If you'd like to build upon the event emitter's behavior, you can create a new JavaScript class that inherits from the event emitter. For example, you could create a class called `Watcher` that would process files placed in a specified filesystem directory. You'd then use this class to create a utility that would watch a filesystem directory (renaming any files placed in it to lowercase) and then copy the files into a separate directory.

There are three steps to extending an event emitter:

1. Creating a class constructor
2. Inheriting the event emitter's behavior
3. Extending the behavior

The following code shows how to create the constructor for your `Watcher` class. The constructor takes, as arguments, the directory to monitor and the directory in which to put the altered files:

```
function Watcher(watchDir, processedDir) {
  this.watchDir     = watchDir;
  this.processedDir = processedDir;
}
```

Next, you need to add logic to inherit the event emitter's behavior:

```
var events = require('events')
  , util = require('util');

util.inherits(Watcher, events.EventEmitter);
```

Note the use of the `inherits` function, which is part of Node's built-in util module. The `inherits` function provides a clean way to inherit another object's behavior.

The `inherits` statement in the previous code snippet is equivalent to the following JavaScript:

```
Watcher.prototype = new events.EventEmitter();
```

After setting up the `Watcher` object, you need to extend the methods inherited from `EventEmitter` with two new methods, as shown in the following listing.

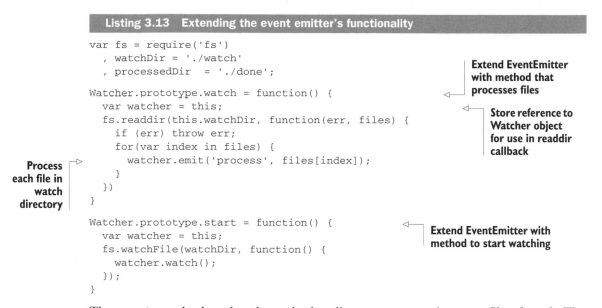

Listing 3.13 Extending the event emitter's functionality

```
var fs = require('fs')
  , watchDir = './watch'
  , processedDir  = './done';

Watcher.prototype.watch = function() {
  var watcher = this;
  fs.readdir(this.watchDir, function(err, files) {
    if (err) throw err;
    for(var index in files) {
      watcher.emit('process', files[index]);
    }
  })
}

Watcher.prototype.start = function() {
  var watcher = this;
  fs.watchFile(watchDir, function() {
    watcher.watch();
  });
}
```

Extend EventEmitter with method that processes files

Store reference to Watcher object for use in readdir callback

Process each file in watch directory

Extend EventEmitter with method to start watching

The `watch` method cycles through the directory, processing any files found. The `start` method starts the directory monitoring. The monitoring leverages Node's `fs.watchFile` function, so when something happens in the watched directory, the `watch` method is triggered, cycling through the watched directory and emitting a `process` event for each file found.

Now that you've defined the `Watcher` class, you can put it to work by creating a `Watcher` object using the following code:

```
var watcher = new Watcher(watchDir, processedDir);
```

With your newly created `Watcher` object, you can use the `on` method, inherited from the event emitter class, to set the logic used to process each file, as shown in this snippet:

```
watcher.on('process', function process(file) {
  var watchFile      = this.watchDir + '/' + file;
  var processedFile  = this.processedDir + '/' + file.toLowerCase();

  fs.rename(watchFile, processedFile, function(err) {
    if (err) throw err;
  });
});
```

Now that all the necessary logic is in place, you can start the directory monitor using the following code:

```
watcher.start();
```

After putting the `Watcher` code into a script and creating watch and done directories, you should be able to run the script using Node, drop files into the watch directory, and see the files pop up, renamed to lowercase, in the done directory. This is an example of how the event emitter can be a useful class from which to create new classes.

By learning how to use callbacks to define one-off asynchronous logic and how to use event emitters to dispatch asynchronous logic repeatedly, you're one step closer to mastering control of a Node application's behavior. In a single callback or event emitter listener, however, you may want to include logic that performs additional asynchronous tasks. If the order in which these tasks are performed is important, you may be faced with a new challenge: how to control exactly when each task, in a series of asynchronous tasks, executes.

Before we get to controlling when tasks execute—coming up in section 3.3—let's take a look at some of the challenges you'll likely encounter as you write asynchronous code.

3.2.3 Challenges with asynchronous development

When creating asynchronous applications, you have to pay close attention to how your application flows and keep a watchful eye on application state: the conditions of the event loop, application variables, and any other resources that change as program logic executes.

Node's event loop, for example, keeps track of asynchronous logic that hasn't completed processing. As long as there's uncompleted asynchronous logic, the Node process won't exit. A continually running Node process is desirable behavior for something like a web server, but it isn't desirable to continue running processes that are expected to end after a period of time, like command-line tools. The event loop will keep track of any database connections until they're closed, preventing Node from exiting.

Application variables can also change unexpectedly if you're not careful. Listing 3.14 shows an example of how the order in which asynchronous code executes can lead to confusion. If the example code was executing synchronously, you'd expect the output to be "The color is blue." Because the example is asynchronous, however, the value of the `color` variable changes before `console.log` executes, and the output is "The color is green."

Listing 3.14 How scope behavior can lead to bugs

```
function asyncFunction(callback) {
  setTimeout(callback, 200);
}

var color = 'blue';

asyncFunction(function() {
  console.log('The color is ' + color);    <- This is executed last (200 ms later).
});

color = 'green';
```

To "freeze" the contents of the `color` variable, you can modify your logic and use a JavaScript closure. In listing 3.15, you wrap the call to `asyncFunction` in an anonymous function that takes a `color` argument. You then execute the anonymous function immediately, sending it the current contents of `color`. By making `color` an argument for the anonymous function, it becomes local to the scope of that function, and when the value of `color` is changed outside of the anonymous function, the local version is unaffected.

Listing 3.15 Using an anonymous function to preserve a global variable's value

```
function asyncFunction(callback) {
  setTimeout(callback, 200);
}
var color = 'blue';

(function(color) {
  asyncFunction(function() {
    console.log('The color is ' + color);
  })
})(color);

color = 'green';
```

This is but one of many JavaScript programming tricks you'll come across in your Node development.

> **CLOSURES** For more information on closures, see the Mozilla JavaScript documentation: https://developer.mozilla.org/en-US/docs/JavaScript/Guide/Closures.

Now that you understand how you can use closures to control your application state, let's look at how you can sequence asynchronous logic in order to keep the flow of your application under control.

3.3 Sequencing asynchronous logic

During the execution of an asynchronous program, there are some tasks that can happen any time, independent of what the rest of the program is doing, without causing problems. But there are also some tasks, however, that should happen only before or after certain other tasks.

The concept of sequencing groups of asynchronous tasks is called *flow control* by the Node community. There are two types of flow control: *serial* and *parallel*, as figure 3.9 shows.

Tasks that need to happen one after the other are called *serial*. A simple example would be the tasks of creating a directory and then storing a file in it. You wouldn't be able to store the file before creating the directory.

Tasks that don't need to happen one after the other are called *parallel*. It isn't necessarily important when these tasks start and stop relative to one another, but they should all be completed before further logic executes. One example would be downloading a number of files that will later be compressed into a zip archive. The files can be downloaded simultaneously, but all of the downloads should be completed before creating the archive.

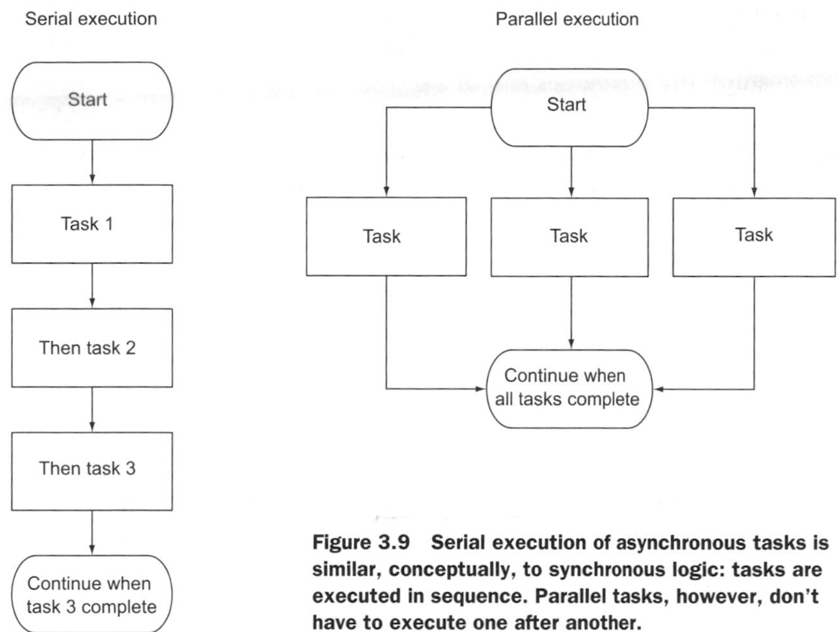

Figure 3.9 Serial execution of asynchronous tasks is similar, conceptually, to synchronous logic: tasks are executed in sequence. Parallel tasks, however, don't have to execute one after another.

Keeping track of serial and parallel flow control involves programmatic bookkeeping. When you implement serial flow control, you need to keep track of the task currently executing or maintain a queue of unexecuted tasks. When you implement parallel flow control, you need to keep track of how many tasks have executed to completion.

Flow control tools handle the bookkeeping for you, which makes grouping asynchronous serial or parallel tasks easy. Although there are plenty of community-created add-ons that deal with sequencing asynchronous logic, implementing flow control yourself demystifies it and helps you gain a deeper understanding of how to deal with the challenges of asynchronous programming.

In this section we'll show you the following:

- When to use serial flow control
- How to implement serial flow control
- How to implement parallel flow control
- How to leverage third-party modules for flow control

Let's start by looking at when and how you handle serial flow control in an asychronous world.

3.3.1 *When to use serial flow control*

In order to execute a number of asynchronous tasks in sequence, you could use callbacks, but if you have a significant number of tasks, you'll have to organize them. If you don't, you'll end up with messy code due to excessive callback nesting.

The following code is an example of executing tasks in sequence using callbacks. The example uses `setTimeout` to simulate tasks that take time to execute: the first task takes one second, the next takes half of a second, and the last takes one-tenth of a second. `setTimeout` is only an artificial simulation; in real code you could be reading files, making HTTP requests, and so on. Although this example code is short, it's arguably a bit messy, and there's no easy way to programmatically add an additional task.

```
setTimeout(function() {
  console.log('I execute first.');
  setTimeout(function() {
    console.log('I execute next.');
    setTimeout(function() {
      console.log('I execute last.');
    }, 100);
  }, 500);
}, 1000);
```

Alternatively, you can use a flow-control tool such as Nimble to execute these tasks. Nimble is straightforward to use and benefits from having a very small codebase (a mere 837 bytes, minified and compressed). You can install Nimble with the following command:

```
npm install nimble
```

Now, use the code in the next listing to re-implement the previous code snippet using serial flow control.

Listing 3.16 Serial control using a community-created add-on

```
var flow = require('nimble');

flow.series([                          <- Provide an array of functions for Nimble to
  function (callback) {                   execute, one after the other.
    setTimeout(function() {
      console.log('I execute first.');
      callback();
    }, 1000);
  },
  function (callback) {
    setTimeout(function() {
      console.log('I execute next.');
      callback();
    }, 500);
  },
  function (callback) {
    setTimeout(function() {
      console.log('I execute last.');
      callback();
    }, 100);
  }
]);
```

Although the implementation using flow control means more lines of code, it's generally easier to read and maintain. You're likely not going to use flow control all the time, but if you run into a situation where you want to avoid callback nesting, it's a handy tool for improving code legibility.

Now that you've seen an example of the use of serial flow control with a specialized tool, let's look at how to implement it from scratch.

3.3.2 Implementing serial flow control

In order to execute a number of asynchronous tasks in sequence using serial flow control, you first need to put the tasks in an array, in the desired order of execution. This array, as figure 3.10 shows, will act as a queue: when you finish one task, you extract the next task in sequence from the array.

Each task exists in the array as a function. When a task has completed, the task should call a handler function to indicate error status and results. The handler function in this implementation will halt execution if there's an error. If there isn't an error, the handler will pull the next task from the queue and execute it.

To demonstrate an implementation of serial flow control, we'll make a simple application that will display a single article's title and URL from a randomly chosen RSS feed. The list of possible RSS feeds will be specified in a text file. The application's output will look something like the following text:

```
Of Course ML Has Monads!
http://lambda-the-ultimate.org/node/4306
```

Our example requires the use of two helper modules from the npm repository. First, open a command-line prompt, and then enter the following commands to create a directory for the example and install the helper modules:

```
mkdir random_story
cd random_story
npm install request
npm install htmlparser
```

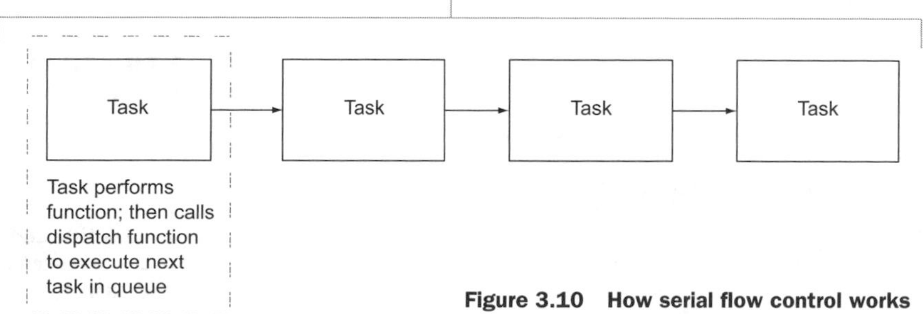

Figure 3.10 How serial flow control works

The request module is a simplified HTTP client that you can use to fetch RSS data. The htmlparser module has functionality that will allow you to turn raw RSS data into JavaScript data structures.

Next, create a file named random_story.js inside your new directory that contains the code shown here.

Listing 3.17 Serial flow control implemented in a simple application

```
var fs = require('fs');
var request = require('request');
var htmlparser = require('htmlparser');
var configFilename = './rss_feeds.txt';

function checkForRSSFile () {
  fs.exists(configFilename, function(exists) {
    if (!exists)
      return next(new Error('Missing RSS file: ' + configFilename));

    next(null, configFilename);
  });
}

function readRSSFile (configFilename) {
  fs.readFile(configFilename, function(err, feedList) {
    if (err) return next(err);

    feedList = feedList
               .toString()
               .replace(/^\s+|\s+$/g, '')
               .split("\n");
    var random = Math.floor(Math.random()*feedList.length);
    next(null, feedList[random]);
  });
}

function downloadRSSFeed (feedUrl) {
  request({uri: feedUrl}, function(err, res, body) {
    if (err) return next(err);
    if (res.statusCode != 200)
      return next(new Error('Abnormal response status code'))

    next(null, body);
  });
}

function parseRSSFeed (rss) {
  var handler = new htmlparser.RssHandler();
  var parser = new htmlparser.Parser(handler);
  parser.parseComplete(rss);

  if (!handler.dom.items.length)
    return next(new Error('No RSS items found'));

  var item = handler.dom.items.shift();
  console.log(item.title);
  console.log(item.link);
}
```

Annotations:
- Task 1: Make sure file containing the list of RSS feed URLs exists.
- Whenever there is an error, return early.
- Task 2: Read and parse file containing the feed URLs.
- Convert list of feed URLs to a string and then into an array of feed URLs.
- Select random feed URL from array of feed URLs.
- Task 3: Do an HTTP request and get data for the selected feed.
- Task 4: Parse RSS data into array of items.
- Display title and URL of the first feed item, if it exists.

```
var tasks = [ checkForRSSFile,
              readRSSFile,
              downloadRSSFeed,
              parseRSSFeed ];

function next(err, result) {
  if (err) throw err;

  var currentTask = tasks.shift();

  if (currentTask) {
    currentTask(result);
  }
}

next();
```

Add each task to be performed to an array in execution order.

A function called next executes each task.

Throw exception if task encounters an error.

Next task comes from array of tasks.

Execute current task.

Start serial execution of tasks.

Before trying out the application, create the file rss_feeds.txt in the same directory as the application script. Put the URLs of RSS feeds into the text file, one on each line of the file. After you've created this file, open a command line and enter the following commands to change to the application directory and execute the script:

```
cd random_story
node random_story.js
```

Serial flow control, as this example implementation shows, is essentially a way of putting callbacks into play when they're needed, rather than simply nesting them.

Now that you know how to implement serial flow control, let's look at how you can execute asynchronous tasks in parallel.

3.3.3 *Implementing parallel flow control*

In order to execute a number of asynchronous tasks in parallel, you again need to put the tasks in an array, but this time the order of the tasks is unimportant. Each task should call a handler function that will increment the number of completed tasks. When all tasks are complete, the handler function should perform some subsequent logic.

For a parallel flow control example, we'll make a simple application that will read the contents of a number of text files and output the frequency of word use throughout the files. Reading the contents of the text files will be done using the asynchronous `readFile` function, so a number of file reads could be done in parallel. How this application works is shown in figure 3.11.

The output will look something like the following text (although it will likely be much longer):

```
would: 2
wrench: 3
writeable: 1
you: 24
```

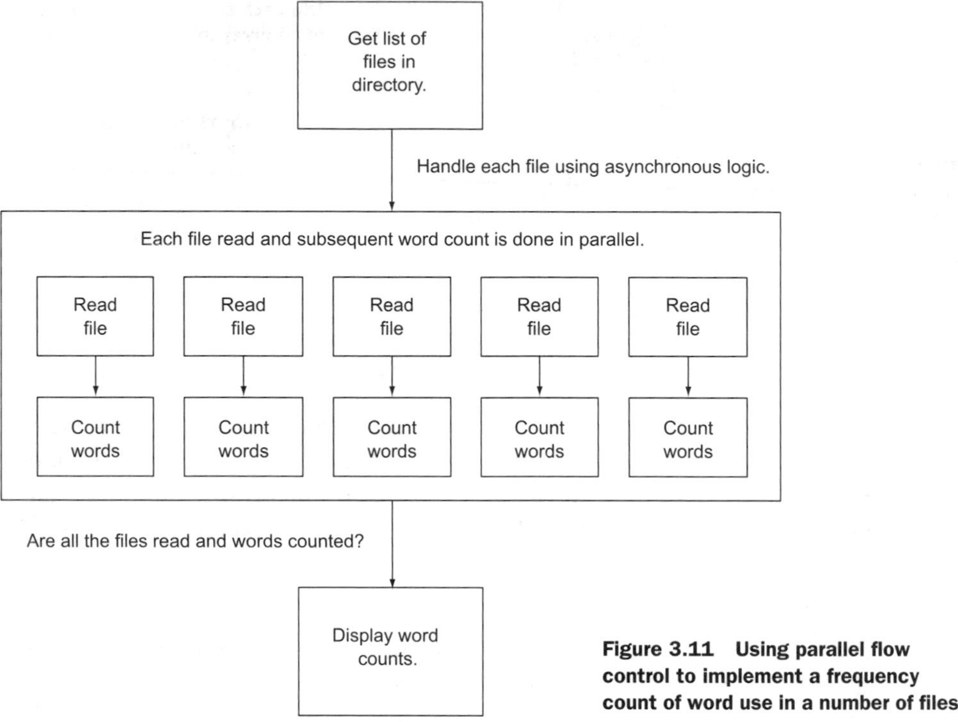

Figure 3.11 Using parallel flow control to implement a frequency count of word use in a number of files

Open a command-line prompt and enter the following commands to create two directories: one for the example, and another within that to contain the text files you want to analyze:

```
mkdir word_count
cd word_count
mkdir text
```

Next, create a file named word_count.js inside the word_count directory that contains the code that follows.

Listing 3.18 Parallel flow control implemented in a simple application

```
var fs = require('fs');
var completedTasks = 0;
var tasks = [];
var wordCounts = {};
var filesDir = './text';

function checkIfComplete() {
  completedTasks++;
  if (completedTasks == tasks.length) {
    for (var index in wordCounts) {
      console.log(index +': ' + wordCounts[index]);
    }
  }
}
```

When all tasks have completed, list each word used in the files and how many times it was used.

```
function countWordsInText(text) {
  var words = text
    .toString()
    .toLowerCase()
    .split(/\W+/)
    .sort();
  for (var index in words) {                              <- Count word occurrences in text.
    var word = words[index];
    if (word) {
      wordCounts[word] =
        (wordCounts[word]) ? wordCounts[word] + 1 : 1;
    }
  }
}
                                                          Get a list of the files in the text directory.
fs.readdir(filesDir, function(err, files) {               <-
  if (err) throw err;
  for(var index in files) {
    var task = (function(file) {                          <- Define a task to handle each file.
      return function() {                                    Each task includes a call to a
        fs.readFile(file, function(err, text) {              function that will asynchronously
          if (err) throw err;                                read the file and then count the
          countWordsInText(text);                            file's word usage.
          checkIfComplete();
        });
      }
    })(filesDir + '/' + files[index]);                       Add each task to an array of functions to
    tasks.push(task);                                     <- call in parallel.
  }
  for(var task in tasks) {                                <- Start executing every task in parallel.
    tasks[task]();
  }
});
```

Before trying out the application, create some text files in the text directory you created earlier. After you've created these files, open a command line and enter the following commands to change to the application directory and execute the script:

```
cd word_count
node word_count.js
```

Now that you've learned how serial and parallel flow control work under the hood, let's look at how to leverage community-created tools that allow you to easily benefit from flow control in your applications, without having to implement it yourself.

3.3.4 Leveraging community tools

Many community add-ons provide convenient flow-control tools. Some popular add-ons include Nimble, Step, and Seq. Although each of these is worth checking out, we'll use Nimble again for another example.

> **COMMUNITY ADD-ONS FOR FLOW CONTROL** For more information about community add-ons for flow control, see the article "Virtual Panel: How to Survive Asynchronous Programming in JavaScript" by Werner Schuster and Dio Synodinos on InfoQ: http://mng.bz/wKnV.

The next listing is an example of using Nimble to sequence tasks in a script that uses parallel flow control to download two files simultaneously and then archives them.

> **THE FOLLOWING EXAMPLE WON'T WORK IN MICROSOFT WINDOWS** Because the Windows operating system doesn't come with the `tar` and `curl` commands, the following example won't work in this operating system.

In this example, we use serial control to make sure that the downloading is done before proceeding to archiving.

Listing 3.19 Using a community add-on flow-control tool in a simple application

```
var flow = require('nimble')
var exec = require('child_process').exec;

function downloadNodeVersion(version, destination, callback) {
  var url = 'http://nodejs.org/dist/node-v' + version + '.tar.gz';
  var filepath = destination + '/' + version + '.tgz';
  exec('curl ' + url + ' >' + filepath, callback);
}

flow.series([
  function (callback) {
    flow.parallel([
      function (callback) {
        console.log('Downloading Node v0.4.6...');
        downloadNodeVersion('0.4.6', '/tmp', callback);
      },
      function (callback) {
        console.log('Downloading Node v0.4.7...');
        downloadNodeVersion('0.4.7', '/tmp', callback);
      }
    ], callback);
  },
  function(callback) {
    console.log('Creating archive of downloaded files...');
    exec(
      'tar cvf node_distros.tar /tmp/0.4.6.tgz /tmp/0.4.7.tgz',
      function(error, stdout, stderr) {
        console.log('All done!');
        callback();
      }
    );
  }
]);
```

Download Node source code for given version

Execute series of tasks in sequence

Execute downloads in parallel

Create archive file

The script defines a helper function that will download any specified release version of the Node source code. Two tasks are then executed in series: the parallel downloading of two versions of Node and the bundling of the downloaded versions into a new archive file.

3.4 Summary

In this chapter, you've learned how to organize your application logic into reusable modules, and how to make asynchronous logic behave the way you want it to.

Node's module system, which is based on the CommonJS module specification (www.commonjs.org/specs/modules/1.0/), allows you to easily reuse modules by populating the `exports` and `module.exports` objects. The module lookup system affords you a lot of flexibility in terms of where you can put modules and have them be found by application code when you `require` them. In addition to allowing you to include modules in your application's source tree, you can also use the node_modules folder to share module code between multiple applications. Within a module, the package.json file can be used to specify which file in the module's source tree is first evaluated when the module is required.

To manage asynchronous logic, you can use callbacks, event emitters, and flow control. Callbacks are appropriate for one-off asynchronous logic, but their use requires care to prevent messy code. Event emitters can be helpful for organizing asynchronous logic, since they allow it to be associated with a conceptual entity and to be easily managed through the use of listeners.

Flow control allows you to manage how asynchronous tasks execute, either one after another or simultaneously. Implementing your own flow control is possible, but community add-ons can save you the trouble. Which flow-control add-on you prefer is largely a matter of taste and project or design constraints.

Now that you've spent this chapter and the last preparing for development, it's time to sink your teeth into one of Node's most important features: its HTTP APIs. In the next chapter, you'll learn the basics of web application development using Node.

Part 2

Web application development with Node

Node's inclusion of built-in HTTP functionality makes Node a natural fit for web application development. This type of development is the most popular use for Node, and part 2 of this book focuses on it.

You'll first learn how to use Node's built-in HTTP functionality. You'll then learn about how to use middleware to add more functionality, such as the ability to process data submitted in forms. Finally, you'll learn how to use the popular Express web framework to speed up your development and how to deploy the applications you've created.

Building Node web applications

This chapter covers

- Handling HTTP requests with Node's API
- Building a RESTful web service
- Serving static files
- Accepting user input from forms
- Securing your application with HTTPS

In this chapter, you'll become familiar with the tools Node provides for creating HTTP servers, and you'll get acquainted with the fs (filesystem) module, which is necessary for serving static files. You'll also learn how to handle other common web application needs, such as creating low-level RESTful web services, accepting user input through HTML forms, monitoring file upload progress, and securing a web application with Node's Secure Sockets Layer (SSL).

At Node's core is a powerful streaming HTTP parser consisting of roughly 1,500 lines of optimized C, written by the author of Node, Ryan Dahl. This parser, in combination with the low-level TCP API that Node exposes to JavaScript, provides you with a very low-level, but very flexible, HTTP server.

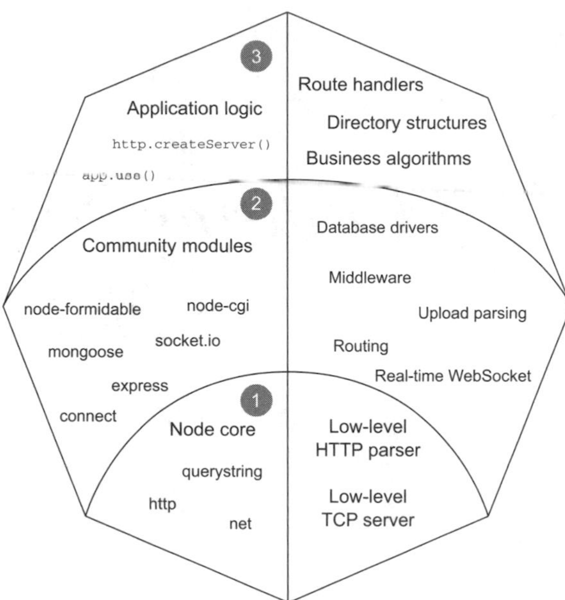

1 Node's core APIs are always lightweight and low-level. This leaves opinions, syntactic sugar, and specific details up to the community modules.

2 Community modules are where Node thrives. Community members take the low-level core APIs and create fun and easy-to-use modules that allow you to get tasks done easily.

3 The application logic layer is where your app is implemented. The size of this layer depends on the number of community modules used and the complexity of the application.

Figure 4.1 Overview of the layers that make up a Node web application

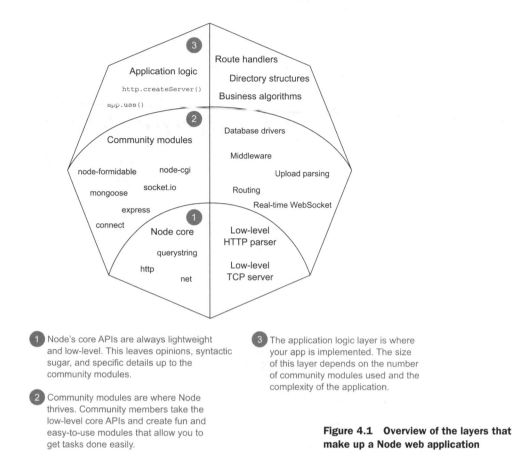

Like most modules in Node's core, the http module favors simplicity. High-level "sugar" APIs are left for third-party frameworks, such as Connect or Express, that greatly simplify the web application building process. Figure 4.1 illustrates the anatomy of a Node web application, showing that the low-level APIs remain at the core, and that abstractions and implementations are built on top of those building blocks.

This chapter will cover some of Node's low-level APIs directly. You can safely skip this chapter if you're more interested in higher-level concepts and web frameworks, like Connect or Express, which will be covered in later chapters. But before creating rich web applications with Node, you'll need to become familiar with the fundamental HTTP API, which can be built upon to create higher-level tools and frameworks.

4.1 HTTP server fundamentals

As we've mentioned throughout this book, Node has a relatively low-level API. Node's HTTP interface is similarly low-level when compared with frameworks or languages such as PHP in order to keep it fast and flexible.

To get you started creating robust and performant web applications, this section will focus on the following topics:

- How Node presents incoming HTTP requests to developers
- How to write a basic HTTP server that responds with "Hello World"
- How to read incoming request headers and set outgoing response headers
- How to set the status code of an HTTP response

Before you can accept incoming requests, you need to create an HTTP server. Let's take a look at Node's HTTP interface.

4.1.1 How Node presents incoming HTTP requests to developers

Node provides HTTP server and client interfaces through the http module:

```
var http = require('http');
```

To create an HTTP server, call the `http.createServer()` function. It accepts a single argument, a callback function, that will be called on each HTTP request received by the server. This *request* callback receives, as arguments, the request and response objects, which are commonly shortened to `req` and `res`:

```
var http = require('http');
  var server = http.createServer(function(req, res){
  // handle request
  });
```

For every HTTP request received by the server, the request callback function will be invoked with new `req` and `res` objects. Prior to the callback being triggered, Node will parse the request up through the HTTP headers and provide them as part of the `req` object. But Node doesn't start parsing the body of the request until the callback has been fired. This is different from some server-side frameworks, like PHP, where both the headers and the body of the request are parsed before your application logic runs. Node provides this lower-level interface so you can handle the body data as it's being parsed, if desired.

Node will not automatically write any response back to the client. After the request callback is triggered, it's your responsibility to end the response using the `res.end()` method (see figure 4.2). This allows you to run any asynchronous logic you want during the lifetime of the request before ending the response. If you fail to end the response, the request will hang until the client times out or it will just remain open.

Node servers are long-running processes that serve many requests throughout their lifetimes.

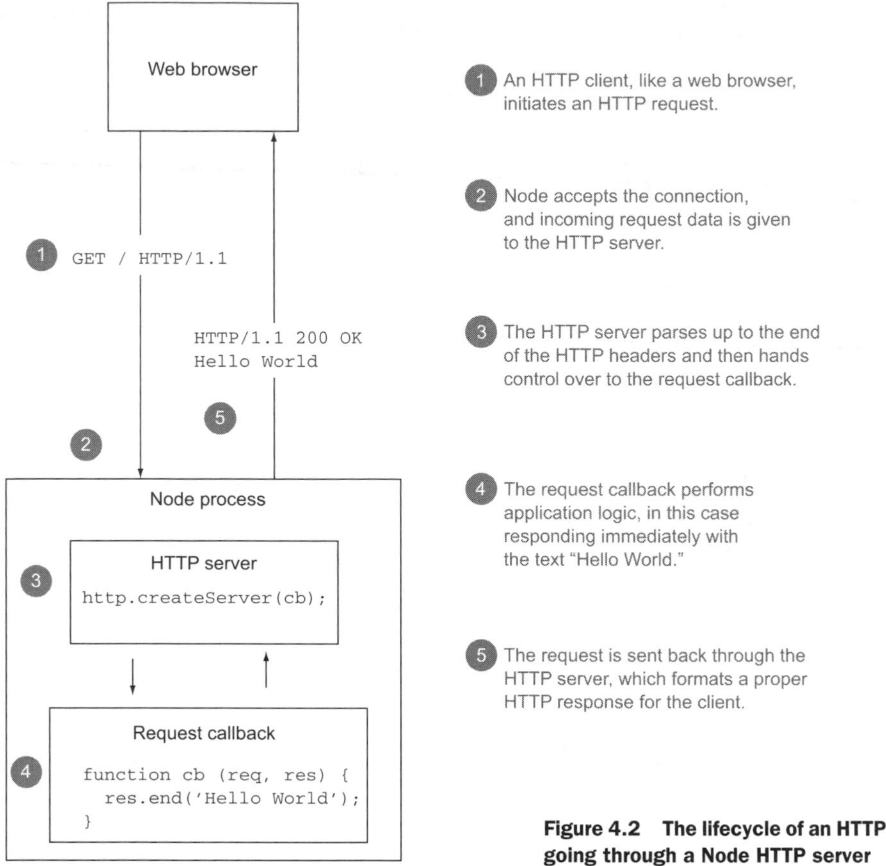

Figure 4.2 The lifecycle of an HTTP request going through a Node HTTP server

4.1.2 A basic HTTP server that responds with "Hello World"

To implement a simple Hello World HTTP server, let's flesh out the request callback function from the previous section.

First, call the `res.write()` method, which writes response data to the socket, and then use the `res.end()` method to end the response:

```
var http = require('http');
var server = http.createServer(function(req, res){
  res.write('Hello World');
  res.end();
});
```

As shorthand, `res.write()` and `res.end()` can be combined into one statement, which can be nice for small responses:

```
res.end('Hello World');
```

The last thing you need to do is bind to a port so you can listen for incoming requests. You do this by using the `server.listen()` method, which accepts a combination of arguments, but for now the focus will be on listening for connections on a specified port. During development, it's typical to bind to an unprivileged port, such as 3000:

```
var http = require('http');
var server = http.createServer(function(req, res){
  res.end('Hello World');
});
server.listen(3000);
```

With Node now listening for connections on port 3000, you can visit http://localhost:3000 in your browser. When you do, you should receive a plain-text page consisting of the words "Hello World."

Setting up an HTTP server is just the start. You'll need to know how to set response status codes and header fields, handle exceptions appropriately, and use the APIs Node provides. First we'll take a closer look at responding to incoming requests.

4.1.3 Reading request headers and setting response headers

The Hello World example in the previous section demonstrates the bare minimum required for a proper HTTP response. It uses the default status code of 200 (indicating success) and the default response headers. Usually, though, you'll want to include any number of other HTTP headers with the response. For example, you'll have to send a `Content-Type` header with a value of `text/html` when you're sending HTML content so that the browser knows to render the result as HTML.

Node offers several methods to progressively alter the header fields of an HTTP response: the `res.setHeader(field, value)`, `res.getHeader(field)`, and `res.removeHeader(field)` methods. Here's an example of using `res.setHeader()`:

```
var body = 'Hello World';
res.setHeader('Content-Length', body.length);
res.setHeader('Content-Type', 'text/plain');
res.end(body);
```

You can add and remove headers in any order, *but* only up to the first `res.write()` or `res.end()` call. After the first part of the response body is written, Node will flush the HTTP headers that have been set.

4.1.4 Setting the status code of an HTTP response

It's common to want to send back a different HTTP status code than the default of 200. A common case would be sending back a 404 Not Found status code when a requested resource doesn't exist.

To do this, you set the `res.statusCode` property. This property can be assigned at any point during the application's response, as long as it's before the first call to `res.write()` or `res.end()`. As shown in the following example, this means `res.statusCode = 302` can be placed above the `res.setHeader()` calls, or below them:

```
var url = 'http://google.com';
var body = '<p>Redirecting to <a href="' + url + '">'
         + url + '</a></p>';

res.setHeader('Location', url);
res.setHeader('Content-Length', body.length);
res.setHeader('Content-Type', 'text/html');
res.statusCode = 302;
res.end(body);
```

Node's philosophy is to provide small but robust networking APIs, not to compete with high-level frameworks such as Rails or Django, but to serve as a tremendous platform for similar frameworks to build upon. Because of this design, neither high-level concepts like sessions nor fundamentals such as HTTP cookies are provided within Node's core. Those are left for third-party modules to provide.

Now that you've seen the basic HTTP API, it's time to put it to use. In the next section, you'll make a simple, HTTP-compliant application using this API.

4.2 Building a RESTful web service

Suppose you want to create a to-do list web service with Node, involving the typical create, read, update, and delete (CRUD) actions. These actions can be implemented in many ways, but in this section we'll focus on creating a RESTful web service—a service that utilizes the HTTP method verbs to expose a concise API.

In 2000, representational state transfer (REST) was introduced by Roy Fielding,[1] one of the prominent contributors to the HTTP 1.0 and 1.1 specifications. By convention, HTTP verbs, such as `GET`, `POST`, `PUT`, and `DELETE`, are mapped to retrieving, creating, updating, and removing the resources specified by the URL. RESTful web services have gained in popularity because they're simple to utilize and implement in comparison to protocols such as the Simple Object Access Protocol (SOAP).

Throughout this section, cURL (http://curl.haxx.se/download.html) will be used, in place of a web browser, to interact with your web service. cURL is a powerful command-line HTTP client that can be used to send requests to a target server.

To create a compliant REST server, you need to implement the four HTTP verbs. Each verb will cover a different task for the to-do list:

- `POST`—Add items to the to-do list
- `GET`—Display a listing of the current items, or display the details of a specific item
- `DELETE`—Remove items from the to-do list
- `PUT`—Should modify existing items, but for brevity's sake we'll skip `PUT` in this chapter

To illustrate the end result, here's an example of creating a new item in the to-do list using the `curl` command:

---

1 Roy Thomas Fielding, "Architectural Styles and the Design of Network-based Software Architectures" (PhD diss, University of California, Irvine, 2000), www.ics.uci.edu/~fielding/pubs/dissertation/top.htm.

```
wavded@dev: ~
wavded@dev ~» curl -d 'buy node in action' http://localhost:3000
OK
```

And here's an example of viewing the items in the to-do list:

```
wavded@dev: ~
wavded@dev ~» curl http://localhost:3000
0) buy node in action
```

4.2.1 Creating resources with POST requests

In RESTful terminology, the creation of a resource is typically mapped to the `POST` verb. Therefore, `POST` will create an entry in the to-do list.

In Node, you can check which HTTP method (verb) is being used by checking the `req.method` property (as shown in listing 4.1). When you know which method the request is using, your server will know which task to perform.

When Node's HTTP parser reads in and parses request data, it makes that data available in the form of `data` events that contain chunks of parsed data ready to be handled by the program:

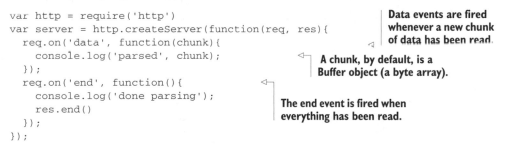

```
var http = require('http')
var server = http.createServer(function(req, res){
  req.on('data', function(chunk){
    console.log('parsed', chunk);
  });
  req.on('end', function(){
    console.log('done parsing');
    res.end()
  });
});
```

Data events are fired whenever a new chunk of data has been read.

A chunk, by default, is a Buffer object (a byte array).

The end event is fired when everything has been read.

By default, the `data` events provide `Buffer` objects, which are Node's version of byte arrays. In the case of textual to-do items, you don't need binary data, so setting the stream encoding to `ascii` or `utf8` is ideal; the `data` events will instead emit strings. This can be set by invoking the `req.setEncoding(encoding)` method:

```
req.setEncoding('utf8')
req.on('data', function(chunk){
  console.log(chunk);
});
```

A chunk is now a utf8 string instead of a Buffer.

In the case of a to-do list item, you need to have the entire string before it can be added to the array. One way to get the whole string is to concatenate all of the chunks of data until the `end` event is emitted, indicating that the request is complete. After the `end` event has occurred, the `item` string will be populated with the entire contents of the request body, which can then be pushed to the `items` array. When the item has been added, you can end the request with the string `OK` and Node's default status code of 200. The following listing shows this in the todo.js file.

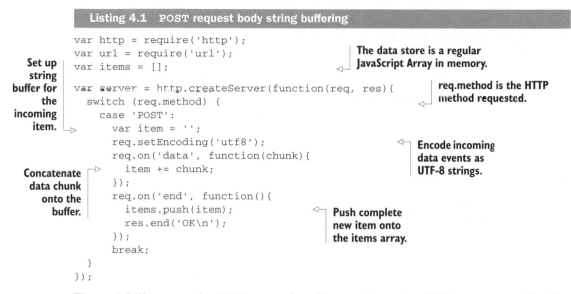

Listing 4.1 POST request body string buffering

```
var http = require('http');
var url = require('url');
var items = [];

var server = http.createServer(function(req, res){
  switch (req.method) {
    case 'POST':
      var item = '';
      req.setEncoding('utf8');
      req.on('data', function(chunk){
        item += chunk;
      });
      req.on('end', function(){
        items.push(item);
        res.end('OK\n');
      });
      break;
  }
});
```

Annotations:
- The data store is a regular JavaScript Array in memory.
- req.method is the HTTP method requested.
- Set up string buffer for the incoming item.
- Encode incoming data events as UTF-8 strings.
- Concatenate data chunk onto the buffer.
- Push complete new item onto the items array.

Figure 4.3 illustrates the HTTP server handling an incoming HTTP request and buffering the input before acting on the request at the end.

The application can now add items, but before you try it out using cURL, you should complete the next task so you can get a listing of the items as well.

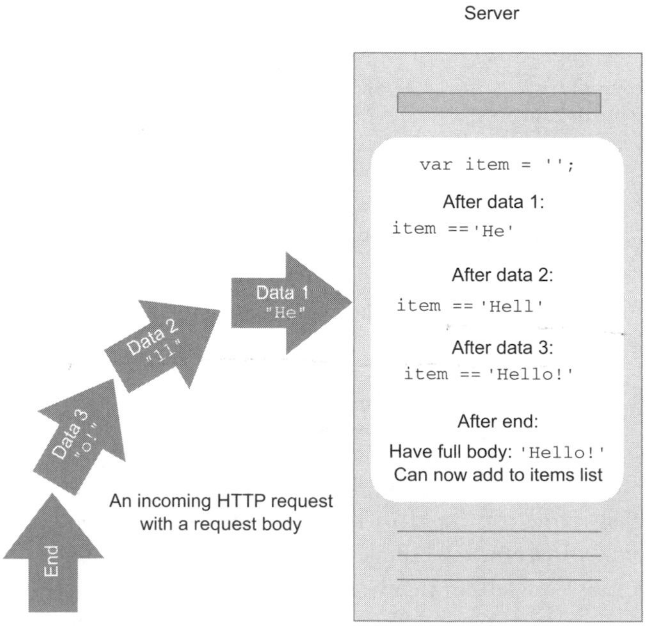

Figure 4.3 Concatenating data events to buffer the request body

4.2.2 *Fetching resources with GET requests*

To handle the GET verb, add it to the same switch statement as before, followed by the logic for listing the to-do items. In the following example, the first call to res.write() will write the header with the default fields, as well as the data passed to it:

```
...
case 'GET':
items.forEach(function(item, i){
  res.write(i + ') ' + item + '\n');
});
res.end();
break;
...
```

Now that the app can display the items, it's time to give it a try! Fire up a terminal, start the server, and POST some items using curl. The -d flag automatically sets the request method to POST and passes in the value as POST data:

```
$ curl -d 'buy groceries' http://localhost:3000
OK
$ curl -d 'buy node in action' http://localhost:3000
OK
```

Next, to GET the list of to-do list items, you can execute curl without any flags, as GET is the default verb:

```
$ curl http://localhost:3000
0) buy groceries
1) buy node in action
```

SETTING THE CONTENT-LENGTH HEADER

To speed up responses, the Content-Length field should be sent with your response when possible. In the case of the item list, the body can easily be constructed ahead of time in memory, allowing you to access the string length and flush the entire list in one shot. Setting the Content-Length header implicitly disables Node's chunked encoding, providing a performance boost because less data needs to be transferred.

An optimized version of the GET handler could look something like this:

```
var body = items.map(function(item, i){
  return i + ') ' + item;
}).join('\n');
res.setHeader('Content-Length', Buffer.byteLength(body));
res.setHeader('Content-Type', 'text/plain; charset="utf-8"');
res.end(body);
```

You may be tempted to use the body.length value for the Content-Length, but the Content-Length value should represent the byte length, not character length, and the two will be different if the string contains multibyte characters. To avoid this problem, Node provides the Buffer.byteLength() method.

The following Node REPL session illustrates the difference by using the string length directly, as the five-character string is comprised of seven bytes:

```
$ node
> 'etc …'.length
5
> Buffer.byteLength('etc …')
7
```

> **The Node REPL**
>
> Node, like many other languages, provides a REPL (read-eval-print-loop) interface, available by running `node` from the command line without any arguments. A REPL allows you to write snippets of code and to get immediate results as each statement is written and executed. It can be great for learning a programming language, running simple tests, or even debugging.

4.2.3 Removing resources with DELETE requests

Finally, the `DELETE` verb will be used to remove an item. To accomplish this, the app will need to check the requested URL, which is how the HTTP client will specify which item to remove. In this case, the identifier will be the array index in the `items` array; for example, `DELETE /1` or `DELETE /5`.

The requested URL can be accessed with the `req.url` property, which may contain several components depending on the request. For example, if the request was `DELETE /1?api-key=foobar`, this property would contain both the pathname and query string `/1?api-key=foobar`.

To parse these sections, Node provides the url module, and specifically the `.parse()` function. The following node REPL session illustrates the use of this function, parsing the URL into an object, including the `pathname` property you'll use in the `DELETE` handler:

```
$ node
> require('url').parse('http://localhost:3000/1?api-key=foobar')
{ protocol: 'http:',
  slashes: true,
  host: 'localhost:3000',
  port: '3000',
  hostname: 'localhost',
  href: 'http://localhost:3000/1?api-key=foobar',
  search: '?api-key=foobar',
  query: 'api-key=foobar',
  pathname: '/1',
  path: '/1?api-key=foobar' }
```

`url.parse()` parses out only the pathname for you, but the item ID is still a string. In order to work with the ID within the application, it should be converted to a number. A simple solution is to use the `String#slice()` method, which returns a portion of the string between two indexes. In this case, it can be used to skip the first character, giving you just the number portion, still as a string. To convert this string to a number, it can be passed to the JavaScript global function `parseInt()`, which returns a `Number`.

Listing 4.2 first does a couple of checks on the input value, because you can never trust user input to be valid, and then it responds to the request. If the number is "not a number" (the JavaScript value `NaN`), the status code is set to 400 indicating a Bad Request. Following that, the code checks if the item exists, responding with a 404 Not Found error if it doesn't. After the input has been validated, the item can be removed from the `items` array, and then the app will respond with 200, OK.

Listing 4.2 `DELETE` request handler

```
...
case 'DELETE':
  var path = url.parse(req.url).pathname;
  var i = parseInt(path.slice(1), 10);

  if (isNaN(i)) {
    res.statusCode = 400;
    res.end('Invalid item id');
  } else if (!items[i]) {
    res.statusCode = 404;
    res.end('Item not found');
  } else {
    items.splice(i, 1);
    res.end('OK\n');
  }
  break;
...
```

- Add DELETE case to the switch statement
- Check that number is valid
- Ensure requested index exists
- Delete requested item

You might be thinking that 15 lines of code to remove an item from an array is a bit much, but we promise that this is much easier to write with higher-level frameworks providing additional sugar APIs. Learning these fundamentals of Node is crucial for understanding and debugging, and it enables you to create more powerful applications and frameworks.

A complete RESTful service would also implement the `PUT` HTTP verb, which should modify an existing item in the to-do list. We encourage you to try implementing this final handler yourself, using the techniques used in this REST server so far, before you move on to the next section, in which you'll learn how to serve static files from your web application.

4.3 Serving static files

Many web applications share similar, if not identical, needs, and serving static files (CSS, JavaScript, images) is certainly one of these. Although writing a robust and efficient static file server is nontrivial, and robust implementations already exist within Node's community, implementing your own static file server in this section will illustrate Node's low-level filesystem API.

In this section you'll learn how to

- Create a simple static file server
- Optimize the data transfer with `pipe()`
- Handle user and filesystem errors by setting the status code

Let's start by creating a basic HTTP server for serving static assets.

4.3.1 Creating a static file server

Traditional HTTP servers like Apache and IIS are first and foremost file servers. You might currently have one of these file servers running on an old website, and moving it over to Node, replicating this basic functionality, is an excellent exercise to help you better understand the HTTP servers you've probably used in the past.

Each static file server has a root directory, which is the base directory files are served from. In the server you'll create, you'll define a `root` variable, which will act as the static file server's root directory:

```
var http = require('http');
var parse = require('url').parse;
var join = require('path').join;
var fs = require('fs');

var root = __dirname;

...
```

`__dirname` is a *magic* variable provided by Node that's assigned the directory path to the file. It's magic because it could be assigned different values in the same program if you have files spread about in different directories. In this case, the server will be serving static files relative to the same directory as this script, but you could configure `root` to specify any directory path.

The next step is accessing the `pathname` of the URL in order to determine the requested file's path. If a URL's `pathname` is /index.html, and your `root` file directory is /var/www/example.com/public, you can simply join these using the path module's `.join()` method to form the absolute path /var/www/example.com/public/index.html. The following code shows how this could be done:

```
var http = require('http');
var parse = require('url').parse;
var join = require('path').join;
var fs = require('fs');

var root = __dirname;

var server = http.createServer(function(req, res){
  var url = parse(req.url);
  var path = join(root, url.pathname);
});

server.listen(3000);
```

> **Directory traversal attack**
>
> The file server built in this section is a simplified one. If you want to run this in production, you should validate the input more thoroughly to prevent users from getting access to parts of the filesystem you don't intend them to via a directory traversal attack. Wikipedia has an explanation of how this type of attack works (http://en.wikipedia.org/wiki/Directory_traversal_attack).

Now that you have the path, the contents of the file need to be transferred. This can be done using high-level streaming disk access with `fs.ReadStream`, one of Node's `Stream` classes. This class emits data events as it incrementally reads the file from disk. The next listing implements a simple but fully functional file server.

Listing 4.3 Bare-bones `ReadStream` static file server

```
var http = require('http');
var parse = require('url').parse;
var join = require('path').join;
var fs = require('fs');

var root = __dirname;

var server = http.createServer(function(req, res){
  var url = parse(req.url);
  var path = join(root, url.pathname);          // Construct absolute path
  var stream = fs.createReadStream(path);       // Create fs.ReadStream
  stream.on('data', function(chunk){            // Write file data to response
    res.write(chunk);
  });
  stream.on('end', function(){
    res.end();                                  // End response when file is complete
  });
});

server.listen(3000);
```

This file server would work in most cases, but there are many more details you'll need to consider. Next up, you'll learn how to optimize the data transfer while making the code for the server even shorter.

OPTIMIZING DATA TRANSFER WITH STREAM#PIPE()

Although it's important to know how the `fs.ReadStream` works and what flexibility its events provide, Node also provides a higher-level mechanism for performing the same task: `Stream#pipe()`. This method allows you to greatly simplify your server code.

> **Pipes and plumbing**
>
> A helpful way to think about pipes in Node is to think about plumbing. If you have water coming from a source (such as a water heater) and you want to direct it to a destination (like a kitchen faucet), you can route that water from its source to its destination by adding a pipe to connect the two. Water can then flow from the source *through the pipe* to the destination.
>
> The same concept is true for pipes in Node, but instead of water you're dealing with data coming from a source (called a `ReadableStream`) that you can then "pipe" to some destination (called a `WritableStream`). You hook up the plumbing with the `pipe` method:
>
> ```
> ReadableStream#pipe(WritableStream);
> ```

(continued)
An example of using pipes is reading a file (`ReadableStream`) and writing its contents to another file (`WritableStream`):

```
var readStream = fs.createReadStream('./original.txt')
var writeStream = fs.createWriteStream('./copy.txt')
readStream#pipe(writeStream);
```

Any `ReadableStream` can be piped into any `WritableStream`. For example, an HTTP request (`req`) object is a `ReadableStream`, and you can stream its contents to a file:

```
req.pipe(fs.createWriteStream('./req-body.txt'))
```

For an in-depth look at streams in Node, including a list of available built-in streams, check out the stream handbook on GitHub: https://github.com/substack/stream-handbook.

```
var server = http.createServer(function(req, res){
  var url = parse(req.url);
  var path = join(root, url.pathname);
  var stream = fs.createReadStream(path);
  stream.pipe(res);
});
```

res.end() called internally by stream.pipe()

Figure 4.4 shows an HTTP server in the act of reading a static file from the filesystem and then piping the result to the HTTP client using `pipe()`.

At this point, you can test to confirm that the static file server is functioning by executing the following `curl` command. The `-i`, or `--include` flag, instructs cURL to output the response header:

```
$ curl http://localhost:3000/static.js -i
HTTP/1.1 200 OK
Connection: keep-alive
Transfer-Encoding: chunked

var http = require('http');
var parse = require('url').parse;
var join = require('path').join;
...
```

As previously mentioned, the root directory used is the directory that the static file server script is in, so the preceding `curl` command requests the server's script itself, which is sent back as the response body.

This static file server isn't complete yet, though—it's still prone to errors. A single unhandled exception, such as a user requesting a file that doesn't exist, will bring down your entire server. In the next section, you'll add error handling to the file server.

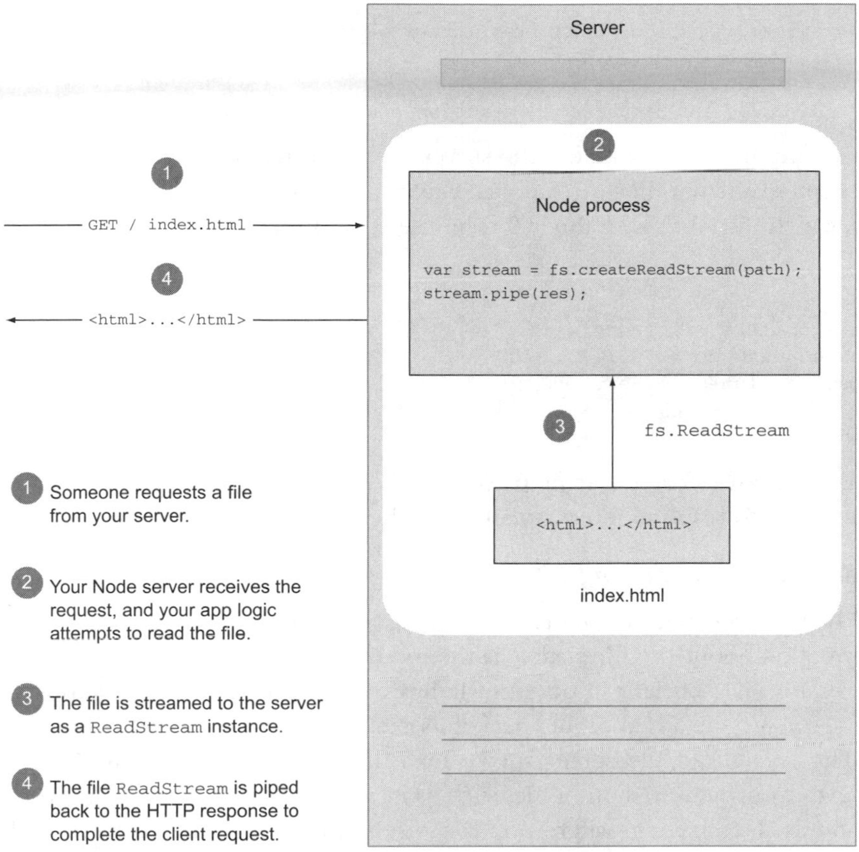
Server
1
GET / index.html
4
<html>...</html>
2
Node process
var stream = fs.createReadStream(path);
stream.pipe(res);
3
fs.ReadStream
<html>...</html>
index.html
1 Someone requests a file from your server.
2 Your Node server receives the request, and your app logic attempts to read the file.
3 The file is streamed to the server as a ReadStream instance.
4 The file ReadStream is piped back to the HTTP response to complete the client request.

Figure 4.4 A Node HTTP server serving a static file from the filesystem using `fs.ReadStream`

4.3.2 *Handling server errors*

Our static file server is not yet handling errors that could occur as a result of using `fs.ReadStream`. Errors will be thrown in the current server if you access a file that doesn't exist, access a forbidden file, or run into any other file I/O–related problem. In this section, we'll touch on how you can make the file server, or any Node server, more robust.

In Node, anything that inherits from `EventEmitter` has the potential of emitting an `error` event. A stream, like `fs.ReadStream`, is simply a specialized `EventEmitter` that contains predefined events such as `data` and `end`, which we've already looked at. By default, `error` events will be thrown when no listeners are present. This means that if you don't listen for these errors, they'll crash your server.

To illustrate this, try requesting a file that doesn't exist, such as /notfound.js. In the terminal session running your server, you'll see the stack trace of an exception printed to stderr, similar to the following:

```
stream.js:99
throw arguments[1]; // Unhandled 'error' event.
^
Error: ENOENT, No such file or directory
  ➥ '/Users/tj/projects/node-in-action/source/notfound.js'
```

To prevent errors from killing the server, you need to listen for errors by registering an `error` event handler on the `fs.ReadStream` (something like the following snippet), which responds with the 500 response status indicating an internal server error:

```
...
stream.pipe(res);
stream.on('error', function(err){
  res.statusCode = 500;
  res.end('Internal Server Error');
});
...
```

Registering an `error` event helps you catch any foreseen or unforeseen errors and enables you to respond more gracefully to the client.

4.3.3 Preemptive error handling with fs.stat

The files transferred are static, so the `stat()` system call can be utilized to request information about the files, such as the modification time, byte size, and more. This information is especially important when providing conditional `GET` support, where a browser may issue a request to check if its cache is stale.

The refactored file server shown in listing 4.4 makes a call to `fs.stat()` and retrieves information about a file, such as its size, or an error code. If the named file doesn't exist, `fs.stat()` will respond with a value of `ENOENT` in the `err.code` field, and you can return the error code 404, indicating that the file is not found. If you receive other errors from `fs.stat()`, you can return a generic 500 error code.

Listing 4.4 Checking for a file's existence and responding with `Content-Length`

```
var server = http.createServer(function(req, res){
  var url = parse(req.url);                              <- Parse URL to obtain path name
  var path = join(root, url.pathname);                   <- Construct absolute path
  fs.stat(path, function(err, stat){                     <- Check for file's existence
    if (err) {
      if ('ENOENT' == err.code) {                        <- File doesn't exist
        res.statusCode = 404;
        res.end('Not Found');
      } else {                                           <- Some other error
        res.statusCode = 500;
        res.end('Internal Server Error');
      }
    } else {
      res.setHeader('Content-Length', stat.size);        <- Set Content-Length using stat object
      var stream = fs.createReadStream(path);
      stream.pipe(res);
      stream.on('error', function(err){
```

```
        res.statusCode = 500;
        res.end('Internal Server Error');
      });
    }
  });
});
```

Now that we've taken a low-level look at file serving with Node, let's take a look at an equally common, and perhaps more important, feature of web application development: getting user input from HTML forms.

4.4 Accepting user input from forms

Web applications commonly gather user input through form submissions. Node doesn't handle the workload (like validation or file uploads) for you—Node just provides you with the body data. Although this may seem inconvenient, it leaves opinions to third-party frameworks in order to provide a simple and efficient low-level API.

In this section, we'll take a look at how you can do the following:

- Handle submitted form fields
- Handle uploaded files using formidable
- Calculate upload progress in real time

Let's dive into how you process incoming form data using Node.

4.4.1 Handling submitted form fields

Typically two `Content-Type` values are associated with form submission requests:

- `application/x-www-form-urlencoded`—The default for HTML forms
- `multipart/form-data`—Used when the form contains files, or non-ASCII or binary data

In this section, you'll rewrite the to-do list application from the previous section to utilize a form and a web browser. When you're done, you'll have a web-based to-do list that looks like the one in figure 4.5.

In this to-do list application, a `switch` is used on the request method, `req.method`, to form simple request routing. This is shown in listing 4.5. Any URL that's not *exactly* "/" is considered a 404 Not Found response. Any HTTP verb that is not `GET` or `POST` is

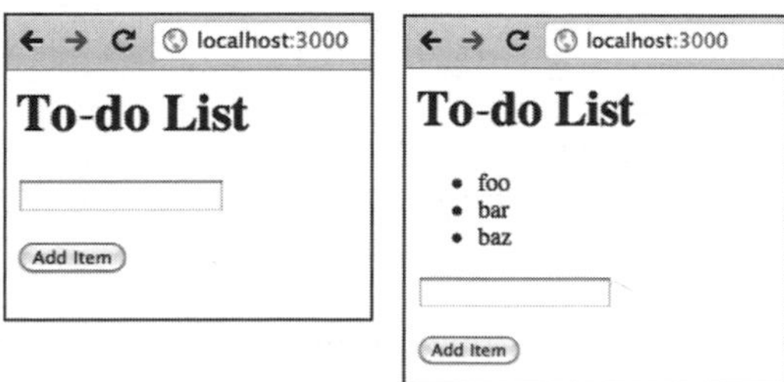

Figure 4.5 A to-do-list application utilizing an HTML form and a web browser. The left screenshot shows the state of the application when it's first loaded and the right shows what the applications looks like after some items have been added.

a 400 Bad Request response. The handler functions `show()`, `add()`, `badRequest()`, and `notFound()` will be implemented throughout the rest of this section.

Listing 4.5 HTTP server supporting GET and POST

```
var http = require('http');
var items = [];

var server = http.createServer(function(req, res){
  if ('/' == req.url) {
    switch (req.method) {
      case 'GET':
        show(res);
        break;
      case 'POST':
        add(req, res);
        break;
      default:
        badRequest(res);
    }
  } else {
    notFound(res);
  }
});

server.listen(3000);
```

Although markup is typically generated using template engines, the example in the following listing uses string concatenation for simplicity. There's no need to assign `res.statusCode` because it defaults to 200 OK. The resulting HTML page in a browser is shown in figure 4.5.

Listing 4.6 To-do list form and item list

```
function show(res) {
  var html = '<html><head><title>Todo List</title></head><body>'
           + '<h1>Todo List</h1>'
           + '<ul>'
           + items.map(function(item){
               return '<li>' + item + '</li>'
             }).join('')
           + '</ul>'
           + '<form method="post" action="/">'
           + '<p><input type="text" name="item" /></p>'
           + '<p><input type="submit" value="Add Item" /></p>'
           + '</form></body></html>';
  res.setHeader('Content-Type', 'text/html');
  res.setHeader('Content-Length', Buffer.byteLength(html));
  res.end(html);
}
```

For simple apps, inlining the HTML instead of using a template engine works well.

The `notFound()` function accepts the response object, setting the status code to 404 and response body to Not Found:

```
function notFound(res) {
  res.statusCode = 404;
  res.setHeader('Content-Type', 'text/plain');
  res.end('Not Found');
}
```

The implementation of the 400 Bad Request response is nearly identical to `notFound()`, indicating to the client that the request was invalid:

```
function badRequest(res) {
  res.statusCode = 400;
  res.setHeader('Content-Type', 'text/plain');
  res.end('Bad Request');
}
```

Finally, the application needs to implement the `add()` function, which will accept both the `req` and `res` objects. This is shown in the following code:

```
var qs = require('querystring');

function add(req, res) {
  var body = '';
  req.setEncoding('utf8');
  req.on('data', function(chunk){ body += chunk });
  req.on('end', function(){
    var obj = qs.parse(body);
    items.push(obj.item);
    show(res);
  });
}
```

For simplicity, this example assumes that the `Content-Type` is `application/x-www-form-urlencoded`, which is the default for HTML forms. To parse this data, you simply concatenate the `data` event chunks to form a complete body string. Because you're not dealing with binary data, you can set the request encoding type to `utf8` with `res.setEncoding()`. When the request emits the `end` event, all `data` events have completed, and the `body` variable contains the entire body as a string.

Buffering too much data

Buffering works well for small request bodies containing a bit of JSON, XML, and the like, but the buffering of this data can be problematic. It can create an application availability vulnerability if the buffer isn't properly limited to a maximum size, which we'll discuss further in chapter 7. Because of this, it's often beneficial to implement a streaming parser, lowering the memory requirements and helping prevent resource starvation. This process incrementally parses the data chunks as they're emitted, though this is more difficult to use and implement.

THE QUERYSTRING MODULE

In the server's `add()` function implementation, you utilized Node's querystring module to parse the body. Let's take a look at a quick REPL session demonstrating how Node's `querystring.parse()` function works—this is the function used in the server.

Imagine the user submitted an HTML form to your to-do list with the text "take ferrets to the vet":

```
$ node
> var qs = require('querystring');
> var body = 'item=take+ferrets+to+the+vet';
> qs.parse(body);
{ item: 'take ferrets to the vet' }
```

After adding the item, the server returns the user back to the original form by calling the same `show()` function previously implemented. This is only the route taken for this example; other approaches could potentially display a message such as "Added to-do list item" or could redirect the user back to /.

Try it out. Add a few items and you'll see the to-do items output in the unordered list. You can also implement the delete functionality that we did in the REST API previously.

4.4.2 Handling uploaded files using formidable

Handling uploads is another very common, and important, aspect of web development. Imagine you're trying to create an application where you upload your photo collection and share it with others using a link on the web. You can do this using a web browser through HTML form file uploads.

The following example shows a form that uploads a file with an associated `name` field:

```
<form method="post" action="/" enctype="multipart/form-data">
<p><input type="text" name="name" /></p>
<p><input type="file" name="file" /></p>
<p><input type="submit" value="Upload" /></p>
</form>
```

To handle file uploads properly and accept the file's content, you need to set the `enctype` attribute to `multipart/form-data`, a MIME type suited for BLOBs (binary large objects).

Parsing multipart requests in a performant and streaming fashion is a nontrivial task, and we won't cover the details in this book, but Node's community has provided several modules to perform this function. One such module, formidable, was created by Felix Geisendörfer for his media upload and transformation startup, Transloadit, where performance and reliability are key.

What makes formidable a great choice for handling file uploads is that it's a streaming parser, meaning it can accept chunks of data as they arrive, parse them, and emit specific parts, such as the part headers and bodies previously mentioned. Not only is this approach fast, but the lack of buffering prevents memory bloat, even for very large files such as videos, which otherwise could overwhelm a process.

Now, back to our photo-sharing example. The HTTP server in the following listing implements the beginnings of the file upload server. It responds to GET with an HTML form, and it has an empty function for POST, in which formidable will be integrated to handle file uploading.

Listing 4.7 HTTP server setup prepared to accept file uploads

```
var http = require('http');
var server = http.createServer(function(req, res){
  switch (req.method) {
    case 'GET':
      show(req, res);
      break;
    case 'POST':
      upload(req, res);
      break;
  }
});

function show(req, res) {                                    Serve HTML form with file input
  var html = ''
    + '<form method="post" action="/" enctype="multipart/form-data">'
    + '<p><input type="text" name="name" /></p>'
    + '<p><input type="file" name="file" /></p>'
    + '<p><input type="submit" value="Upload" /></p>'
    + '</form>';
  res.setHeader('Content-Type', 'text/html');
  res.setHeader('Content-Length', Buffer.byteLength(html));
  res.end(html);
}

function upload(req, res) {
  // upload logic
}
```

Now that the GET request is taken care of, it's time to implement the upload() function, which is invoked by the request callback when a POST request comes in. The upload() function needs to accept the incoming upload data, which is where formidable comes in. In the rest of this section, you'll learn what's needed in order to integrate formidable into your web application:

1. Install formidable through npm.
2. Create an IncomingForm instance.
3. Call form.parse() with the HTTP request object.
4. Listen for form events field, file, and end.
5. Use formidable's high-level API.

The first step to utilizing formidable in the project is to install it. This can be done by executing the following command, which installs the module locally into the ./node_modules directory:

```
$ npm install formidable
```

To access the API, you need to `require()` it, along with the initial http module:

```
var http = require('http');
var formidable = require('formidable');
```

The first step to implementing the `upload()` function is to respond with 400 Bad Request when the request doesn't appear to contain the appropriate type of content:

```
function upload(req, res) {
  if (!isFormData(req)) {
    res.statusCode = 400;
    res.end('Bad Request: expecting multipart/form-data');
    return;
  }
}

function isFormData(req) {
  var type = req.headers['content-type'] || '';
  return 0 == type.indexOf('multipart/form-data');
}
```

The helper function `isFormData()` checks the `Content-Type` header field for `multipart/form-data` by using the JavaScript `String.indexOf()` method to assert that `multipart/form-data` is at the beginning of the field's value.

Now that you know that it's a multipart request, you need to initialize a new `formidable.IncomingForm` form and then issue the `form.parse(req)` method call, where `req` is the request object. This allows formidable to access the request's `data` events for parsing:

```
function upload(req, res) {
  if (!isFormData(req)) {
    res.statusCode = 400;
    res.end('Bad Request');
    return;
  }

  var form = new formidable.IncomingForm();
  form.parse(req);
}
```

The `IncomingForm` object emits many events itself, and by default it streams file uploads to the /tmp directory. As shown in the following listing, formidable issues events when form elements have been processed. For example, a `file` event is issued when a file has been received and processed, and `field` is issued on the complete receipt of a field.

Listing 4.8 Using formidable's API

```
...
var form = new formidable.IncomingForm();

form.on('field', function(field, value){
  console.log(field);
  console.log(value);
});

form.on('file', function(name, file){
  console.log(name);
  console.log(file);
});

form.on('end', function(){
  res.end('upload complete!');
});

form.parse(req);
...
```

By examining the first two `console.log()` calls in the `field` event handler, you can see that "my clock" was entered in the `name` text field:

```
name
my clock
```

The `file` event is emitted when a file upload is complete. The `file` object provides you with the file size, the path in the form.uploadDir directory (/tmp by default), the original basename, and the MIME type. The `file` object looks like the following when it's passed to `console.log()`:

```
{ size: 28638,
  path: '/tmp/d870ede4d01507a68427a3364204cdf3',
  name: 'clock.png',
  type: 'image/png',
  lastModifiedDate: Sun, 05 Jun 2011 02:32:10 GMT,
  length: [Getter],
  filename: [Getter],
  mime: [Getter],
  ...
}
```

Formidable also provides a higher-level API, essentially wrapping the API we've already looked at into a single callback. When a function is passed to `form.parse()`, an `error` is passed as the first argument if something goes wrong. Otherwise, two objects are passed: `fields` and `files`.

The `fields` object may look something like the following `console.log()` output:

```
{ name: 'my clock' }
```

The `files` object provides the same `File` instances that the `file` event emits, keyed by name like `fields`.

It's important to note that you can listen for these events even while using the callback, so functions like progress reporting aren't hindered. The following code shows how this more concise API can be used to produce the same results that we've already discussed:

```
var form = new formidable.IncomingForm();
form.parse(req, function(err, fields, files){
  console.log(fields);
  console.log(files);
  res.end('upload complete!');
});
```

Now that you have the basics, we'll look at calculating upload progress, a process that comes quite naturally to Node and its event loop.

4.4.3 Calculating upload progress

Formidable's `progress` event emits the number of bytes received and bytes expected. This allows you to implement a progress bar. In the following example, the percentage is computed and logged by invoking `console.log()` each time the `progress` event is fired:

```
form.on('progress', function(bytesReceived, bytesExpected){
  var percent = Math.floor(bytesReceived / bytesExpected * 100);
  console.log(percent);
});
```

This script will yield output similar to the following:

```
1
2
4
5
6
8
...
99
100
```

Now that you understand this concept, the next obvious step would be to relay that progress back to the user's browser. This is a fantastic feature for any application expecting large uploads, and it's a task that Node is well suited for. By using the WebSocket protocol, for instance, or a real-time module like Socket.IO, it would be possible in just a few lines of code. We'll leave that as an exercise for you to figure out.

We have one final, and very important, topic to cover: securing your application.

4.5 Securing your application with HTTPS

A frequent requirement for e-commerce sites, and sites dealing with sensitive data, is to keep traffic to and from the server private. Standard HTTP sessions involve the client and server exchanging information using unencrypted text. This makes HTTP traffic fairly trivial to eavesdrop on.

The Hypertext Transfer Protocol Secure (HTTPS) protocol provides a way to keep web sessions private. HTTPS combines HTTP with the TLS/SSL transport layer. Data sent using HTTPS is encrypted and is therefore harder to eavesdrop on. In this section, we'll cover some basics on securing your application using HTTPS.

If you'd like to take advantage of HTTPS in your Node application, the first step is getting a private key and a certificate. The private key is, essentially, a "secret" needed to decrypt data sent between the server and client. The private key is kept in a file on the server in a place where it can't be easily accessed by untrusted users. In this section, you'll generate what's called a *self-signed certificate*. These kinds of SSL certificates can't be used in production websites because browsers will display a warning message when a page is accessed with an untrusted certificate, but it's useful for development and testing encrypted traffic.

To generate a private key, you'll need OpenSSL, which will already be installed on your system if you installed Node. To generate a private key, which we'll call key.pem, open up a command-line prompt and enter the following:

```
openssl genrsa 1024 > key.pem
```

In addition to a private key, you'll need a certificate. Unlike a private key, a certificate can be shared with the world; it contains a public key and information about the certificate holder. The public key is used to encrypt traffic sent from the client to the server.

The private key is used to create the certificate. Enter the following to generate a certificate called key-cert.pem.

```
openssl req -x509 -new -key key.pem > key-cert.pem
```

Now that you've generated your keys, put them in a safe place. In the HTTPS server in the following listing we reference keys stored in the same directory as our server script, but keys are more often kept elsewhere, typically ~/.ssh. The following code will create a simple HTTPS server using your keys.

Listing 4.9 HTTPS server options

```
var https = require('https');
var fs = require('fs');

var options = {
  key:  fs.readFileSync('./key.pem'),
  cert: fs.readFileSync('./key-cert.pem')
};

https.createServer(options, function (req, res) {
  res.writeHead(200);
  res.end("hello world\n");
}).listen(3000);
```

SSL key and cert given as options

options object is passed in first

https and http modules have almost identical APIs

Once the HTTPS server code is running, you can connect to it securely using a web browser. To do so, navigate to https://localhost:3000/ in your web browser. Because the certificate used in our example isn't backed by a Certificate Authority, a warning will be displayed. You can ignore this warning here, but if you're deploying a public site, you should always properly register with a Certificate Authority (CA) and get a real, trusted certificate for use with your server.

4.6 Summary

In this chapter, we've introduced the fundamentals of Node's HTTP server, showing you how to respond to incoming requests and how to handle asynchronous exceptions to keep your application reliable. You've learned how to create a RESTful web application, serve static files, and even create an upload progress calculator.

You may also have seen that starting with Node from a web application developer's point of view can seem daunting. As seasoned web developers, we promise that it's worth the effort. This knowledge will aid in your understanding of Node for debugging, authoring open source frameworks, or contributing to existing frameworks.

This chapter's fundamental knowledge will prepare you for diving into Connect, a higher-level framework that provides a fantastic set of bundled functionality that every web application framework can take advantage of. Then there's Express—the icing on the cake! Together, these tools will make everything you've learned in this chapter easier, more secure, and more enjoyable.

Before we get there, though, you'll need somewhere to store your application data. In the next chapter, we'll look at the rich selection of database clients created by the Node community, which will help power the applications you create throughout the rest of the book.

5 Storing Node application data

This chapter covers

- In-memory and filesystem data storage
- Conventional relational database storage
- Nonrelational database storage

Almost every application, web-based or otherwise, requires data storage of some kind, and the applications you build with Node are no different. The choice of an appropriate storage mechanism depends on five factors:

- What data is being stored
- How quickly data needs to be read and written to maintain adequate performance
- How much data exists
- How data needs to be queried
- How long and reliably the data needs to be stored

Methods of storing data range from keeping data in server memory to interfacing with a full-blown database management system (DBMS), but all methods require trade-offs of one sort or another.

Mechanisms that support long-term persistence of complex structured data, along with powerful search facilities, incur significant performance costs, so using them is not always the best strategy. Similarly, storing data in server memory maximizes performance, but it's less reliably persistent because data will be lost if the application restarts or the server loses power.

So how will you decide which storage mechanism to use in your applications? In the world of Node application development, it isn't unusual to use different storage mechanisms for different use cases. In this chapter, we'll talk about three different options:

- Storing data without installing and configuring a DBMS
- Storing data using a relational DBMS—specifically, MySQL and PostgreSQL
- Storing data using NoSQL databases—specifically, Redis, MongoDB, and Mongoose

You'll use some of these storage mechanisms to build applications later in the book, and by the end of this chapter you'll know how to use these storage mechanisms to address your own application needs.

To start, let's look at the easiest and lowest level of storage possible: serverless data storage.

5.1 Serverless data storage

From the standpoint of system administration, the most convenient storage mechanisms are those that don't require you to maintain a DBMS, such as in-memory storage and file-based storage. Removing the need to install and configure a DBMS makes the applications you build much easier to install.

The lack of a DBMS makes serverless data storage a perfect fit for Node applications that users will run on their own hardware, like web applications and other TCP/IP applications. It's also great for command-line interface (CLI) tools: a Node-driven CLI tool might require storage, but it's likely the user won't want to go through the hassle of setting up a MySQL server in order to use the tool.

In this section, you'll learn when and how to use in-memory storage and file-based storage, both of which are primary forms of serverless data storage. Let's start with the simplest of the two: in-memory storage.

5.1.1 In-memory storage

In the example applications in chapters 2 and 4, in-memory storage was used to keep track of details about chat users and tasks. In-memory storage uses variables to store data. Reading and writing this data is fast, but as we mentioned earlier, you'll lose the data during server and application restarts.

The ideal use of in-memory storage is for small bits of frequently accessed data. One such application would be a counter that keeps track of the number of page views since the last application restart. For example, the following code will start a web server on port 8888 that counts each request:

```
var http = require('http');
var counter = 0;

var server = http.createServer(function(req, res) {
  counter++;
  res.write('I have been accessed ' + counter + ' times.');
  res.end();
}).listen(8888);
```

For applications that need to store information that can persist beyond application and server restarts, file-based storage may be more suitable.

5.1.2 File-based storage

File-based storage uses a filesystem to store data. Developers often use this type of storage for application configuration information, but it also allows you to easily persist data that can survive application and server restarts.

> **Concurrency issues**
>
> File-based storage, although easy to use, isn't suitable for all types of applications. If a multiuser application, for example, stored records in a file, there could be concurrency issues. Two users could load the same file at the same time and modify it; saving one version would overwrite the other, causing one user's changes to be lost. For multiuser applications, database management systems are a more sensible choice because they're designed to deal with concurrency issues.

To illustrate the use of file-based storage, let's create a simple command-line variant of chapter 4's web-based Node to-do list application. Figure 5.1 shows this variant in operation.

The application will store tasks in a file named .tasks in whatever directory the script runs from. Tasks will be converted to JSON before being stored, and they'll be converted from JSON when they're read from the file.

To create the application, you'll need to write the starting logic and then define helper functions to retrieve and store tasks.

```
1. Shell
$ node cli_tasks.js add Floss the cat.
Saved.
$ node cli_tasks.js list
Floss the cat.
$ node cli_tasks.js add Buy some hats.
Saved.
$ node cli_tasks.js list
Floss the cat.
Buy some hats.
$
```

Figure 5.1 A command-line to-do list tool

WRITING THE STARTING LOGIC

The logic begins by requiring the necessary modules, parsing the task command and description from the command-line arguments, and specifying the file in which tasks should be stored. This is shown in the following code.

Listing 5.1 Gather argument values and resolve file database path

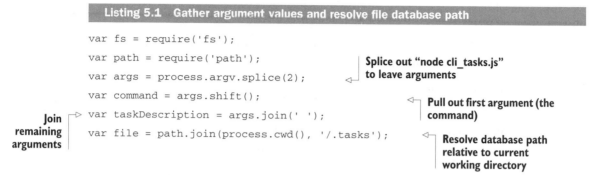

```
var fs = require('fs');
var path = require('path');
var args = process.argv.splice(2);
var command = args.shift();
var taskDescription = args.join(' ');
var file = path.join(process.cwd(), '/.tasks');
```

- Splice out "node cli_tasks.js" to leave arguments
- Pull out first argument (the command)
- Join remaining arguments
- Resolve database path relative to current working directory

If you provide an action argument, the application either outputs a list of stored tasks or adds a task description to the task store, as shown in the following listing. If you don't provide the argument, usage help will be displayed.

Listing 5.2 Determining what action the CLI script should take

```
switch (command) {
  case 'list':
    listTasks(file);
    break;

  case 'add':
    addTask(file, taskDescription);
    break;

  default:
    console.log('Usage: ' + process.argv[0]
      + ' list|add [taskDescription]');
}
```

- 'list' will list all tasks stored
- 'add' will add new task
- Anything else will show usage help

DEFINING A HELPER FUNCTION TO RETRIEVE TASKS

The next step is to define a helper function called `loadOrInitializeTaskArray` in the application logic to retrieve existing tasks. As listing 5.3 shows, `loadOrInitializeTaskArray` loads a text file in which JSON-encoded data is stored. Two asynchronous `fs` module functions are used in the code. These functions are non-blocking, allowing the event loop to continue instead of having it sit and wait for the filesystem to return results.

Listing 5.3 Loading JSON-encoded data from a text file

```
function loadOrInitializeTaskArray(file, cb) {
  fs.exists(file, function(exists) {
    var tasks = [];
    if (exists) {
      fs.readFile(file, 'utf8', function(err, data) {
```

- Check if .tasks file already exists
- Read to-do data from .tasks file

```
        if (err) throw err;
        var data = data.toString();
        var tasks = JSON.parse(data || '[]');     <-- Parse JSON-encoded to-do data into array of tasks
        cb(tasks);
      });
    } else {
      cb([]);                                     <-- Create empty array of tasks if tasks file doesn't exist
    }
  });
}
```

Next, you use the `loadOrInitializeTaskArray` helper function to implement the `listTasks` functionality.

Listing 5.4 List tasks function

```
function listTasks(file) {
  loadOrInitializeTaskArray(file, function(tasks) {
    for(var i in tasks) {
      console.log(tasks[i]);
    }
  });
}
```

DEFINING A HELPER FUNCTION TO STORE TASKS

Now you need to define another helper function, `storeTasks`, to store JSON-serialized tasks into a file.

Listing 5.5 Storing a task to disk

```
function storeTasks(file, tasks) {
  fs.writeFile(file, JSON.stringify(tasks), 'utf8', function(err) {
    if (err) throw err;
    console.log('Saved.');
  });
}
```

Then you can use the `storeTasks` helper function to implement the `addTask` functionality.

Listing 5.6 Adding a task

```
function addTask(file, taskDescription) {
  loadOrInitializeTaskArray(file, function(tasks) {
    tasks.push(taskDescription);
    storeTasks(file, tasks);
  });
}
```

Using the filesystem as a data store enables you to add persistence to an application relatively quickly and easily. It's also a great way to handle application configuration. If application configuration data is stored in a text file and encoded in JSON, the logic defined earlier in `loadOrInitializeTaskArray` could be repurposed to read the file and parse the JSON.

In chapter 13, you'll learn more about manipulating the filesystem with Node. Now let's move on to look at the traditional data storage workhorses of applications: relational database management systems.

5.2 Relational database management systems

Relational database management systems (RDBMSs) allow complex information to be stored and easily queried. RDBMSs have traditionally been used for relatively high-end applications, such as content management, customer relationship management, and shopping carts. They can perform well when used correctly, but they require specialized administration knowledge and access to a database server. They also require knowledge of SQL, although there are object-relational mappers (ORMs) with APIs that can write SQL for you in the background. RDBMS administration, ORMs, and SQL are beyond the scope of this book, but you'll find many online resources that cover these technologies.

Developers have many relational database options, but most choose open source databases, primarily because they're well supported, they work well, and they don't cost anything. In this section, we'll look at MySQL and PostgreSQL, the two most popular full-featured relational databases. MySQL and PostgreSQL have similar capabilities, and both are solid choices. If you haven't used either, MySQL is easier to set up and has a larger user base. If you happen to use the proprietary Oracle database, you'll want to use the db-oracle module (https://github.com/mariano/node-db-oracle), which is also outside the scope of this book.

Let's start with MySQL and then look at PostgreSQL.

5.2.1 MySQL

MySQL is the world's most popular SQL database, and it's well supported by the Node community. If you're new to MySQL and interested in learning about it, you'll find the official tutorial online (http://dev.mysql.com/doc/refman/5.0/en/tutorial.html). For those new to SQL, many online tutorials and books, including Chris Fehily's *SQL: Visual QuickStart Guide* (Peachpit Press, 2008), are available to help you get up to speed.

USING MYSQL TO BUILD A WORK-TRACKING APP

To see how Node takes advantage of MySQL, let's look at an application that requires an RDBMS. Let's say you're creating a serverless web application to keep track of how you spend your workdays. You'll need to record the date of the work, the time spent on the work, and a description of the work performed.

The application you'll build will have a form in which details about the work performed can be entered, as shown in figure 5.2.

Once the work information has been entered, it can be archived or deleted so it doesn't show above the fields used to enter more work, as shown in figure 5.3. Clicking the Archived Work link will then display any work items that have been archived.

You could build this web application using the filesystem as a simple data store, but it would be tricky to build reports with the data. If you wanted to create a report on

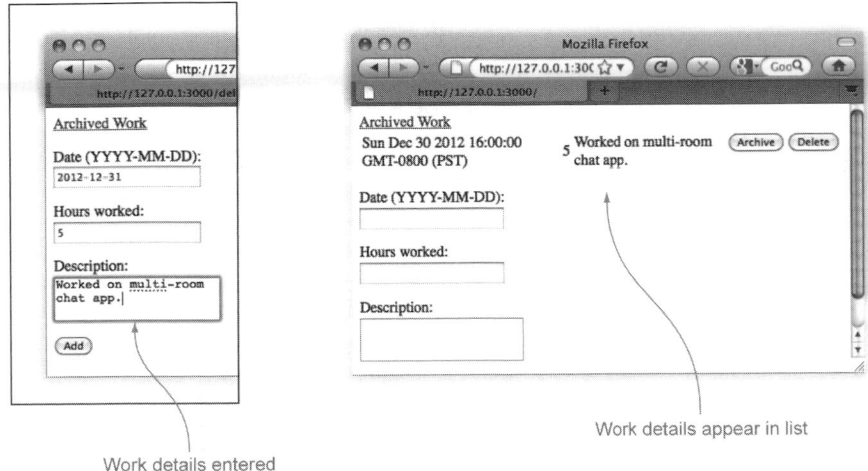

Figure 5.2 Recording details of work performed

the work you did last week, for example, you'd have to read every work record stored and check the record's date. Having application data in an RDBMS gives you the ability to generate reports easily using SQL queries.

To build a work-tracking application, you'll need to do the following:

- Create the application logic
- Create helper functions needed to make the application work
- Write functions that let you add, delete, update, and retrieve data with MySQL
- Write code that renders the HTML records and forms

The application will leverage Node's built-in http module for web server functionality and will use a third-party module to interact with a MySQL server. A custom module named *timetrack* will contain application-specific functions for storing, modifying, and retrieving data using MySQL. Figure 5.4 provides an overview of the application.

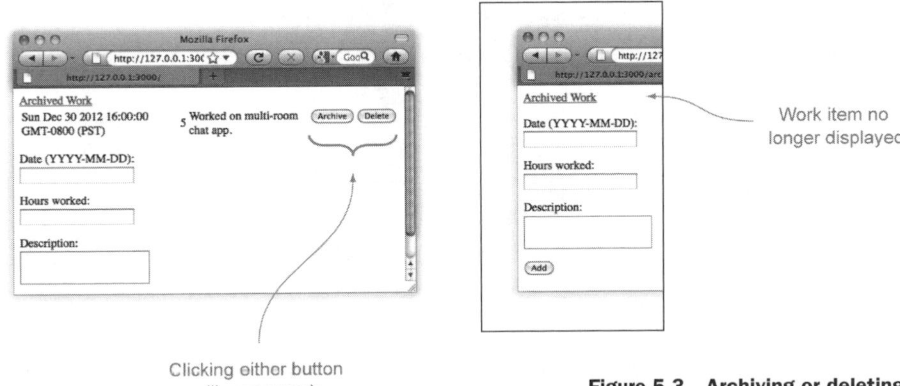

Figure 5.3 Archiving or deleting details of work performed

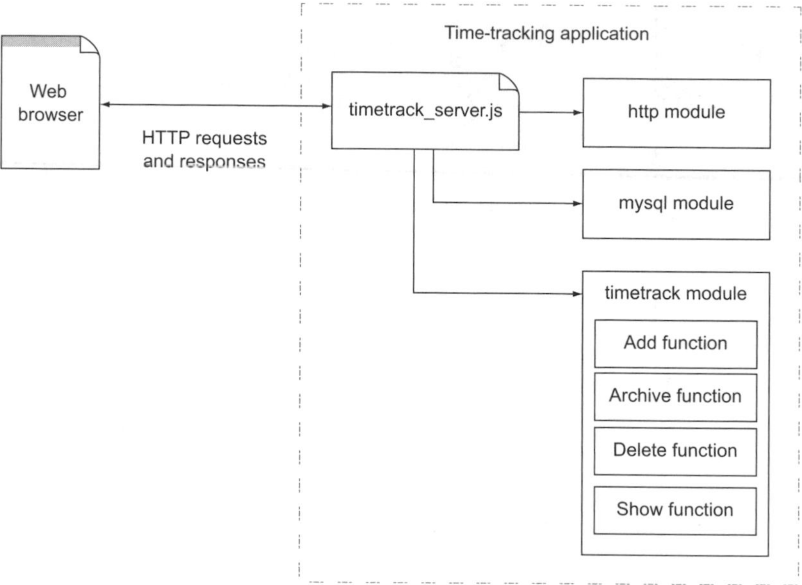

Figure 5.4 How the work-tracking application will be structured

The end result, as shown in figure 5.5, will be a simple web application that allows you to record work performed and review, archive, and delete the work records.

To allow Node to talk to MySQL, we'll use Felix Geisendörfer's popular node-mysql module (https://github.com/felixge/node-mysql). To begin, install the MySQL Node module using the following command:

```
npm install mysql
```

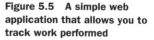

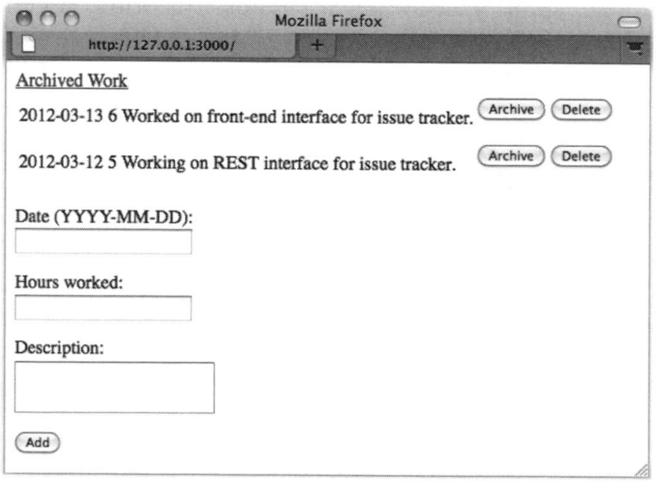

Figure 5.5 A simple web application that allows you to track work performed

CREATING THE APPLICATION LOGIC

Next, you need to create two files for application logic. The application will be composed of two files: timetrack_server.js, used to start the application, and timetrack.js, a module containing application-related functionality.

To start, create a file named timetrack_server.js and include the code in listing 5.7. This code includes Node's HTTP API, application-specific logic, and a MySQL API. Fill in the `host`, `user`, and `password` settings with those that correspond to your MySQL configuration.

Listing 5.7 Application setup and database connection initialization

```
var http = require('http');
var work = require('./lib/timetrack');
var mysql = require('mysql');                   <-- Require MySQL API

var db = mysql.createConnection({               <-- Connect to MySQL
  host:     '127.0.0.1',
  user:     'myuser',
  password: 'mypassword',
  database: 'timetrack'
});
```

Next, add the logic in listing 5.8 to define the basic web application behavior. The application allows you to browse, add, and delete work performance records. In addition, the app will let you archive work records. Archiving a work record hides it on the main page, but archived records remain browsable on a separate web page.

Listing 5.8 HTTP request routing

```
var server = http.createServer(function(req, res) {
  switch (req.method) {
    case 'POST':                                <-- Route HTTP POST requests
      switch(req.url) {
        case '/':
          work.add(db, req, res);
          break;
        case '/archive':
          work.archive(db, req, res);
          break;
        case '/delete':
          work.delete(db, req, res);
          break;
      }
      break;
    case 'GET':                                 <-- Route HTTP GET requests
      switch(req.url) {
        case '/':
          work.show(db, res);
          break;
        case '/archived':
          work.showArchived(db, res);
      }
```

```
      break;
    }
  });
```

The code in listing 5.9 is the final addition to timetrack_server.js. This logic creates a database table if none exists and starts the HTTP server listening to IP address 127.0.0.1 on TCP/IP port 3000. All node-mysql queries are performed using the query function.

Listing 5.9 Database table creation

```
db.query(
  "CREATE TABLE IF NOT EXISTS work ("                    <-- Table-creation SQL
  + "id INT(10) NOT NULL AUTO_INCREMENT, "
  + "hours DECIMAL(5,2) DEFAULT 0, "
  + "date DATE, "
  + "archived INT(1) DEFAULT 0, "
  + "description LONGTEXT,"
  + "PRIMARY KEY(id))",
  function(err) {
    if (err) throw err;
    console.log('Server started...');
    server.listen(3000, '127.0.0.1');                    <-- Start HTTP server
  }
);
```

CREATING HELPER FUNCTIONS THAT SEND HTML, CREATE FORMS, AND RECEIVE FORM DATA

Now that you've fully defined the file you'll use to start the application, it's time to create the file that defines the rest of the application's functionality. Create a directory named lib, and inside this directory create a file named timetrack.js. Inside this file, insert the logic from listing 5.10, which includes the Node querystring API and defines helper functions for sending web page HTML and receiving data submitted through forms.

Listing 5.10 Helper functions: sending HTML, creating forms, receiving form data

```
var qs = require('querystring');

exports.sendHtml = function(res, html) {                <-- Send HTML response
  res.setHeader('Content-Type', 'text/html');
  res.setHeader('Content-Length', Buffer.byteLength(html));
  res.end(html);
};

exports.parseReceivedData = function(req, cb) {        <-- Parse HTTP POST data
  var body = '';
  req.setEncoding('utf8');
  req.on('data', function(chunk){ body += chunk });
  req.on('end', function() {
    var data = qs.parse(body);
    cb(data);
  });
};
```

```
exports.actionForm = function(id, path, label) {          <-- Render simple form
  var html = '<form method="POST" action="' + path + '">' +
    '<input type="hidden" name="id" value="' + id + '">' +
    '<input type="submit" value="' + label + '" />' +
    '</form>';
  return html;
};
```

ADDING DATA WITH MYSQL

With the helper functions in place, it's time to define the logic that will add a work record to the MySQL database. Add the code in the next listing to timetrack.js.

Listing 5.11 Adding a work record

```
exports.add = function(db, req, res) {
  exports.parseReceivedData(req, function(work) {          <-- Parse HTTP POST data
    db.query(
      "INSERT INTO work (hours, date, description) " +     <-- SQL to add work record
      " VALUES (?, ?, ?)",
      [work.hours, work.date, work.description],           <-- Work record data
      function(err) {
        if (err) throw err;
        exports.show(db, res);                             <-- Show user a list of work records
      }
    );
  });
};
```

Note that you use the question mark character (?) as a placeholder to indicate where a parameter should be placed. Each parameter is automatically escaped by the `query` method before being added to the query, preventing SQL injection attacks.

Note also that the second argument of the `query` method is now a list of values to substitute for the placeholders.

DELETING MYSQL DATA

Next, you need to add the following code to timetrack.js. This logic will delete a work record.

Listing 5.12 Deleting a work record

```
exports.delete = function(db, req, res) {
  exports.parseReceivedData(req, function(work) {          <-- Parse HTTP POST data
    db.query(
      "DELETE FROM work WHERE id=?",                       <-- SQL to delete work record
      [work.id],                                           <-- Work record ID
      function(err) {
        if (err) throw err;
        exports.show(db, res);                             <-- Show user a list of work records
      }
    );
  });
};
```

UPDATING MYSQL DATA

To add logic that will update a work record, flagging it as archived, add the following code to timetrack.js.

Listing 5.13 Archiving a work record

```
exports.archive = function(db, req, res) {
  exports.parseReceivedData(req, function(work) {      <-- Parse HTTP POST data
    db.query(
      "UPDATE work SET archived=1 WHERE id=?",       <-- SQL to update work record
      [work.id],                                     <-- Work record ID
      function(err) {
        if (err) throw err;
        exports.show(db, res);                       <-- Show user a list of work records
      }
    );
  });
};
```

RETRIEVING MYSQL DATA

Now that you've defined the logic that will add, delete, and update a work record, you can add the logic in listing 5.14 to retrieve work-record data—archived or unarchived—so it can be rendered as HTML. When issuing the query, a callback is provided that includes a `rows` argument for the returned records.

Listing 5.14 Retrieving work records

```
exports.show = function(db, res, showArchived) {
  var query = "SELECT * FROM work " +                 <-- SQL to fetch work records
    "WHERE archived=? " +
    "ORDER BY date DESC";
  var archiveValue = (showArchived) ? 1 : 0;
  db.query(
    query,
    [archiveValue],                     <-- Desired work-record archive status
    function(err, rows) {
      if (err) throw err;
      html = (showArchived)
        ? ''
        : '<a href="/archived">Archived Work</a><br/>';
      html += exports.workHitlistHtml(rows);          <-- Format results as HTML table
      html += exports.workFormHtml();
      exports.sendHtml(res, html);                <-- Send HTML response to user
    }
  );
};

exports.showArchived = function(db, res) {
  exports.show(db, res, true);                    <-- Show only archived work records
};
```

RENDERING MYSQL RECORDS

Add the logic in the following listing to timetrack.js. It'll do the rendering of work records to HTML.

Listing 5.15 Rendering work records to an HTML table

```
exports.workHitlistHtml = function(rows) {
  var html = '<table>';
  for(var i in rows) {                              // Render each work record as HTML table row
    html += '<tr>';
    html += '<td>' + rows[i].date + '</td>';
    html += '<td>' + rows[i].hours + '</td>';
    html += '<td>' + rows[i].description + '</td>';
    if (!rows[i].archived) {                        // Show archive button if work record isn't already archived
      html += '<td>' + exports.workArchiveForm(rows[i].id) + '</td>';
    }
    html += '<td>' + exports.workDeleteForm(rows[i].id) + '</td>';
    html += '</tr>';
  }
  html += '</table>';
  return html;
};
```

RENDERING HTML FORMS

Finally, add the following code to timetrack.js to render the HTML forms needed by the application.

Listing 5.16 HTML forms for adding, archiving, and deleting work records

```
exports.workFormHtml = function() {
  var html = '<form method="POST" action="/">' +    // Render blank HTML form for entering new work record
    '<p>Date (YYYY-MM-DD):<br/><input name="date" type="text"><p/>' +
    '<p>Hours worked:<br/><input name="hours" type="text"><p/>' +
    '<p>Description:<br/>' +
    '<textarea name="description"></textarea></p>' +
    '<input type="submit" value="Add" />' +
    '</form>';
  return html;
};

exports.workArchiveForm = function(id) {            // Render Archive button form
  return exports.actionForm(id, '/archive', 'Archive');
};

exports.workDeleteForm = function(id) {             // Render Delete button form
  return exports.actionForm(id, '/delete', 'Delete');
};
```

TRYING IT OUT

Now that you've fully defined the application, you can run it. Make sure that you've created a database named timetrack using your MySQL administration interface of choice. Then start the application by entering the following into your command line:

```
node timetrack_server.js
```

Finally, navigate to http://127.0.0.1:3000/ in a web browser to use the application.

MySQL may be the most popular relational database, but PostgreSQL is, for many, the more respected of the two. Let's look at how you can use PostgreSQL in your application.

5.2.2 PostgreSQL

PostgreSQL is well regarded for its standards compliance and robustness, and many Node developers favor it over other RDBMSs. Unlike MySQL, PostgreSQL supports recursive queries and many specialized data types. PostgreSQL can also use a variety of standard authentication methods, such as Lightweight Directory Access Protocol (LDAP) and Generic Security Services Application Program Interface (GSSAPI). For those using replication for scalability or redundancy, PostgreSQL supports synchronous replication, a form of replication in which data loss is prevented by verifying replication after each data operation.

If you're new to PostgreSQL and interested in learning it, you'll find the official tutorial online (www.postgresql.org/docs/7.4/static/tutorial.html).

The most mature and actively developed PostgreSQL API module is Brian Carlson's node-postgres (https://github.com/brianc/node-Postgres).

> **UNTESTED FOR WINDOWS** While the node-postgres module is intended to work for Windows, the module's creator primarily tests using Linux and OS X, so Windows users may encounter issues, such as a fatal error during installation. Because of this, Windows users may want to use MySQL instead of PostgreSQL.

Install node-postgres via npm using the following command:

```
npm install pg
```

CONNECTING TO POSTGRESQL

Once you've installed the node-postgres module, you can connect to PostgreSQL and select a database to query using the following code (omit the `:mypassword` portion of the connection string if no password is set):

```
var pg = require('pg');
var conString = "tcp://myuser:mypassword@localhost:5432/mydatabase";

var client = new pg.Client(conString);
client.connect();
```

INSERTING A ROW INTO A DATABASE TABLE

The `query` method performs queries. The following example code shows how to insert a row into a database table:

```
client.query(
  'INSERT INTO users ' +
  "(name) VALUES ('Mike')"
);
```

Placeholders ($1, $2, and so on) indicate where to place a parameter. Each parameter is escaped before being added to the query, preventing SQL injection attacks. The following example shows the insertion of a row using placeholders:

```
client.query(
  "INSERT INTO users " +
  "(name, age) VALUES ($1, $2)",
  ['Mike', 39]
);
```

To get the primary key value of a row after an insert, you can use a `RETURNING` clause to specify the name of the column whose value you'd like to return. You then add a callback as the last argument of the `query` call, as the following example shows:

```
client.query(
  "INSERT INTO users " +
  "(name, age) VALUES ($1, $2) " +
  "RETURNING id",
  ['Mike', 39],
  function(err, result) {
    if (err) throw err;
    console.log('Insert ID is ' + result.rows[0].id);
  }
);
```

CREATING A QUERY THAT RETURNS RESULTS

If you're creating a query that will return results, you'll need to store the client `query` method's return value to a variable. The `query` method returns an object that has inherited `EventEmitter` behavior to take advantage of Node's built-in functionality. This object emits a `row` event for each retrieved database row. Listing 5.17 shows how you can output data from each row returned by a query. Note the use of `EventEmitter` listeners that define what to do with database table rows and what to do when data retrieval is complete.

Listing 5.17 Selecting rows from a PostgreSQL database

```
var query = client.query(
  "SELECT * FROM users WHERE age > $1",
  [40]
);

query.on('row', function(row) {      <-- Handle return of a row
  console.log(row.name)
});

query.on('end', function() {         <-- Handle query completion
  client.end();
});
```

An `end` event is emitted after the last row is fetched, and it may be used to close the database or continue with further application logic.

Relational databases may be classic workhorses, but another breed of database manager that doesn't require the use of SQL is becoming increasingly popular.

5.3 NoSQL databases

In the early days of the database world, nonrelational databases were the norm. But relational databases slowly gained in popularity and over time became the mainstream choice for applications both on and off the web. In recent years, a resurgent interest in nonrelational DBMSs has emerged as their proponents claimed advantages in scalability and simplicity, and these DBMSs target a variety of usage scenarios. They're popularly referred to as "NoSQL" databases, interpreted as "No SQL" or "Not Only SQL."

Although relational DBMSs sacrifice performance for reliability, many NoSQL databases put performance first. For this reason, NoSQL databases may be a better choice for real-time analytics or messaging. NoSQL databases also usually don't require data schemas to be predefined, which is useful for applications in which stored data is hierarchical but whose hierarchy varies.

In this section, we'll look at two popular NoSQL databases: Redis and MongoDB. We'll also look at Mongoose, a popular API that abstracts access to MongoDB, adding a number of time-saving features. The setup and administration of Redis and MongoDB are out of the scope of this book, but you'll find quick-start instructions on the web for Redis (http://redis.io/topics/quickstart) and MongoDB (http://docs.mongodb.org/manual/installation/#installation-guides) that should help you get up and running.

5.3.1 Redis

Redis is a data store well suited to handling simple data that doesn't need to be stored for long-term access, such as instant messages and game-related data. Redis stores data in RAM, logging changes to it to disk. The downside to this is that storage space is limited, but the advantage is that Redis can perform data manipulation quickly. If a Redis server crashes and the contents of RAM are lost, the disk log can be used to restore the data.

Redis provides a vocabulary of primitive but useful commands (http://redis.io/commands) that work on a number of data structures. Most of the data structures supported by Redis will be familiar to developers, as they're analogous to those frequently used in programming: hash tables, lists, and key/value pairs (which are used like simple variables). Hash table and key/value pair types are illustrated in figure 5.6. Redis also supports a less-familiar data structure called a *set*, which we'll talk about later in this chapter.

We won't go into all of Redis's commands in this chapter, but we'll run through a number of examples that will be applicable for most applications. If you're new to Redis and want to get an idea of its usefulness before trying these examples, a great place to start is the "Try Redis" tutorial (http://try.redis.io/). For an in-depth look at leveraging Redis for your applications, check out Josiah L. Carlson's book, *Redis in Action* (Manning, 2013).

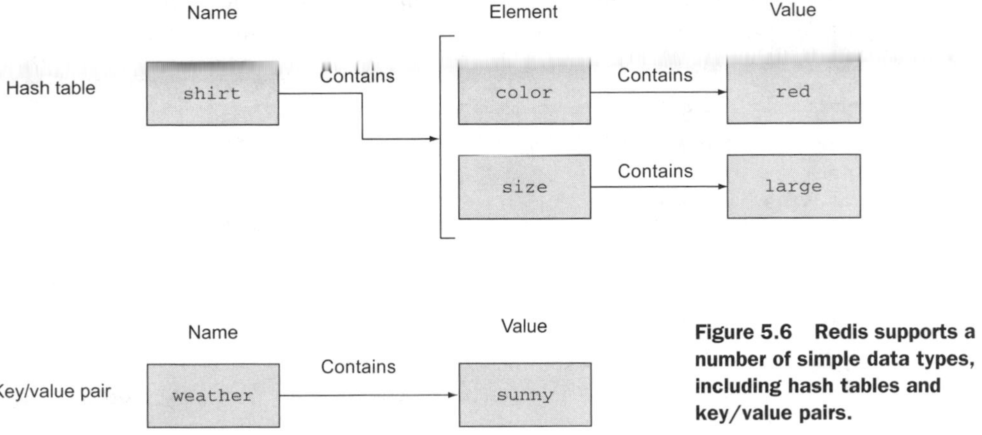

Figure 5.6 Redis supports a number of simple data types, including hash tables and key/value pairs.

The most mature and actively developed Redis API module is Matt Ranney's node_redis (https://github.com/mranney/node_redis) module. Install this module using the following npm command:

```
npm install redis
```

CONNECTING TO A REDIS SERVER

The following code establishes a connection to a Redis server using the default TCP/IP port running on the same host. The Redis client you've created has inherited `EventEmitter` behavior that emits an `error` event when the client has problems communicating with the Redis server. As the following example shows, you can define your own error-handling logic by adding a listener for the `error` event type:

```
var redis = require('redis');
var client = redis.createClient(6379, '127.0.0.1');

client.on('error', function (err) {
    console.log('Error ' + err);
});
```

MANIPULATING DATA IN REDIS

After you've connected to Redis, your application can start manipulating data immediately using the `client` object. The following example code shows the storage and retrieval of a key/value pair:

```
client.set('color', 'red', redis.print);
client.get('color', function(err, value) {
  if (err) throw err;
  console.log('Got: ' + value);
});
```

The print function prints the results of an operation or an error if one occurs.

STORING AND RETRIEVING VALUES USING A HASH TABLE

Listing 5.18 shows the storage and retrieval of values in a slightly more complicated data structure: a *hash table*, also known as a *hash map*. A hash table is essentially a table of identifiers, called *keys*, that are associated with corresponding *values*.

The hmset Redis command sets hash table elements, identified by a key, to a value. The hkeys Redis command lists the keys of each element in a hash table.

Listing 5.18 Storing data in elements of a Redis hash table

```
client.hmset('camping', {
  'shelter': '2-person tent',
  'cooking': 'campstove'
}, redis.print);                                   <-- Set hash table elements

client.hget('camping', 'cooking', function(err, value) {   <-- Get "cooking" element's value
  if (err) throw err;
  console.log('Will be cooking with: ' + value);
});

client.hkeys('camping', function(err, keys) {       <-- Get hash table keys
  if (err) throw err;
  keys.forEach(function(key, i) {
    console.log('   ' + key);
  });
});
```

STORING AND RETRIEVING DATA USING THE LIST

Another data structure Redis supports is the list. A Redis list can theoretically hold over four billion elements, memory permitting.

The following code shows the storage and retrieval of values in a list. The lpush Redis command adds a value to a list. The lrange Redis command retrieves a range of list items using start and end arguments. The -1 end argument in the following code signifies the last item of the list, so this use of lrange will retrieve all list items:

```
client.lpush('tasks', 'Paint the bikeshed red.', redis.print);
client.lpush('tasks', 'Paint the bikeshed green.', redis.print);
client.lrange('tasks', 0, -1, function(err, items) {
  if (err) throw err;
  items.forEach(function(item, i) {
    console.log('   ' + item);
  });
});
```

A Redis list is an ordered list of strings. If you were creating a conference-planning application, for example, you might use a list to store the conference's itinerary.

Redis lists are similar, conceptually, to arrays in many programming languages, and they provide a familiar way to manipulate data. One downside to lists, however, is their retrieval performance. As a Redis list grows in length, retrieval becomes slower (O(n) in big O notation).

> **BIG O NOTATION** In computer science, *big O notation* is a way of categorizing algorithms by complexity. Seeing an algorithm's description in big O notation gives you a quick idea of the performance ramifications of using the algorithm. If you're new to big O, Rob Bell's "A Beginner's Guide to Big O Notation" provides a great overview (http://mng.bz/UJu7).

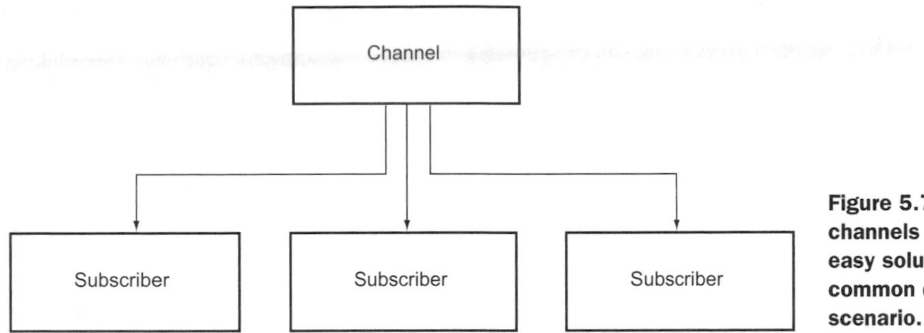

Figure 5.7 Redis channels provide an easy solution to a common data-delivery scenario.

STORING AND RETRIEVING DATA USING SETS

A Redis set is an unordered group of strings. If you were creating a conference-planning application, for example, you might use a set to store attendee information. Sets have better retrieval performance than lists. The time it takes to retrieve a set member is independent of the size of the set (O(1) in big O notation).

Sets must contain unique elements—if you try to store two identical values in a set, the second attempt to store the value will be ignored.

The following code illustrates the storage and retrieval of IP addresses. The `sadd` Redis command attempts to add a value to the set, and the `smembers` command returns stored values. In this example, we've twice attempted to add the IP address 204.10.37.96, but as you can see, when we display the set members, the address has only been stored once:

```
client.sadd('ip_addresses', '204.10.37.96', redis.print);
client.sadd('ip_addresses', '204.10.37.96', redis.print);
client.sadd('ip_addresses', '72.32.231.8', redis.print);
client.smembers('ip_addresses', function(err, members) {
  if (err) throw err;
  console.log(members);
});
```

DELIVERING DATA WITH CHANNELS

It's worth noting that Redis goes beyond the traditional role of data store by providing *channels*. Channels are data-delivery mechanisms that provide publish/subscribe functionality, as shown conceptually in figure 5.7. They're useful for chat and gaming applications.

A Redis client can either subscribe or publish to any given channel. Subscribing to a channel means you get any message sent to the channel. Publishing a message to a channel sends the message to all clients subscribed to that channel.

Listing 5.19 shows an example of how Redis's publish/subscribe functionality can be used to implement a TCP/IP chat server.

Listing 5.19 A simple chat server implemented with Redis pub/sub functionality

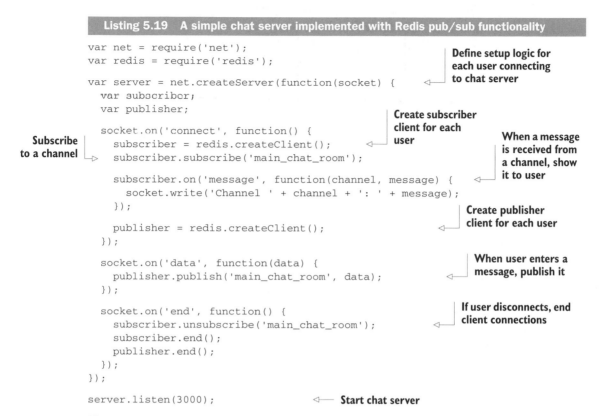

```
var net = require('net');
var redis = require('redis');

var server = net.createServer(function(socket) {
  var subscriber;
  var publisher;

  socket.on('connect', function() {
    subscriber = redis.createClient();
    subscriber.subscribe('main_chat_room');

    subscriber.on('message', function(channel, message) {
      socket.write('Channel ' + channel + ': ' + message);
    });

    publisher = redis.createClient();
  });

  socket.on('data', function(data) {
    publisher.publish('main_chat_room', data);
  });

  socket.on('end', function() {
    subscriber.unsubscribe('main_chat_room');
    subscriber.end();
    publisher.end();
  });
});

server.listen(3000);
```

Define setup logic for each user connecting to chat server

Create subscriber client for each user

Subscribe to a channel

When a message is received from a channel, show it to user

Create publisher client for each user

When user enters a message, publish it

If user disconnects, end client connections

Start chat server

MAXIMIZING NODE_REDIS PERFORMANCE

When you're deploying a Node.js application that uses the node_redis API to production, you may want to consider using Pieter Noordhuis's hiredis module (https://github.com/pietern/hiredis-node). This module will speed up Redis performance significantly because it takes advantage of the official hiredis C library. The node_redis API will automatically use hiredis, if it's installed, instead of the JavaScript implementation.

You can install hiredis using the following npm command:

```
npm install hiredis
```

Note that because the hiredis library compiles from C code, and Node's internal APIs change occasionally, you may have to recompile hiredis when upgrading Node.js. Use the following npm command to rebuild hiredis:

```
npm rebuild hiredis
```

Now that we've looked at Redis, which excels at high-performance handling of data primitives, let's look at a more generally useful database: MongoDB.

5.3.2 MongoDB

MongoDB is a general-purpose nonrelational database. It's used for the same sorts of applications that you'd use an RDBMS for.

A MongoDB database stores documents in *collections*. Documents in a collection, as shown in figure 5.8, need not share the same schema—each document could conceivably have a different schema. This makes MongoDB more flexible than conventional RDBMSs, as you don't have to worry about predefining schemas.

The most mature, actively maintained MongoDB API module is Christian Amor Kvalheim's node-mongodb-native (https://github.com/mongodb/node-mongodb-native). You can install this module using the following npm command. Windows users, note that the installation requires msbuild.exe, which is installed by Microsoft Visual Studio:

```
npm install mongodb
```

Connecting to MongoDB

After installing node-mongodb-native and running your MongoDB server, use the following code to establish a server connection:

```
var mongodb = require('mongodb');
var server = new mongodb.Server('127.0.0.1', 27017, {});

var client = new mongodb.Db('mydatabase', server, {w: 1});
```

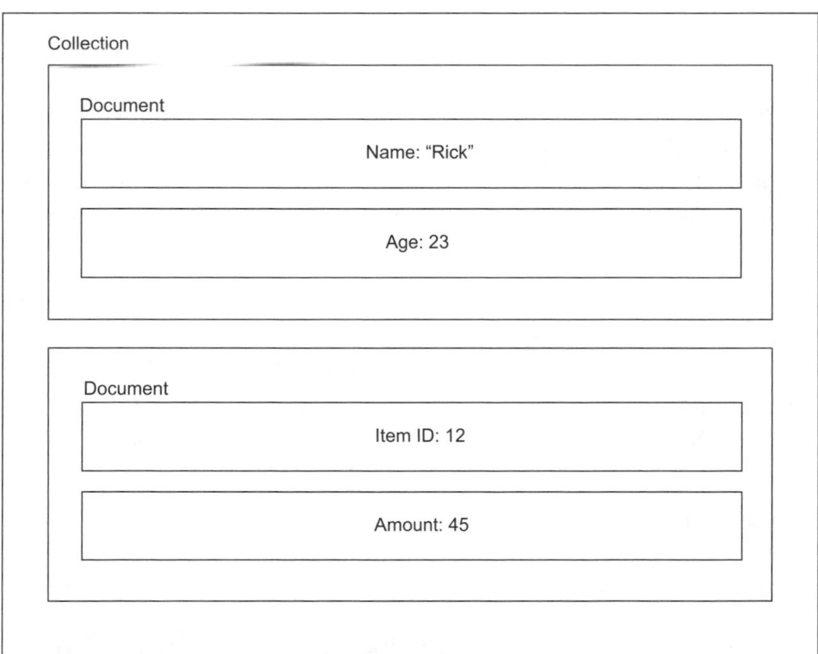

Figure 5.8 Each item in a MongoDB collection can have a completely different schema.

ACCESSING A MONGODB COLLECTION

The following snippet shows how you can access a collection once the database connection is open. If at any time after completing your database operations you want to close your MongoDB connection, execute `client.close()`:

```
client.open(function(err) {
  if (err) throw err;
  client.collection('test_insert', function(err, collection) {
    if (err) throw err;
    console.log('We are now able to perform queries.');     <-- Put MongoDB query code here
  });
});
```

INSERTING A DOCUMENT INTO A COLLECTION

The following code inserts a document into a collection and prints its unique document ID:

```
collection.insert(
  {
    "title": "I like cake",
    "body": "It is quite good."
  },
  {safe: true},                     <-- Safe mode indicates database operation should be completed before callback is executed
  function(err, documents) {
    if (err) throw err;
    console.log('Document ID is: ' + documents[0]._id);
  }
);
```

> **SAFE MODE** Specifying `{safe: true}` in a query indicates that you want the database operation to complete before executing the callback. If your callback logic is in any way dependent on the database operation being complete, you'll want to use this option. If your callback logic isn't dependent, you can get away with using `{}` instead.

Although you can use `console.log` to display `documents[0]._id` as a string, it's not actually a string. Document identifiers from MongoDB are encoded in *binary JSON* (BSON). BSON is a data interchange format primarily used by MongoDB instead of JSON to move data to and from the MongoDB server. In most cases, it's more space efficient than JSON and can be parsed more quickly. Taking less space and being easier to scan means database interactions end up being faster.

UPDATING DATA USING DOCUMENT IDS

BSON document identifiers can be used to update data. The following listing shows how to update a document using its ID.

Listing 5.20 Updating a MongoDB document

```
var _id = new client.bson_serializer
                    .ObjectID('4e650d344ac74b5a01000001');
collection.update(
```

```
  {_id: _id},
  {$set: {"title": "I ate too much cake"}},
  {safe: true},
  function(err) {
    if (err) throw err;
  }
);
```

SEARCHING FOR DOCUMENTS

To search for documents in MongoDB, use the `find` method. The following example shows logic that will display all items in a collection with a title of "I like cake":

```
collection.find({"title": "I like cake"}).toArray(
  function(err, results) {
    if (err) throw err;
    console.log(results);
  }
);
```

DELETING DOCUMENTS

Want to delete something? You can delete a record by referencing its internal ID (or any other criteria) using code similar to the following:

```
var _id = new client
              .bson_serializer
              .ObjectID('4e6513f0730d319501000001');
collection.remove({_id: _id}, {safe: true}, function(err) {
  if (err) throw err;
});
```

MongoDB is a powerful database, and node-mongodb-native offers high-performance access to it, but you may want to use an API that abstracts database access, handling the details for you in the background. This allows you to develop faster, while maintaining fewer lines of code. The most popular of these APIs is called Mongoose.

5.3.3 Mongoose

LearnBoost's Mongoose is a Node module that makes using MongoDB painless. Mongoose's models (in model-view-controller parlance) provide an interface to MongoDB collections as well as additional useful functionality, such as schema hierarchies, middleware, and validation. A schema hierarchy allows the association of one model with another, enabling, for example, a blog post to contain associated comments. Middleware allows the transformation of data or the triggering of logic during model data operations, making possible tasks like the automatic pruning of child data when a parent is removed. Mongoose's validation support lets you determine what data is acceptable at the schema level, rather than having to manually deal with it.

Although we'll focus solely on the basic use of Mongoose as a data store, if you decide to use Mongoose in your application, you'll definitely benefit from reading its online documentation and learning about all it has to offer (http://mongoosejs.com/).

In this section, we'll walk you through the basics of Mongoose, including how to do the following:

- Open and close a MongoDB connection
- Register a schema
- Add a task
- Search for a document
- Update a document
- Remove a document

First, you can install Mongoose via npm using the following command:

```
npm install mongoose
```

OPENING AND CLOSING A CONNECTION

Once you've installed Mongoose and have started your MongoDB server, the following example code will establish a MongoDB connection, in this case to a database called tasks:

```
var mongoose = require('mongoose');
var db = mongoose.connect('mongodb://localhost/tasks');
```

If at any time in your application you want to terminate your Mongoose-created connection, the following code will close it:

```
mongoose.disconnect();
```

REGISTERING A SCHEMA

When managing data using Mongoose, you'll need to register a schema. The following code shows the registration of a schema for tasks:

```
var Schema = mongoose.Schema;
var Tasks = new Schema({
  project: String,
  description: String
});
mongoose.model('Task', Tasks);
```

Mongoose schemas are powerful. In addition to defining data structures, they also allow you to set defaults, process input, and enforce validation. For more on Mongoose schema definition, see Mongoose's online documentation (http://mongoosejs.com/docs/schematypes.html).

ADDING A TASK

Once a schema is registered, you can access it and put Mongoose to work. The following code shows how to add a task using a model:

```
var Task = mongoose.model('Task');
var task = new Task();
task.project = 'Bikeshed';
task.description = 'Paint the bikeshed red.';
task.save(function(err) {
```

```
  if (err) throw err;
  console.log('Task saved.');
});
```

SEARCHING FOR A DOCUMENT

Searching with Mongoose is similarly easy. The `Task` model's `find` method allows you to find all documents, or to select specific documents using a JavaScript object to specify your filtering criteria. The following example code searches for tasks associated with a specific project and outputs each task's unique ID and description:

```
var Task = mongoose.model('Task');
Task.find({'project': 'Bikeshed'}, function(err, tasks) {
  for (var i = 0; i < tasks.length; i++) {
    console.log('ID:' + tasks[i]._id);
    console.log(tasks[i].description);
  }
});
```

UPDATING A DOCUMENT

Although it's possible to use a model's `find` method to zero in on a document that you can subsequently change and save, Mongoose models also have an `update` method expressly for this purpose. The following snippet shows how you can update a document using Mongoose:

```
var Task = mongoose.model('Task');
Task.update(
  {_id: '4e65b793d0cf5ca508000001'},          <-- Update using internal ID
  {description: 'Paint the bikeshed green.'},
  {multi: false},                          <-- Only update one document
  function(err, rows_updated) {
    if (err) throw err;
    console.log('Updated.');
  }
);
```

REMOVING A DOCUMENT

It's easy to remove a document in Mongoose once you've retrieved it. You can retrieve and remove a document using its internal ID (or any other criteria, if you use the `find` method instead of `findById`) using code similar to the following:

```
var Task = mongoose.model('Task');
Task.findById('4e65b3dce1592f7d08000001', function(err, task) {
  task.remove();
});
```

You'll find much to explore in Mongoose. It's an all-around great tool that enables you to pair the flexibility and performance of MongoDB with the ease of use traditionally associated with relational database management systems.

5.4 Summary

Now that you've gained a healthy understanding of data storage technologies, you have the basic knowledge you need to deal with common application data storage scenarios.

If you're creating multiuser web applications, you'll most likely use a DBMS of some sort. If you prefer the SQL-based way of doing things, MySQL and PostgreSQL are well-supported RDBMSs. If you find SQL limiting in terms of performance or flexibility, Redis and MongoDB are rock-solid options. MongoDB is a great general-purpose DBMS, whereas Redis excels in dealing with frequently changing, less complex data.

If you don't need the bells and whistles of a full-blown DBMS and want to avoid the hassle of setting one up, you have several options. If speed and performance are key, and you don't care about data persisting beyond application restarts, in-memory storage may be a good fit. If you aren't concerned about performance and don't need to do complex queries on your data—as with a typical command-line application—storing data in files may suit your needs.

Don't be afraid to use more than one type of storage mechanism in an application. If you were building a content management system, for example, you might store web application configuration options using files, stories using MongoDB, and user-contributed story-ranking data using Redis. How you handle persistence is limited only by your imagination.

With the basics of web application development and data persistence under your belt, you've learned the fundamentals you need to create simple web applications. You're now ready to move on to testing, an important skill you'll need to ensure that what you code today works tomorrow.

6 Connect

In this chapter

- Setting up a Connect application
- How Connect middleware works
- Why middleware ordering matters
- Mounting middleware and servers
- Creating configurable middleware
- Using error-handling middleware

Connect is a framework that uses modular components called *middleware* to implement web application logic in a reusable manner. In Connect, a middleware component is a function that intercepts the request and response objects provided by the HTTP server, executes logic, and then either ends the response or passes it to the next middleware component. Connect "connects" the middleware together using what's called the *dispatcher*.

Connect allows you to write your own middleware but also includes several common components that can be used in your applications for request logging, static file serving, request body parsing, and session managing, among others. Connect serves as an abstraction layer for developers who want to build their own higher-level web frameworks, because Connect can be easily expanded and built upon. Figure 6.1 shows how a Connect application is composed of the dispatcher, as well as an arrangement of middleware.

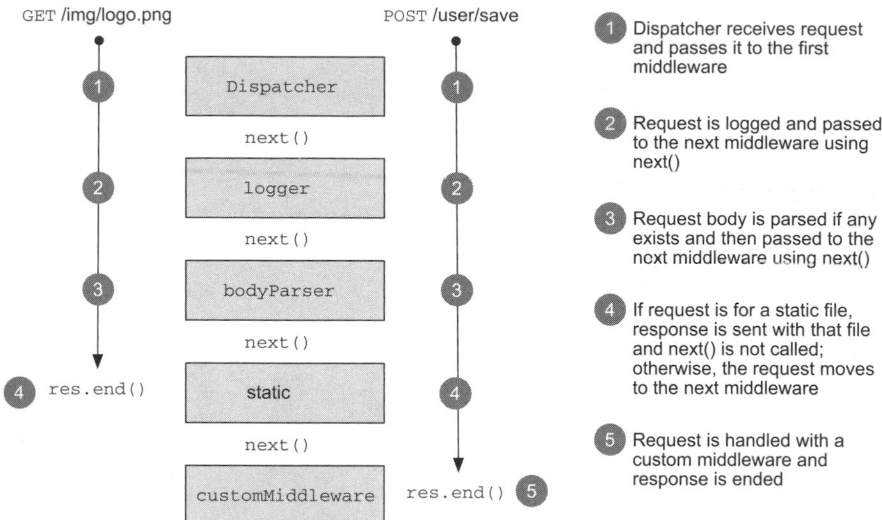
GET /img/logo.png
POST /user/save
Dispatcher
next()
logger
next()
bodyParser
next()
static
next()
customMiddleware
res.end()
res.end()
1 Dispatcher receives request and passes it to the first middleware
2 Request is logged and passed to the next middleware using next()
3 Request body is parsed if any exists and then passed to the next middleware using next()
4 If request is for a static file, response is sent with that file and next() is not called; otherwise, the request moves to the next middleware
5 Request is handled with a custom middleware and response is ended

Figure 6.1 The lifecycle of two HTTP requests making their way through a Connect server

> **Connect and Express**
>
> The concepts discussed in this chapter are directly applicable to the higher-level framework Express because it extends and builds upon Connect with additional higher-level sugar. After reading this chapter, you'll have a firm understanding of how Connect middleware works and how to compose components together to create an application.
>
> In chapter 8 we'll use Express to make writing web applications more enjoyable with a higher-level API than Connect provides. In fact, much of the functionality that Connect now provides originated in Express, before the abstraction was made (leaving lower-level building blocks to Connect and reserving the expressive sugar for Express).

To start off, let's create a basic Connect application.

6.1 Setting up a Connect application

Connect is a third-party module, so it isn't included by default when you install Node. You can download and install Connect from the npm registry using the command shown here:

```
$ npm install connect
```

Now that installing is out of the way, let's begin by creating a basic Connect application. To do this, you require the connect module, which is a function that returns a bare Connect application when invoked.

In chapter 4, we discussed how `http.createServer()` accepts a callback function that acts on incoming requests. The "application" that Connect creates is actually a JavaScript function designed to take the HTTP request and dispatch it to the middleware you've specified.

Listing 6.1 shows what the minimal Connect application looks like. This bare application has no middleware added to it, so the dispatcher will respond to any HTTP request that it receives with a 404 Not Found status.

Listing 6.1 A minimal Connect application

```
var connect = require('connect');
var app = connect();
app.listen(3000);
```

When you fire up the server and send it an HTTP request (with `curl` or a web browser), you'll see the text "Cannot GET /" indicating that this application isn't configured to handle the requested URL. This is the first example of how Connect's dispatcher works—it invokes each attached middleware component, one by one, until one of them decides to respond to the request. If it gets to the end of the list of middleware and none of the components respond, the application will respond with a 404.

Now that you've learned how to create a bare-bones Connect app and how the dispatcher works, let's take a look at how you can make the application *do something* by defining and adding middleware.

6.2 How Connect middleware works

In Connect, a middleware component is a JavaScript function that by convention accepts three arguments: a request object, a response object, and an argument commonly named `next`, which is a callback function indicating that the component is done and the next middleware component can be executed.

The concept of middleware was initially inspired by Ruby's Rack framework, which provided a very similar modular interface, but due to the streaming nature of Node the API isn't identical. Middleware components are great because they're designed to be small, self-contained, and reusable across applications.

In this section, you'll learn the basics of middleware by taking that bare-bones Connect application from the previous section and building two simple layers of middleware that together make up the app:

- A `logger` middleware component to log requests to the console
- A `hello` middleware component to respond to the request with "hello world"

Let's start by creating a simple middleware component that logs requests coming in to the server.

6.2.1 Middleware that does logging

Suppose you want to create a log file that records the request method and URL of requests coming in to your server. To do this, you'd create a function, which we'll call `logger`, that accepts the request and response objects and the `next` callback function.

The `next` function can be called from within the middleware to tell the dispatcher that the middleware has done its business and that control can be passed to the next middleware component. A callback function is used, rather than the method returning, so that asynchronous logic can be run within the middleware component, with the dispatcher only moving on to the next middleware component after the previous one has completed. Using `next()` is a nice mechanism to handle the flow between middleware components.

For the `logger` middleware component, you could invoke `console.log()` with the request method and URL, outputting something like "GET /user/1," and then invoke the `next()` function to pass control to the next component:

```
function logger(req, res, next) {
  console.log('%s %s', req.method, req.url);
  next();
}
```

And there you have it, a perfectly valid middleware component that prints out the request method and URL of each HTTP request received and then calls `next()` to pass control back to the dispatcher. To use this middleware in the application, invoke the `.use()` method, passing it the middleware function:

```
var connect = require('connect');
var app = connect();
app.use(logger);
app.listen(3000);
```

After issuing a few requests to your server (again, you can use `curl` or a web browser) you'll see output similar to the following on your console:

```
GET /
GET /favicon.ico
GET /users
GET /user/1
```

Logging requests is just one layer of middleware. You still have to send some sort of response to the client. That will come in your next middleware component.

6.2.2 Middleware that responds with "hello world"

The second middleware component in this app will send a response to the HTTP request. It's the same code that's in the "hello world" server callback function on the Node homepage:

```
function hello(req, res) {
  res.setHeader('Content-Type', 'text/plain');
  res.end('hello world');
}
```

You can use this second middleware component with your app by invoking the `.use()` method, which can be called any number of times to add more middleware.

Listing 6.2 ties the whole app together. The addition of the `hello` middleware component in this listing will make the server first invoke the `logger`, which prints text to the console, and then respond to every HTTP request with the text "hello world."

Listing 6.2 Using multiple Connect middleware components

```
var connect = require('connect');

function logger(req, res, next) {
  console.log('%s %s', req.method, req.url);
  next();
}

function hello(req, res) {
  res.setHeader('Content-Type', 'text/plain');
  res.end('hello world');
}

connect()
  .use(logger)
  .use(hello)
  .listen(3000);
```

Prints HTTP method and request URL and calls next()

Ends response to HTTP request with "hello world"

In this case, the `hello` middleware component doesn't have a `next` callback argument. That's because this component finishes the HTTP response and never needs to give control back to the dispatcher. For cases like this, the `next` callback is optional, which is convenient because it matches the signature of the `http.createServer` callback function. This means that if you've already written an HTTP server using just the http module, you already have a perfectly valid middleware component that you can reuse in your Connect application.

The `use()` function returns an instance of a Connect application to support method chaining, as shown previously. Note that chaining the `.use()` calls is not required, as shown in the following snippet:

```
var app = connect();
app.use(logger);
app.use(hello);
app.listen(3000);
```

Now that you have a simple "hello world" application working, we'll look at why the ordering of middleware `.use()` calls is important, and how you can use the ordering strategically to alter how your application works.

6.3 Why middleware ordering matters

Connect tries not to make assumptions, in order to maximize flexibility for application and framework developers. One example of this is that Connect allows you to define the order in which middleware is executed. It's a simple concept, but one that's often overlooked.

In this section, you'll see how the ordering of middleware in your application can dramatically affect the way it behaves. Specifically, we'll cover the following:

- Stopping the execution of remaining middleware by omitting `next()`
- Using the powerful middleware-ordering feature to your advantage
- Leveraging middleware to perform authentication

Let's first see how Connect handles a middleware component that does explicitly call `next()`.

6.3.1 When middleware doesn't call next()

Consider the previous "hello world" example, where the `logger` middleware component is used first, followed by the `hello` component. In that example, Connect logs to stdout and then responds to the HTTP request. But consider what would happen if the ordering were switched, as follows.

Listing 6.3 Wrong: `hello` middleware component before `logger` component

```
var connect = require('connect');

function logger(req, res, next) {
  console.log('%s %s', req.method, req.url);
  next();
}

function hello(req, res) {
  res.setHeader('Content-Type', 'text/plain');
  res.end('hello world');
}

var app = connect()
  .use(hello)
  .use(logger)
  .listen(3000);
```

Always calls next(), so subsequent middleware is invoked

Doesn't call next(), because component responds to request

logger will never be invoked because hello doesn't call next()

In this example, the `hello` middleware component will be called first and will respond to the HTTP request as expected. But `logger` will never be called because `hello` never calls `next()`, so control is never passed back to the dispatcher to invoke the next middleware component. The moral here is that when a component doesn't call `next()`, no remaining middleware in the chain of command will be invoked.

In this case, placing `hello` in front of `logger` is rather useless, but when leveraged properly, the ordering can be used to your benefit.

6.3.2 Using middleware order to perform authentication

You can use order of middleware to your advantage, such as in the case of authentication. Authentication is relevant to almost any kind of application. Your users need a way to log in, and you need a way to prevent people who are not logged in from accessing the content. The order of the middleware can help you implement your authentication.

Suppose you've written a middleware component called `restrictFileAccess` that grants file access only to valid users. Valid users are able to continue to the next middleware component, whereas if the user isn't valid, `next()` isn't called. The following listing shows how the `restrictFileAccess` middleware component should follow the `logger` component but precede the `serveStaticFiles` component.

Listing 6.4 Using middleware precedence to restrict file access

```
var connect = require('connect');
connect()
  .use(logger)
  .use(restrictFileAccess)
  .use(serveStaticFiles)
  .use(hello);
```

next() will only be called if user is valid

Now that we've discussed middleware precedence and how it's an important tool for constructing application logic, let's take a look at another of Connect's features that helps you use middleware.

6.4 Mounting middleware and servers

Connect includes the concept of *mounting*, a simple yet powerful organizational tool that allows you to define a path prefix for middleware or entire applications. Mounting allows you to write middleware as if you were at the root level (the / base `req.url`) and use it on any path prefix without altering the code.

For example, when a middleware component or server is mounted at /blog, a `req.url` of /article/1 in the code will be accessible at /blog/article/1 by a client request. This separation of concerns means you can reuse the blog server in multiple places without needing to alter the code for different sources. For example, if you decide you want to host your articles at /articles (/articles/article/1) instead of /blog, you only need to make a change to the mount path prefix.

Let's look at another example of how you can use mounting. It's common for applications to have their own administration area, such as for moderating comments and approving new users. In our example, this admin area will reside at /admin in the application. Now you need a way to make sure that /admin is only available to authorized users and that the rest of the site is available to all users.

Besides rewriting requests from the / base `req.url`, mounting also will only invoke middleware or applications when a request is made within the path prefix (the mount point). In the following listing, the second and third `use()` calls have the string `'/admin'` as the first argument, followed by the middleware component. This means that the following components will only be used when a request is made with a /admin prefix. Let's look at the syntax for mounting a middleware component or server in Connect.

Listing 6.5 The syntax for mounting a middleware component or server

```
var connect = require('connect');

connect()
  .use(logger)
  .use('/admin', restrict)
  .use('/admin', admin)
  .use(hello)
  .listen(3000);
```

When a string is the first argument to .use(), Connect will only invoke the middleware when the prefix URL matches.

Armed with that knowledge of mounting middleware and servers, let's enhance the "hello world" application with an admin area. We'll use mounting and add two new middleware components:

- A `restrict` component that ensures a valid user is accessing the page
- An `admin` component that'll present the administration area to the user

Let's begin by looking at a middleware component that restricts users without valid credentials from accessing resources.

6.4.1 *Middleware that does authentication*

The first middleware component you need to add will perform authentication. This will be a generic authentication component, not specifically tied to the /admin `req.url` in any way. But when you mount it onto the application, the authentication component will only be invoked when the request URL begins with /admin. This is important, because you only want to authenticate users who attempt to access the /admin URL; you want regular users to pass through as normal.

Listing 6.6 implements crude Basic authentication logic. Basic authentication is a simple authentication mechanism that uses the HTTP `Authorization` header field with Base64-encoded credentials (see the Wikipedia article for more details: http://wikipedia.org/wiki/Basic_access_authentication). Once the credentials are decoded by the middleware component, the username and password are checked for correctness. If they're valid, the component will invoke `next()`, meaning the request is okay to continue processing; otherwise it will throw an error.

Listing 6.6 A middleware component that performs HTTP Basic authentication

```
function restrict(req, res, next) {
  var authorization = req.headers.authorization;
  if (!authorization) return next(new Error('Unauthorized'));

  var parts = authorization.split(' ')
  var scheme = parts[0]
  var auth = new Buffer(parts[1], 'base64').toString().split(':')
  var user = auth[0]
  var pass = auth[1];

  authenticateWithDatabase(user, pass, function (err) {
    if (err) return next(err);
```

A function that checks credentials against a database

Informs dispatcher that an error occurred

```
    next();
  });
}
```

Calls next() with no arguments when given valid credentials

Again, notice how this middleware doesn't do any checking of `req.url` to ensure that /admin is what is actually being requested, because Connect is handling this for you. This allows you to write generic middleware. The `restrict` middleware component could be used to authenticate another part of the site or another application.

> **INVOKING NEXT WITH AN ERROR ARGUMENT** Notice in the previous example how the `next` function is invoked with an `Error` object passed in as the argument. When you do this, you're notifying Connect that an application error has occurred, which means that only error-handling middleware will be executed for the remainder of this HTTP request. Error-handing middleware is a topic you'll learn about a little later in this chapter. For now, just know that it tells Connect that your middleware has finished and that an error occurred in the process.

When authorization is complete, and no errors have occurred, Connect will continue on to the next middleware component, which in this case is `admin`.

6.4.2 A middleware component that presents an administration panel

The `admin` middleware component implements a primitive router using a `switch` statement on the request URL. The `admin` component will present a redirect message when / is requested, and it'll return a JSON array of usernames when /users is requested. The usernames are hardcoded for this example, but a real application would more likely grab them from a database.

Listing 6.7 Routing `admin` requests

```
function admin(req, res, next) {
  switch (req.url) {
    case '/':
      res.end('try /users');
      break;
    case '/users':
      res.setHeader('Content-Type', 'application/json');
      res.end(JSON.stringify(['tobi', 'loki', 'jane']));
      break;
  }
}
```

The important thing to note here is that the strings used are / and /users, not /admin and /admin/users. The reason for this is that Connect removes the prefix from the `req.url` before invoking the middleware, treating URLs as if they were mounted at /. This simple technique makes applications and middleware more flexible because they don't care where they're used.

For example, mounting would allow a blog application to be hosted at http://foo.com/blog or at http://bar.com/posts without requiring any change to the blog application code for the change in URL. This is because Connect alters the `req.url` by stripping off the prefix portion when mounted. The end result is that the blog app can be written with paths relative to /, and doesn't need to know about /blog or /posts. The requests will use the same middleware components and share the same state. Consider the server setup used here, which reuses the hypothetical blog application by mounting it at two different mount points:

```
var connect = require('connect');

connect()
  .use(logger)
  .use('/blog', blog)
  .use('/posts', blog)
  .use(hello)
  .listen(3000);
```

TESTING IT ALL OUT

Now that the middleware is taken care of, it's time to take your application for a test drive using `curl`. You can see that regular URLs other than /admin will invoke the `hello` component as expected:

```
$ curl http://localhost
hello world

$ curl http://localhost/foo
hello world
```

You can also see that the `restrict` component will return an error to the user when no credentials are given or incorrect credentials are used:

```
$ curl http://localhost/admin/users
Error: Unauthorized
  at Object.restrict [as handle]
  (E:\transfer\manning\node.js\src\ch7\multiple_connect.js:24:35)
  at next
  (E:\transfer\manning\node.js\src\ch7\node_modules\
  ➥connect\lib\proto.js:190:15)
  ...

$ curl --user jane:ferret http://localhost/admin/users
Error: Unauthorized
  at Object.restrict [as handle]
  (E:\transfer\manning\node.js\src\ch7\multiple_connect.js:24:35)
  at next
  (E:\transfer\manning\node.js\src\ch7\node_modules\
  ➥connect\lib\proto.js:190:15)
  ...
```

Finally, you can see that only when authenticated as "tobi" will the `admin` component be invoked and the server respond with the JSON array of users:

```
$ curl --user tobi:ferret http://localhost/admin/users
["tobi","loki","jane"]
```

See how simple yet powerful mounting is? Now let's take a look at some techniques for creating configurable middleware.

6.5 Creating configurable middleware

You've learned some middleware basics; now we'll go into detail and look at how you can create more generic and reusable middleware. Reusability is one of the major benefits of writing middleware, and in this section we'll create middleware that allows you to configure logging, routing requests, URLs, and more. You'll be able to reuse these components in your applications with just some additional configuration, rather than needing to re-implement the components from scratch to suit your specific applications.

Middleware commonly follows a simple convention in order to provide configuration capabilities to developers: using a function that returns another function. (This is a powerful JavaScript feature, typically called a *closure*.) The basic structure for configurable middleware of this kind looks like this:

```
function setup(options) {
  // setup logic                    <- Additional middleware initialization here

  return function(req, res, next) {
    // middleware logic             <- Options still accessible even though outer function has returned

  }
}
```

This type of middleware is used as follows:

```
app.use(setup({some: 'options'}))
```

Notice that the `setup` function is invoked in the `app.use` line, where in our previous examples we were just passing a reference to the function.

In this section, we'll apply this technique to build three reusable configurable middleware components:

- A logger component with a configurable printing format
- A router component that invokes functions based on the requested URL
- A URL rewriter component that converts URL slugs to IDs

Let's start by expanding our logger component to make it more configurable.

6.5.1 Creating a configurable logger middleware component

The `logger` middleware component you created earlier in this chapter was *not* configurable. It was hardcoded to print out the request's `req.method` and `req.url` when invoked. But what if you want to change what the logger displays at some point in the future? You could modify your `logger` component manually, but a better solution would be to make the logger configurable from the start, instead of hardcoding the values. So let's do that.

In practice, using configurable middleware is just like using any of the middleware you've created so far, except that you can pass additional arguments to the middleware component to alter its behavior. Using the configurable component in your application might look a little like the following example, where `logger` can accept a string that describes the format that it should print out:

```
var app = connect()
  .use(logger(':method :url'))
  .use(hello);
```

To implement the configurable `logger` component, you first need to define a `setup` function that accepts a single string argument (in this example, we'll name it `format`). When `setup` is invoked, a function is returned, and it's the actual middleware component Connect will use. The returned component retains access to the `format` variable, even after the `setup` function has returned, because it's defined within the same JavaScript closure. The `logger` then replaces the tokens in the `format` string with the associated request properties on the `req` object, logs to stdout, and calls `next()`, as shown in the following listing.

Listing 6.8 A configurable `logger` middleware component for Connect

```
function setup(format) {                    <- Setup function can be called multiple
                                               times with different configurations
  var regexp = /:(\w+)/g;                   <- Logger component uses a regexp to match request properties

  return function logger(req, res, next) {  <- Actual logger component that Connect will use

    var str = format.replace(regexp, function(match, property){  <- Use regexp to format
      return req[property];                                         log entry for request
    });

    console.log(str);                       <- Print request log entry to console

    next();                                 <- Pass control to next middleware component
  }
}

module.exports = setup;                     <- Directly export logger setup function
```

Because we've created this `logger` middleware component as configurable middleware, you can `.use()` the logger multiple times in a single application with different configurations or reuse this logger code in any number of future applications you might develop. This simple concept of configurable middleware is used throughout the Connect community, and it's used for all core Connect middleware to maintain consistency.

Now let's write a middleware component with a little more involved logic. Let's create a router to map incoming requests to business logic!

6.5.2 Building a routing middleware component

Routing is a crucial web application concept. Put simply, it's a method of mapping incoming request URLs to functions that employ business logic. Routing comes in many shapes and sizes, ranging from highly abstract controllers used by frameworks like Ruby on Rails to simpler, less abstract, routing based on HTTP methods and paths, such as the routing provided by frameworks like Express and Ruby's Sinatra.

A simple router in your application might look something like listing 6.9. In this example, HTTP verbs and paths are represented by a simple object and some callback functions; some paths contain tokens prefixed with a colon (:) that represent path segments that accept user input, matching paths like /user/12. The result is an application with a collection of handler functions that will be invoked when the request method and URL match one of the routes that's been defined.

Listing 6.9 Using the `router` middleware component

```
var connect = require('connect');
var router = require('./middleware/router');
var routes = {
  GET: {
    '/users': function(req, res){
      res.end('tobi, loki, ferret');
    },
    '/user/:id': function(req, res, id){
      res.end('user ' + id);
    }
  },
  DELETE: {
    '/user/:id': function(req, res, id){
      res.end('deleted user ' + id);
    }
  }
};

connect()
  .use(router(routes))
  .listen(3000);
```

- router component, defined later in this section
- Routes are stored as an object
- Each entry maps to request URL and contains callback function to be invoked
- Pass routes object to router setup function

Because there are no restrictions on the number of middleware components in an application or on the number of times a middleware component can be used, it's possible to define several routers in a single application. This could be useful for organizational purposes. Suppose you have both user-related routes and administration routes. You could separate these into module files and require them for the `router` component, as shown in the following snippet:

```
var connect = require('connect');
var router = require('./middleware/router');

connect()
  .use(router(require('./routes/user')))
  .use(router(require('./routes/admin')))
  .listen(3000);
```

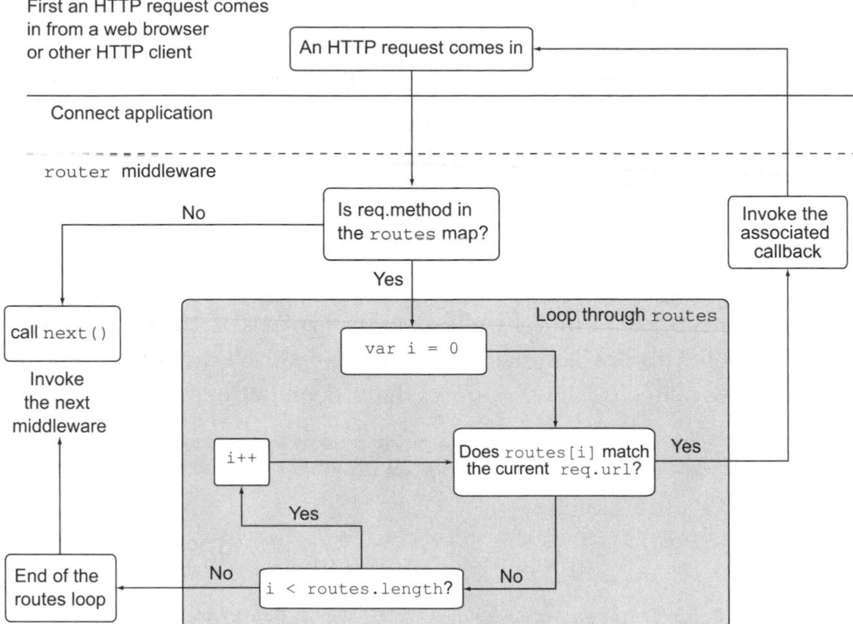

Figure 6.2 Flowchart of the router component's logic

Now let's build this router middleware. This will be more complicated than the middleware examples we've gone over so far, so let's quickly run through the logic this router will implement, as illustrated in figure 6.2.

You can see how the flowchart almost acts as pseudocode for the middleware, which can help you implement the actual code for the router. The middleware in its entirety is shown in the following listing.

Listing 6.10 Simple routing middleware

```
var parse = require('url').parse;
module.exports = function route(obj) {
  return function(req, res, next){
    if (!obj[req.method]) {                        // Check to make sure req.method is defined
      next();                                      // If not, invoke next() and
      return;                                      // stop any further execution
    }
    var routes = obj[req.method]                   // Lookup paths for req.method
    var url = parse(req.url)                       // Parse URL for matching against pathname
    var paths = Object.keys(routes)                // Store paths for req.method as array

    for (var i = 0; i < paths.length; i++) {       // Loop through paths
      var path = paths[i];
      var fn = routes[path];
      path = path
        .replace(/\//g, '\\/')
        .replace(/:(\w+)/g, '([^\\/]+)');
      var re = new RegExp('^' + path + '$');       // Construct regular expression
```

```
        var captures = url.pathname.match(re)
        if (captures) {
          var args = [req, res].concat(captures.slice(1));
          fn.apply(null, args);
          return;
        }
      }
      next();
    }
};
```

Attempt match against pathname

Pass the capture groups

Return when match is found to prevent following next() call

This router is a great example of configurable middleware, as it follows the traditional format of having a setup function return a middleware component for Connect applications to use. In this case, it accepts a single argument, the `routes` object, which contains the map of HTTP verbs, request URLs, and callback functions. It first checks to see if the current `req.method` is defined in the `routes` map, and stops further processing in the router if it isn't (by invoking `next()`). After that, it loops through the defined paths and checks to see if one matches the current `req.url`. If it finds a match, then the match's associated callback function will be invoked, hopefully completing the HTTP request.

This is a complete middleware component with a couple of nice features, but you could easily expand on it. For example, you could utilize the power of closures to cache the regular expressions, which would otherwise be compiled for each request.

Another great use of middleware is for rewriting URLs. We'll look at that next, with a middleware component that handles blog post slugs instead of IDs in the URL.

6.5.3 Building a middleware component to rewrite URLs

Rewriting URLs can be very helpful. Suppose you want to accept a request to /blog/posts/my-post-title, look up the post ID based on the end portion of the post's title (commonly known as the *slug* part of the URL), and then transform the URL to /blog/posts/<post-id>. This is a perfect task for middleware!

The small blog application in the following snippet first rewrites the URL based on the slug with a `rewrite` middleware component, and then passes control to the `showPost` component:

```
var connect = require('connect')
var url = require('url')
var app = connect()
  .use(rewrite)
  .use(showPost)
  .listen(3000)
```

The `rewrite` middleware implementation in listing 6.11 parses the URL to access the pathname, and then matches the pathname with a regular expression. The first capture group (the slug) is passed to a hypothetical `findPostIdBySlug` function that looks up the blog post ID by slug. When it's successful, you can then re-assign the request URL (`req.url`) to whatever you like. In this example, the ID is appended to /blog/post/ so that the subsequent middleware can perform the blog post lookup via ID.

Listing 6.11 Middleware that rewrites the request URL based on a slug name

```
var path = url.parse(req.url).pathname;

function rewrite(req, res, next) {
  var match = path.match(/^\/blog\/posts\/(.+)/)
  if (match) {
    findPostIdBySlug(match[1], function(err, id) {
      if (err) return next(err);
      if (!id) return next(new Error('User not found'));
      req.url = '/blog/posts/' + id;
      next();
    });
  } else {
    next();
  }
}
```

Only perform lookup on /blog/posts requests

If there was a lookup error, inform error handler and stop processing

If there was no matching ID for slug name, call next() with "User not found" Error argument

Overwrite req.url property so that subsequent middleware can utilize real ID

> **WHAT THESE EXAMPLES DEMONSTRATE** The important takeaway from these examples is that you should focus on small and configurable pieces when building your middleware. Build lots of tiny, modular, and reusable middleware components that collectively make up your application. Keeping your middleware small and focused really helps break down complicated application logic into smaller pieces.

Next up, let's take a look at a final middleware concept in Connect: handing application errors.

6.6 Using error-handling middleware

All applications have errors, whether at the system level or the user level, and being well prepared for error situations—even ones you aren't anticipating—is a smart thing to do. Connect implements an error-handling variant of middleware that follows the same rules as regular middleware but accepts an error object along with the request and response objects.

Connect error handling is intentionally minimal, allowing the developer to specify how errors should be handled. For example, you could pass only system and application errors through the middleware (for example, "foo is undefined") or user errors ("password is invalid") or a combination of both. Connect lets you choose which is best for your application.

In this section, we'll make use of both types, and you'll learn how error-handling middleware works. You'll also learn some useful patterns that can be applied while we look at the following:

- Using Connect's default error handler
- Handing application errors yourself
- Using multiple error-handling middleware components

Let's jump in with a look at how Connect handles errors without any configuration.

6.6.1 *Connect's default error handler*

Consider the following middleware component, which will throw a `ReferenceError` error because the function `foo()` isn't defined by the application:

```
var connect = require('connect')

connect()
  .use(function hello(req, res) {
    foo();
    res.setHeader('Content-Type', 'text/plain');
    res.end('hello world');
  })
.listen(3000)
```

By default, Connect will respond with a 500 status code, a response body containing the text "Internal Server Error," and more information about the error itself. This is fine, but in any kind of real application, you'd probably like to do more specialized things with those errors, like send them off to a logging daemon.

6.6.2 *Handing application errors yourself*

Connect also offers a way for you to handle application errors yourself using error-handling middleware. For instance, in development you might want to respond with a JSON representation of the error to the client for quick and easy reporting, whereas in production you'd want to respond with a simple "Server error," so as not to expose sensitive internal information (such as stack traces, filenames, and line numbers) to a potential attacker.

An error-handling middleware function must be defined to accept four arguments—`err`, `req`, `res`, and `next`—as shown in the following listing, whereas regular middleware takes the arguments `req`, `res`, and `next`.

Listing 6.12 Error-handling middleware in Connect

```
function errorHandler() {
  var env = process.env.NODE_ENV || 'development';
  return function(err, req, res, next) {

    res.statusCode = 500;
    switch (env) {
      case 'development':
        res.setHeader('Content-Type', 'application/json');
        res.end(JSON.stringify(err));
        break;
      default:
        res.end('Server error');
    }
  }
}
```

Error-handling middleware defines four arguments

errorHandler middleware component behaves differently depending on value of NODE_ENV

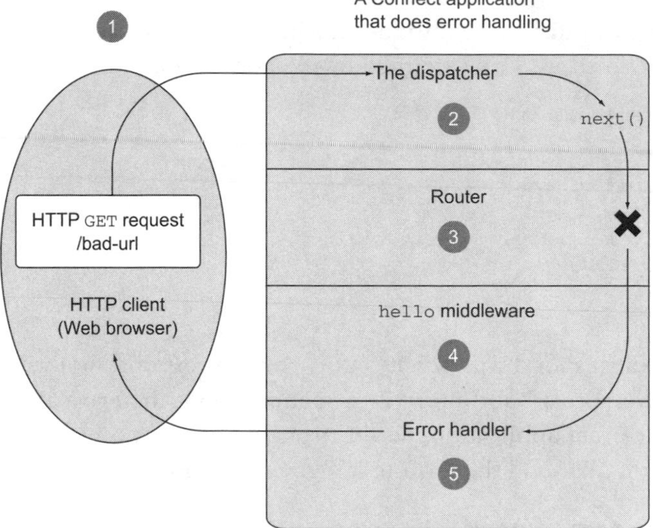

1 HTTP request to a URL that will throw an error on the server.

2 Passes the request down the middleware stack as usual.

3 Uh-oh! The `router` middleware has some kind of error!

4 The `hello` middleware gets skipped, since it was not defined as error-handling middleware.

5 The `errorHandler` middleware gets the `Error` that was created by the `logger` middleware, and can respond to the request in the context of the `Error`.

Figure 6.3 The lifecycle of an HTTP request causing an error in a Connect server

> **USE NODE_ENV TO SET THE APPLICATION'S MODE** A common Connect convention is to use the `NODE_ENV` environment variable (`process.env.NODE_ENV`) to toggle the behavior between different server environments, like production and development.

When Connect encounters an error, it'll switch to invoking only error-handling middleware, as you can see in figure 6.3.

For example, in our previous admin application, if the routing middleware component for the user routes caused an error, both the blog and admin middleware components would be skipped, because they don't act as error-handling middleware—they only define three arguments. Connect would then see that `errorHandler` accepts the error argument and would invoke it:

```
connect()
  .use(router(require('./routes/user')))
  .use(router(require('./routes/blog'))) // Skipped
  .use(router(require('./routes/admin'))) // Skipped
  .use(errorHandler());
```

6.6.3 Using multiple error-handling middleware components

Using a variant of middleware for error handling can be useful for separating error-handling concerns. Suppose your app has a web service mounted at /api. You might want any web application errors to render an HTML error page to the user, but /api requests to return more verbose errors, perhaps always responding with JSON so that receiving clients can easily parse the errors and react properly.

To see how this /api scenario works, implement this small example as you read along. Here `app` is the main web application and `api` is mounted to /api:

```
var api = connect()
  .use(users)
  .use(pets)
  .use(errorHandler);

var app = connect()
  .use(hello)
  .use('/api', api)
  .use(errorPage)
  .listen(3000);
```

This configuration is easily visualized in figure 6.4.

Now you need to implement each of the application's middleware components:

- The `hello` component will respond with "Hello World\n."
- The `users` component will throw a `notFoundError` when a user doesn't exist.
- The `pets` component will cause a `ReferenceError` to be thrown to demonstrate the error handler.
- The `errorHandler` component will handle any errors from the `api` app.
- The `errorPage` component will handle any errors from the main `app` app.

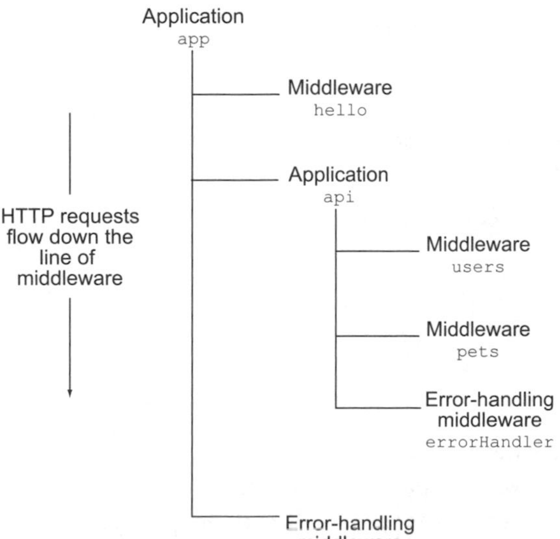

Figure 6.4 Layout of an application with two error-handling middleware components

IMPLEMENTING THE HELLO MIDDLEWARE COMPONENT

The `hello` component is simply a function that matches "/hello" with a regular expression, as shown in the following snippet:

```
function hello(req, res, next) {
  if (req.url.match(/^\/hello/)) {
    res.end('Hello World\n');
  } else {
    next();
  }
}
```

There's no possible way for an error to occur in such a simple function.

IMPLEMENTING THE USERS MIDDLEWARE COMPONENT

The `users` component is slightly more complex. As you can see in listing 6.13, you match the `req.url` using a regular expression and then check if the user index exists by using `match[1]`, which is the first capture group for your match. If the user exists, it's serialized as JSON; otherwise an error is passed to the `next()` function with its `notFound` property set to `true`, allowing you to unify error-handling logic later in the error-handling component.

Listing 6.13 A component that searches for a user in the database

```
var db = {
  users: [
    { name: 'tobi' },
    { name: 'loki' },
    { name: 'jane' }
  ]
};

function users(req, res, next) {
  var match = req.url.match(/^\/user\/(.+)/)
  if (match) {
    var user = db.users[match[1]];
    if (user) {
      res.setHeader('Content-Type', 'application/json');
      res.end(JSON.stringify(user));
    } else {
      var err = new Error('User not found');
      err.notFound = true;
      next(err);
    }
  } else {
    next();
  }
}
```

IMPLEMENTING THE PETS MIDDLEWARE COMPONENT

The following code snippet shows the partially implemented `pets` component. It illustrates how you can apply logic to the errors, based on properties such as the err.notFound Boolean assigned in the users component. Here the undefined foo() function will trigger an exception, which will not have an err.notFound property:

```
function pets(req, res, next) {
  if (req.url.match(/^\/pet\/(.+)/)) {
    foo();
  } else {
    next();
  }
}
```

IMPLEMENTING THE ERRORHANDER MIDDLEWARE COMPONENT

Finally, it's time for the errorHandler component! Contextual error messages are especially important for web services—they allow web services to provide appropriate feedback to the consumer without giving away too much information. You certainly don't want to expose errors such as "{"error":"foo is not defined"}", or even worse, full stack traces, because an attacker could use this information against you. You should only respond with error messages that you know are safe, as the following errorHandler implementation does.

Listing 6.14 An error-handling component that doesn't expose unnecessary data

```
function errorHandler(err, req, res, next) {
  console.error(err.stack);
  res.setHeader('Content-Type', 'application/json');
  if (err.notFound) {
    res.statusCode = 404;
    res.end(JSON.stringify({ error: err.message }));
  } else {
    res.statusCode = 500;
    res.end(JSON.stringify({ error: 'Internal Server Error' }));
  }
}
```

This error-handling component uses the err.notFound property set earlier to distinguish between server errors and client errors. Another approach would be to check whether the error is an instanceof some other kind of error (such as a Validation-Error from some validation module) and respond accordingly.

Using the err.notFound property, if the server were to accept an HTTP request to, say, /user/ronald, which doesn't exist in your database, the users component would throw a notFound error, and when it got to the errorHandler component it would trigger the err.notFound code path, which returns a 404 status code along with the err.message property as a JSON object. Figure 6.5 shows what the raw output looks like in a web browser.

IMPLEMENTING THE ERRORPAGE MIDDLEWARE COMPONENT

The errorPage component is the second error-handling component in this example application. Because the previous error-handling component never calls next(err), this component will only be invoked by an error occurring in the hello component.

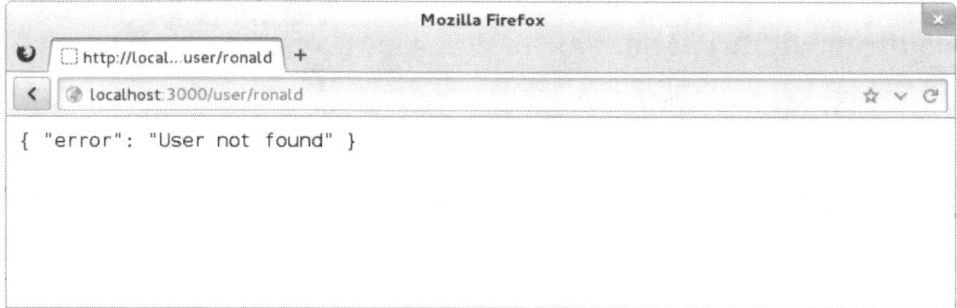

Figure 6.5 The JSON object output of the "User not found" error

That component is very unlikely to generate an error, so there's very little chance that this `errorPage` component will ever be invoked. That said, we'll leave implementing this second error-handling component up to you, because it literally is optional in this example.

Your application is finally ready. You can fire up the server, which we set to listen on port `3000` back in the beginning. You can play around with it using a browser or `curl` or any other HTTP client. Try triggering the various routes of the error handler by requesting an invalid user or requesting one of the `pets` entries.

To re-emphasize, error handling is a *crucial* aspect of any kind of application. Error-handling middleware components offer a clean way to unify the error-handling logic in your application in a centralized location. You should always include at least one error-handling middleware component in your application by the time it hits production.

6.7 Summary

In this chapter, you've learned everything you need to know about the small but powerful Connect framework. You've learned how the dispatcher works and how to build middleware to make your applications modular and flexible. You've learned how to mount middleware to a particular base URL, which enables you to create applications inside of applications. You've also been exposed to configurable middleware that takes in settings and thus can be repurposed and tweaked. Lastly, you learned how to handle errors that occur within middleware.

Now that the fundamentals are out of the way, it's time to learn about the middleware that Connect provides out of the box. That's covered in the next chapter.

7 Connect's built-in middleware

This chapter covers

- Middleware for parsing cookies, request bodies, and query strings
- Middleware that implements core web application needs
- Middleware that handles web application security
- Middleware for serving static files

In the previous chapter, you learned what middleware is, how to create it, and how to use it with Connect. But Connect's real power comes from its bundled middleware, which meets many common web application needs, such as session management, cookie parsing, body parsing, request logging, and much more. This middleware ranges in complexity and provides a great starting point for building simple web servers or higher-level web frameworks.

Throughout this chapter, we'll explain and demonstrate the more commonly used bundled middleware components. Table 7.1 provides an overview of the middleware we'll cover.

First up, we'll look at middleware that implements the various parsers needed to build proper web applications, because these are the foundation for most of the other middleware.

Table 7.1 Connect middleware quick reference guide

Middleware component	Section	Description
`cookieParser()`	7.1.1	Provides `req.cookies` and `req.signedCookies` for subsequent middleware to use.
`bodyParser()`	7.1.2	Provides `req.body` and `req.files` for subsequent middleware to use.
`limit()`	7.1.3	Restricts request body sizes based on a given byte length limit. Must go before the `bodyParser` middleware component.
`query()`	7.1.4	Provides `req.query` for subsequent middleware to use.
`logger()`	7.2.1	Logs configurable information about incoming HTTP requests to a stream, like stdout or a log file.
`favicon()`	7.2.2	Responds to /favicon.ico HTTP requests. Usually placed before the `logger` middleware component so that you don't have to see it in your log files.
`methodOverride()`	7.2.3	Allows you to fake `req.method` for browsers that can't use the proper method. Depends on `bodyParser`.
`vhost()`	7.2.4	Uses a given middleware component and/or HTTP server instances based on a specified hostname (such as nodejs.org).
`session()`	7.2.5	Sets up an HTTP session for a user and provides a persistent `req.session` object in between requests. Depends on `cookieParser`.
`basicAuth()`	7.3.1	Provides HTTP Basic authentication for your application.
`csrf()`	7.3.2	Protects against cross-site request forgery attacks in HTTP forms. Depends on `session`.
`errorHandler()`	7.3.3	Returns stack traces to the client when a server-side error occurs. Useful for development; *don't* use for production.
`static()`	7.4.1	Serves files from a given directory to HTTP clients. Works really well with Connect's mounting feature.
`compress()`	7.4.2	Optimizes HTTP responses using gzip compression.
`directory()`	7.4.3	Serves directory listings to HTTP clients, providing the optimal result based on the client's `Accept` request header (plain text, JSON, or HTML).

7.1 Middleware for parsing cookies, request bodies, and query strings

Node's core doesn't provide modules for higher-level web application concepts like parsing cookies, buffering request bodies, or parsing complex query strings, so Connect provides those out of the box for your application to use. In this section, we'll cover the four built-in middleware components that parse request data:

- `cookieParser()`—Parses cookies from web browsers into `req.cookies`
- `bodyParser()`—Consumes and parses the request body into `req.body`
- `limit()`—Goes hand in hand with `bodyParser()` to keep requests from getting too big
- `query()`—Parses the request URL query string into `req.query`

Let's start off with cookies, which are often used by web browsers to simulate state because HTTP is a stateless protocol.

7.1.1 cookieParser(): parsing HTTP cookies

Connect's cookie parser supports regular cookies, signed cookies, and special JSON cookies out of the box. By default, regular unsigned cookies are used, populating the `req.cookies` object. But if you want signed cookie support, which is required by the `session()` middleware, you'll want to pass a secret string when creating the `cookieParser()` instance.

> **SETTING COOKIES ON THE SERVER SIDE** The `cookieParser()` middleware doesn't provide any helpers for setting outgoing cookies. For this, you should use the `res.setHeader()` function with `Set-Cookie` as the header name. Connect patches Node's default `res.setHeader()` function to special-case the `Set-Cookie` headers so that it just works, as you'd expect it to.

BASIC USAGE

The secret passed as the argument to `cookieParser()` is used to sign and unsign cookies, allowing Connect to determine whether the cookies' contents have been tampered with (because only your application knows the secret's value). Typically the secret should be a reasonably large string, potentially randomly generated.

In the following example, the secret is *tobi is a cool ferret*:

```
var connect = require('connect');
var app = connect()
  .use(connect.cookieParser('tobi is a cool ferret'))
  .use(function(req, res){
    console.log(req.cookies);
    console.log(req.signedCookies);
    res.end('hello\n');
  }).listen(3000);
```

The `req.cookies` and `req.signedCookies` properties get set to objects representing the parsed `Cookie` header that was sent with the request. If no cookies are sent with the request, the objects will both be empty.

REGULAR COOKIES

If you were to fire some HTTP requests off to the preceding server using `curl(1)` without the `Cookie` header field, both of the `console.log()` calls would output an empty object:

```
$ curl http://localhost:3000/
{}
{}
```

Now try sending a few cookies. You'll see that both cookies are available as properties of `req.cookies`:

```
$ curl http://localhost:3000/ -H "Cookie: foo=bar, bar=baz"
{ foo: 'bar', bar: 'baz' }
{}
```

SIGNED COOKIES

Signed cookies are better suited for sensitive data, as the integrity of the cookie data can be verified, helping to prevent man-in-the-middle attacks. Signed cookies are placed in the `req.signedCookies` object when valid. The reasoning behind having two separate objects is that it shows the developer's intention. If you were to place both signed and unsigned cookies in the same object, a regular cookie could be crafted to contain data to mimic a signed cookie.

A signed cookie looks something like `tobi.DDm3AcVxE9oneYnbmpqxoyhyKsk`, where the content to the left of the period (`.`) is the cookie's value, and the content to the right is the secret hash generated on the server with SHA-1 HMAC (hash-based message authentication code). When Connect attempts to unsign the cookie, it will fail if either the value or HMAC has been altered.

Suppose, for example, you set a signed cookie with a key of `name` and a value of `luna`. `cookieParser` would encode the cookie to `luna.PQLM0wNvqOQEObZXUkWbS5m6Wlg`. The hash portion is checked on each request, and when the cookie is sent intact, it will be available as `req.signedCookies.name`:

```
$ curl http://localhost:3000/ -H "Cookie:
➥ name=luna.PQLM0wNvqOQEObZXUkWbS5m6Wlg"
{}
{ name: 'luna' }
GET / 200 4ms
```

If the cookie's value were to change, as shown in the next `curl` command, the `name` cookie would be available as `req.cookies.name` because it wasn't valid. It might still be of use for debugging or application-specific purposes:

```
$ curl http://localhost:3000/ -H "Cookie:
➥name=manny.PQLM0wNvqOQEObZXUkWbS5m6Wlg"
{ name: 'manny.PQLM0wNvqOQEObZXUkWbS5m6Wlg' }
{}
GET / 200 1ms
```

JSON COOKIES

The special JSON cookie is prefixed with `j:`, which informs Connect that it is intended to be serialized JSON. JSON cookies can be either signed or unsigned.

Frameworks such as Express can use this functionality to provide developers with a more intuitive cookie interface, instead of requiring them to manually serialize and parse JSON cookie values. Here's an example of how Connect parses JSON cookies:

```
$ curl http://localhost:3000/ -H 'Cookie: foo=bar,
bar=j:{"foo":"bar"}'
{ foo: 'bar', bar: { foo: 'bar' } }
{}
GET / 200 1ms
```

As mentioned, JSON cookies can also be signed, as illustrated in the following request:

```
$ curl http://localhost:3000/ -H "Cookie:
➥cart=j:{\"items\":[1]}.sD5p6xFFBO/4ketA1OP43bcjS3Y"
{}
{ cart: { items: [ 1 ] } }
GET / 200 1ms
```

SETTING OUTGOING COOKIES

As noted earlier, the `cookieParser()` middleware doesn't provide any functionality for writing outgoing headers to the HTTP client via the `Set-Cookie` header. Connect, however, provides explicit support for multiple `Set-Cookie` headers via the `res.setHeader()` function.

Say you wanted to set a cookie named `foo` with the string value `bar`. Connect enables you to do this in one line of code by calling `res.setHeader()`. You can also set the various options of a cookie, like its expiration date, as shown in the second `setHeader()` call here:

```
var connect = require('connect');

var app = connect()
  .use(function(req, res){
    res.setHeader('Set-Cookie', 'foo=bar');
    res.setHeader('Set-Cookie', 'tobi=ferret;
  ➥Expires=Tue, 08 Jun 2021 10:18:14 GMT');
    res.end();
  }).listen(3000);
```

If you check out the headers that this server sends back to the HTTP request by using the `--head` flag of `curl`, you can see the `Set-Cookie` headers set as you would expect:

```
$ curl http://localhost:3000/ --head
HTTP/1.1 200 OK
Set-Cookie: foo=bar
Set-Cookie: tobi=ferret; Expires=Tue, 08 Jun 2021 10:18:14 GMT
Connection: keep-alive
```

That's all there is to sending cookies with your HTTP response. You can store any kind of text data in cookies, but it has become usual to store a single session cookie on the client side so that you can have full user state on the server. This session technique is encapsulated in the `session()` middleware, which you'll learn about a little later in this chapter.

Another extremely common need in web application development is parsing incoming request bodies. Next we'll look at the `bodyParser()` middleware and how it will make your life as a Node developer easier.

7.1.2 bodyParser(): parsing request bodies

A common need for all kinds of web applications is accepting input from the user. Let's say you wanted to accept file uploads using the `<input type="file">` HTML tag. One line of code adding the `bodyParser()` middleware component is all it takes. This is an extremely helpful component, and it's actually an aggregate of three other smaller components: `json()`, `urlencoded()`, and `multipart()`.

The `bodyParser()` component provides a `req.body` property for your application to use by parsing JSON, x-www-form-urlencoded, and `multipart/form-data` requests. When the request is a `multipart/form-data` request, like a file upload, the `req.files` object will also be available.

BASIC USAGE

Suppose you want to accept registration information for your application though a JSON request. All you have to do is add the `bodyParser()` component before any other middleware that will access the `req.body` object. Optionally, you can pass in an options object that will be passed through to the subcomponents mentioned previously (`json()`, `urlencoded()`, and `multipart()`):

```
var app = connect()
  .use(connect.bodyParser())
  .use(function(req, res){
    // .. do stuff to register the user ..
    res.end('Registered new user: ' + req.body.username);
  });
```

PARSING JSON DATA

The following `curl(1)` request could be used to submit data to your application, sending a JSON object with the `username` property set to `tobi`:

```
$ curl -d '{"username":"tobi"}' -H "Content-Type: application/json"
  ➥http://localhost
Registered new user: tobi
```

PARSING REGULAR <FORM> DATA

Because `bodyParser()` parses data based on the `Content-Type`, the input format is abstracted, so that all your application needs to care about is the resulting `req.body` data object.

For example, the following `curl(1)` command will send `x-www-form-urlencoded` data, but the middleware will work as expected without any additional changes to the code. It will provide the `req.body.name` property just as before:

```
$ curl -d name=tobi http://localhost
Registered new user: tobi
```

PARSING MULTIPART <FORM> DATA

The `bodyParser` parses `multipart/form-data`, typical for file uploads. It's backed by the third-party module formidable, discussed earlier in chapter 4.

To test this functionality, you can log both the `req.body` and `req.files` objects to inspect them:

```
var app = connect()
  .use(connect.bodyParser())
  .use(function(req, res){
    console.log(req.body);
    console.log(req.files);
    res.end('thanks!');
  });
```

Now you can simulate a browser file upload using `curl(1)` with the `-F` or `--form` flag, which expects the name of the field and the value. The following example will upload a single image named `photo.png`, as well as the field `name` containing `tobi`:

```
$ curl -F image=@photo.png -F name=tobi http://localhost
thanks!
```

If you take a look at the output of the application, you'll see something very similar to the following example output, where the first object represents `req.body` and the second is `req.files`. As you can see in the output, `req.files.image.path` would be available to your application, and you could rename the file on disk, transfer the data to a worker for processing, upload to a content delivery network, or do anything else your app requires:

```
{ name: 'tobi' }
{ image:
   { size: 4,
     path: '/tmp/95cd49f7ea6b909250abbd08ea954093',
     name: 'photo.png',
     type: 'application/octet-stream',
     lastModifiedDate: Sun, 11 Dec 2011 20:52:20 GMT,
     length: [Getter],
     filename: [Getter],
     mime: [Getter] } }
```

Now that we've looked at the body parsers, you may be wondering about security. If `bodyParser()` buffers the `json` and `x-www-form-urlencoded` request bodies in memory, producing one large string, couldn't an attacker produce extremely large bodies of JSON to deny service to valid visitors? The answer to that is essentially yes, and this is why the `limit()` middleware component exists. It allows you to specify what an acceptable request body size is. Let's take a look.

7.1.3 limit(): request body limiting

Simply parsing request bodies is not enough. Developers also need to properly classify acceptable requests and place limits on them when appropriate. The `limit()` middleware component is designed to help filter out huge requests, whether they are intended to be malicious or not.

For example, an innocent user uploading a photo may accidentally send an uncompressed RAW image consisting of several hundred megabytes, or a malicious user may craft a massive JSON string to lock up `bodyParser()`, and in turn V8's `JSON.parse()` method. You must configure your server to handle these situations.

WHY IS LIMIT() NEEDED?

Let's take a look at how a malicious user can render a vulnerable server useless. First, create the following small Connect application named server.js, which does nothing other than parse request bodies using the `bodyParser()` middleware component:

```
var connect = require('connect');

var app = connect()
  .use(connect.bodyParser());

app.listen(3000);
```

Now create a file named dos.js, as shown in the following listing. You can see how a malicious user could use Node's HTTP client to attack the preceding Connect application, simply by writing several megabytes of JSON data.

Listing 7.1 Performing a denial of service attack on a vulnerable HTTP server

```
var http = require('http');

var req = http.request({
    method: 'POST',
    port: 3000,
    headers: {
      'Content-Type': 'application/json'          <-- Notify server that you're sending JSON data
      }
});

req.write('[');                                   <-- Begin sending a very large array object
var n = 300000;
while (n--) {
  req.write('"foo",');                            <-- Array contains 300,000 "foo" string entries
}
req.write('"bar"]');

req.end();
```

Fire up the server and run the attack script:

```
    $ node server.js &
    $ node dos.js
```

You'll see that it can take V8 up to 10 seconds (depending on your hardware) to parse such a large JSON string. This is bad, but thankfully it's exactly what the `limit()` middleware component was designed to prevent.

BASIC USAGE

By adding the `limit()` component *before* `bodyParser()`, you can specify a maximum size for the request body either by the number of bytes (like `1024`) or by using a string representation in any of the following ways: `1gb`, `25mb`, or `50kb`.

If you set `limit()` to `32kb` and run the server and attack script again, you'll see that Connect will terminate the request at 32 kilobytes:

```
var app = connect()
  .use(connect.limit('32kb'))
```

```
  .use(connect.bodyParser())
  .use(hello);

http.createServer(app).listen(3000);
```

WRAPPING LIMIT() FOR GREATER FLEXIBILITY

Limiting every request body to a small size like `32kb` is not feasible for applications accepting user uploads, because most image uploads will be larger than this, and files such as videos will definitely be much larger. But it may be a reasonable size for bodies formatted as JSON or XML, for example.

A good idea for applications needing to accept varying sizes of request bodies would be to wrap the `limit()` middleware component in a function based on some type of configuration. For example, you could wrap the component to specify a `Content-Type`, as shown in the following listing.

Listing 7.2 Limiting body size based on a request's `Content-Type`

```
function type(type, fn) {                              ⊲ fn, in this case, is a limit() instance
  return function(req, res, next){
    var ct = req.headers['content-type'] || '';
    if (0 != ct.indexOf(type)) {                       ⊲ Returned middleware first checks content-type
      return next();
    }
    fn(req, res, next);                                ⊲ Middleware then invokes passed in limit() component
  }
}

var app = connect()
  .use(type('application/x-www-form-urlencoded', connect.limit('64kb')))
  .use(type('application/json', connect.limit('32kb')))      ⊲ Handles forms, JSON
  .use(type('image', connect.limit('2mb')))          ⊲ Handles image uploads up to 2 MB
  .use(type('video', connect.limit('300mb')))        ⊲ Handles video uploads up to 300 MB
  .use(connect.bodyParser())
  .use(hello);
```

Another way to use this middleware would be to provide the `limit` option to `bodyParser()`, and the latter could call `limit()` transparently.

The next middleware component we'll cover is a small, but very useful, component that parses the request's query strings for your application to use.

7.1.4 query(): query-string parser

You've already learned about `bodyParser()`, which can parse `POST` form requests, but what about the `GET` form requests? That's where the `query()` middleware component comes in. It parses the query string, when one is present, and provides the `req.query` object for your application to use. For developers coming from PHP, this is similar to the `$_GET` associative array. Much like `bodyParser()`, `query()` should be placed before any middleware that will use it.

BASIC USAGE

The following application utilizes the `query()` middleware component, which will respond with a JSON representation of the query string sent by the request. Query-string parameters are usually used for controlling the display of the data being sent back:

```
var app = connect()
  .use(connect.query())
  .use(function(req, res, next){
    res.setHeader('Content-Type', 'application/json');
    res.end(JSON.stringify(req.query));
  });
```

Suppose you were designing a music library app. You could offer a search engine and use the query string to build up the search parameters, something like this: `/songSearch?artist=Bob%20Marley&track=Jammin`. This example query would produce a `res.query` object like this:

```
{ artist: 'Bob Marley', track: 'Jammin' }
```

The `query()` component uses the same third-party qs module as `bodyParser()`, so complex query strings like `?images[]=foo.png&images[]=bar.png` produce the following object:

```
{ images: [ 'foo.png', 'bar.png' ] }
```

When no query-string parameters are given in the HTTP request, like `/songSearch`, then `req.query` will default to an empty object:

```
{}
```

That's all there is to it. Next we'll look at the built-in middleware that covers core web application needs, such as logging and sessions.

7.2 Middleware that implements core web application functions

Connect aims to implement and provide built-in middleware for the most common web application needs, so that they don't need to be re-implemented over and over by every developer. Core web application functions like logging, sessions, and virtual hosting are all provided by Connect out of the box.

In this section, you'll learn about five very useful middleware components that you'll likely use in your applications:

- `logger()`—Provides flexible request logging
- `favicon()`—Takes care of the /favicon.ico request without you having to think about it
- `methodOverride()`—Enables incapable clients to transparently overwrite `req.method`
- `vhost()`—Sets up multiple websites on a single server (virtual hosting)
- `session()`—Manages session data

Up until now you've created your own custom logging middleware, but Connect provides a very flexible solution named `logger()`, so let's explore that first.

7.2.1 logger(): logging requests

`logger()` is a flexible request-logging middleware component with customizable log formats. It also has options for buffering log output to decrease disk writes, and for specifying a log stream if you want to log to something other than the console, such as a file or socket.

BASIC USAGE

To use Connect's `logger()` component in your own application, invoke it as a function to return a `logger()` middleware instance, as shown in the following listing.

Listing 7.3 Using the `logger()` middleware component

```
var connect = require('connect');

var app = connect()
  .use(connect.logger())
  .use(hello)
  .listen(3000);
```

With no arguments, default logger options will be used

hello is hypothetical middleware component that responds with "Hello World"

By default, the logger uses the following format, which is extremely verbose, but it provides useful information about each HTTP request. This is similar to how other web servers, such as Apache, create their log files:

```
':remote-addr - - [:date] ":method :url HTTP/:http-version" :status
  ➥:res[content-length] ":referrer" ":user-agent"'
```

Each of the `:something` pieces are *tokens*, and in an actual log entry they'd contain real values from the HTTP request that's being logged. For example, a simple `curl(1)` request would generate a log line similar to the following:

```
127.0.0.1 - - [Wed, 28 Sep 2011 04:27:07 GMT]
                    ➥"GET / HTTP/1.1" 200 - "-"
                    ➥"curl/7.19.7 (universal-apple-darwin10.0)
                    ➥libcurl/7.19.7 OpenSSL/0.9.8l zlib/1.2.3"
```

CUSTOMIZING LOG FORMATS

The most basic use of `logger()` doesn't require any customization. But you may want a custom format that records other information, or that's less verbose, or that provides custom output. To customize the log format, you pass a custom string of tokens. For example, the following format would output something like `GET /users 15 ms`:

```
var app = connect()
  .use(connect.logger(':method :url :response-time ms'))
  .use(hello);
```

By default, the following tokens are available for use (note that the header names are not case-sensitive):

- `:req[header]` ex: `:req[Accept]`
- `:res[header]` ex: `:res[Content-Length]`

- `:http-version`
- `:response-time`
- `:remote-addr`
- `:date`
- `:method`
- `:url`
- `:referrer`
- `:user-agent`
- `:status`

Defining custom tokens is easy. All you have to do is provide a token name and callback function to the `connect.logger.token` function. For example, say you wanted to log each request's query string. You might define it like this:

```
var url = require('url');

connect.logger.token('query-string', function(req, res){
  return url.parse(req.url).query;
});
```

`logger()` also comes with other predefined formats than the default one, such as `short` and `tiny`. Another predefined format is `dev`, which produces concise output for development, for situations when you're usually the only user on the site and you don't care about the details of the HTTP requests. This format also color-codes the response status codes by type: responses with a status code in the 200s are green, 300s are blue, 400s are yellow, and 500s are red. This color scheme makes it great for development.

To use a predefined format, you simply provide the name to `logger()`:

```
var app = connect()
  .use(connect.logger('dev'))
  .use(hello);
```

Now that you know how to format the logger's output, let's take a look at the options you can provide to it.

LOGGER OPTIONS: STREAM, IMMEDIATE, AND BUFFER

As mentioned previously, you can use options to tweak how `logger()` behaves.

One such option is `stream`, which allows you to pass a Node `Stream` instance that the logger will write to instead of stdout. This would allow you to direct the logger output to its own log file, independent of your server's own output using a `Stream` instance created from `fs.createWriteStream`.

When you use these options, it's generally recommended to also include the `format` property. The following example uses a custom format and logs to /var/log/myapp.log with the append flag, so that the file isn't truncated when the application boots:

```
var fs = require('fs')
var log = fs.createWriteStream('/var/log/myapp.log', { flags: 'a' })
```

```
var app = connect()
  .use(connect.logger({ format: ':method :url', stream: log }))
  .use('/error', error)
  .use(hello);
```

Another useful option is `immediate`, which writes the log line when the request is first received, rather than waiting for the response. You might use this option if you're writing a server that keeps its requests open for a long time, and you want to know when the connection begins. Or you might use it for debugging a critical section of your app. This means that tokens such as `:status` and `:response-time` can't be used, because they're related to the response. To enable immediate mode, pass `true` for the `immediate` value, as shown here:

```
var app = connect()
  .use(connect.logger({ immediate: true }))
  .use('/error', error)
  .use(hello);
```

The third option available is `buffer`, which is useful when you want to minimize the number of writes to the disk where your log file resides. This is especially useful if your log file is being written over a network, and you want to minimize the amount of network activity. The `buffer` option takes a numeric value specifying the interval in milliseconds between flushes of the buffer, or you can just pass `true` to use the default interval.

That's it for logging! Next we'll look at the favicon-serving middleware component.

7.2.2 favicon(): serving a favicon

A favicon is that tiny website icon your browser displays in the address bar and bookmarks. To get this icon, the browser makes a request for a file at /favicon.ico. It's usually best to serve favicon files as soon as possible, so the rest of your application can simply ignore them. The `favicon()` middleware component will serve Connect's favicon by default (when no arguments are passed to it). This favicon is shown in figure 7.1.

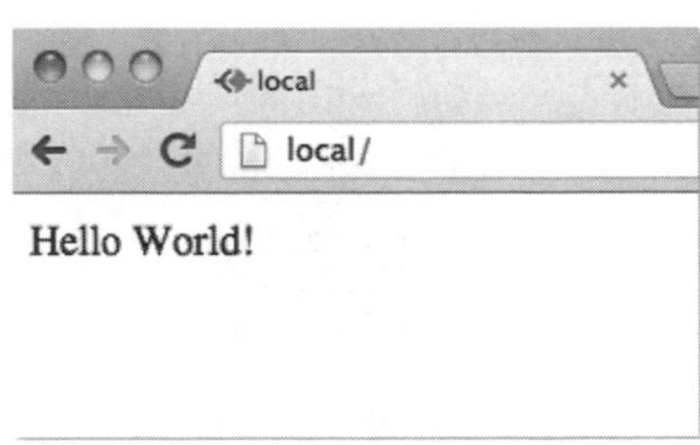

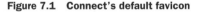

Figure 7.1 Connect's default favicon

Basic usage

Typically `favicon()` is used at the very top of the stack, so even logging is ignored for favicon requests. The icon is then cached in memory for fast subsequent responses.

The following example shows `favicon()` requesting a custom .ico file by passing the file path as the only argument:

```
connect()
  .use(connect.favicon(__dirname + '/public/favicon.ico'))
  .use(connect.logger())
  .use(function(req, res) {
```

```
    res.end('Hello World!\n');
  });
```

Optionally, you can pass in a maxAge argument to specify how long browsers should cache the favicon in memory.

Next we have another small but helpful middleware component: methodOverride(). It provides the means to fake the HTTP request method when client capabilities are limited.

7.2.3 methodOverride(): faking HTTP methods

An interesting problem arises in the browser when you're building a server that utilizes special HTTP verbs, like PUT or DELETE. The browser <form> methods can only be GET or POST, restricting you from using any other methods in your application.

A common workaround is to add an <input type=hidden> with the value set to the method name you want to use, and then have the server check that value and "pretend" it's the request method for this request. The methodOverride() middleware component is the server-side half of this technique.

BASIC USAGE

By default, the HTML input name is _method, but you can pass a custom value to methodOverride(), as shown in the following snippet:

```
connect()
  .use(connect.methodOverride('__method__'))
  .listen(3000)
```

To demonstrate how methodOverride() is implemented, let's create a tiny application to update user information. The application will consist of a single form that will respond with a simple success message when the form is submitted by the browser and processed by the server, as illustrated in figure 7.2.

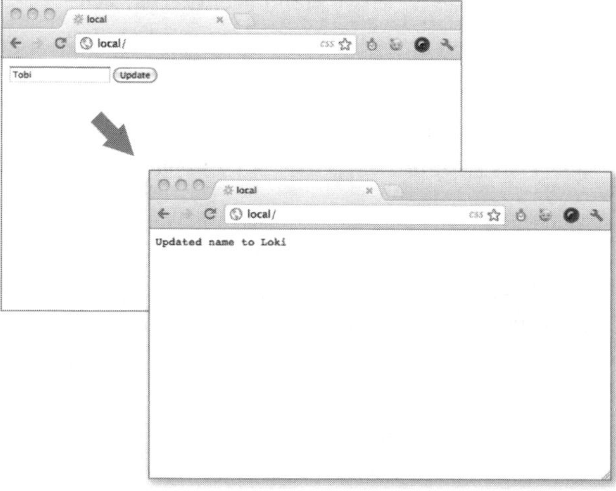

Figure 7.2 Using methodOverride() to simulate a PUT request to update a form in the browser

The application updates the user data through the use of two separate middleware components. In the `update` function, `next()` is called when the request method is not `PUT`. As mentioned previously, most browsers don't respect the form attribute `method="put"`, so the application in the following listing won't function properly.

Listing 7.4 A broken user-update application

```
var connect = require('connect');

function edit(req, res, next) {
  if ('GET' != req.method) return next();
  res.setHeader('Content-Type', 'text/html');
  res.write('<form method="put">');
  res.write('<input type="text" name="user[name]" value="Tobi" />');
  res.write('<input type="submit" value="Update" />');
  res.write('</form>');
  res.end();
}

function update(req, res, next) {
  if ('PUT' != req.method) return next();
  res.end('Updated name to ' + req.body.user.name);
}

var app = connect()
  .use(connect.logger('dev'))
  .use(connect.bodyParser())
  .use(edit)
  .use(update);

app.listen(3000);
```

The update application needs to look something like listing 7.5. Here an additional input with the name `_method` has been added to the form, and `methodOverride()` has been added below the `bodyParser()` component because it references `req.body` to access the form data.

Listing 7.5 A user-update application with `methodOverride()` implemented

```
var connect = require('connect');

function edit(req, res, next) {
  if ('GET' != req.method) return next();
  res.setHeader('Content-Type', 'text/html');
  res.write('<form method="post">');
  res.write('<input type="hidden" name="_method" value="put" />');
  res.write('<input type="text" name="user[name]" value="Tobi" />');
  res.write('<input type="submit" value="Update" />');
  res.write('</form>');
  res.end();
}

function update(req, res, next) {
  if ('PUT' != req.method) return next();
  res.end('Updated name to ' + req.body.user.name);
}
```

```
var app = connect()
  .use(connect.logger('dev'))
  .use(connect.bodyParser())
  .use(connect.methodOverride())
  .use(edit)
  .use(update)
  .listen(3000);
```

ACCESSING THE ORIGINAL REQ.METHOD

`methodOverride()` alters the original `req.method` property, but Connect copies over the original method, which you can always access with `req.originalMethod`. This means the previous form would output values like these:

```
console.log(req.method);
  // "PUT"
console.log(req.originalMethod);
  // "POST"
```

This may seem like quite a bit of work for a simple form, but we promise this will be more enjoyable when we discuss higher-level features from Express in chapter 8 and templating in chapter 11.

The next thing we'll look at is `vhost()`, which is a small middleware component for serving applications based on hostnames.

7.2.4 *vhost(): virtual hosting*

The `vhost()` (virtual host) middleware component is a simple, lightweight way to route requests via the `Host` request header. This task is commonly performed by a reverse proxy, which then forwards the request to a web server running locally on a different port. The `vhost()` component does this in the same Node process by passing control to a Node HTTP server associated with the `vhost` instance.

BASIC USAGE

Like all the middleware that Connect provides out of the box, a single line is all it takes to get up and running with the `vhost()` component. It takes two arguments: The first is the hostname string that this `vhost` instance will match against. The second is the `http.Server` instance that will be used when an HTTP request with a matching hostname is made (all Connect apps are subclasses of `http.Server`, so an application instance will work as well).

```
var connect = require('connect');

var server = connect()
var app = require('./sites/expressjs.dev');

server.use(connect.vhost('expressjs.dev', app));

server.listen(3000);
```

In order to use the preceding ./sites/expressjs.dev module, it should assign the HTTP server to `module.exports` as in the following example:

```
var http = require('http')
```

```
module.exports = http.createServer(function(req, res){
  res.end('hello from expressjs.com\n');
});
```

USING MULTIPLE VHOST() INSTANCES

Like any other middleware, you can use `vhost()` more than once in an application to map several hosts to their associated applications:

```
var app = require('./sites/expressjs.dev');
server.use(connect.vhost('expressjs.dev', app));

var app = require('./sites/learnboost.dev');
server.use(connect.vhost('learnboost.dev', app));
```

Rather than setting up the `vhost()` middleware manually like this, you could generate a list of hosts from the filesystem. That's shown in the following example, with the `fs.readdirSync()` method returning an array of directory entries:

```
var connect = require('connect')
var fs = require('fs');

var app = connect()
var sites = fs.readdirSync('source/sites');

sites.forEach(function(site){
  console.log('  ... %s', site);
  app.use(connect.vhost(site, require('./sites/' + site)));
});

app.listen(3000);
```

The benefit of using `vhost()` instead of a reverse proxy is simplicity. It allows you to manage all of your applications as a single unit. This is ideal for serving several smaller sites, or for serving sites that are largely comprised of static content, but it also has the downside that if one site causes a crash, all of your sites will be taken down (because they all run in the same process).

Next we'll take a look at one of the most fundamental middleware components that Connect provides: the session management component appropriately named `session()`, which relies on `cookieParser()` for cookie signing.

7.2.5 *session(): session management*

In chapter 4, we explained that Node provides all the means to implement concepts like sessions, but it doesn't provide them out of the box. Following Node's general philosophy of having a small core and a large user-land, session management has been left to be created as a third-party add-on to Node. And that's exactly what the `session()` middleware component is for.

Connect's `session()` component provides robust, intuitive, and community-backed session management with numerous session stores ranging from the default memory store to stores based on Redis, MongoDB, CouchDB, and cookies. In this section we'll look at setting up the middleware, working with session data, and utilizing the Redis key/value store as an alternative session store.

First let's set up the middleware and explore the options available.

BASIC USAGE

As previously mentioned, the `session()` middleware component requires signed cookies to function, so you should use `cookieParser()` somewhere above it and pass a secret.

Listing 7.6 implements a small pageview count application with minimal setup, where no options are passed to `session()` at all and the default in-memory data store is used. By default, the cookie name is connect.sid and it's set to be `httpOnly`, meaning client-side scripts can't access its value. But these are options you can tweak, as you'll soon see.

Listing 7.6 A Connect pageview counter using sessions

```
var connect = require('connect');

var app = connect()
  .use(connect.favicon())
  .use(connect.cookieParser('keyboard cat'))
  .use(connect.session())
  .use(function(req, res, next){
    var sess = req.session;
    if (sess.views) {
      res.setHeader('Content-Type', 'text/html');
      res.write('<p>views: ' + sess.views + '</p>');
      res.end();
      sess.views++;
    } else {
      sess.views = 1;
      res.end('welcome to the session demo. refresh!');
    }
});

app.listen(3000);
```

SETTING THE SESSION EXPIRATION DATE

Suppose you want sessions to expire in 24 hours, to send the session cookie only when HTTPS is used, and to configure the cookie name. You might pass an object like the one shown here:

```
var hour = 3600000;
var sessionOpts = {
    key: 'myapp_sid',
    cookie: { maxAge: hour * 24, secure: true }
};

...
  .use(connect.cookieParser('keyboard cat'))
  .use(connect.session(sessionOpts))
...
```

When using Connect (and, as you'll see in the next chapter, "Express") you'll often set `maxAge`, specifying a number of milliseconds from that point in time. This method of expressing future dates is often written more intuitively, essentially expanding to `new Date(Date.now() + maxAge)`.

Now that sessions are set up, let's look at the methods and properties available when working with session data.

Working with session data

Connect's session data management is very simple. The basic principle is that any properties assigned to the `req.session` object are saved when the request is complete; then they're loaded on subsequent requests from the same user (browser). For example, saving shopping cart information is as simple as assigning an object to the `cart` property, as shown here:

```
req.session.cart = { items: [1,2,3] };
```

When you access `req.session.cart` on subsequent requests, the `.items` array will be available. Because this is a regular JavaScript object, you can call methods on the nested objects in subsequent requests, as in the following example, and they'll be saved as you expect:

```
req.session.cart.items.push(4);
```

One important thing to keep in mind is that this session object gets serialized as JSON in between requests, so the `req.session` object has the same restrictions as JSON: cyclic properties aren't allowed, `function` objects can't be used, `Date` objects can't be serialized correctly, and so on. Keep those restrictions in mind when using the session object.

Connect will save session data for you automatically, but internally it's calling the `Session#save([callback])` method, which is also available as a public API. Two additional helpful methods are `Session#destroy()` and `Session#regenerate()`, which are often used when authenticating a user to prevent session fixation attacks. When you build applications with Express in later chapters, you'll use these methods for authentication.

Now let's move on to manipulating session cookies.

Manipulating session cookies

Connect allows you to provide global cookie settings for sessions, but it's also possible to manipulate a specific cookie via the `Session#cookie` object, which defaults to the global settings.

Before you start tweaking properties, let's extend the previous session application to inspect the session cookie properties by writing each property into individual <p> tags in the response HTML, as shown here:

```
...
res.write('<p>views: ' + sess.views + '</p>');
res.write('<p>expires in: ' + (sess.cookie.maxAge / 1000) + 's</p>');
res.write('<p>httpOnly: ' + sess.cookie.httpOnly + '</p>');
res.write('<p>path: ' + sess.cookie.path + '</p>');
res.write('<p>domain: ' + sess.cookie.domain + '</p>');
```

```
res.write('<p>secure: ' + sess.cookie.secure + '</p>');
...
```

Connect allows all of the cookie properties, such as `expires`, `httpOnly`, `secure`, `path`, and `domain`, to be altered programmatically on a per-session basis. For example, you could expire an active session in 5 seconds like this:

```
req.session.cookie.expires = new Date(Date.now() + 5000);
```

An alternative, more intuitive API for expiry is the `.maxAge` accessor, which allows you to get and set the value in milliseconds relative to the current time. The following will also expire the session in 5 seconds:

```
req.session.cookie.maxAge = 5000;
```

The remaining properties, `domain`, `path`, and `secure`, limit the cookie *scope*, restricting it by domain, path, or to secure connections, whereas `httpOnly` prevents client-side scripts from accessing the cookie data. These properties can be manipulated in the same manner:

```
req.session.cookie.path = '/admin';
req.session.cookie.httpOnly = false;
```

So far you've been using the default memory store to store session data, so let's take a look at how you can plug in alternative data stores.

SESSION STORES

The built-in `connect.session.MemoryStore` is a simple, in-memory data store, which is ideal for running application tests because no other dependencies are necessary. But during development and in production, it's best to have a persistent, scalable database backing your session data.

Just about any database can act as a session store, but low-latency key/value stores work best for such volatile data. The Connect community has created several session stores for databases, including CouchDB, MongoDB, Redis, Memcached, PostgreSQL, and others.

Here you'll use Redis with the connect-redis module. In chapter 5 you learned about interacting with Redis using the node_redis module. Now you'll learn how to use Redis to store your session data in Connect. Redis is a good backing store because it supports key expiration, it provides great performance, and it's easy to install.

You should have Redis installed and running from chapter 5, but try invoking the `redis-server` command just to be sure:

```
$ redis-server
[11790] 16 Oct 16:11:54 * Server started, Redis version 2.0.4
[11790] 16 Oct 16:11:54 * DB loaded from disk: 0 seconds
[11790] 16 Oct 16:11:54 * The server is now ready to accept
  ➥connections on port 6379
[11790] 16 Oct 16:11:55 - DB 0: 522 keys (0 volatile) in 1536 slots HT.
```

Next, you need to install connect-redis by adding it to your package.json file and running `npm install`, or by executing `npm install connect-redis` directly. The connect-redis module exports a function that should be passed `connect`, as shown here:

```
var connect = require('connect')
var RedisStore = require('connect-redis')(connect);

var app = connect()
  .use(connect.favicon())
  .use(connect.cookieParser('keyboard cat'))
  .use(connect.session({ store: new RedisStore({ prefix: 'sid' }) }))
...
```

Passing the `connect` reference to `connect-redis` allows it to inherit from `connect.session.Store.prototype`. This is important because in Node a single process may use multiple versions of a module simultaneously; by passing your specific version of Connect, you can be sure that connect-redis uses the proper copy.

The instance of `RedisStore` is passed to `session()` as the `store` value, and any options you want to use, such as a key prefix for your sessions, can be passed to the `RedisStore` constructor.

Whew! `session` was a lot to cover, but that finishes up all the core concept middleware. Next we'll go over the built-in middleware that handles web application security. This is a very important subject for applications needing to secure their data.

7.3 Middleware that handles web application security

As we've stated many times, Node's core API is intentionally low-level. This means it provides no built-in security or best practices when it comes to building web applications. Fortunately, Connect steps in to implement these security practices for use in your Connect applications.

This section will teach you about three more of Connect's built-in middleware components, this time with a focus on security:

- `basicAuth()`—Provides HTTP Basic authentication for protecting data
- `csrf()`—Implements protection against cross-site request forgery (CSRF) attacks
- `errorHandler()`—Helps you debug during development

First, `basicAuth()` implements HTTP Basic authentication for safeguarding restricted areas of your application.

7.3.1 basicAuth(): HTTP Basic authentication

In chapter 6's section 6.4, you created a crude Basic authentication middleware component. Well, it turns out that Connect provides a real implementation of this out of the box. As previously mentioned, Basic authentication is a very simple HTTP authentication mechanism, and it should be used with caution because user credentials can be trivial for an attacker to intercept unless Basic authentication is served over HTTPS.

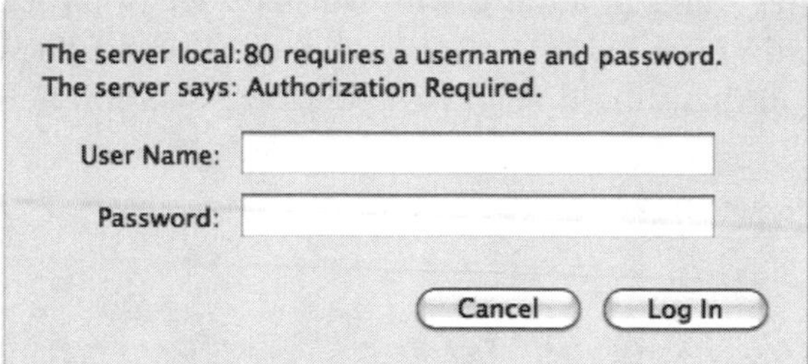
The server local:80 requires a username and password.
The server says: Authorization Required.
User Name:
Password:
Cancel
Log In

Figure 7.3 Basic authentication prompt

That being said, it can be useful for adding quick and dirty authentication to a small or personal application.

When your application has the `basicAuth()` component in use, web browsers will prompt for credentials the first time the user attempts to connect to your application, as shown in figure 7.3.

BASIC USAGE

The `basicAuth()` middleware component provides three means of validating credentials. The first is to pass it a single username and password, as shown here:

```
var app = connect()
  .use(connect.basicAuth('tj', 'tobi'));
```

PROVIDING A CALLBACK FUNCTION

The second way of validating credentials is to pass `basicAuth()` a callback, which must return `true` in order to succeed. This is useful for checking the credentials against a hash:

```
var users = {
    tobi: 'foo',
    loki: 'bar',
    jane: 'baz'
};

var app = connect()
  .use(connect.basicAuth(function(user, pass){
    return users[user] === pass;
  });
```

PROVIDING AN ASYNCHRONOUS CALLBACK FUNCTION

The final option is similar, except this time a callback is passed to `basicAuth()` with three arguments defined, which enables the use of asynchronous lookups. This is useful when authenticating from a file on disk, or when querying from a database.

Listing 7.7 A Connect `basicAuth` middleware component doing asynchronous lookups

```
var app = connect();

app.use(connect.basicAuth(function(user, pass, callback){
  User.authenticate({ user: user, pass: pass }, gotUser);
```

Performs a database validation function

```
  function gotUser(err, user) {
    if (err) return callback(err);
    callback(null, user);
  }
}));
```

Runs asynchronous callback when database has responded

Provides basicAuth() callback with user object from database

AN EXAMPLE WITH CURL(1)

Suppose you want to restrict access to all requests coming to your server. You might set up the application like this:

```
var connect = require('connect');

var app = connect()
  .use(connect.basicAuth('tobi', 'ferret'))
  .use(function (req, res) {
    res.end("I'm a secret\n");
  });

app.listen(3000);
```

Now try issuing an HTTP request to the server with `curl(1)`, and you'll see that you're unauthorized:

```
$ curl http://localhost -i
HTTP/1.1 401 Unauthorized
WWW-Authenticate: Basic realm="Authorization Required"
Connection: keep-alive
Transfer-Encoding: chunked

Unauthorized
```

Issuing the same request with HTTP Basic authorization credentials (notice the beginning of the URL) will provide access:

```
$ curl --user tobi:ferret http://localhost -i
HTTP/1.1 200 OK
Date: Sun, 16 Oct 2011 22:42:06 GMT
Cache-Control: public, max-age=0
Last-Modified: Sun, 16 Oct 2011 22:41:02 GMT
ETag: "13-1318804862000"
Content-Type: text/plain; charset=UTF-8
Accept-Ranges: bytes
Content-Length: 13
Connection: keep-alive

I'm a secret
```

Continuing on with the security theme of this section, let's look at the `csrf()` middleware component, which is designed to help protect against cross-site request forgery attacks.

7.3.2 csrf(): cross-site request forgery protection

Cross-site request forgery (CSRF) is a form of attack that exploits the trust that a web browser has in a site. The attack works by having an authenticated user on your application visit a different site that an attacker has either created or compromised, and then making requests on the user's behalf without them knowing about it.

This is a complicated attack, so let's go through it with an example. Suppose that in your application the request `DELETE /account` will trigger a user's account to be destroyed (though only while the user is logged in). Now suppose that user visits a forum that happens to be vulnerable to CSRF. An attacker could post a script that issues the `DELETE /account` request, thus destroying the user's account. This is a bad situation for your application to be in, and the `csrf()` middleware component can help protect against such an attack.

The `csrf()` component works by generating a 24-character unique ID, the *authenticity token*, and assigning it to the user's session as `req.session._csrf`. This token can then be included as a hidden form input named `_csrf`, and the CSRF component can validate the token on submission. This process is repeated for each interaction.

BASIC USAGE

To ensure that `csrf()` can access `req.body._csrf` (the hidden input value) and `req.session._csrf`, you'll want to make sure that you add the `csrf()` below `bodyParser()` and `session()`, as shown in the following example:

```
connect()
  .use(connect.bodyParser())
  .use(connect.cookieParser('secret'))
  .use(connect.session())
  .use(connect.csrf());
```

Another aspect of web development is ensuring verbose logs and detailed error reporting are available both in production and development environments. Let's look at the `errorHandler()` middleware component, which is designed to do exactly that.

7.3.3 errorHandler(): development error handling

The `errorHandler()` middleware component bundled with Connect is ideal for development, providing verbose HTML, JSON, and plain-text error responses based on the `Accept` header field. It's meant for use during development and shouldn't be part of the production configuration.

BASIC USAGE

Typically this component should be the last used so it can catch all errors:

```
var app = connect()
  .use(connect.logger('dev'))
  .use(function(req, res, next){
    setTimeout(function () {
       next(new Error('something broke!'));
     }, 500);
  })
.use(connect.errorHandler());
```

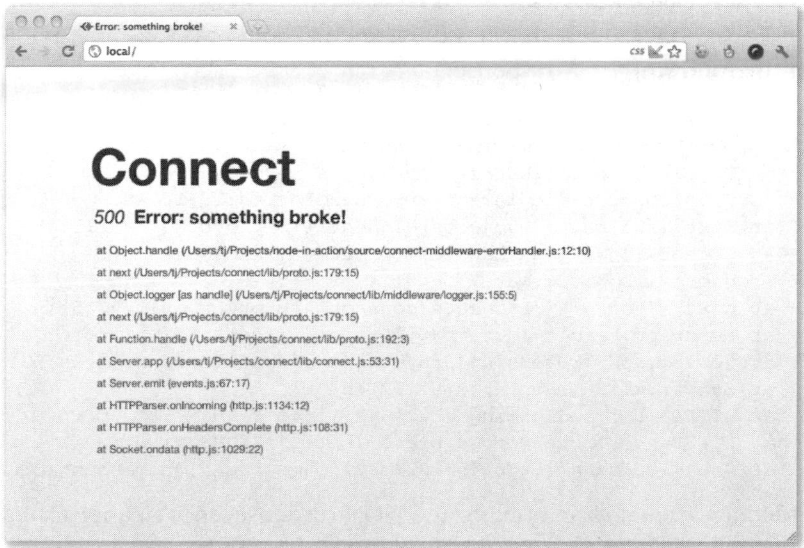

Figure 7.4 Connect's default `errorHandler()` middleware as displayed in a web browser

RECEIVING AN HTML ERROR RESPONSE

If you view any page in your browser with the setup shown here, you'll see a Connect error page like the one shown in figure 7.4, displaying the error message, the response status, and the entire stack trace.

RECEIVING A PLAIN-TEXT ERROR RESPONSE

Now suppose you're testing an API built with Connect. It's far from ideal to respond with a large chunk of HTML, so by default `errorHandler()` will respond with `text/plain`, which is ideal for command-line HTTP clients such as `curl(1)`. This is illustrated in the following stdout:

```
$ curl http://localhost/
Error: something broke!
    at Object.handle (/Users/tj/Projects/node-in-action/source
    ➥/connect-middleware-errorHandler.js:12:10)
    at next (/Users/tj/Projects/connect/lib/proto.js:179:15)
    at Object.logger [as handle] (/Users/tj/Projects/connect
    ➥/lib/middleware/logger.js:155:5)
    at next (/Users/tj/Projects/connect/lib/proto.js:179:15)
    at Function.handle (/Users/tj/Projects/connect/lib/proto.js:192:3)
    at Server.app (/Users/tj/Projects/connect/lib/connect.js:53:31)
    at Server.emit (events.js:67:17)
    at HTTPParser.onIncoming (http.js:1134:12)
    at HTTPParser.onHeadersComplete (http.js:108:31)
    at Socket.ondata (http.js:1029:22)
```

RECEIVING A JSON ERROR RESPONSE

If you send an HTTP request that has the `Accept: application/json` HTTP header, you'll get the following JSON response:

```
$ curl http://localhost/ -H "Accept: application/json"
{"error":{"stack":"Error: something broke!\n
        ➥at Object.handle (/Users/tj/Projects/node-in action
        ➥/source/connect-middleware-errorHandler.js:12:10)\n
        ➥at next (/Users/tj/Projects/connect/lib/proto.js:179:15)\n
        ➥at Object.logger [as handle] (/Users/tj/Projects
        ➥/connect/lib/middleware/logger.js:155:5)\n
        ➥at next (/Users/tj/Projects/connect/lib/proto.js:179:15)\n
        ➥at Function.handle (/Users/tj/Projects/connect/lib/proto.js:192:3)\n
        ➥at Server.app (/Users/tj/Projects/connect/lib/connect.js:53:31)\n
        ➥at Server.emit (events.js:67:17)\n
        ➥at HTTPParser.onIncoming (http.js:1134:12)\n
        ➥at HTTPParser.onHeadersComplete (http.js:108:31)\n
        ➥at Socket.ondata (http.js:1029:22)","message":"something broke!"}}
```

We've added additional formatting to the JSON response, so it's easier to read on the page, but when Connect sends the JSON response, it gets compacted nicely by `JSON.stringify()`.

Are you feeling like a Connect security guru now? Maybe not yet, but you should have enough of the basics down to make your applications secure, all using Connect's built-in middleware. Now let's move on to a very common web application function: serving static files.

7.4 Middleware for serving static files

Serving static files is another requirement common to many web applications that's not provided by Node's core. Fortunately, Connect has you covered here as well.

In this section, you'll learn about three more of Connect's built-in middleware components, this time focusing on serving files from the filesystem, much like regular HTTP servers do:

- `static()`—Serves files from the filesystem from a given root directory
- `compress()`—Compresses responses, ideal for use with `static()`
- `directory()`—Serves pretty directory listings when a directory is requested

First we'll show you how to serve static files with a single line of code using the `static` component.

7.4.1 static(): static file serving

Connect's `static()` middleware component implements a high-performance, flexible, feature-rich static file server supporting HTTP cache mechanisms, `Range` requests, and more. Even more important, it includes security checks for malicious paths, disallows access to hidden files (beginning with a `.`) by default, and rejects poison null bytes. In essence, `static()` is a very secure and compliant static file-serving middleware component, ensuring compatibility with the various HTTP clients out there.

BASIC USAGE

Suppose your application follows the typical scenario of serving static assets from a directory named ./public. This can be achieved with a single line of code:

```
app.use(connect.static('public'));
```

With this configuration, `static()` will check for regular files that exist in ./public/ based on the request URL. If a file exists, the response's `Content-Type` field value will be defaulted based on the file's extension, and the data will be transferred. If the requested path doesn't represent a file, the `next()` callback will be invoked, allowing subsequent middleware (if any) to handle the request.

To test it out, create a file named ./public/foo.js with `console.log('tobi')`, and issue a request to the server using `curl(1)` with the `-i` flag, telling it to print the HTTP headers. You'll see that the HTTP cache-related header fields are set appropriately, the `Content-Type` reflects the .js extension, and the content is transferred:

```
$ curl http://localhost/foo.js -i
HTTP/1.1 200 OK
Date: Thu, 06 Oct 2011 03:06:33 GMT
Cache-Control: public, max-age=0
Last-Modified: Thu, 06 Oct 2011 03:05:51 GMT
ETag: "21-1317870351000"
Content-Type: application/javascript
Accept-Ranges: bytes
Content-Length: 21
Connection: keep-alive

console.log('tobi');
```

Because the request path is used as is, files nested within directories are served as you'd expect. For example, you might have a `GET /javascripts/jquery.js` request and a `GET /stylesheets/app.css` request on your server, which would serve the files ./public/javascripts/jquery.js and ./public/stylesheets/app.css, respectively.

USING STATIC() WITH MOUNTING

Sometimes applications prefix pathnames with /public, /assets, /static, and so on. With the mounting concept that Connect implements, serving static files from multiple directories is simple. Just mount the app at the location you want. As mentioned in chapter 6, the middleware itself has no knowledge that it's mounted, because the prefix is removed.

For example, a request to `GET /app/files/js/jquery.js` with `static()` mounted at /app/files will appear to the middleware as `GET /js/jquery`. This works out well for the prefixing functionality because /app/files won't be part of the file resolution:

```
app.use('/app/files', connect.static('public'));
```

The original request of `GET /foo.js` won't work anymore, because the middleware isn't invoked unless the mount point is present, but the prefixed version `GET /app/files/foo.js` will transfer the file:

```
$ curl http://localhost/foo.js
Cannot get /foo.js

$ curl http://localhost/app/files/foo.js
console.log('tobi');
```

ABSOLUTE VS. RELATIVE DIRECTORY PATHS

Keep in mind that the path passed into the `static()` component is relative to the current working directory. That means passing in `"public"` as your path will essentially resolve to `process.cwd() + "public"`.

Sometimes, though, you may want to use absolute paths when specifying the base directory, and the `__dirname` variable helps with that:

```
app.use('/app/files', connect.static(__dirname + '/public'));
```

SERVING INDEX.HTML WHEN A DIRECTORY IS REQUESTED

Another useful feature of `static()` is its ability to serve index.html files. When a request for a directory is made and an index.html file lives in that directory, it will be served.

Now that you can serve static files with a single line of code, let's take a look at how you can compress the response data using the `compress()` middleware component to decrease the amount of data being transferred.

7.4.2 compress(): compressing static files

The zlib module provides developers with mechanisms for compressing and decompressing data with gzip and deflate. Connect 2.0 and above provide zlib at the HTTP server level for compressing outgoing data with the `compress()` middleware component.

The `compress()` component autodetects accepted encodings via the `Accept-Encoding` header field. If this field isn't present, the identity encoding is used, meaning the response is untouched. Otherwise, if the field contains `gzip`, `deflate`, or both, the response will be compressed.

BASIC USAGE

You should generally add `compress()` high in the Connect stack, because it wraps the `res.write()` and `res.end()` methods.

In the following example, the static files served will support compression:

```
var connect = require('connect');

var app = connect()
  .use(connect.compress())
  .use(connect.static('source'));

app.listen(3000);
```

In the snippet that follows, a small 189-byte JavaScript file is served. By default, `curl(1)` doesn't send the `Accept-Encoding` field, so you receive plain text:

```
$ curl http://localhost/script.js -i
HTTP/1.1 200 OK
```

```
Date: Sun, 16 Oct 2011 18:30:00 GMT
Cache-Control: public, max-age=0
Last-Modified: Sun, 16 Oct 2011 18:29:55 GMT
ETag: "189-1318789795000"
Content-Type: application/javascript
Accept-Ranges: bytes
Content-Length: 189
Connection: keep-alive

console.log('tobi');
console.log('loki');
console.log('jane');
console.log('tobi');
console.log('loki');
console.log('jane');
console.log('tobi');
console.log('loki');
console.log('jane');
```

The following `curl(1)` command adds the `Accept-Encoding` field, indicating that it's willing to accept gzip-compressed data. As you can see, even for such a small file, the data transferred is reduced considerably because the data is quite repetitive:

```
$ curl http://localhost/script.js -i -H "Accept-Encoding: gzip"
HTTP/1.1 200 OK
Date: Sun, 16 Oct 2011 18:31:45 GMT
Cache-Control: public, max-age=0
Last-Modified: Sun, 16 Oct 2011 18:29:55 GMT
ETag: "189-1318789795000"
Content-Type: application/javascript
Accept-Ranges: bytes
Content-Encoding: gzip
Vary: Accept-Encoding
Connection: keep-alive
Transfer-Encoding: chunked

K??+??I???O?P/?O?T??JF?????J?K???v?!?_?
```

You could try the same example with `Accept-Encoding: deflate`.

USING A CUSTOM FILTER FUNCTION

By default, `compress()` supports the MIME types `text/*`, `*/json`, and `*/javascript`, as defined in the default `filter` function:

```
exports.filter = function(req, res){
  var type = res.getHeader('Content-Type') || '';
  return type.match(/json|text|javascript/);
};
```

To alter this behavior, you can pass a `filter` in the options object, as shown in the following snippet, which will only compress plain text:

```
function filter(req) {
  var type = req.getHeader('Content-Type') || '';
  return 0 == type.indexOf('text/plain');
}
```

```
connect()
  .use(connect.compress({ filter: filter }))
```

SPECIFYING COMPRESSION AND MEMORY LEVELS

Node's zlib bindings provide options for tweaking performance and compression characteristics, and they can also be passed to the `compress()` function.

In the following example, the compression `level` is set to `3` for less but faster compression, and `memLevel` is set to `8` for faster compression by using more memory. These values depend entirely on your application and the resources available to it. Consult Node's zlib documentation for details:

```
connect()
  .use(connect.compress({ level: 3, memLevel: 8 }))
```

Next is the `directory()` middleware component, which helps `static()` to serve directory listings in all kinds of formats.

7.4.3 directory(): directory listings

Connect's `directory()` is a small directory-listing middleware component that provides a way for users to browse remote files. Figure 7.5 illustrates the interface provided by this component, complete with a search input field, file icons, and clickable breadcrumbs.

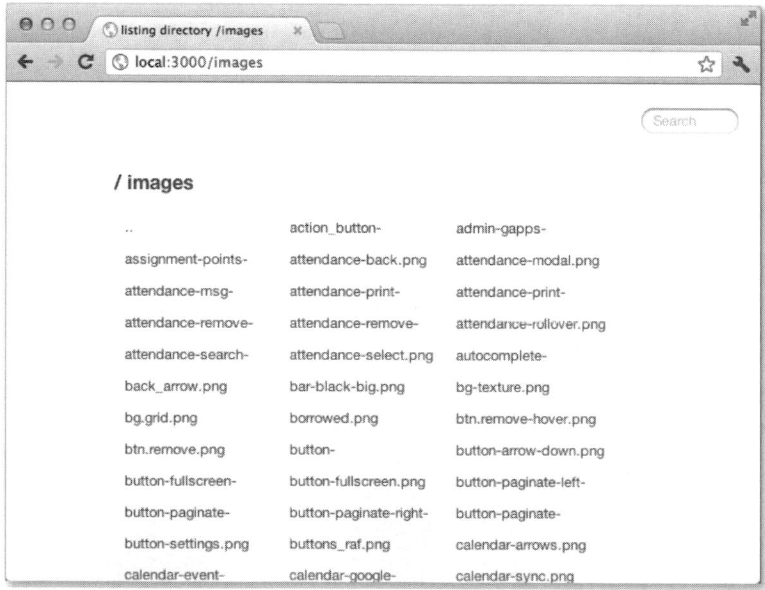

Figure 7.5 Serving directory listings with Connect's `directory()` middleware component

BASIC USAGE

This component is designed to work with `static()`, which will perform the actual file serving; `directory()` simply serves the listings. The setup can be as simple as the following snippet, where the request `GET /` serves the ./public directory:

```
var connect = require('connect');

var app = connect()
  .use(connect.directory('public'))
  .use(connect.static('public'));

app.listen(3000);
```

USING DIRECTORY() WITH MOUNTING

Through the use of middleware mounting, you can prefix both the `directory()` and `static()` middleware components to any path you like, such as `GET /files` in the following example. Here the `icons` option is used to enable icons, and `hidden` is enabled for both components to allow the viewing and serving of hidden files:

```
var app = connect()
  .use('/files', connect.directory('public',
    ➥{ icons: true, hidden: true }))
  .use('/files', connect.static('public', { hidden: true }));

app.listen(3000);
```

It's now possible to navigate through files and directories with ease.

7.5 Summary

The real power of Connect comes from its rich suite of bundled reusable middleware, which provides implementations for common web application functions like session management, robust static file serving, and compression of outgoing data, among others. Connect's goal is to give developers some functionality right out of the box, so that everyone isn't constantly rewriting the same pieces of code (possibly less efficiently) for their own applications or frameworks.

Connect is perfectly capable when used for building entire web applications using combinations of middleware, as you've seen throughout this chapter. But Connect is typically used as a building block for higher-level frameworks; for example, it doesn't provide any routing or templating helpers. This low-level approach makes Connect great as a base for higher-level frameworks, which is exactly how Express integrates with it.

You might be thinking, why not just use Connect for building a web application? That's perfectly possible, but the higher-level Express web framework makes full use of Connect's functionality, while taking application development one step further. Express makes application development quicker and more enjoyable with an elegant view system, powerful routing, and several request- and response-related methods. We'll explore Express in the next chapter.

8 Express

This chapter covers

- Starting a new Express application
- Configuring your application
- Creating Express views
- Handling file uploads and downloads

Things are about to get even more fun. The Express web framework (http://expressjs.com) is built on top of Connect, providing tools and structure that make writing web applications easier, faster, and more fun. Express offers a unified view system that lets you use nearly any template engine you want, plus simple utilities for responding with various data formats, transferring files, routing URLs, and more.

In comparison to application frameworks such as Django or Ruby on Rails, Express is extremely small. The philosophy behind Express is that applications vary greatly in their requirements and implementations, and a lightweight framework allows you to craft exactly what you need and nothing more. Both Express and the entire Node community are focused on smaller, more modular bits of functionality rather than monolithic frameworks.

Throughout this chapter, you'll learn how to use Express to create applications by building a photo sharing application from start to finish. During the build, you'll learn how to do the following:

- Generate the initial application structure
- Configure Express and your application
- Render views and integrate template engines
- Handle forms and file uploads
- Handle resource downloads

The final stock photo application will have a list view that will look like figure 8.1.

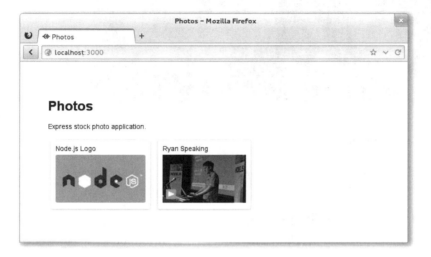

Figure 8.1 The photo list view

It'll also include a form for uploading new photos, as shown in figure 8.2.

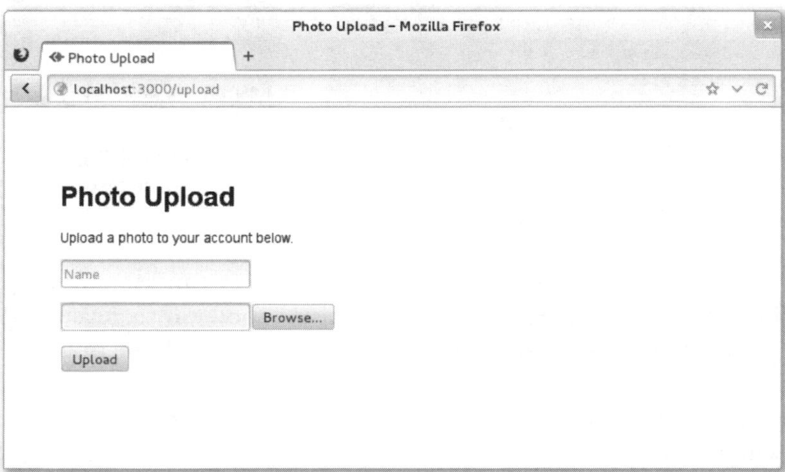

Figure 8.2 The photo upload view

Figure 8.3 Downloading a file

Finally, it'll have a mechanism for downloading photos, as shown in figure 8.3. Let's get started by looking at the application's structure.

8.1 Generating the application skeleton

Express doesn't force application structure on the developer—you can place routes in as many files as you want, public assets in any directory you want, and so on. A minimal Express application can be as small as the following listing, which implements a fully functional HTTP server.

Listing 8.1 A minimal Express application

```
var express = require('express');
var app = express();

app.get('/', function(req, res){      <- Respond to any web request to /
  res.send('Hello');                  <- Send "Hello" as response text
});

app.listen(3000);      <- Listen on port 3000
```

The express(1) executable script bundled with Express can set up an application skeleton for you. Using the generated application is a good way to get started if you're new to Express, as it sets up an application complete with templates, public assets, configuration, and more.

The default application skeleton that express(1) generates consists of only a few directories and files, as shown in figure 8.4. This structure is designed to get developers up and running with Express in seconds, but the application's structure is entirely up to you and your team to create.

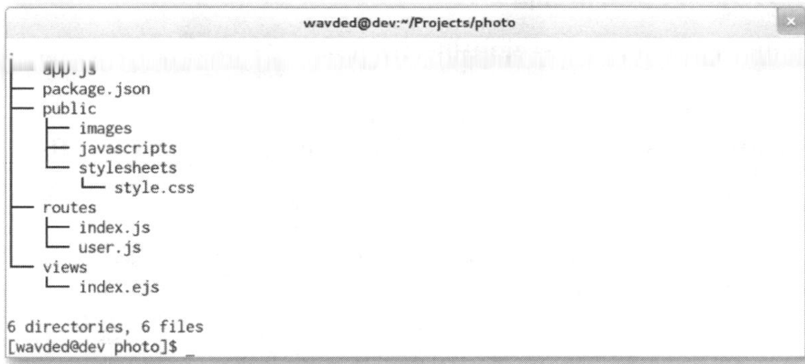

Figure 8.4 Default application skeleton structure using EJS templates

In this chapter's example, we'll use EJS templates, which are similar in structure to HTML. EJS is similar to PHP, JSP (for Java), and ERB (for Ruby), where server-side JavaScript is embedded in an HTML document and executed prior to being sent to the client. We'll look at EJS more closely in chapter 11.

By the end of this chapter, you'll have an application with a similar but expanded structure, as shown in figure 8.5.

In this section you'll do the following:

- Install Express globally with npm
- Generate the application
- Explore the application and install dependencies

Let's get started.

Figure 8.5 Final application structure

8.1.1 Installing the Express executable

First you'll want to install Express globally with npm:

```
$ npm install -g express
```

Once it's installed, you can use the `--help` flag to see the options available, as shown in figure 8.6.

```
wavded@dev:~/Projects/photo
[wavded@dev photo]$ express --help

  Usage: express [options]

  Options:

    -h, --help          output usage information
    -V, --version       output the version number
    -s, --sessions      add session support
    -e, --ejs           add ejs engine support (defaults to jade)
    -J, --jshtml        add jshtml engine support (defaults to jade)
    -H, --hogan         add hogan.js engine support
    -c, --css <engine>  add stylesheet <engine> support (less|stylus) (defaults to plain c
ss)
    -f, --force         force on non-empty directory

[wavded@dev photo]$ _
```

Figure 8.6 Express help

Some of these options will generate small portions of the application for you. For example, you can specify a template engine to generate a dummy template file for the chosen template engine. Similarly, if you specify a CSS preprocessor using the `--css` option, a dummy template file will be generated for it. If you use the `--sessions` option, session middleware will be enabled.

Now that the executable is installed, let's generate what will become the photo application.

8.1.2 Generating the application

For this application, you'll use the `-e` (or `--ejs`) flag to use the EJS templating engine. Execute `express -e photo`.

A fully functional application will be created in the photo directory. It will contain a package.json file to describe the project and dependencies, the application file itself, the public file directories, and a directory for routes (see figure 8.7).

8.1.3 Exploring the application

Let's take a closer look at what was generated. Open the package.json file in your editor to see the application's dependencies, as shown in figure 8.8. Express can't guess which version of the dependencies you'll want, so it's good practice to supply the major, minor, and patch levels of the module so you don't introduce any surprise bugs. For example, `"express": "3.0.0"` is explicit and will provide you with identical code on each installation.

```
wavded@dev:~/Projects
[wavded@dev Projects]$ express -e photo

   create : photo
   create : photo/package.json
   create : photo/app.js
   create : photo/public
   create : photo/public/javascripts
   create : photo/public/images
   create : photo/routes
   create : photo/routes/index.js
   create : photo/routes/user.js
   create : photo/views
   create : photo/views/index.ejs
   create : photo/public/stylesheets
   create : photo/public/stylesheets/style.css

   install dependencies:
     $ cd photo && npm install

   run the app:
     $ node app

[wavded@dev Projects]$ _
```

Figure 8.7 Generating the Express application

```
wavded@dev:~/Projects/photo
[wavded@dev Projects]$ cd photo
[wavded@dev photo]$ cat package.json
{
  "name": "application-name",
  "version": "0.0.1",
  "private": true,
  "scripts": {
    "start": "node app"
  },
  "dependencies": {
    "express": "3.0.0",
    "ejs": "*"
  }
[wavded@dev photo]$ _
```

Figure 8.8 Generated package.json contents

To add the latest version of a module, in this case EJS, you can pass npm the `--save` flag on installation. Execute the following command, and then open package.json again to see the change:

```
$ npm install ejs --save
```

Now look at the application file generated by `express(1)`, shown in the following listing. For now you'll leave this file as is. You should be familiar with these middleware components from the Connect chapter, but it's worth taking a look at how the default middleware configuration is set up.

Listing 8.2 Generated Express application skeleton

```
var express = require('express')
  , routes = require('./routes')
  , user = require('./routes/user')
```

```
  , http = require('http')
  , path = require('path');

var app = express();

app.configure(function(){
  app.set('port', process.env.PORT || 3000);
  app.set('views', __dirname + '/views');
  app.set('view engine', 'ejs');
  app.use(express.favicon());                          <-- Serve default favicon
  app.use(express.logger('dev'));                      <-- Output development-friendly colored logs
  app.use(express.bodyParser());                       <-- Parse request bodies
  app.use(express.methodOverride());
  app.use(app.router);
  app.use(express.static(path.join(__dirname, 'public')));   <-- Serve static files from ./public
});

app.configure('development', function(){
  app.use(express.errorHandler());                     <-- Display styled HTML error pages in development
});

app.get('/', routes.index);                            <-- Specify application routes
app.get('/users', user.list);

http.createServer(app).listen(app.get('port'), function(){
  console.log("Express server listening on port " + app.get('port'));
});
```

You've got the package.json and app.js files, but the application won't run yet because the dependencies haven't been installed. Whenever you generate a package.json file from `express(1)`, you'll need to install the dependencies (as shown in figure 8.9). Execute `npm install` to do this, and then execute `node app.js` to fire up the application. Check out the application by visiting http://localhost:3000 in your browser. The default application looks like the one in figure 8.10.

Now that you've seen the generated application, let's dive into the environment-specific configuration.

```
wavded@dev:~/Projects/photo
[wavded@dev photo]$ npm install
ejs@0.8.3 node_modules/ejs

express@3.0.0 node_modules/express
├── methods@0.0.1
├── fresh@0.1.0
├── range-parser@0.0.4
├── cookie@0.0.4
├── crc@0.2.0
├── commander@0.6.1
├── debug@0.7.0
├── mkdirp@0.3.3
├── send@0.1.0 (mime@1.2.6)
└── connect@2.6.0 (pause@0.0.1, bytes@0.1.0, formidable@1.0.11, qs@0.5.1, send@0.0.4)
[wavded@dev photo]$ node app.js
Express server listening on port 3000
```

Figure 8.9 Install dependencies and run application

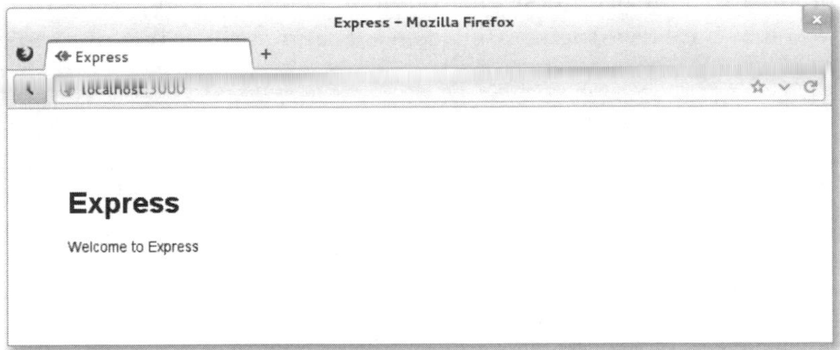

Figure 8.10 Default Express application

8.2 Configuring Express and your application

Your application's requirements will depend on the environment in which it's running. For example, you may want verbose logging when your product's in development, but a leaner set of logs and gzip compression when it's in production. In addition to configuring environment-specific functionality, you may want to define some application-level settings so Express knows what template engine you're using and where it can find the templates. Express also lets you define custom configuration key/value pairs.

Express has a minimalistic environment-driven configuration system, consisting of five methods, all driven by the `NODE_ENV` environment variable:

- `app.configure()`
- `app.set()`
- `app.get()`
- `app.enable()`
- `app.disable()`

In this section, you'll see how to use the configuration system to customize how Express behaves, as well as how to use it for your own purposes throughout development.

Let's take a closer look at what "environment-based configuration" means.

> **Setting environment variables**
>
> To set an environment variable in UNIX systems, you can use this command:
>
> ```
> $ NODE_ENV=production node app
> ```
>
> In Windows, you can use this code:
>
> ```
> $ set NODE_ENV=production
> $ node app
> ```
>
> These environment variables will be available in your application on the `process.env` object.

8.2.1 Environment-based configuration

Although the `NODE_ENV` environment variable originated in Express, many other Node frameworks have adopted it as a means to notify the Node application which environment it's operating within, defaulting to development.

As shown in listing 8.3, the `app.configure()` method accepts optional strings representing the environment, and a function. When the environment matches the string passed, the callback is immediately invoked; when only a function is given, it will be invoked for all environments. These environment names are completely arbitrary. For example, you may have development, stage, test, and production, or prod for short.

Listing 8.3 Using app.configure() to set environment-specific options

```
app.configure(function(){
  app.set('views', __dirname + '/views');      <— All environments
  app.set('view engine', 'ejs');
  ...
});

app.configure('development', function(){
  app.use(express.errorHandler());     <— Development only
});
```

To illustrate that app.configure() is purely sugar, the following listing would be equivalent to the preceding one. You're not forced to use this feature; for example, you could load the configuration from JSON or YAML.

Listing 8.4 Using conditionals to set environment-specific options

```
var env = process.env.NODE_ENV || 'development';      <— Default to "development"

app.set('views', __dirname + '/views');
app.set('view engine', 'ejs');                <— All environments
...

if ('development' == env) {                   <— Development only, using if
  app.use(express.errorHandler());                statement instead of app.configure
}
```

Express uses the configuration system internally, allowing you to customize how Express behaves, but it's also available for your own use. For the application you're building in this chapter, you'll only use a single setting, photos, whose value is the directory that will be used to store the uploaded images. This value could be changed in production to permit saving and serving photos from a different volume with more disk space:

```
app.configure(function(){
  ...
  app.set('photos', __dirname + '/public/photos');
  ...
});

app.configure('production', function(){
  ...
  app.set('photos', '/mounted-volume/photos');
  ...
});
```

Express also provides Boolean variants of app.set() and app.get(). For example, app.enable(setting) is equivalent to app.set(setting, true), and app.enabled (setting) can be used to check if the value was enabled. The methods app.disable (setting) and app.disabled(setting) complement the truthful variants.

Now that you've seen how to take advantage of the configuration system for your own use, let's look at rendering views in Express.

8.3 Rendering views

In this chapter's application, we'll utilize EJS templates, though as previously mentioned almost any template engine in the Node community can be used. If you're not familiar with EJS, don't worry. It's similar to templating languages found in other languages (PHP, JSP, ERB). We'll cover some basics of EJS in this chapter, but we'll discuss EJS and several other template engines in greater detail in chapter 11.

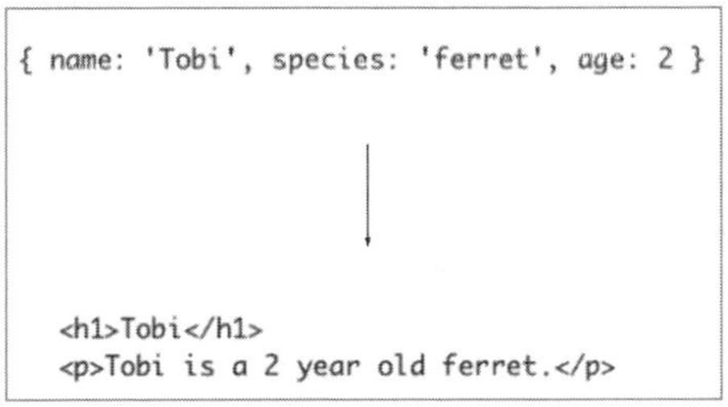

```
{ name: 'Tobi', species: 'ferret', age: 2 }

<h1>Tobi</h1>
<p>Tobi is a 2 year old ferret.</p>
```

Figure 8.11 HTML template plus data = HTML view of data

Whether it's rendering an entire HTML page, an HTML fragment, or an RSS feed, rendering views is crucial for nearly every application. The concept is simple: you pass data to a *view*, and that data is transformed, typically to HTML for web applications. You're likely familiar with the idea of views, because most frameworks provide similar functionality; figure 8.11 illustrates how a view forms a new representation for the data.

Express provides two ways to render views: at the application level with `app.render()`, and at the request or response level with `res.render()`, which uses the former internally. In this chapter, you'll only use `res.render()`. If you look in ./routes/index.js, a single function is exported: the `index` function. This function invokes `res.render()` in order to render the ./views/index.ejs template, as shown in the following code:

```
exports.index = function(req, res){
  res.render('index', { title: 'Express' });
};
```

In this section, you'll see how to do the following:

- Configure the Express view system
- Look up view files
- Expose data when rendering views

Before looking at `res.render()` more closely, let's configure the view system.

8.3.1 View system configuration

Configuring the Express view system is simple. But even though `express(1)` generated the configuration for you, it's still useful to know what's going on behind the scenes so you can make changes. We'll focus on three areas:

- Adjusting the view lookup
- Configuring the default template engine
- Enabling view caching to reduce file I/O

First up is the `views` setting.

CHANGING THE LOOKUP DIRECTORY

The following snippet shows the views setting that the Express executable created:

```
app.set('views', __dirname + '/views');
```

This specifies the directory that Express will use during view lookup. It's a good idea to use __dirname so that your application isn't dependent on the current working directory being the application's root.

> **__dirname**
>
> __dirname (with two leading underscores) is a global variable in Node that identifies the directory in which the currently running file *exists*. Often in development this directory will be the same as your current working directory (CWD), but in production the Node executable may run from another directory. Using __dirname helps keep paths consistent across environments.

The next setting is view engine.

DEFAULT TEMPLATE ENGINE

When express(1) generated the application, the view engine setting was assigned ejs because EJS was the template engine selected by the -e command-line option. This setting enables you to render index rather than index.ejs. Otherwise Express requires the extension in order to determine which template engine is to be used.

You might be wondering why Express even considers extensions. The use of extensions allows you to use multiple template engines within a single Express application, while providing a clean API for common use cases, because most applications will use one template engine.

Suppose, for example, you find writing RSS feeds easier with another template engine, or perhaps you're migrating from one template engine to another. You might use Jade as the default, and EJS for the /feed route, as indicated in the following listing by the .ejs extension.

Listing 8.5 Specifying the template engine using a file extension

```
app.set('view engine', 'jade');

app.get('/', function(){
  res.render('index');
 });

app.get('/feed', function(){
  res.render('rss.ejs')
;
});
```

- .jade is assumed because it's set as view engine
- Because .ejs extension is provided, use EJS template engine

KEEPING PACKAGE.JSON IN SYNC Keep in mind that any additional template engines you wish to use should be added to your package.json dependencies object.

VIEW CACHING

The `view cache` setting is enabled by default in the production environment and prevents subsequent `render()` calls from performing disk I/O. The contents of the templates are saved in memory, greatly improving performance. The side effect of enabling this setting is that you can no longer edit the template files without restarting the server, which is why it's disabled in development. If you're running a staging environment, you'll likely want to enable this option.

As illustrated in figure 8.12, when `view cache` is disabled, the template is read from disk on every request. This is what allows you to make changes to a template without restarting the application. When `view cache` is enabled, the disk is only hit once per template.

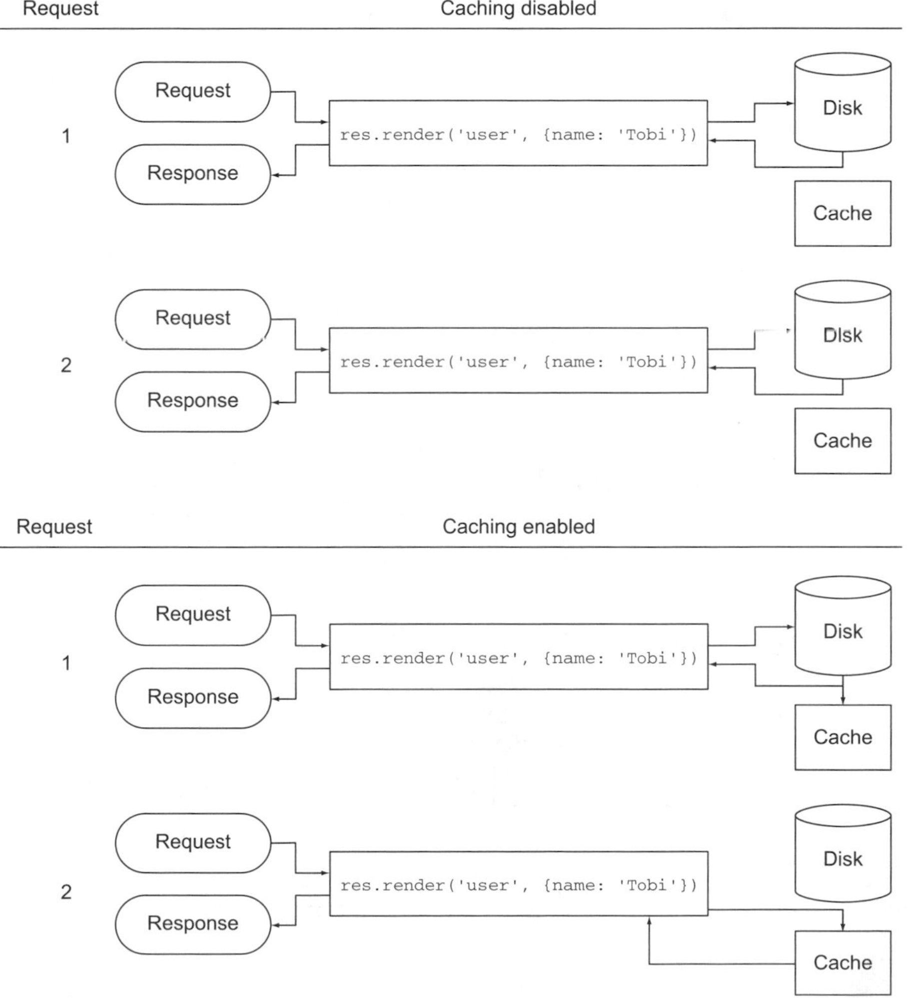

Figure 8.12 The view cache setting

You've seen how the view-caching mechanism helps improve performance in a nondevelopment environment. Now let's see how Express locates views in order to render them.

8.3.2 View lookup

Now that you know how to configure the view system, let's take a look at how Express looks up the view, which is where the target view file is located. Don't worry about creating these templates yet; you'll do that later.

The process of looking up a view is similar to how Node's `require()` works. When `res.render()` or `app.render()` is invoked, Express will first check whether a file exists at an absolute path. Next, Express will look relative to the `views` directory setting discussed in section 8.3.1. Finally, Express will try an index file.

This process is represented as a flowchart in figure 8.13.

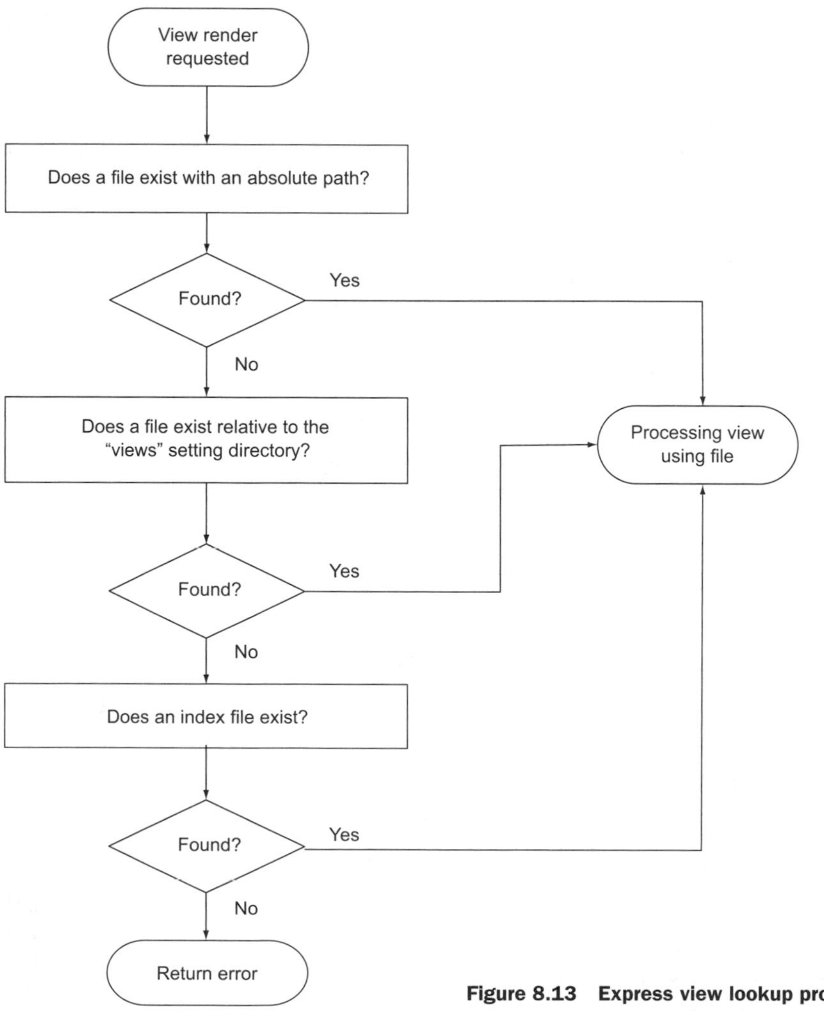

Figure 8.13 Express view lookup process

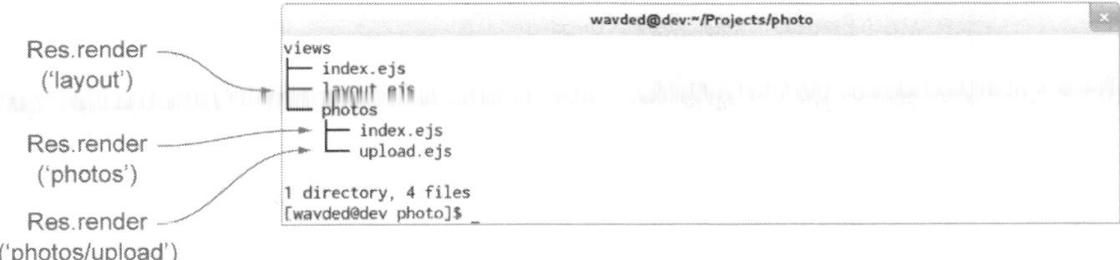

Figure 8.14 Express view lookup

Because `ejs` is set as the default engine, the render call omits the .ejs extension, but it's still resolved correctly.

As the application evolves, you'll need more views, and sometimes several for a single resource. Using `view lookup` can help with organization—for example, you can use subdirectories related to the resource and create views within them, as illustrated by the photos directory in figure 8.14.

Adding subdirectories allows you to eliminate redundant parts of names such as upload-photo.ejs and show-photo.ejs. Express will then add the `view engine` extension and resolve the view as ./views/photos/upload.ejs.

Express will check to see if a file named *index* resides in that directory. When files are named with a pluralized resource, such as *photos*, this typically implies a resource listing. An example is `res.render('photos')` in figure 8.14.

Now that you know how Express looks up views, let's start creating the photo listings and put this feature to work.

8.3.3 Exposing data to views

Express provides several mechanisms for exposing local variables to the views being rendered, but first you need something to render. In this section, you'll use some dummy data to populate the initial photo listing view.

Before getting databases involved, let's create this placeholder data. Create a file named ./routes/photos.js, which will contain the photo-specific routes. Now create a `photos` array in this same file that will act as the faux database. This is shown in the following code.

Listing 8.6 Dummy photo data to populate the view

```
var photos = [];
photos.push({
  name: 'Node.js Logo',
  path: 'http://nodejs.org/images/logos/nodejs-green.png'
});

photos.push({
  name: 'Ryan Speaking',
  path: 'http://nodejs.org/images/ryan-speaker.jpg'
});
...
```

Now that you have some content, you'll need a route to display it.

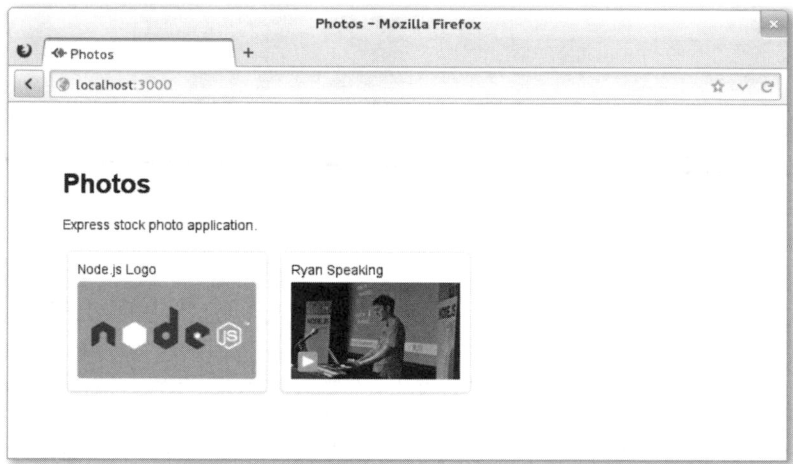

Figure 8.15 Initial photo listing view

CREATING THE PHOTO LISTING VIEW

To start displaying the dummy photo data, you need to define a route that will render an EJS photos view, as shown in figure 8.15.

To get started, open up ./routes/photos.js and export a function named `list` (shown in the following code). In practice, this function can be named whatever you like. Route functions are identical to regular Connect middleware functions, accepting request and response objects, as well as the `next()` callback, which isn't used in this example. This is the first and main method of passing objects to a view, by passing an object to `res.render()`.

Listing 8.7 List route

```
exports.list = function(req, res){
  res.render('photos', {
    title: 'Photos',
    photos: photos
  });
};
```

In ./app.js you can then require the photos module to get access to the `exports.list` function you just wrote. To display the photos for the index page, /, pass the `photos.list` function to the `app.get()` method, which is used to map the HTTP method `GET` and the path matching / to this function.

Listing 8.8 Adding `photos.list` route

```
...
var routes = require('./routes');
var photos = require('./routes/photos');
...
app.get('/', photos.list);
```

Replaces app.get('/', routes.index)

With the dummy data and route set up, you can write the photo view. You'll have several photo-related views, so create a directory named ./views/photos and index.ejs inside of it. Using a JavaScript `forEach`, you can then iterate through each `photo` in the `photos` object that was passed to `res.render()`. Each photo name and image is then displayed, as the following listing shows.

Listing 8.9 A view template to list photos

```
<!DOCTYPE html>
<html>
  <head>
    <title><%= title %></title>
    <link rel='stylesheet' href='/stylesheets/style.css' />
  </head>
  <body>
    <h1>Photos</h1>
    <p>Express stock photo application.</p>
    <div id="photos">
      <% photos.forEach(function(photo) { %>
        <div class="photo">
          <h2><%=photo.name%></h2>
          <img src='<%=photo.path%>'/>
        </div>
      <% }) %>
    </div>
  </body>
</html>
```

EJS outputs escaped values by using <%= value %>

EJS executes vanilla JS using <% code %>

This view will produce markup similar to the following listing.

Listing 8.10 HTML produced by the photos/index.ejs template

```
...
<h1>Photos</h1>
<p>Express stock photo application.</p>
<div id="photos">
  <div class="photo">
    <h2>Node.js Logo</h2>
    <img src="http://nodejs.org/images/logos/nodejs-green.png" />
  </div>
...
```

If you're interested in styling your application, here's the CSS used for ./public/stylesheets/style.css.

Listing 8.11 CSS used to style this chapter's tutorial application

```
body {
  padding: 50px;
  font: 14px "Helvetica Neue", Helvetica, Arial, sans-serif;
}
a { color: #00B7FF; }
.photo {
```

```
  display: inline-block;
  margin: 5px;
  padding: 10px;
  border: 1px solid #eee;
  border-radius: 5px;
  box-shadow: 0 1px 2px #ddd;
}
.photo h2 {
  margin: 0;
  margin-bottom: 5px;
  font-size: 14px;
  font-weight: 200;
}
.photo img { height: 100px; }
```

Fire up the application with `node app`, and take a look at http://localhost:3000 in your browser. You'll see the photo display shown earlier in figure 8.15.

METHODS OF EXPOSING DATA TO VIEWS

You've seen how you can pass local variables directly to `res.render()` calls, but you can also use a few other mechanisms for this. For example, `app.locals` can be used for application-level variables and `res.locals` for request-level local variables.

The values passed directly to `res.render()` will take precedence over values set in `res.locals` and `app.locals`, as figure 8.16 shows.

By default, Express exposes only one application-level variable, `settings`, to views, which is the object containing all of the values set with `app.set()`. For example, using `app.set('title', 'My Application')` would expose `settings.title` in the template, as shown in the following EJS snippet:

```
<html>
  <head>
     <title><%=settings.title%></title>
  </head>
  <body>
    <h1><%=settings.title%></h1>
    <p>Welcome to <%=settings.title%>.</p>
  </body>
```

Internally, Express exposes this object with the following JavaScript:

```
app.locals.settings = app.settings;
```

That's all there is to it.

For convenience, `app.locals` is also a JavaScript function. When an object is passed, all the keys will be merged, so if you have existing objects that you want to expose in their entirety, such as some i18n data, you can do the following:

```
var i18n = {
  prev: 'Prev',
  next: 'Next',
  save: 'Save
};

app.locals(i18n);
```

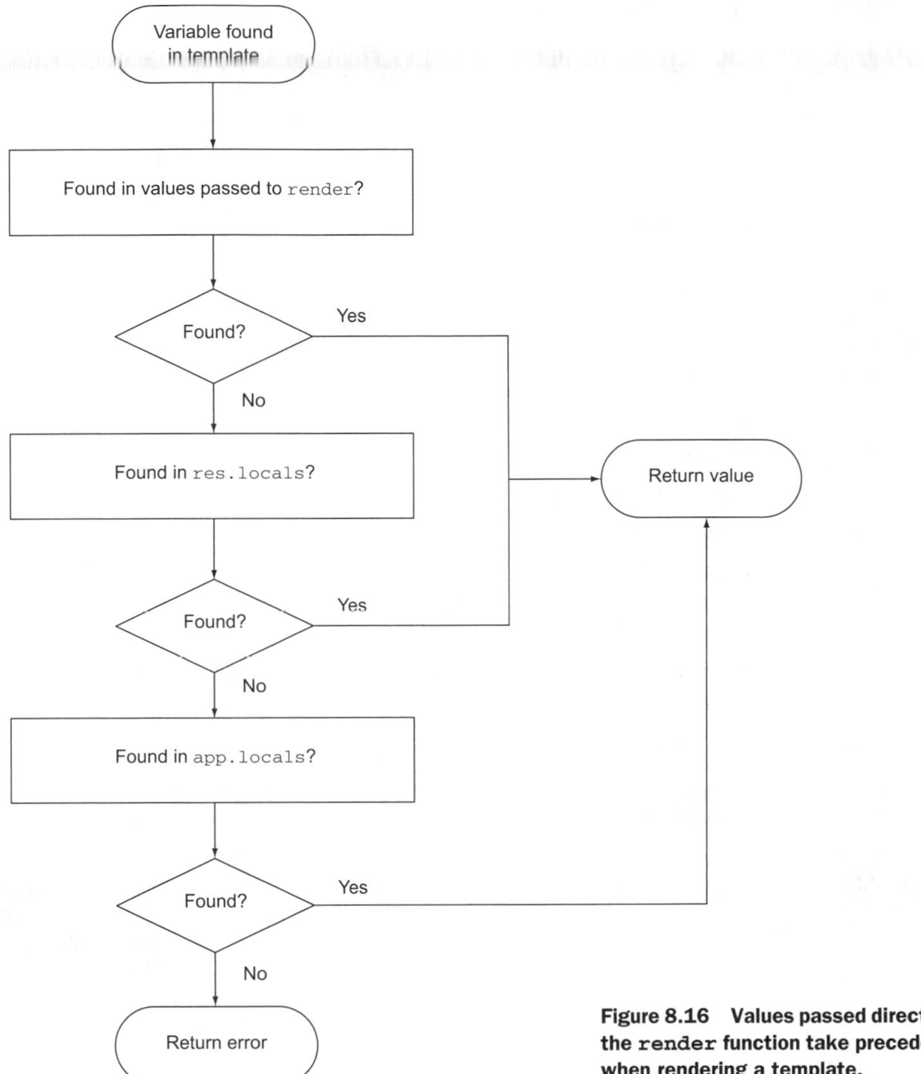

Figure 8.16 Values passed directly to the `render` function take precedence when rendering a template.

This will expose `prev`, `next`, and `save` to all templates. This feature exposes view helpers to help reduce logic within templates. For example, if you have the Node module helpers.js with a few functions exported, you could expose all of these functions to the views by doing the following:

```
app.locals(require('./helpers'));
```

Let's add a way to upload files to this site and learn how Express uses Connect's `bodyParser` middleware component to make that possible.

8.4 Handling forms and file uploads

Let's implement the photo upload feature. Make sure you have the `photos` setting defined for this application, as discussed earlier in section 8.2.1. This will give you the freedom to change the photo directory in various environments. For now they'll be saved in ./public/photos, as the following code shows. Create this directory.

Listing 8.12 A custom setting that allows a photo upload destination to be set

```
...
app.configure(function(){
  app.set('views', __dirname + '/views');
  app.set('view engine', 'ejs');
  app.set('photos', __dirname + '/public/photos');
...
```

There are three main steps involved in implementing the photo upload feature:

- Define the photo model
- Create a photo upload form
- Display a photo listing

8.4.1 Implementing the photo model

We'll use the simple Mongoose model we discussed in chapter 5 to make the model. Install Mongoose with `npm install mongoose --save`. Then create the file ./models/Photo.js with the model definition shown here.

Listing 8.13 A model for your photos

```
var mongoose = require('mongoose');
mongoose.connect('mongodb://localhost/photo_app');

var schema = new mongoose.Schema({
  name: String,
  path: String
});

module.exports = mongoose.model('Photo', schema);
```

Set up connection to mongodb on localhost and use photo_app as database

Mongoose provides all the CRUD methods (`Photo.create`, `Photo.update`, `Photo.remove`, and `Photo.find`) on the model, so you're done.

8.4.2 Creating a photo upload form

With the photo model in place, you can now implement the upload form and related routes. Much like the other pages, you'll need a `GET` route and a `POST` route for the uploads page.

You'll pass the photos directory the `POST` handler and return a route callback, so the handler has access to the directory. Add the new routes to app.js below the default (/) route:

```
...
app.get('/upload', photos.form);
app.post('/upload', photos.submit(app.get('photos')));
...
```

CREATING THE PHOTO UPLOAD FORM

Next you'll create the upload form shown in figure 8.17. This form contains an optional photo name and a file input for the image.

Create the file views/photos/upload.ejs with the following EJS code.

Listing 8.14 A form for uploading photos

```
<!DOCTYPE html>
<html>
  <head>
    <title><%= title %></title>
    <link rel='stylesheet' href='/stylesheets/style.css' />
  </head>
  <body>
    <h1><%= title %></h1>
    <p>Upload a photo to your account below.</p>
    <form method='post' enctype='multipart/form-data'>
      <p><input
                type='text', name='photo[name]', placeholder='Name'/>
                </p>
      <p><input type='file', name='photo[image]'/></p>
      <p><input type='submit', value='Upload'/></p>
    </form>
  </body>
</html>
```

Let's now look at adding a route for the photo upload.

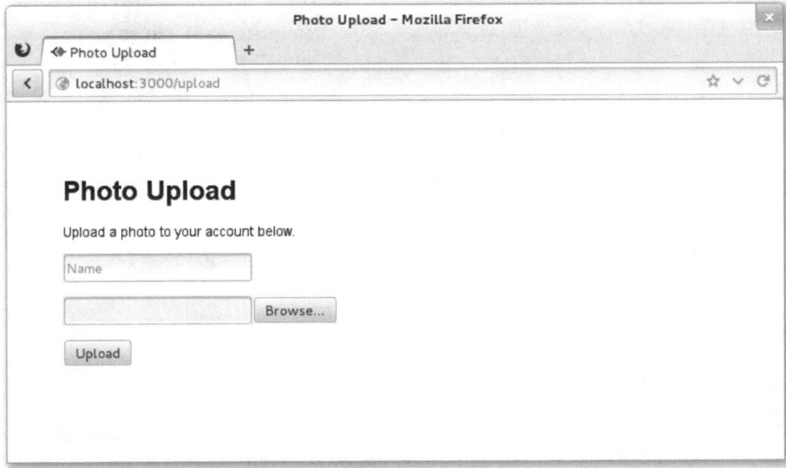

Figure 8.17 Photo upload form

ADDING A ROUTE FOR THE PHOTO UPLOAD PAGE

Now you have a photo upload form, but no way to display it. The `photos.form` function will do this. In ./routes/photos.js, export the `form` function, which will render ./views/photos/upload.ejs.

Listing 8.15 Add the form route

```
exports.form = function(req, res){
  res.render('photos/upload', {
    title: 'Photo upload'
  });
};
```

HANDLING PHOTO SUBMISSIONS

Next you'll need a route to handle the form submission. As discussed in chapter 7, the `bodyParser()` and, more specifically, the `multipart()` middleware component (which `bodyParser` includes), will provide you with a `req.files` object representing files that have been uploaded and saved to disk. This object can be accessed via `req.files.photo.image`, and the field in the upload form, `photo[name]`, can be accessed via `req.body.photo.name`.

The file is "moved" with `fs.rename()` to its new destination within the `dir` passed to `exports.submit()`. Remember, in your case, `dir` is the `photos` setting you defined in app.js. After the file is moved, a new `Photo` object is populated and saved with the photo's name and path. Upon a successful save, the user is redirected to the index page, as the following code shows.

Listing 8.16 Adding photo submit route definition

```
var Photo = require('../models/Photo');          <-- Require the Photo model
var path = require('path');
var fs = require('fs');
var join = path.join;                            <-- Reference path.join so you
                                                     can name variables "path"
...

exports.submit = function (dir) {
  return function(req, res, next){
    var img = req.files.photo.image;
    var name = req.body.photo.name || img.name;  <-- Default to original filename
    var path = join(dir, img.name);

    fs.rename(img.path, path, function(err){     <-- Rename file
      if (err) return next(err);                 <-- Delegate errors

      Photo.create({
        name: name,
        path: img.name
      }, function (err) {
        if (err) return next(err);               <-- Delegate errors
        res.redirect('/');                       <-- Perform HTTP redirect to index page
      });
    });
  };
};
```

Great! Now you can upload photos. Next you'll implement the logic necessary to display them on the index page.

8.4.3 Showing a list of uploaded photos

In section 8.3.3, you implemented the route `app.get('/', photos.list)` using dummy data. Now it's time to replace it with the real thing.

Previously the route callback did little more than pass the dummy array of photos to the template, as shown here:

```
exports.list = function(req, res){
  res.render('photos', {
    title: 'Photos',
    photos: photos
  });
};
```

The updated version uses `Photo.find`, provided in Mongoose, to grab every photo you ever uploaded. Note that this example will perform poorly with a large collection of photos. You'll learn how to implement pagination in the next chapter.

Once the callback is invoked with an array of `photos`, the rest of the route remains the same as it was before introducing the asynchronous query.

Listing 8.17 Modified list route

```
exports.list = function(req, res, next){
  Photo.find({}, function(err, photos){        // {} finds all records in photo collection
    if (err) return next(err);
    res.render('photos', {
      title: 'Photos',
      photos: photos
    });
  });
};
```

Let's also update the ./views/photos/index.ejs template so it's relative to ./public/photos.

Listing 8.18 Modified view to use settings for photos path

```
...
<% photos.forEach(function(photo) { %>
  <div class="photo">
    <h2><%=photo.name%></h2>
    <img src='/photos/<%=photo.path%>'/>
  </div>
<% }) %>
...
```

The index page will now display a dynamic list of photos uploaded through the application, as shown in figure 8.18.

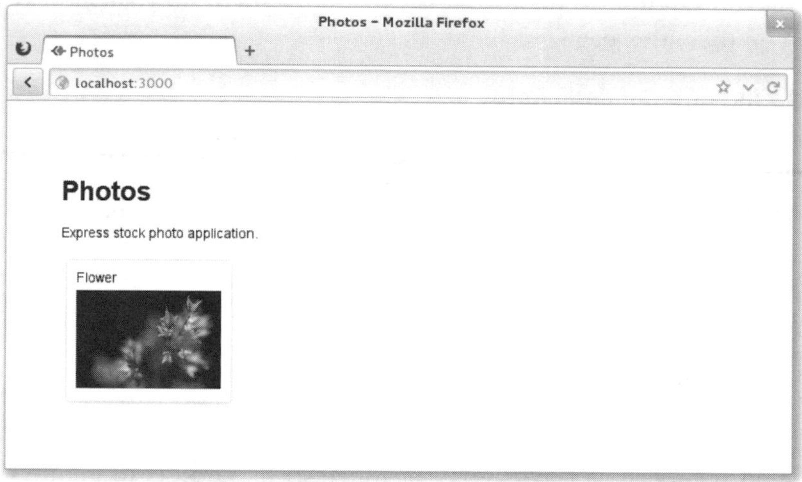

Figure 8.18 The photo application as it appears at this point

So far the routes you've defined have been simple: they don't accept wildcards. Let's dive into the routing capabilities of Express.

8.5 Handling resource downloads

You've been serving static files with the `express.static()` middleware component, but Express provides several helpful response methods for dealing with file transfers. These include `res.sendfile()` for transferring files and the `res.download()` variant, which prompts the browser to save the file.

In this section, you'll tweak your application so that original photos can be downloaded by adding a `GET /photo/:id/download` route.

8.5.1 Creating the photo download route

First you'll need to add a link to the photos so that users can download them. Open up ./views/photos/index.ejs and revise it to match the following listing. This change adds a link around the `img` tag pointing to the `GET /photo/:id/download` route.

Listing 8.19 Add a download hyperlink

```
...
<% photos.forEach(function(photo) { %>
  <div class="photo">
    <h2><%=photo.name%></h2>
    <a href='/photo/<%=photo.id%>/download'>
      <img src='/photos/<%=photo.path%>'/>

    </a>
  </div>
<% }) %>
...
```

Mongoose provides ID field that can be used to look up specific record

Back in app.js, define the following route anywhere you like among the others:

```
app.get('/photo/:id/download', photos.download(app.get('photos')));
```

Before you can try this out, you need the download route. Let's implement it.

8.5.2 Implementing the photo download route

In ./routes/photos.js, export a download function, as shown in listing 8.20. This route loads up the requested photo and transfers the file at that given path. `res.sendfile()` is provided by Express and is backed by the same code as `express.static()`, so you get HTTP cache, range, and other features for free. This method also takes the same options, so you can pass values like `{ maxAge: oneYear }` as the second argument.

Listing 8.20 Photo download route

```
exports.download = function(dir){                    <- Set directory you'll serve files from
  return function(req, res, next){                 <- Set route callback
    var id = req.params.id;
    Photo.findById(id, function(err, photo){          <- Load photo record
      if (err) return next(err);
      var path = join(dir, photo.path);           <- Construct absolute path to file
      res.sendfile(path);            <- Transfer file
    });
  };
};
```

If you fire up the application, you should now be able to click the photos when you're authenticated.

The result you get may not be what you'd expected. With `res.sendfile()`, the data is transferred and interpreted by the browser. In the case of images, the browser will display them within the window, as shown in figure 8.19. Next we'll look at `res.download()`, which will prompt the browser for download.

Figure 8.19 Photo transferred with `res.sendfile()`

SENDFILE CALLBACK ARGUMENT A callback can also be provided as the second or third argument (when using options) to notify the application when a download is complete. For example, you could use a callback to decrement a user's download credits.

TRIGGER A BROWSER DOWNLOAD

Replacing `res.sendfile()` with `res.download()` will alter the behavior of browsers when files are transferred. The `Content-Disposition` header field will be set to the file's name, and the browser will prompt for download accordingly.

Figure 8.20 shows how the original image's name (littlenice_by_dhor.jpeg) was used as the downloaded file's name. Depending on your application, this might not be ideal.

Let's look at `res.download()`'s optional filename argument next.

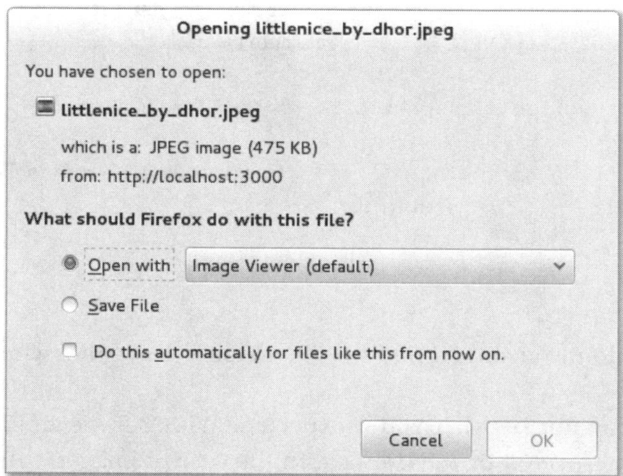

Figure 8.20 Photo transferred with `res.download()`

SETTING A DOWNLOAD'S FILENAME

The second argument of `res.download()` allows you to define a custom name to be used when downloading rather than defaulting to the original filename. Listing 8.21 changes the previous implementation to provide the name given when the photo was uploaded, such as Flower.jpeg.

Listing 8.21 Photo download route with explicit filename

```
...
var path = join(dir, photo.path);
res.download(path, photo.name+'.jpeg');
...
```

If you fire up the application and try clicking a photo now, you should be prompted to download it, as shown in figure 8.21.

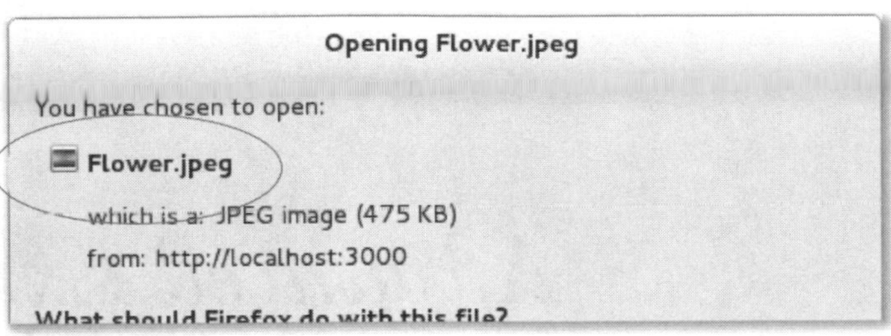

Figure 8.21 Photo transferred with `res.download()` and a custom filename

8.6 Summary

In this chapter, you learned how to create an Express application from scratch and how to deal with common web development tasks.

You learned how a typical Express application's directories are structured and how to use environmental variables and the `app.configure` method to change application behavior for different environments.

The most basic components of Express applications are routes and views. You learned how to render views and how to expose data to them by setting `app.locals` and `res.locals` and by passing values directly using `res.render()`. You also learned how basic routing works.

In the next chapter, we'll go into more advanced things you can do with Express, such as using authentication, routing, middleware, and REST APIs.

9 Advanced Express

This chapter covers

- Implementing authentication
- URL routing
- Creating a REST API
- Handling errors

In this chapter, you'll learn a number of advanced Express techniques that will enable you to take more advantage of the framework's functionality.

To demonstrate these techniques, you'll create a simple application that allows people to register and post public messages that are displayed, in reverse chronological order, for visitors to see. This type of application is known as a "shoutbox" application. Figure 9.1 shows the front and user registration pages. Figure 9.2 shows the login and post pages.

For this application, you'll add logic to do the following:

- Authenticate users
- Implement validation and pagination
- Provide a public representational state transfer (REST) API to send and receive messages

Let's dive in by leveraging Express for user authentication.

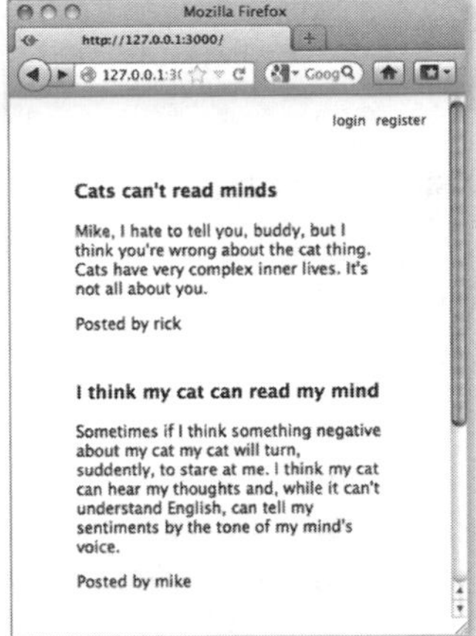

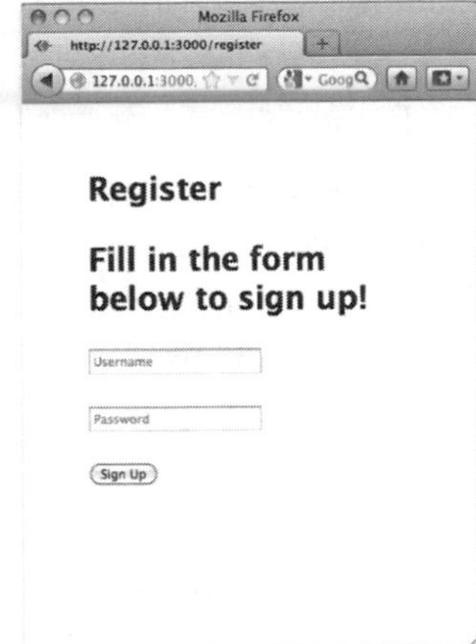

Figure 9.1 The front and registration pages of the shoutbox application

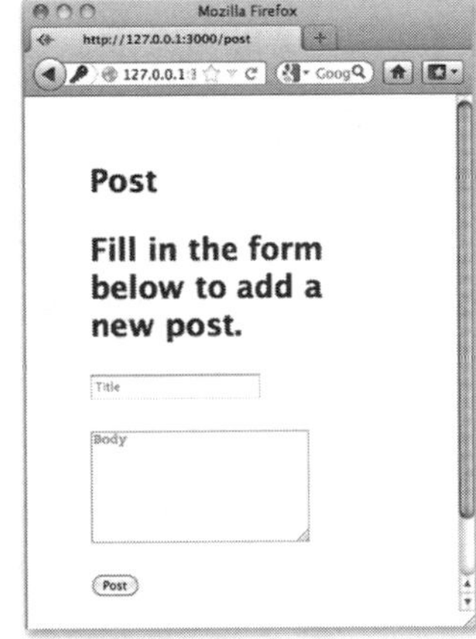

Figure 9.2 The login and post pages of the shoutbox application

9.1 Authenticating users

In this section you'll start working on the shoutbox application by creating an authentication system for it from scratch. Within this section you'll implement the following:

- Logic to store and authenticate registered users
- Registration functionality
- Login functionality
- Middleware to load user information, on request, for logged-in users

For user authentication, you'll need some way to store the data. For this application you'll be using Redis, which you learned about in section 5.3.1. It's a quick install and has a minimal learning curve, which makes it a good candidate since we're focusing on application logic, not the database layer. The database interaction within this chapter translates well to nearly every database available, so if you're feeling adventurous you may want to replace Redis with your favorite database. Let's create a `User` model.

9.1.1 Saving and loading users

In this section you'll follow a series of steps to implement user loading, saving, and authentication. You'll do the following:

- Define application dependencies using a package.json file
- Create a user model
- Add logic to load and save user data using Redis
- Secure user passwords using bcrypt
- Add logic to authenticate attempts to log in

Bcrypt is a salted hashing function that's available as a third-party module designed specifically for hashing passwords. Bcrypt is great for passwords because as computers get faster and faster, bcrypt can be made slower to effectively eliminate brute-force attacks.

CREATING A PACKAGE.JSON FILE

To create an application skeleton with support for EJS and sessions, start a command-line session, change to a development directory, and enter `express -e -s shoutbox`. You used the `-e` flag in the previous chapter to enable EJS support in app.js. The `-s` flag similarly enables sessions support.

With the application skeleton created, change to the shoutbox directory. Next, modify the package.json file, which specifies dependencies, to include a couple of additional modules. Change the package.json file so it looks like the contents of the next listing.

Listing 9.1 A package.json file with additional bcrypt and Redis dependencies

```
{
  "name": "shoutbox",
  "version": "0.0.1",
  "private": true,
  "scripts": {
    "start": "node app"
  },
  "dependencies": {
    "express": "3.x",
    "ejs": "*",
    "bcrypt": "0.7.3",
    "redis": "0.7.2"
  }
}
```

To install the dependencies, enter `npm install`. This will install them to ./node_modules.

Finally, execute the following command to create an empty EJS template file that you'll define later. As this template file is included by other template files, you'll get errors if you don't precreate it:

```
touch views/menu.ejs
```

With the application skeleton set up and dependencies installed, you can now define the application's user model.

Creating a user model

You now need to create a lib directory and, within that, a file named user.js. You'll put the code for the user model in this file.

Listing 9.2 specifies the first logic you'll want to add. In this code, the `redis` and `bcrypt` dependencies are required, and then a Redis connection is opened with `redis.createClient()`. The `User` function accepts an object and merges this object's properties into its own. For example, `new User({ name: 'Tobi' })` creates an object and sets the object's `name` property to `Tobi`.

Listing 9.2 Starting to create a user model

```
var redis = require('redis');
var bcrypt = require('bcrypt');
var db = redis.createClient();          <-- Create long-running Redis connection

module.exports = User;                  <-- Export User function from the module

function User(obj) {
  for (var key in obj) {                <-- Iterate keys in the object passed
    this[key] = obj[key];               <-- Merge values
  }
}
```

Saving a user into Redis

The next functionality you'll need is the ability to save a user, storing their data with Redis. The `save()` method shown in listing 9.3 checks if the user already has an ID, and if so it invokes the `update()` method, indexing the user ID by name, and populating a Redis hash with the object's properties. Otherwise, if the user doesn't have an ID, they're considered a new user, the `user:ids` value is incremented, which gives the user a unique ID, and the password is hashed before saving into Redis with the same `update()` method.

Add the code in the following listing to lib/user.js.

Listing 9.3 The user model's save implementation

```
User.prototype.save = function(fn){
  if (this.id) {                                  <-- User already exists
    this.update(fn);
  } else {
    var user = this;
    db.incr('user:ids', function(err, id){         <-- Create unique ID
      if (err) return fn(err);
      user.id = id;                                <-- Set ID so it'll be saved
      user.hashPassword(function(err){             <-- Hash password
        if (err) return fn(err);
        user.update(fn);                           <-- Save user properties
      });
    });
```

```
  }
};

User.prototype.update = function(fn){
  var user = this;
  var id = user.id;
  db.set('user:id:' + user.name, id, function(err) {    <-- Index user ID by name
    if (err) return fn(err);
    db.hmset('user:' + id, user, function(err) {    <-- Use Redis hash to store data
      fn(err);
    });
  });
};
```

SECURING USER PASSWORDS

When the user is first created, it'll need to have a `.pass` property set to the user's password. The user-saving logic will then replace the `.pass` property with a hash generated using the password.

The hash will be *salted*. Per-user salting helps to protect against rainbow table attacks: the salt acts as a private key for the hashing mechanism. You can use bcrypt to generate a 12-character salt for the hash with `genSalt()`.

> **RAINBOW TABLE ATTACKS** Rainbow table attacks use precomputed tables to break hashed passwords. You can read more about it in the Wikipedia article: http://en.wikipedia.org/wiki/Rainbow_table.

After the salt is generated, `bcrypt.hash()` is called, which hashes the `.pass` property and the salt. This final `hash` value then replaces the `.pass` property before `.update()` stores it in Redis, ensuring that plain-text passwords aren't saved, only the hash.

The following listing, which you'll add to lib/user.js, defines a function that creates the salted hash and stores it in the user's `.pass` property.

Listing 9.4 Adding bcrypt encryption support to the user model

```
User.prototype.hashPassword = function(fn){
  var user = this;
  bcrypt.genSalt(12, function(err, salt){    <-- Generate a 12-character salt
    if (err) return fn(err);
    user.salt = salt;    <-- Set salt so it'll be saved
    bcrypt.hash(user.pass, salt, function(err, hash){    <-- Generate hash
      if (err) return fn(err);
      user.pass = hash;    <-- Set hash so it'll be saved
      fn();
    });
  });
};
```

That's all there is to it.

TESTING THE USER-SAVING LOGIC

To try it out, start the Redis server by entering `redis-server` on the command line. Then add the code in listing 9.5, which will create an example user, to the bottom of lib/user.js. You can then run `node lib/user` on the command line to create the example user.

Listing 9.5 Testing the user model

```
var tobi = new User({                          <— Create new user
  name: 'Tobi',
  pass: 'im a ferret',
  age: '2'
});

tobi.save(function(err){                       <— Save user
  if (err) throw err;
  console.log('user id %d', tobi.id);
});
```

You should see output indicating that the user has been created: `user id 1`, for example. After testing the user model, remove the code in listing 9.5 from lib/user.js.

When you use the redis-cli tool that comes with Redis, you can use the `HGETALL` command to fetch each key and value of the hash, as the following command-line session demonstrates.

Listing 9.6 Using the redis-cli tool to examine stored data

```
$ redis-cli                     <— Starting the Redis command line
redis> get user:ids             <— Finding out the ID of the most recently created user
"1"
redis> hgetall user:1           <— Retrieving data in a hash map item
 1) "name"                      <— Properties of a hash map item
 2) "Tobi"
 3) "pass"
 4) "$2a$12$BAOWThTAkNjY7Uht0UdBku46eDGpKpK5iJcf0eLW08sMcfPL7.PN."
 5) "age"
 6) "2"
 7) "id"
 8) "4"
 9) "salt"
10) "$2a$12$BAOWThTAkNjY7Uht0UdBku"
redis> quit                     <— Quitting the Redis command line
```

Having defined logic to save a user, you'll now need to add logic to retrieve user information.

> **OTHER REDIS COMMANDS YOU CAN RUN IN THE REDIS-CLI TOOL** For more information about Redis commands, see the Redis command reference at http://redis.io/commands.

RETRIEVING USER DATA

When a user attempts to log in to a web application, they'll usually enter a username and password into a form, and this data is then submitted to the application for authentication. Once the login form is submitted, you'll need a method for fetching the user via name.

This logic is defined in the following listing as `User.getByName()`. The function first does an ID lookup with `User.getId()` and then passes the ID that it finds to `User.get()`, which gets the Redis hash data for that user. Add the following logic to lib/user.js.

Listing 9.7 Fetching a user from Redis

```
User.getByName = function(name, fn){
  User.getId(name, function(err, id){      // Look up user ID by name
    if (err) return fn(err);
    User.get(id, fn);                      // Grab user with the ID
  });
};

User.getId = function(name, fn){
  db.get('user:id:' + name, fn);           // Get ID indexed by name
};

User.get = function(id, fn){
  db.hgetall('user:' + id, function(err, user){   // Fetch plain-object hash
    if (err) return fn(err);
    fn(null, new User(user));              // Convert plain object to a new User object
  });
};
```

Having retrieved the hashed password, you can now proceed with authenticating the user.

AUTHENTICATING USER LOGINS

The final component needed for user authentication is a method, defined in the following listing, that takes advantage of the functions defined earlier for user data retrieval. Add this logic to lib/user.js.

Listing 9.8 Authenticating a user's name and password

```
User.authenticate = function(name, pass, fn){
  User.getByName(name, function(err, user){              // Look up user by name
    if (err) return fn(err);
    if (!user.id) return fn();                           // User doesn't exist
    bcrypt.hash(pass, user.salt, function(err, hash){    // Hash the given password
      if (err) return fn(err);
      if (hash == user.pass) return fn(null, user);      // Match found
      fn();                                              // Invalid password
    });
  });
};
```

The authentication logic begins by fetching the user by name. If the user isn't found, the callback function is immediately invoked. Otherwise, the user's stored salt and the password submitted are hashed to produce what should be identical to the stored `user.pass` hash. If the submitted and stored hashes don't match, the user has entered invalid credentials. When looking up a key that doesn't exist, Redis will give you an empty hash, which is why the check for `!user.id` is used instead of `!user`.

Now that you're able to authenticate users, you'll need a way for users to register.

9.1.2 Registering new users

To allow users to create new accounts and then sign in, you'll need both registration and login capabilities.

In this section, you'll do the following to implement registration:

- Map registration and login routes to URL paths
- Add route logic to display a registration form
- Add logic to store user data submitted from the form

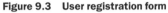

Figure 9.3 User registration form

The form will look like figure 9.3.

This form will be displayed when a user visits /register with a web browser. Later you'll create a similar form that will allow users to log in.

Adding registration routes

To get the registration form to show up, you'll first want to create a route to render the form and return it to the user's browser for display.

Listing 9.9 shows how you should alter app.js, using Node's module system to import a module defining registration route behavior from the routes directory and associating HTTP methods and URL paths to route functions. This forms a sort of "front controller." As you can see, there will be both `GET` and `POST` register routes.

Listing 9.9 Adding registration routes

```
...
var register = require('./routes/register');          <-- Requiring route logic
...
app.get('/register', register.form);           <-- Adding routes
app.post('/register', register.submit);
```

Next, to define the route logic, create an empty file in the routes directory called register.js. Start defining registration route behavior by exporting the following function from routes/register.js—a route that renders the registration template:

```
exports.form = function(req, res){
  res.render('register', { title: 'Register' });
};
```

This route uses an Embedded JavaScript (EJS) template, which you'll create next, to define the registration form HTML.

CREATING A REGISTRATION FORM

To define the registration form's HTML, create a file in the views directory called register.ejs. You can define this form using the HTML/EJS detailed in the following listing.

Listing 9.10 A view template that provides a registration form

```
<!DOCTYPE html>
<html>
  <head>
    <title><%= title %></title>
    <link rel='stylesheet' href='/stylesheets/style.css' />
  </head>
  <body>
    <% include menu %>                                         <-- Navigation links will be added later

    <h1><%= title %></h1>
    <p>Fill in the form below to sign up!</p>

    <% include messages %>                                     <-- Display of messages will be added later

    <form action='/register' method='post'>
      <p>
        <input type='text' name='user[name]' placeholder='Username' />   <-- User must enter a username
      </p>
      <p>
        <input type='password' name='user[pass]'
        ➥ placeholder='Password' />                           <-- User must enter a password
      </p>
      <p>
        <input type='submit' value='Sign Up' />
      </p>
    </form>
  </body>
</html>
```

Note the use of `include messages`, which literally includes another template: messages.ejs. This template, which you'll define next, is used to communicate with the user.

RELAYING FEEDBACK TO USERS

During user registration, and in many other parts of a typical application, it can be necessary to relay feedback to the user. A user, for example, may attempt to register with a username that someone else is already using. In this case, you'll need to let the user know they must choose another name.

In your application, the messages.ejs template will be used to display errors. A number of templates throughout the application will include the messages.ejs template.

To create the messages template, create a file in the views directory called messages.ejs and put the logic in the following snippet into it. The template logic checks if the `locals.messages` variable is set, and, if so, the template cycles through the variable displaying message objects. Each message object has a `type` property (allowing you to use messages for non-error notifications if need be) and a `string` property (the message text). Application logic can queue an error for display by adding to the `res.locals.messages` array. After messages are displayed, `removeMessages` is called to empty the messages queue:

```
<% if (locals.messages) { %>
  <% messages.forEach(function(message) { %>
    <p class='<%= message.type %>'><%= message.string %></p>
  <% }) %>
  <% removeMessages() %>
<% } %>
```

Figure 9.4 shows how the registration form will look when displaying an error message.

Adding a message to `res.locals.messages` is a simple way to communicate with the user, but as `res.locals` doesn't persist across redirects, you need to make it more robust by storing messages between requests using sessions.

Figure 9.4 Registration form error reporting

STORING TRANSIENT MESSAGES IN SESSIONS

A common web application design pattern is the Post/Redirect/Get (PRG) pattern. In this pattern, a user requests a form, the form data is submitted as an HTTP `POST` request, and the user is then redirected to another web page. Where the user is redirected to depends on whether the form data was considered valid by the application. If the form data isn't considered valid, the application redirects the user back to the form page. If the form data is valid, the user is redirected to a new web page. The PRG pattern is primarily used to prevent duplicate form submissions.

In Express, when a user is redirected, the contents of `res.locals` are reset. If you're storing messages to the user in `res.locals`, the messages are lost before they can be displayed. By storing messages in a session variable, however, you can work around this. Messages can then be displayed on the final redirect page.

To accommodate the ability to queue messages to the user in a session variable, you need to add an additional module to your application. Create a file named ./lib/messages.js and add the following code:

```
var express = require('express');
var res = express.response;

res.message = function(msg, type){
  type = type || 'info';
  var sess = this.req.session;
  sess.messages = sess.messages || [];
  sess.messages.push({ type: type, string: msg });
};
```

The `res.message` function provides a way to add messages to a session variable from any Express request. The `express.response` object is the prototype that Express uses for the response objects. Adding properties to this object means they'll then be available to all middleware and routes alike. In the preceding snippet, `express.response` is assigned to a variable named `res` to make it easier to add properties on the object and to improve readability.

To made it even easier to add messages, add the code in the following snippet. The `res.error` function allows you to easily add a message of type `error` to the message queue. It leverages the `res.message` function you previously defined in the module:

```
res.error = function(msg){
  return this.message(msg, 'error');
};
```

The last step is to expose these messages to the templates for output. If you don't do this, you'd have to pass `req.session.messages` to every `res.render()` call in the application, which isn't exactly ideal.

To address this, you'll create middleware that will populate `res.locals.messages` with the contents of `res.session.messages` on each request, effectively exposing the messages to any templates that are rendered. So far, ./lib/messages.js extends the response prototype, but it doesn't export anything. Adding the following snippet to this file, however, will export the middleware you need:

```
module.exports = function(req, res, next){
  res.locals.messages = req.session.messages || [];
  res.locals.removeMessages = function(){
    req.session.messages = [];
  };
  next();
};
```

First, a `messages` template variable is defined to store the session's messages—it's an array that may or may not exist from the previous request (remember that these are session-persisted messages). Next, you'll need a way to remove the messages from the session; otherwise they'll build up, because nothing is clearing them.

Now, all you need to do to integrate this new feature is to `require()` the file in app.js. You should mount this middleware below the session middleware because it depends on `req.session` being defined. Note that because this middleware was designed not to accept options and doesn't return a second function, you can call `app.use(messages)` instead of `app.use(messages())`. For future-proofing, it's typically best for third-party middleware to use `app.use(messages())` regardless of whether or not it accepts options:

```
...
var register = require('./routes/register');
var messages = require('./lib/messages');
...

app.use(express.methodOverride());
app.use(express.cookieParser('your secret here'));
app.use(express.session());
app.use(messages);
...
```

Now you're able to access `messages` and `removeMessages()` within any view, so messages.ejs should work perfectly when included in any template.

With the display of the registration form completed and a way to relay any necessary feedback to the user worked out, let's move on to handling registration submissions.

IMPLEMENTING USER REGISTRATION

Now that the registration form is defined and you've added a way to relay feedback to the user, you need to create the route function that will handle HTTP `POST` requests to /register. This function will be called `submit`.

As discussed in chapter 7, when form data is submitted, the `bodyParser()` middleware will populate `req.body` with the submitted data. The registration form uses the object notation `user[name]`, which translates to `req.body.user.name` once parsed by Connect. Likewise, `req.body.user.pass` is used for the password field.

You need only a small amount of code in the submission route to handle validation, such as ensuring the username isn't already taken, and to save the new user, as listing 9.11 shows.

Once registration is complete, the `user.id` is assigned to the user's session, which you'll later check to verify that the user is authenticated. If validation fails, a message is exposed to templates as the `messages` variable, via `res.locals.messages`, and the user is redirected back to the registration form.

To add this functionality, add the contents of the following listing to routes/register.js.

Listing 9.11 Creating a user with submitted data

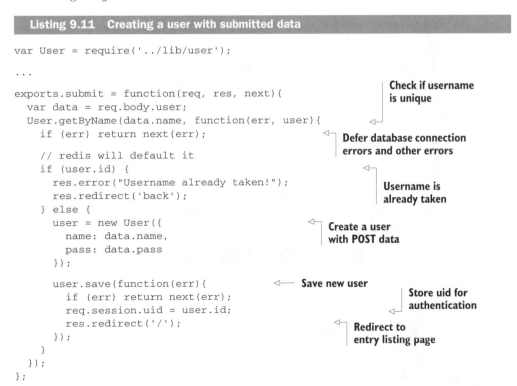

```
var User = require('../lib/user');

...

exports.submit = function(req, res, next){
  var data = req.body.user;
  User.getByName(data.name, function(err, user){     <-- Check if username is unique
    if (err) return next(err);                       <-- Defer database connection errors and other errors

    // redis will default it
    if (user.id) {                                   <-- Username is already taken
      res.error("Username already taken!");
      res.redirect('back');
    } else {
      user = new User({                              <-- Create a user with POST data
        name: data.name,
        pass: data.pass
      });

      user.save(function(err){                       <-- Save new user
        if (err) return next(err);
        req.session.uid = user.id;                   <-- Store uid for authentication
        res.redirect('/');                           <-- Redirect to entry listing page
      });
    }
  });
};
```

You can now fire up the application, visit /register, and register a user. The next thing you'll need is a way for returning registered users to authenticate, via the /login form.

9.1.3 *Logging in registered users*

Adding login functionality is even simpler than registration because the bulk of the necessary logic is already in `User.authenticate()`, the general-purpose authentication method defined earlier.

In this section you'll add the following:

- Route logic to display a login form
- Logic to authenticate user data submitted from the form

Figure 9.5 User login form

The form will look like figure 9.5.

Let's start by modifying app.js so login routes are required and the route paths are established:

```
...
var login = require('./routes/login');
...
app.get('/login', login.form);
app.post('/login', login.submit);
app.get('/logout', login.logout);
...
```

Next, you'll add functionality to display a login form.

DISPLAYING A LOGIN FORM

The first step in implementing a login form is creating a file for login- and logout-related routes: routes/login.js. The route logic you'll need to add to display the login form is nearly identical to the logic used earlier to display the registration form; the only differences are the name of the template displayed and the page title:

```
exports.form = function(req, res){
  res.render('login', { title: 'Login' });
};
```

The EJS login form that you'll define in ./views/login.ejs, shown in listing 9.12, is extremely similar to register.ejs as well; the only differences are the instruction text and the route that data is submitted to.

Listing 9.12 A view template for a login form

```
<!DOCTYPE html>
<html>
  <head>
    <title><%= title %></title>
    <link rel='stylesheet' href='/stylesheets/style.css' />
  </head>
  <body>
```

```
    <% include menu %>
    <h1><%= title %></h1>
    <p>Fill in the form below to sign in!</p>

    <% include messages %>

    <form action='/login' method='post'>
      <p>
        <input type='text' name='user[name]' placeholder='Username' />    <- User must enter a username
      </p>
      <p>
        <input type='password' name='user[pass]'
        ➥ placeholder='Password' />    <- User must enter a password
      </p>
      <p>
        <input type='submit' value='Login' />
      </p>
    </form>
  </body>
</html>
```

Now that you've added the route and template needed to display the login form, the next step is to add logic to handle login attempts.

AUTHENTICATING LOGINS

To handle login attempts, you need to add route logic that will check the submitted username and password and, if they're correct, set a session variable to the user's ID and redirect the user to the home page. The following listing contains this logic, and you should add it to routes/login.js.

Listing 9.13 A route to handle logins

```
var User = require('../lib/user');

...

exports.submit = function(req, res, next){
  var data = req.body.user;
  User.authenticate(data.name, data.pass, function(err, user){    <- Check credentials
    if (err) return next(err);    <- Delegate errors
    if (user) {    <- Handle a user with valid credentials
      req.session.uid = user.id;    <- Store uid for authentication
      res.redirect('/');    <- Redirect to entry listing
    } else {
      res.error("Sorry! invalid credentials.");    <- Expose an error message
      res.redirect('back');    <- Redirect back to login form
    }
  });
};
```

In listing 9.13, if the user is authenticated using `User.authenticate()`, `req.session.uid` is assigned in the same way as in the `POST` /register route: the session will persist this value, which you can use later to retrieve the `User` or other associated user data. If a match isn't found, an error is set and the form is redisplayed.

Users may also prefer to explicitly log out, so you should provide a link for this somewhere in the application. In app.js, you assigned `app.get('/logout', login.logout)`, so in ./routes/login.js the following function will remove the session, which is detected by the `session()` middleware, causing the session to be assigned for subsequent requests:

```
exports.logout = function(req, res){
  req.session.destroy(function(err) {
    if (err) throw err;
    res.redirect('/');
  })
};
```

Now that the registration and login pages have been created, the next thing you need to add is a menu so users can reach them. Let's create one.

CREATING A MENU FOR AUTHENTICATED AND ANONYMOUS USERS

In this section, you'll create a menu for both anonymous and authenticated users, allowing them to sign in, register, submit entries, and log out. Figure 9.6 shows the menu for an anonymous user.

Figure 9.6 User login and registration menu used to access the forms you created

When the user is authenticated, you'll display a different menu showing their username, as well as a link to a page for posting messages to the shoutbox and a link allowing the user to log out. This menu is shown in figure 9.7.

Figure 9.7 Menu when the user is authenticated

Each EJS template you've created, representing an application page, has contained the code `<% include menu %>` after the <body> tag. This includes the ./views/menu.ejs template, which you'll create next with the contents of the following listing.

Listing 9.14 Anonymous and authenticated user menu template

```
<% if (locals.user) { %>
  <div id='menu'>                                    <-- Menu for logged-in users
    <span class='name'><%= user.name %></span>
```

```
    <a href='/post'>post</a>
    <a href='/logout'>logout</a>
  </div>
<% } else { %>
  <div id='menu'>                              <-- Menu for anonymous users
    <a href='/login'>login</a>
    <a href='/register'>register</a>
  </div>
<% } %>
```

In this application, you can assume that if a `user` variable is exposed to the template, that a user is authenticated, because you won't be exposing the variable otherwise; you'll see this next. That means that when this variable is present, you can display the username along with the entry submission and logout links. When an anonymous user is visiting, the site login and register links are displayed.

You may be wondering where this `user` local variable comes from—you haven't written it yet. Next you'll write some code to load the logged-in user's data for each request and make this data available to templates.

9.1.4 User-loading middleware

A common task when you work with a web application is loading user information from a database, typically represented as a JavaScript object. Having this data readily available makes interacting with the user simpler. For this chapter's application you'll load the user data on every request, using middleware.

This middleware script will be placed in ./lib/middleware/user.js, requiring the `User` model from the directory above (./lib). The middleware function is first exported, and then it checks the session for the user ID. When the user ID is present, a user is authenticated, so it's safe to fetch the user data from Redis.

Because Node is single-threaded, there's no thread-local storage. In the case of an HTTP server, the request and response variables are the only contextual objects available. High-level frameworks could build upon Node to provide additional objects to store things like the authenticated user, but Express made the choice to stick with the original objects that Node provides. As a result, contextual data is typically stored on the request object, as shown in listing 9.15 where the user is stored as `req.user`; subsequent middleware and routes can access it using the same property.

You may wonder what the assignment to `res.locals.user` is for. `res.locals` is the request-level object that Express provides to expose data to templates, much like `app.locals`. It's also a function that can be used to merge existing objects into itself.

Listing 9.15 Middleware that loads a logged-in user's data

```
var User = require('../user');

module.exports = function(req, res, next){
  var uid = req.session.uid;                   <-- Get logged-in user ID from session
  if (!uid) return next();
  User.get(uid, function(err, user){           <-- Get logged-in user's data from Redis
    if (err) return next(err);
```

```
    req.user = res.locals.user = user;     <-- Expose user data to
    next();                                     response object
  });
};
```

To use this new middleware, first delete all lines in app.js containing the text "user." You can then require the module as usual, and then pass it to `app.use()`. In this application, `user` is used above the router, so only the routes and middleware following `user` will have access to `req.user`. If you're using middleware that loads data, as this middleware does, you may want to move the `express.static` middleware above it; otherwise each time a static file is served, a needless round trip to the database will have taken place to fetch the user.

The following listing shows how you can enable this middleware in app.js.

Listing 9.16 Enabling user-loading middleware

```
var user = require('./lib/middleware/user');

...
app.use(express.session());
app.use(express.static(__dirname + '/public'));
app.use(user);                          <-- Adds the middleware
app.use(messages);                          to the application
app.use(app.router);
...
```

If you fire up the application again and visit either the /login or /register pages in your browser, you should see the menu. If you'd like to style the menu, add the following lines of CSS to public/stylesheets/style.css.

Listing 9.17 CSS that can be added to style.css to style application menus

```
#menu {
  position: absolute;
  top: 15px;
  right: 20px;
  font-size: 12px;
  color: #888;
}

#menu .name:after {
  content: ' -';
}

#menu a {
  text-decoration: none;
  margin-left: 5px;
  color: black;
}
```

With the menu in place, you should be able to register yourself as a user. Once you've registered a user, you should see the authenticated user menu with the Post link.

In the next section, you'll learn advanced routing techniques while adding the functionality for posting shoutbox messages.

9.2 Advanced routing techniques

The primary function of Express routes is to pair a URL pattern with response logic. Routes can also, however, pair a URL pattern with middleware. This allows you to use middleware to provide reusable functionality to certain routes.

In this section, you'll do the following:

- Validate user-submitted content using route-specific middleware
- Implement route-specific validation
- Implement pagination

Let's explore some of the various ways you can leverage route-specific middleware.

9.2.1 Validating user content submission

To give you something to apply validation to, let's finally add the ability to post to the shoutbox application. To add the ability to post, you'll need to do a few things:

- Create an entry model
- Add entry-related routes
- Create an entry form
- Add logic to create entries using submitted form data

You'll start by creating an entry model.

CREATING AN ENTRY MODEL

Create a file to contain the entry model definition at lib/entry.js. Add the code contained in the following listing to this file. The entry model will be quite similar to the user model created earlier, except it will save data in a Redis list.

Listing 9.18 A model for entries

```
var redis = require('redis');
var db = redis.createClient();                  <— Instantiate Redis client

module.exports = Entry;                         <— Export Entry function from the module

function Entry(obj) {                           Iterate keys in the object passed
  for (var key in obj) {
    this[key] = obj[key];                       <— Merge values
  }
}

Entry.prototype.save = function(fn){            Convert saved entry data to JSON string
  var entryJSON = JSON.stringify(this);

  db.lpush(                                     <— Save JSON string to Redis list
    'entries',
    entryJSON,
    function(err) {
      if (err) return fn(err);
      fn();
    }
  );
};
```

With the basic model fleshed out, you now need to add a function called `getRange`, using the contents of the following listing. This function will allow you to retrieve entries.

Listing 9.19 Logic to retrieve a range of entries

```
Entry.getRange = function(from, to, fn){
  db.lrange('entries', from, to, function(err, items){     <-- Redis lrange function is used to retrieve entries
    if (err) return fn(err);
    var entries = [];

    items.forEach(function(item){
      entries.push(JSON.parse(item));     <-- Decode entries previously stored as JSON
    });

    fn(null, entries);
  });
};
```

With a model created, you can now add routes to list and create entries.

ADDING ENTRY-RELATED ROUTES

Before you add entry-related routes to the application, you'll need to make some modifications to app.js. First, add the following require statement to the top of your app.js file:

```
var entries = require('./routes/entries');
```

Next, also in app.js, change the line containing the text `app.get('/'` to the following to make any requests to the path / return the entry listing:

```
app.get('/', entries.list);
```

You can now begin adding routing logic.

ADDING FRONT-PAGE DISPLAY OF ENTRIES

Start by creating the file routes/entries.js and add the code in the following listing to require the entry model and export a function for rendering a list of entries.

Listing 9.20 Listing entries

```
var Entry = require('../lib/entry');

exports.list = function(req, res, next){
  Entry.getRange(0, -1, function(err, entries) {     <-- Retrieve entries
    if (err) return next(err);

    res.render('entries', {     <-- Render HTTP response
      title: 'Entries',
      entries: entries,
    });
  });
};
```

With route logic defined for listing entries, you now need to add an EJS template to display them. In the views directory, create a file named entries.ejs and put the following EJS in it.

Listing 9.21 Modified entries.ejs including pagination

```
<!DOCTYPE html>
<html>
  <head>
    <title><%= title %></title>
    <link rel='stylesheet' href='/stylesheets/style.css' />
  </head>
  <body>
    <% include menu %>

    <% entries.forEach(function(entry) { %>
      <div class='entry'>
        <h3><%= entry.title %></h3>
        <p><%= entry.body %></p>
        <p>Posted by <%= entry.username %></p>
      </div>
    <% }) %>
  </body>
</html>
```

Now, when you run the application, the front page will display a list of entries. As no entries have yet been created, however, let's move on to adding the necessary components to create some.

CREATING AN ENTRY FORM

Now you have the ability to list entries, but no way to add them. You'll add this capability next, starting by adding the following lines to the routing section of app.js:

```
app.get('/post', entries.form);
app.post('/post', entries.submit);
```

Next, add the following route to routes/entries.js. This route logic will render a template containing a form:

```
exports.form = function(req, res){
  res.render('post', { title: 'Post' });
};
```

Next, use the EJS template in the following listing to create a template for the form and save it to views/post.ejs.

Listing 9.22 A form into which post data can be entered

```
<!DOCTYPE html>
<html>
  <head>
    <title><%= title %></title>
    <link rel='stylesheet' href='/stylesheets/style.css' />
  </head>
```

```
  <body>
    <% include menu %>

    <h1><%= title %></h1>
    <p>Fill in the form below to add a new post.</p>

    <% include messages %>

    <form action='/post' method='post'>
      <p>
        <input type='text' name='entry[title]' placeholder='Title' />
      </p>
      <p>
        <textarea name='entry[body]' placeholder='Body'></textarea>
      </p>
      <p>
        <input type='submit' value='Post' />
      </p>
    </form>
  </body>
</html>
```

Entry title text

Entry body text

With form display taken care of, let's move on to creating entries from the submitted form data.

Implementing entry creation

To add the capability to create entries from submitted form data, add the logic in the next listing to the file routes/entries.js. This logic will add entries when form data is submitted.

Listing 9.23 Add an entry using submitted form data

```
exports.submit = function(req, res, next){
  var data  = req.body.entry;

  var entry = new Entry({
    "username": res.locals.user.name,
    "title": data.title,
    "body": data.body
  });

  entry.save(function(err) {
    if (err) return next(err);
    res.redirect('/');
  });
};
```

Now when you use a browser to access /post on your application, you'll be able to add entries if you're logged in.

With that taken care of, let's move on to route-specific middleware and how you can use it to validate form data.

9.2.2 *Route-specific middleware*

Suppose you want the entry text field in the post entry form to be required. The first way you might think of to address this problem is to simply add it straight in your route callback, as shown in the following snippet. This approach isn't ideal, however, because it tightly ties the validation logic to this particular form. In many cases validation logic can be abstracted into reusable components, making development easier, faster, and more declarative:

```
...
exports.submit = function(req, res, next){
  var data  = req.body.entry;

  if (!data.title) {
    res.error("Title is required.");
    res.redirect('back');
    return;
  }

  if (data.title.length < 4) {
    res.error("Title must be longer than 4 characters.");
    res.redirect('back');
    return;
  }
...
```

Express routes can optionally accept middleware of their own, applied only when that route is matched, before the final route callback. The route callbacks themselves that you've been using throughout the chapter aren't treated specially. These are the same as any other middleware, even the ones you're about to create for validation!

Let's get started with route-specific middleware by looking at a simple, but inflexible, way to implement validation as route-specific middleware.

FORM VALIDATION USING ROUTE-SPECIFIC MIDDLEWARE

The first possibility is to write a few simple, yet specific, middleware components to perform validation. Extending the `POST` /post route with this middleware might look something like the following:

```
app.post('/post',
  requireEntryTitle,
  requireEntryTitleLengthAbove(4),
  entries.submit
);
```

Note in the previous snippet that the route definition, which normally has only a path and routing logic as arguments, has two additional arguments specifying validation middleware.

The two example middleware components in the following listing illustrate how the original validations can be abstracted out. But they're still not very modular and only work for the single field `entry[title]`.

Listing 9.24 Two more potential, but imperfect, attempts at validation middleware

```
function requireEntryTitle(req, res, next) {
  var title = req.body.entry.title;
  if (title) {
    next();
  } else {
    res.error("Title is required.");
    res.redirect('back');
  }
}

function requireEntryTitleLengthAbove(len) {
  return function(req, res, next) {
    var title = req.body.entry.title;
    if (title.length > len) {
      next();
    } else {
      res.error("Title must be longer than " + len);
      res.redirect('back');
    }
  }
}
```

A more viable solution would be to abstract the validators and pass the target field name. Let's take a look at approaching it this way.

BUILDING FLEXIBLE VALIDATION MIDDLEWARE

You can pass the field name, as shown in the following snippet. This allows you to reuse validation logic, lessening the amount of code you need to write.

```
app.post('/post',
          validate.required('entry[title]'),
          validate.lengthAbove('entry[title]', 4),
          entries.submit);
```

Swap the line `app.post('/post', entries.submit);` in the routing section of app.js with this snippet. It's worth noting that the Express community has created many similar libraries for public consumption, but understanding how validation middleware works, and how to author your own, is invaluable.

So let's get on with it. Create a file named ./lib/middleware/validate.js using the program code in the next listing. In it you'll export several middleware components—in this case, `validate.required()` and `validate.lengthAbove()`. The implementation details here aren't important; the point of this example is that a small amount of effort can go a long way if the code is common within the application.

Listing 9.25 Validation middleware implementation

```
function parseField(field) {              <-- Parse entry[name] notation
  return field
    .split(/\[|\]/)
    .filter(function(s){ return s });
}
```

```
function getField(req, field) {          <- Look up property based
  var val = req.body;                       on parseField() results
  field.forEach(function(prop){
    val = val[prop];
  });
  return val;
}

exports.required = function(field){
  field = parseField(field);              <- Parse field once
  return function(req, res, next){
    if (getField(req, field)) {           <- On each request, check if field has a value
      next();                             <- If it does, move on to next middleware component
    } else {
      res.error(field.join(' ') + ' is required');    <- If it doesn't, display an error
      res.redirect('back');
    }
  }
};

exports.lengthAbove = function(field, len){
  field = parseField(field);
  return function(req, res, next){
    if (getField(req, field).length > len) {
      next();
    } else {
      res.error(field.join(' ') + ' must have more than '
      ➥ + len + ' characters');
      res.redirect('back');
    }
  }
};
```

To make this middleware available to your application, add the following line at the top of app.js:

```
var validate = require('./lib/middleware/validate');
```

If you try the application now, you'll find that the validation will be in effect. This validation API could be made even more fluent, but we'll leave that for you to investigate.

9.2.3 Implementing pagination

Pagination is another great candidate for route-specific middleware. In this section, you'll write a small middleware function that will make it easy to paginate any resource you have available.

Designing a pager API

The API for the `page()` middleware you'll create will look like the following snippet, where `Entry.count` is a function that will look up the total count of entries, and `5` is the number to display per page, defaulting to `10`. In apps.js, change the line containing `app.get('/'` to the contents of the following snippet:

```
app.get('/', page(Entry.count, 5), entries.list);
```

To make the application ready for the pagination middleware, add the lines in the following snippet to the top of app.js. This will require the pagination middleware you'll be creating and the entry model:

```
...
var page = require('./lib/middleware/page');
var Entry = require('./lib/entry');
...
```

Next, you need to implement `Entry.count()`. With Redis, this is simple. Open up lib/entry.js and add the following function, which utilizes the `LLEN` command to get the list's cardinality (the number of elements):

```
Entry.count = function(fn){
  db.llen('entries', fn);
};
```

You're now ready to implement the middleware itself.

IMPLEMENTING PAGINATION MIDDLEWARE

For pagination, you'll use the query-string `?page=N` value to determine the current page. Add the following middleware function to ./lib/middleware/page.js.

Listing 9.26 Pagination middleware

```
module.exports = function(fn, perpage){
  perpage = perpage || 10;                          // Default to 10 per page
  return function(req, res, next){                  // Return middleware function
    var page = Math.max(
      parseInt(req.param('page') || '1', 10),
      1
    ) - 1;                                          // Parse page param as a base 10 integer

    fn(function(err, total){                        // Invoke the function passed
      if (err) return next(err);                    // Delegate errors

      req.page = res.locals.page = {                // Store page properties for future reference
        number: page,
        perpage: perpage,
        from: page * perpage,
        to: page * perpage + perpage - 1,
        total: total,
        count: Math.ceil(total / perpage)
      };

      next();                                       // Pass control to next middleware component
    });
  }
};
```

The middleware in listing 9.26 grabs the value assigned to `?page=N`; for example, `?page=1`. It then fetches the total number of results and exposes the `page` object with some precomputed values to any views that may later be rendered. These values are computed outside of the template to allow for a cleaner template containing less logic.

USING THE PAGER IN A ROUTE

Now you need to update the `entries.list` route. All you have to change is the original `Entry.getRange(0, -1)` to use the range that the `page()` middleware defined, as the following code shows:

```
exports.list = function(req, res, next){
  var page = req.page;
  Entry.getRange(page.from, page.to, function(err, entries){
    if (err) return next(err);
  ...
```

> **What's req.param() all about?**
>
> `req.param()` is similar to PHP's `$_REQUEST` associative array. It allows you to check the query string, route, or body. For example, `?page=1`, `/:page` with the value `/1`, or even posting JSON with `{"page":1}` would all be equivalent. If you were to access `req.query.page` directly, only the query-string value would be used.

CREATING A TEMPLATE FOR PAGINATION LINKS

Next, you need a template to implement the pager itself. Add the following listing to ./views/pager.ejs, which is a simple pager that consists of Previous and Next buttons.

Listing 9.27 An EJS template for rendering paging buttons

```
<div id='pager'>
  <% if (page.count > 1) { %>
    <% if (page.number) { %>
      <a id='prev' href='/?page=<%= page.number %>'>Prev</a>
    <% } %>
    <% if (page.number < page.count - 1) { %>
      <% if (page.number) { %>
          
      <% } %>
      <a id='next' href='/?page=<%= page.number + 2 %>'>Next</a>
    <% } %>
  <% } %>
</div>
```

- Don't show page controls if there's only one page
- If not on first page, show a link to previous page
- If not on last page, show a link to next page

INCLUDING PAGINATION LINKS IN A TEMPLATE

Now that you're all set up with the pager middleware and pager template, you can use EJS's `include` directive to add the template to the entry listing template ./views/entries.ejs.

Listing 9.28 Modified entries.ejs including pagination

```
<!DOCTYPE html>
<html>
  <head>
    <title><%= title %></title>
    <link rel='stylesheet' href='/stylesheets/style.css' />
  </head>
```

```
  <body>
    <% include menu %>

    <% entries.forEach(function(entry) { %>
      <div class='entry'>
        <h3><%= entry.title %></h3>
        <p><%= entry.body %></p>
        <p>Posted by <%= entry.username %></p>
      </div>
    <% }) %>

    <% include pager %>

  </body>
</html>
```

ENABLING CLEAN PAGINATION URLS

You might be wondering how to implement paging using only the pathname, such as /entries/2, instead of a URL parameter, such as ?page=2. Fortunately, only two changes need to be made to the pagination implementation to make this possible:

1. Change the route path to accept a page number.
2. Modify the page template.

The first step is to change the entries listing route path to accept a page number. You could do this by calling `app.get()` with the string `/:page`, but you'll want to consider / equivalent to `/0`, so make it optional using the string `/:page?`. In route paths, strings like `:page` are called route *parameters*, or *params* for short.

With the parameter being optional, both `/15` and / are valid, and the `page()` middleware defaults the page to 1. Because this route is top-level—`/5` and not `/entries/5`, for example—the `:page` parameter may potentially consume routes such as `/upload`. The simple solution is to move this route definition down below the others so that it's the last route defined. This way, more specific routes will be matched before ever reaching this route.

To implement this, the first step is to remove the existing route path in app.js for `/`. Remove the following line:

```
app.get('/', page(Entry.count, 5), entries.list);
```

Next, you'll want to add the following route path to app.js. Add this after all of the other route definitions:

```
app.get('/:page?', page(Entry.count, 5), entries.list);
```

The only other change necessary is to the pager template. The query string needs to be removed so the value becomes part of the path rather than a URL parameter. Change views/pager.ejs to the following:

```
<div id='pager'>
  <% if (page.count > 1) { %>
    <% if (page.number) { %>
      <a id='prev' href='/<%= page.number %>'>Prev</a>
    <% } %>
```

```
    <% if (page.number < page.count - 1) { %>
      <% if (page.number) { %>
          
      <% } %>
      <a id='next' href='/<%= page.number + 2 %>'>Next</a>
    <% } %>
  <% } %>
</div>
```

Now if you start up your application, you'll notice paging URLs are clean.

9.3 Creating a public REST API

In this section, you'll implement a RESTful public API for the shoutbox application, so that third-party applications can access and add to publication data. The idea of REST is that application data can be queried and changed using verbs and nouns, represented by HTTP methods and URLs, respectively. A REST request will typically return data in a machine-readable form, such as JSON or XML.

To implement an API, you'll do the following:

- Design an API that allows users to show, list, remove, and post entries
- Add Basic authentication
- Implement routing
- Provide JSON and XML responses

Various techniques can be used to authenticate and sign API requests, but implementing the more complex solutions are beyond the scope of this book. To illustrate how you could integrate authentication, you'll use the `basicAuth()` middleware bundled by Connect.

9.3.1 Designing the API

Before proceeding with the implementation, it's a good idea to rough out the routes that will be involved. For this application, you'll prefix the RESTful API with the /api path, but this is a design choice you can alter. For example, you may wish to use a subdomain such as http://api.myapplication.com.

The following snippet illustrates why it can be a good choice to move the callback functions into separate Node modules, versus defining them inline with the `app.VERB()` calls. A single list of routes gives you a clear picture of what you and the rest of your team has implemented, and where the implementation callback lives:

```
app.get('/api/user/:id', api.user);
app.get('/api/entries/:page?', api.entries);
app.post('/api/entry', api.add);
```

9.3.2 Adding Basic authentication

As previously mentioned, there are many ways to approach API security and restrictions that fall outside the scope of this book. But it's worth illustrating the process with Basic authentication.

The `api.auth` middleware will abstract this process, because the implementation will live in the soon-to-be-created ./routes/api.js module. If you recall from chapter 6, `app.use()` can be passed a pathname. This is the mount point, meaning that request pathnames beginning with /api and any HTTP verb will cause this middleware to be invoked.

The line `app.use('/api', api.auth)`, as shown in the following snippet, should be placed before the middleware that loads user data. This is so that you can later modify the user-loading middleware to load data for authenticated API users:

```
...
var api = require('./routes/api');
...
app.use('/api', api.auth);
app.use(user);
...
```

Next, create the ./routes/api.js file, and require both express and the user model, as shown in the following snippet. As mentioned in chapter 7, the `basicAuth()` middleware accepts a function to perform the authentication, taking the function signature `(username, password, callback)`. Your `User.authentication` function is a perfect fit:

```
var express = require('express');
var User = require('../lib/user');

exports.auth = express.basicAuth(User.authenticate);
```

Authentication is ready to roll. Let's move on to implementing the API routes.

9.3.3 *Implementing routing*

The first route you'll implement is `GET /api/user/:id`. The logic for this route will have to first fetch the user by ID, responding with a 404 Not Found code if the user doesn't exist. If the user exists, the user data will be passed to `res.send()` to be serialized, and the application will respond with a JSON representation of this data. Add the logic in the following snippet to routes/api.js:

```
exports.user = function(req, res, next){
  User.get(req.params.id, function(err, user){
    if (err) return next(err);
    if (!user.id) return res.send(404);
    res.json(user);
  });
};
```

Next, add the following route path to app.js:

```
app.get('/api/user/:id', api.user);
```

You're now ready to test it.

TESTING USER DATA RETRIEVAL

Fire up the application and test it out with the cURL command-line tool. The following snippet shows how you can test the application's REST authentication. Credentials are provided in the URL `tobi:ferret`, which cURL uses to produce the `Authorization` header field:

```
$ curl http://tobi:ferret@127.0.0.1:3000/api/user/1 -v
```

The following listing shows the result of a successful test.

Listing 9.29 Testing output

```
* About to connect() to local port 80 (#0)
*   Trying 127.0.0.1... connected
* Connected to local (127.0.0.1) port 80 (#0)
* Server auth using Basic with user 'tobi'
> GET /api/user/1 HTTP/1.1
> Authorization: Basic Zm9vYmFyYmF6Cg==
> User-Agent: curl/7.21.4 (universal-apple-darwin11.0) libcurl/7.21.4
➥ OpenSSL/0.9.8r zlib/1.2.5
> Host: local
> Accept: */*
>
< HTTP/1.1 200 OK
< X-Powered-By: Express
< Content-Type: application/json; charset=utf-8
< Content-Length: 150
< Connection: keep-alive
<
{
  "name": "tobi",
  "pass":
  ➥ "$2a$12$P.mzcfvmumS3MMO1EBN9wutf0Eiyw5X0VcGroeoVPGE7MLVtziYqK",
  "id": "1",
  "salt": "$2a$12$P.mzcfvmumS3MMO1EBN9wu"
}
```

Display of HTTP headers sent

Display of HTTP headers received

Display of JSON data received

REMOVING SENSITIVE USER DATA

As you can see by the JSON response, both the user's password and salt are provided in the response. To alter this, you can implement `.toJSON()` on the `User.prototype` in lib/user.js:

```
User.prototype.toJSON = function(){
  return {
    id: this.id,
    name: this.name
  }
};
```

If `.toJSON` exists on an object, it will be used by `JSON.stringify` calls to get the JSON format. If the cURL request shown earlier was to be issued again, you'd now receive only the ID and name properties:

```
{
  "id": "1",
  "name": "tobi"
}
```

The next thing you'll add to the API is the ability to create entries.

ADDING ENTRIES

The processes for adding an entry via the HTML form and through an API are nearly identical, so you'll likely want to reuse the previously implemented `entries.submit()` route logic.

When adding entries, however, the route logic stores the name of the user, adding the entry in addition to the other details. For this reason, you'll need to modify the user-loading middleware to populate `res.locals.user` with the user data loaded by the `basicAuth` middleware. The `basicAuth` middleware stores this data in a property of the request object: `req.remoteUser`. Adding a check for this in the user-loading middleware is straightforward: simply change the `module.exports` definition in lib/middleware/user.js as follows to make the user-loading middleware work with the API:

```
...
module.exports = function(req, res, next){
  if (req.remoteUser) {
    res.locals.user = req.remoteUser;
  }
  var uid = req.session.uid;
  if (!uid) return next();
  User.get(uid, function(err, user){
    if (err) return next(err);
    req.user = res.locals.user = user;
    next();
  });
};
```

With this change made, you'll now be able to add entries via the API.

One more change you'll want to implement, however, is an API-friendly response, rather than redirection to the application's homepage. To add this functionality, change the `entry.save` call in routes/entries.js to the following:

```
...
  entry.save(function(err) {
    if (err) return next(err);
    if (req.remoteUser) {
      res.json({message: 'Entry added.'});
    } else {
      res.redirect('/');
    }
  });
...
```

Finally, to activate the entry-adding API in your application, add the contents of the following snippet to the routing section of api.js:

```
app.post('/api/entry', entries.submit);
```

By using the following cURL command, you can test adding an entry via the API. Here the title and body data is sent using the same field names that are in the HTML form:

```
$ curl -F entry[title]='Ho ho ho' -F entry[body]='Santa loves you'
  ➥http://tobi:ferret@127.0.0.1:3000/api/entry
```

Now that you've added the ability to create entries, you need to add the ability to retrieve entry data.

ADDING ENTRY LISTING SUPPORT

The next API route you'll implement is `GET /api/entries/:page?`. The route implementation is nearly identical to the existing entry listing route in ./routes/entries.js. You'll want to use the already defined `page()` middleware to provide you with the `req.page` object used for pagination, as you did previously.

Because the routing logic will be accessing entries, you'll require the `Entry` model at the top of routes/api.js using the following line:

```
var Entry = require('../lib/entry');
```

Next, you'll add the line in the following snippet to the app.js routing section:

```
app.get('/api/entries/:page?', page(Entry.count), api.entries);
```

Now add the routing logic in the following snippet to routes/api.js. The difference between this route logic and the similar logic in routes/entries.js reflects the fact that you're no longer rendering a template, but JSON instead:

```
exports.entries = function(req, res, next){
  var page = req.page;
  Entry.getRange(page.from, page.to, function(err, entries){
    if (err) return next(err);
    res.json(entries);
  });
};
```

The following cURL command will request entry data from the API:

```
$ curl http://tobi:ferret@127.0.0.1:3000/api/entries
```

This cURL command should result in output similar to the following JSON:

```
[
  {
    "username": "rick",
    "title": "Cats can't read minds",
    "body": "I think you're wrong about the cat thing."
  },
  {
    "username": "mike",
    "title": "I think my cat can read my mind",
    "body": "I think cat can hear my thoughts."
  },
...
```

With basic API implementation covered, let's move on to look at how APIs can support multiple response formats.

9.3.4 Enabling content negotiation

Content negotiation is what enables a client to specify what formats it's willing to accept, and which it would prefer. In this section, you'll provide JSON and XML representations of the API content so that the API consumers can decide what they want.

HTTP provides the content negotiation mechanism via the `Accept` header field. For example, a client that prefers HTML, but that is willing to accept plain text, could set the following request header:

```
Accept: text/plain; q=0.5, text/html
```

The *qvalue* or *quality value* (`q=0.5` in this example) indicates that even though `text/html` is specified second, it's favored by 50 percent over `text/plain`. Express parses this information and provides a normalized `req.accepted` array:

```
[{ value: 'text/html', quality: 1 },
 { value: 'text/plain', quality: 0.5 }]
```

Express also provides the `res.format()` method, which accepts an array of MIME types and callbacks. Express will determine what the client is willing to accept and what you're willing to provide, and it'll invoke the appropriate callback.

IMPLEMENTING CONTENT NEGOTIATION

Implementing content negotiation for the `GET /api/entries` route might look something like listing 9.30. JSON is supported as it was before—you serialize the entries as JSON with `res.send()`. The XML callback iterates the entries and writes to the socket as it does so. Note that there's no need to set the `Content-Type` explicitly; `res.format()` will set it to the associated type automatically.

Listing 9.30 Implementing content negotiation

```
exports.entries = function(req, res, next){
  var page = req.page;
  Entry.getRange(page.from, page.to, function(err, entries){      <-- Fetch entry data
    if (err) return next(err);

    res.format({                                <-- Respond differently based on Accept header value
      'application/json': function(){
        res.send(entries);                      <-- JSON response
      },

      'application/xml': function(){
        res.write('<entries>\n');               <-- XML response
        entries.forEach(function(entry){
          res.write('  <entry>\n');
          res.write('    <title>' + entry.title + '</title>\n');
          res.write('    <body>' + entry.body + '</body>\n');
          res.write('    <username>' + entry.username
            + '</username>\n');
```

```
        res.write('  </entry>\n');
      });
      res.end('</entries>');
    }
  })
 });
};
```

If you set a default response format callback, this will execute if a user hasn't requested a format you've explicitly handled.

The `res.format()` method also accepts an extension name that maps to an associated MIME type. For example, `json` and `xml` can be used in place of `application/json` and `application/xml`, as the following snippet shows:

```
...
res.format({
  json: function(){
    res.send(entries);
  },

  xml: function(){
    res.write('<entries>\n');
    entries.forEach(function(entry){
      res.write('  <entry>\n');
      res.write('    <title>' + entry.title + '</title>\n');
      res.write('    <body>' + entry.body + '</body>\n');
      res.write('    <username>' + entry.username + '</username>\n');
      res.write('  </entry>\n');
    });
    res.end('</entries>');
  }
})
...
```

RESPONDING WITH XML

Writing a bunch of custom logic in the route in order to respond with XML may not be the cleanest way to go, so let's use the view system to clean this up.

Create a template named ./views/entries/xml.ejs with the following EJS iterating the entries to generate <entry> tags.

Listing 9.31 Using an EJS template to generate XML

```
<entries>
<% entries.forEach(function(entry){ %>        <- Cycle through each entry
  <entry>
    <title><%= entry.title %></title>          <- Output the fields
    <body><%= entry.body %></body>
    <username><%= entry.username %></username>
  </entry>
<% }) %>
</entries>
```

The XML callback can now be replaced with a single `res.render()` call, passing the `entries` array, as shown in the following code:

```
...
  xml: function(){
    res.render('entries/xml', { entries: entries });
  }
})
...
```

You're now ready to test the XML version of the API. Enter the following in the command line to see the XML output:

```
curl -i -H 'Accept: application/xml'
  ➥http://tobi:ferret@127.0.0.1:3000/api/entries
```

9.4 Error handling

So far, neither the application itself nor the API respond with error or 404 Not Found pages. This means that if a resource isn't found, or if the connection to the database goes down, Express will respond with its default of 404 or 500, respectively. As you can see in figure 9.8, this isn't user friendly, so let's customize it. In this section, you'll implement both 404 and error middleware, which will be used to respond with HTML, JSON, or plain text as accepted by the client.

Let's get started with the missing resources by implementing the 404 middleware.

9.4.1 Handling 404 errors

As previously mentioned, the default behavior when Connect exhausts all middleware without a response is to respond with 404 and a small plain-text string. It looks something like the following response for an entry that doesn't exist:

```
$ curl http://tobi:ferret@127.0.0.1:3000/api/not/a/real/path -i
  ➥-H "Accept: application/json"

HTTP/1.1 404 Not Found
Content-Type: text/plain
Connection: keep-alive
Transfer-Encoding: chunked

Cannot GET /api/not/a/real/path
```

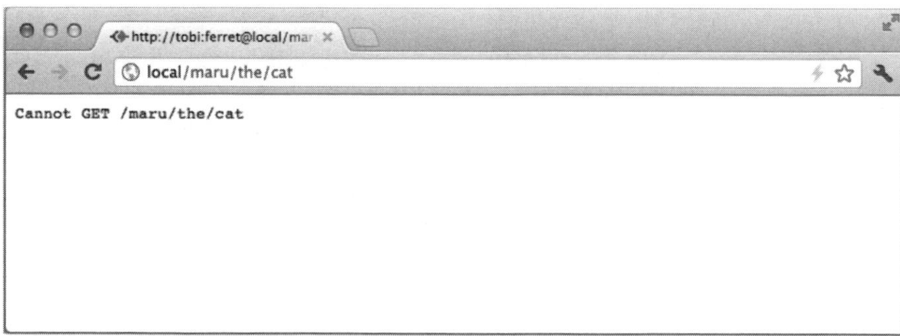

Figure 9.8 A standard Connect 404 error message

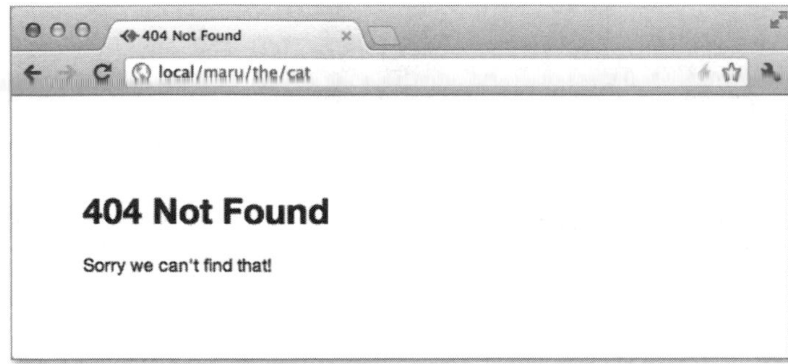

Figure 9.9 A 404 error message that's easier on the eyes than a standard Connect 404 message

Depending on your needs, this may be acceptable, but ideally a JSON API will respond with a JSON response, as the following snippet shows:

```
$ curl http://tobi:ferret@127.0.0.1:3000/api/not/a/real/path
➥-i -H "Accept: application/json"
HTTP/1.1 404 Not Found
Content-Type: application/json; charset=utf-8
Content-Length: 37
Connection: keep-alive

{ "message": "Resource not found" }
```

Implementing the 404 middleware is nothing special; neither Connect nor Express special-case this functionality. A 404 middleware function is a regular middleware function that's used below any other. If it's reached, you can safely assume nothing else decided to respond, so you can go ahead and render a template or respond in any other way you prefer.

Figure 9.9 shows the HTML response for a 404 error you'll create.

ADDING A ROUTE TO RETURN THE ERROR RESPONSE

Open up ./routes/index.js. So far this file only contains the original `exports.index` function that `express(1)` generated. Feel free to get rid of that, because it was replaced with `entries.list`.

The implementation of the error response function will depend on your application's needs. In the following snippet, you'll use the `res.format()` content negotiation method to provide `text/html`, `application/json`, and `text/plain` responses to the client, depending on which they prefer. The response method `res.status(code)` is identical to setting Node's `res.statusCode = code` property, but because it's a method, it's chainable, as you can see by the immediate `.format()` call in the following code.

Listing 9.32 Not Found route logic

```
exports.notfound = function(req, res){
  res.status(404).format({
    html: function(){
      res.render('404');
    },
    json: function(){
      res.send({ message: 'Resource not found' });
```

```
    },
    xml: function() {
      res.write('<error>\n');
      res.write('  <message>Resource not found</message>\n');
      res.end('</error>\n');
    },
    text: function(){
      res.send('Resource not found\n');
    }
  });
};
```

CREATING THE ERROR PAGE TEMPLATE

You haven't created the 404 template yet, so create a new file named ./views/404.ejs containing the following EJS snippet. The design of the template is entirely up to you.

Listing 9.33 Sample 404 page

```
<!DOCTYPE html>
<html>
  <head>
    <title>404 Not Found</title>
    <link rel='stylesheet' href='/stylesheets/style.css' />
  </head>
  <body>
    <% include menu %>

    <h1>404 Not Found</h1>
    <p>Sorry we can't find that!</p>
  </body>
</html>
```

ENABLING THE MIDDLEWARE

Add the `routes.notfound` middleware below the others, and you can now handle 404 errors as you wish:

```
...
app.use(app.router);
app.use(routes.notfound);
...
```

Now that you can handle 404s in style, let's implement a custom error-handling middleware component to provide a better experience for users when an error occurs.

9.4.2 Handling errors

Up until now you've been passing errors to `next()`. But by default Connect will respond with the canned 500 Internal Server Error response, much like the bland default 404 response. Typically, it's not a good idea to leak error details to a client, as it poses a potential security issue, but this default response isn't helpful for the consumers of your API or visitors viewing it from a browser.

In this section, you'll create a generic 5xx template that will be used to respond to clients when an error occurs. It will provide HTML for clients who accept HTML, and JSON for those accepting JSON, such as the API consumers.

The middleware function can live wherever you like, but for now place it in ./routes/index.js alongside the 404 function. The key difference with the `exports.error` middleware here is that it accepts four parameters. As we discussed in chapter 6, error-handling middleware must have no more and no fewer than four parameters.

Using a conditional route to test error pages

If your application is robust, it may be difficult to trigger an error on demand. For this reason, it can be handy to create *conditional* routes. These routes are only enabled via a configuration flag, environment variable, or perhaps an environment type, such as when you're in development.

The following snippet from app.js illustrates how you can add a `/dev/error` route to the application only when the `ERROR_ROUTE` environment variable is specified, creating a faux error with an arbitrary `err.type` property. Add this code to the routing section of app.js:

```
if (process.env.ERROR_ROUTE) {
  app.get('/dev/error', function(req, res, next){
    var err = new Error('database connection failed');
    err.type = 'database';
    next(err);
  });
}
```

Once this is in place, you can fire up the application with this optional route by executing the following command. Visit /dev/error in the browser if you're curious, but you'll be using it in a moment to test the error handler:

```
$ ERROR_ROUTE=1 node app
```

Implementing the error handler

To implement the error handler in ./routes/index.js, listing 9.34 starts off with a call to `console.error(err.stack)`. This is possibly the most important line in this function. It ensures that when an error propagates through Connect, reaching this function, you'll know about it. The error message and stack trace will be written to the stderr stream for later review.

Listing 9.34 Error handler with content negotiation

```
exports.error = function(err, req, res, next){    // Error handlers must accept four arguments
  console.error(err.stack);                       // Log error to stderr stream
  var msg;

  switch (err.type) {                             // An example of special-casing errors
    case 'database':
      msg = 'Server Unavailable';
      res.statusCode = 503;
      break;
    default:
      msg = 'Internal Server Error';
      res.statusCode = 500;
  }
```

```
  res.format({
    html: function(){
      res.render('5xx', { msg: msg, status: res.statusCode });
    },

    json: function(){
      res.send({ error: msg });
    },

    text: function(){
      res.send(msg + '\n');
    }
  });
};
```

Render template when HTML is accepted

Respond with JSON when accepted

Respond with plain text

In order to provide a more meaningful response to the user, without exposing too much information about a given error, you might want to check the properties of the error and respond accordingly. Here the `err.type` property you added on the `/dev/error` route is checked in order to customize the message, and you then respond with HTML, JSON, or plain-text representations, much like the 404 handler.

> **APPLICATION ERROR ALERTS** This unified error handler is a great place to perform additional error-related tasks, like alerting your team that something has gone wrong. Try it out yourself: choose one of the third-party email modules and write an error-handling middleware component that will alert you via email, and then invoke `next(err)` to pass the error to the remaining error-handling middleware.

CREATING THE ERROR PAGE TEMPLATE

The EJS template for the `res.render('5xx')` call will live in ./views/5xx.ejs, as shown in the following listing.

Listing 9.35 Sample 500 error page

```
<!DOCTYPE html>
<html>
  <head>
    <title><%= status %> <%= msg %></title>
    <link rel='stylesheet' href='/stylesheets/style.css' />
  </head>
  <body>
    <% include menu %>

    <h1><%= status %> Error</h1>
    <p><%= msg %></p>
    <p>
      Try refreshing the page, if this problem
      ➥persists then we're already working on it!
    </p>
  </body>
</html>
```

ENABLING THE MIDDLEWARE

By editing app.js and placing the `routes.error` middleware below the others—even below `routes.notfound`—you'll ensure that all errors Connect can see, even potential errors in `routes.notfound`, will hit this middleware component:

```
...
app.use(app.router);
app.use(routes.notfound);
app.use(routes.error);
});
```

Fire up the application with the `ERROR_ROUTE` enabled again, and take a look at the new error page in figure 9.10.

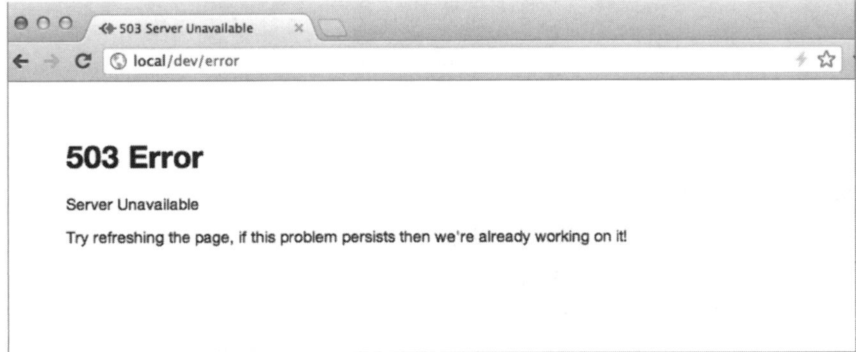

Figure 9.10 An error page

You've now created a fully functioning shoutbox application and have learned some essential Express development techniques in the process.

9.5 Summary

In this chapter, you built a simple web application that employs many aspects of Express's functionality that we didn't touch on in the previous chapter. The techniques you've learned in this chapter should help you go further in your web application development efforts.

You first created a general-purpose user authentication and registration system that uses sessions to store the IDs of logged-in users and any messages the system wants displayed to the users.

You then leveraged the authentication system, through the use of middleware, to create a REST API. The REST API exposes selected application data to developers and, through the use of content negotiation, makes the data available in either JSON or XML.

Having spent the last two chapters honing your web application development skills, you're ready to focus on a subject useful for all types of Node development: automated testing.

10 Testing Node applications

This chapter covers

- Testing logic with Node's assert module
- Using Node unit-testing frameworks
- Simulating and controlling web browsers using Node

As you add features to your application, you run the risk of introducing bugs. An application isn't complete if it's not tested, and as manual testing is tedious and prone to human error, automated testing has become increasingly popular with developers. Automated testing involves writing logic to test your code, rather than running through application functionality by hand.

If the idea of automated testing is new to you, think of it as a robot doing all of the boring stuff for you, allowing you to focus on the interesting stuff. Every time you make a change to the code, you can get the robot to make sure bugs haven't crept in. Although you may not have completed or started your first Node application yet, it's good to get a handle on how you can implement automated testing because you'll be able to write tests as you develop.

In this chapter, we'll look at two types of automated testing: unit testing and acceptance testing. Unit testing tests code logic directly, typically at a function or method level, and it's applicable to all types of applications. Unit-testing methodology can be divided into two major forms: test-driven development (TDD) and

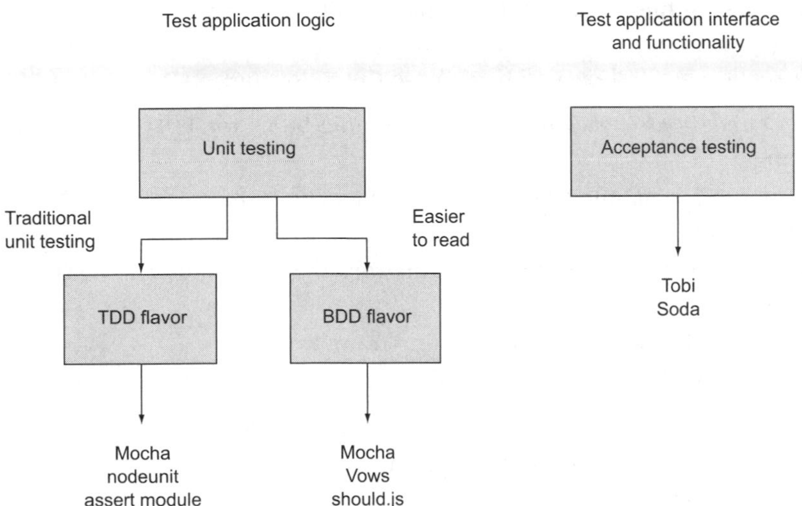

Figure 10.1 Test framework overview

behavior-driven development (BDD). Practically speaking, TDD and BDD are largely the same thing, with the differences mostly being in the language used to describe the tests, as you'll see when we go through some examples. There are other differences between TDD and BDD, but they're beyond the scope of this book.

Acceptance testing is an additional layer of testing most commonly used for web applications. Acceptance testing involves scripting control of a browser and attempting to trigger web application functionality with it.

We'll look at established solutions for both unit and acceptance testing. For unit testing, we'll cover Node's assert module and the Mocha, nodeunit, Vows, and should.js frameworks. For acceptance testing, we'll look at the Tobi and Soda frameworks. Figure 10.1 places the tools alongside their respective testing methodologies and flavors.

Let's start with unit testing.

10.1 Unit testing

Unit testing is a type of automated testing where you write logic to test discrete parts of your application. Writing tests makes you think more critically about your application design choices and helps you avoid pitfalls early. The tests also give you confidence that your recent changes haven't introduced errors. Although unit tests take a bit of work up front to write, they can save you time by lessening the need to manually retest every time you make a change to an application.

Unit testing can be tricky, and asynchronous logic can add new challenges. Asynchronous unit tests can run in parallel, so you've got to be careful to ensure that tests don't interfere with each other. For example, if your tests create temporary files on disk, you'll have to be careful that when you delete the files after a test, you don't delete the working files of another test that hasn't yet finished. For this reason, many unit-testing frameworks include flow control to sequence the running of tests.

In this section, we'll show you how to use the following:

- *Node's built-in assert module*—A good building block for TDD-style automated testing
- *nodeunit*—A longtime favorite TDD-style testing framework of the Node community
- *Mocha*—A relatively new testing framework that can be used for TDD- or BDD-style testing
- *Vows*—A widely used BDD-style testing framework
- *should.js*—A module that builds on Node's assert module to provide BDD-style assertions

Let's start with the assert module, which is included with Node.

10.1.1 The assert module

The basis for most Node unit testing is the built-in assert module, which tests a condition and, if the condition isn't met, throws an error. Node's assert module is taken advantage of by many third-party testing frameworks, but even without a testing framework, you can do useful testing with it.

A SIMPLE EXAMPLE

Suppose you have a simple to-do application that stores items in memory, and you want to assert that it's doing what you think it's doing.

The following listing defines a module containing the core application functionality. Module logic supports creating, retrieving, and deleting to-do items. It also includes a simple `doAsync` method, so we can look at testing asynchronous methods too. Let's call this file todo.js.

Listing 10.1 A model for a to-do list

```
function Todo () {                    <-- Define to-do database
  this.todos = [];
}

Todo.prototype.add = function (item) {                    <-- Add a to-do item
  if (!item) throw new Error('Todo#add requires an item')
  this.todos.push(item);
}

Todo.prototype.deleteAll = function () {                  <-- Delete all to-do items
  this.todos = [];
}

Todo.prototype.getCount = function () {                   <-- Get count of to-do items
  return this.todos.length;
}

Todo.prototype.doAsync = function (cb) {     <-- Call back with "true" after 2 secs
```

```
  setTimeout(cb, 2000, true);
}

module.exports = Todo;        <-- Export Todo function
```

Now you can use Node's assert module to test the code.

In a file called test.js, enter the following code to load the necessary modules, set up a new to-do list, and set a variable that will track testing progress.

Listing 10.2 Set up necessary modules

```
var assert = require('assert');
var Todo = require('./todo');
var todo = new Todo();
var testsCompleted = 0;
```

USING EQUAL TO TEST THE CONTENTS OF A VARIABLE

Next, you can add a test of the to-do application's delete functionality.

Note the use of `equal` in listing 10.3. `equal` is the assert module's most-used assertion, and it tests that the contents of a variable are indeed equal to a value specified in the second argument. In the example here, a to-do item is created, and then all items are deleted.

Listing 10.3 Test to make sure that no to-do items remain after deletion

```
function deleteTest () {
  todo.add('Delete Me');                                     <-- Add some data in order to test delete
  assert.equal(todo.getCount(), 1, '1 item should exist');   <-- Assert data was added correctly
  todo.deleteAll();                                          <-- Delete all records
  assert.equal(todo.getCount(), 0, 'No items should exist'); <-- Assert record was deleted
  testsCompleted++;                                          <-- Note that test has completed
}
```

As there should be no to-dos at the end of this test, the value of `todo.getCount()` should be `0` if the application logic is working properly. If a problem occurs, an exception is thrown. If the variable `todo.getCount()` isn't set to `0`, the assertion will result in a stack trace showing an error message, "No items should exist," outputted to the console. After the assertion, `testsCompleted` is incremented to note that a test has completed.

USING NOTEQUAL TO FIND PROBLEMS IN LOGIC

Next, add the code in the following listing to test.js. This code is a test of the to-do application's add functionality.

Listing 10.4 Test to make sure adding a to-do works

```
function addTest () {
  todo.deleteAll();                                           <-- Delete any existing items
  todo.add('Added');                                          <-- Add item
  assert.notEqual(todo.getCount(), 0, '1 item should exist'); <-- Assert that items exist
  testsCompleted++;                                           <-- Note that test has completed
}
```

The assert module also allows `notEqual` assertions. This type of assertion is useful when the generation of a certain value by application code indicates a problem in logic.

Listing 10.4 shows the use of a `notEqual` assertion. All to-do items are deleted, an item is added, and the application logic then gets all items. If the number of items is `0`, the assertion will fail and an exception will be thrown.

USING ADDITION FUNCTIONALITY: STRICTEQUAL, NOTSTRICTEQUAL, DEEPEQUAL, NOTDEEPEQUAL

In addition to `equal` and `notEqual` functionality, the assert module offers strict versions of assertions called `strictEqual` and `notStrictEqual`. These use the strict equality operator (===) rather than the more permissive version (==).

To compare objects, the assert module offers `deepEqual` and `notDeepEqual`. The *deep* in the names of these assertions indicates that they recursively compare two objects, comparing two object's properties and, if the properties are themselves objects, comparing these as well.

USING OK TO TEST FOR AN ASYNCHRONOUS VALUE BEING TRUE

Now it's time to add a test of the to-do application's `doAsync` method, as shown in listing 10.5. Because this is an asynchronous test, we're providing a callback function (`cb`) to signal to the test runner when the test has completed—we can't rely on the function returning to tell us like we can with synchronous tests. To see if the result of `doAsync` is the value `true`, we use the `ok` assertion. The `ok` assertion provides an easy way to test a value for being `true`.

Listing 10.5 Test to see if the `doAsync` callback is passed `true`

```
function doAsyncTest (cb) {
  todo.doAsync(function (value) {                         <-- Callback will fire 2 secs later
    assert.ok(value,'Callback should be passed true');    <-- Assert value is true
    testsCompleted++;                                     <-- Note that test has completed
    cb();                                                 <-- Trigger callback when done
  })
}
```

TESTING THAT THROWN ERRORS ARE CORRECT

You can also use the assert module to check that thrown error messages are correct, as the following listing shows. The second argument in the `throws` call is a regular expression that looks for the text "requires" in the error message.

Listing 10.6 Test to see if `add` throws when missing a parameter

```
function throwsTest (cb) {
  assert.throws(todo.add, /requires/);     <-- todo.add called with no arguments
  testsCompleted++                         <-- Note that test has completed
}
```

ADDING LOGIC TO RUN YOUR TESTS

Now that you've defined the tests, you can add logic to the file to run each of the tests. The logic in the following listing will run each test, and then print how many tests were run and completed.

Listing 10.7 Running the tests and reporting test completion

```
deleteTest();
addTest();
throwsTest();
doAsyncTest(function () {
  console.log('Completed ' + testsCompleted + ' tests');   <- Indicate completion
})
```

You can run the tests with the following command:

```
$ node test.js
```

If the tests don't fail, the script informs you of the number of tests completed. It also can be smart to keep track of when tests start execution as well as when they complete, to protect against flaws in individual tests. For example, a test may execute without reaching the assertion.

In order to use Node's built-in functionality, each test case had to include a lot of boilerplate to set up the test (such as deleting all items) and to keep track of progress (the "completed" counter). All this boilerplate shifts the focus away from the primary concern of writing test cases, and it's better left to a dedicated framework that can do the heavy lifting while you focus on testing business logic. Let's look at how you can make things easier using nodeunit, a third-party unit-testing framework.

10.1.2 Nodeunit

Using a unit-testing framework simplifies unit testing. Frameworks generally keep track of how many tests have run and they make it easy to run multiple test scripts.

A number of excellent testing frameworks have been created by the Node community. We'll start with a look at nodeunit (https://github.com/caolan/nodeunit) as it's a time-tested favorite of Node developers who prefer TDD-flavored testing. Nodeunit provides a command-line tool that will run all of your application's tests and let you know how many pass and fail, saving you from having to implement your own application-specific testing tool.

In this section, you'll learn how to write tests with nodeunit that can test both Node application code and client-side code run using a web browser. You'll also learn how nodeunit deals with the challenge of keeping track of running tests asynchronously.

INSTALLING NODEUNIT

Enter the following to install nodeunit:

```
$ npm install -g nodeunit
```

Once it has completed, you'll have a new command available named `nodeunit`. This command is given one or more directories or files containing tests, as an argument, and it will run all scripts with the extension .js within the directories passed.

TESTING NODE APPLICATIONS WITH NODEUNIT

To add nodeunit tests to your project, create a directory for them (the directory is usually named *test*). Each test script should populate the `exports` object with tests.

Here's an example nodeunit server-side test file:

```
exports.testPony = function(test) {
  var isPony = true;
  test.ok(isPony, 'This is not a pony.');
  test.done();
}
```

Note that the previous test script doesn't require any modules. Nodeunit automatically includes Node's assert module's methods in an object that it passes to each function exported by a test script. In the preceding example, this object is called `test`.

Once each function exported by the test script has completed, the `done` method should be called. If it isn't called, the test will report a failure of "Undone tests." By requiring that this method be called, nodeunit checks that all tests that were started were also finished.

It also can be helpful to check that all the assertions fire within a test. Why wouldn't assertions fire? When writing unit tests, the danger always exists that the test logic itself is buggy, leading to false positives. Logic in the test may be written in such a way that certain assertions don't evaluate. The following example shows how `test.done()` can fire and report success even though one of the assertions hasn't executed:

```
exports.testPony = function(test) {
  if (false) {
    test.ok(false, 'This should not have passed.');
  }
  test.ok(true, 'This should have passed.');
  test.done();
}
```

If you want to safeguard against this, you could manually implement an assertion counter, such as the one shown in the following listing.

Listing 10.8 Manually counting assertions

```
exports.testPony = function(test) {
  var count = 0;                                        <— Count assertions
  if (false) {
    test.ok(false, 'This should not have passed.');
    count++;                                            <— Increment assertion count
  }
  test.ok(true, 'This should have passed.');
  count++;                                              <— Increment assertion count
  test.equal(count, 2, 'Not all assertions triggered.'); <— Test assertion count
  test.done();
}
```

This is tedious. Nodeunit offers a nicer way to do this by using `test.expect`. This method allows you to specify the number of assertions each test should include. The result is fewer lines of unnecessary code:

```
exports.testPony = function(test) {
  test.expect(2);
  if (false) {
    test.ok(false, 'This should not have passed.');
  }
  test.ok(true, 'This should have passed.');
  test.done();
}
```

In addition to testing Node modules, nodeunit also allows you to test client-side JavaScript, giving you the ability to use one test harness for your web applications. You can learn about that and more advanced techniques by checking out nodeunit's online documentation: https://github.com/caolan/nodeunit.

Now that you've learned how to use a TDD-flavored unit-testing framework, let's look at how you can incorporate a BDD style of unit testing.

10.1.3 Mocha

Mocha is the newest testing framework you'll learn about in this chapter, and it's an easy framework to grasp. Although it defaults to a BDD style, you can also use it in a TDD style. Mocha has a wide variety of features, including global variable leak detection, and, like nodeunit, Mocha supports client-side testing.

> **Global variable leak detection**
>
> You should have little need for global variables that are readable application-wide, and it's considered a programming best practice to minimize your use of them. But in JavaScript it's easy to inadvertently create global variables by forgetting to include the `var` keyword when declaring a variable. Mocha helps detect accidental global variable leaks by throwing an error when you create a global variable during testing.
>
> If you want to disable global leak detection, run `mocha` with the `--ignored-leaks` command-line option. Alternatively, if you want to allow a select number of globals to be used, you can specify them using the `--globals` command-line option followed by a comma-delimited list of allowable global variables.

By default, Mocha tests are defined and their logic is set up using BDD-flavored functions called `describe`, `it`, `before`, `after`, `beforeEach`, and `afterEach`. Alternatively, you can use Mocha's TDD interface, which replaces the use of `describe` with `suite`, `it` with `test`, `before` with `setup`, and `after` with `teardown`. For our example, we'll stick with the default BDD interface.

TESTING NODE APPLICATIONS WITH MOCHA

Let's dive right in and create a small project called *memdb*—a small in-memory database—and use Mocha to test it. First, you need to create the directories and files for the project:

```
$ mkdir -p memdb/test
$ cd memdb
$ touch index.js
$ touch test/memdb.js
```

The *test* directory is where the tests will live, but before you write any tests you need to install Mocha:

```
$ npm install -g mocha
```

By default, Mocha will use the BDD interface. The following listing shows what it looks like.

Listing 10.9 Basic structure for Mocha test

```
var memdb = require('..');

describe('memdb', function(){
  describe('.save(doc)', function(){
    it('should save the document', function(){

    });
  });
});
```

Mocha also supports TDD and qunit, and exports style interfaces, which are detailed on the project's site (http://visionmedia.github.com/mocha), but to illustrate the concept of different interfaces, here's the exports interface:

```
module.exports = {
  'memdb': {
    '.save(doc)': {
      'should save the document': function(){

      }
    }
  }
}
```

All of these interfaces provide the same functionality, but for now let's stick to the BDD interface and write the first test, shown in the following listing, in test/memdb.js. This test uses Node's assert module to perform the assertions.

Listing 10.10 Describing the `memdb.save` functionality

```
var memdb = require('..');
var assert = require('assert');

describe('memdb', function(){
  describe('.save(doc)', function(){
```

Describe memdb functionality

Describe .save() method's functionality

```
    it('should save the document', function(){
      var pet = { name: 'Tobi' };
      memdb.save(pet);
      var ret = memdb.first({ name: 'Tobi' });
      assert(ret == pet);
    })
  })
})
```

Describe the expectation

Ensure the pet was found

To run the tests, all you need to do is execute mocha. Mocha will look in the ./test directory by default for JavaScript files to execute. Because you haven't implemented the .save() method yet, you'll see that the single test defined fails, as shown in figure 10.2.

Let's make it pass! Add the code in the following listing to index.js.

Listing 10.11 Added save functionality

```
var db = [];

exports.save = function(doc){
  db.push(doc);
};

exports.first = function(obj) {
  return db.filter(function(doc){
    for (var key in obj) {
      if (doc[key] != obj[key]) {
        return false;
      }
    }
    return true;
  }).shift();
};
```

Add the doc to database array

Select docs that match every property in obj

Not a match; return false and don't select this doc

They all matched; return and select the doc

Only want the first doc or null

Run the tests again with Mocha and see success, as shown in figure 10.3.

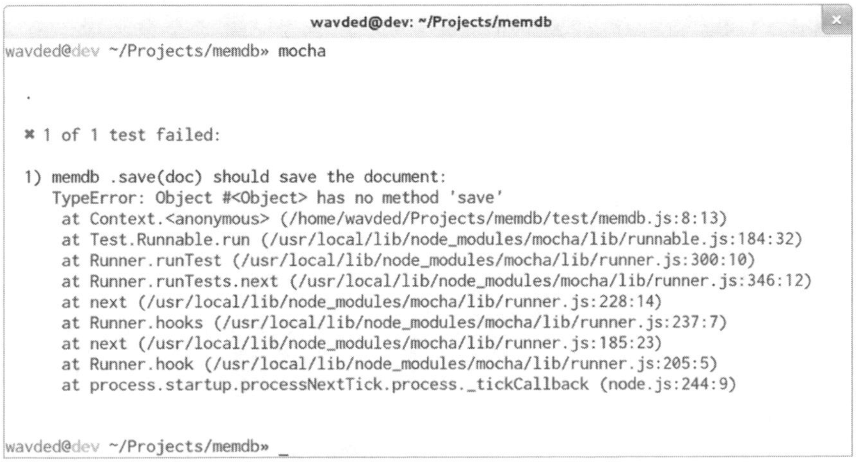

```
wavded@dev: ~/Projects/memdb
wavded@dev ~/Projects/memdb» mocha

  .

  ✖ 1 of 1 test failed:

  1) memdb .save(doc) should save the document:
     TypeError: Object #<Object> has no method 'save'
      at Context.<anonymous> (/home/wavded/Projects/memdb/test/memdb.js:8:13)
      at Test.Runnable.run (/usr/local/lib/node_modules/mocha/lib/runnable.js:184:32)
      at Runner.runTest (/usr/local/lib/node_modules/mocha/lib/runner.js:300:10)
      at Runner.runTests.next (/usr/local/lib/node_modules/mocha/lib/runner.js:346:12)
      at next (/usr/local/lib/node_modules/mocha/lib/runner.js:228:14)
      at Runner.hooks (/usr/local/lib/node_modules/mocha/lib/runner.js:237:7)
      at next (/usr/local/lib/node_modules/mocha/lib/runner.js:185:23)
      at Runner.hook (/usr/local/lib/node_modules/mocha/lib/runner.js:205:5)
      at process.startup.processNextTick.process._tickCallback (node.js:244:9)

wavded@dev ~/Projects/memdb» _
```

Figure 10.2 Failing test in Mocha

```
wavded@dev: ~/Projects/memdb
wavded@dev ~/Projects/memdb» mocha

  .

  ✓ 1 test complete (2ms)

wavded@dev ~/Projects/memdb» _
```

Figure 10.3 Successful test in Mocha

DEFINING SETUP AND CLEANUP LOGIC USING MOCHA HOOKS

This test case makes the assumption that `memdb.first()` functions appropriately, so you'll want to add a few test cases for it as well, with expectations defined using the `it()` function. The revised test file, listing 10.12, includes a new concept—the concept of Mocha *hooks*. For example, the BDD interface exposes `beforeEach()`, `afterEach()`, `before()`, and `after()`, which take callbacks, allowing you to define setup and cleanup logic before and after test cases and suites defined with `describe()`.

Listing 10.12 Adding a `beforeEach` hook

```
var memdb = require('..');
var assert = require('assert');

describe('memdb', function(){
  beforeEach(function(){
    memdb.clear();
  })

  describe('.save(doc)', function(){
    it('should save the document', function(){
      var pet = { name: 'Tobi' };
      memdb.save(pet);
      var ret = memdb.first({ name: 'Tobi' });
      assert(ret == pet);
    })
  })

  describe('.first(obj)', function(){
    it('should return the first matching doc', function(){
      var tobi = { name: 'Tobi' };
      var loki = { name: 'Loki' };

      memdb.save(tobi);
      memdb.save(loki);

      var ret = memdb.first({ name: 'Tobi' });
      assert(ret == tobi);

      var ret = memdb.first({ name: 'Loki' });
      assert(ret == loki);
    })

    it('should return null when no doc matches', function(){
      var ret = memdb.first({ name: 'Manny' });
```

Annotations:
- Clear database before each test case to keep tests stateless
- The first expectation for .first()
- Save two documents
- Make sure each one can be returned properly
- The second expectation for .first()

```
      assert(ret == null);
    })
  })
})
```

Ideally test cases share no state whatsoever. To achieve this with memdb, you simply need to remove all the documents by implementing the `.clear()` method in index.js:

```
exports.clear = function(){
  db = [];
};
```

Running Mocha again should show you that three tests have passed.

TESTING ASYNCHRONOUS LOGIC

One thing we haven't yet dealt with in Mocha testing is testing asynchronous logic. To show how this is done, let's make a small change to one of the functions defined earlier in index.js. By changing the `save` function to the following, a callback can be optionally provided that will execute after a small delay (meant to simulate some sort of asynchronous operation):

```
exports.save = function(doc, cb){
  db.push(doc);
  if (cb) {
    setTimeout(function() {
      cb();
    }, 1000);
  }
};
```

Mocha test cases can be defined as async simply by adding an argument to a function defining testing logic. The argument is commonly named *done*. The following listing shows how you could change the initial `.save()` test to work with asynchronous code.

Listing 10.13 Testing asynchronous logic

```
describe('.save(doc)', function(){
  it('should save the document', function(done){
    var pet = { name: 'Tobi' };
    memdb.save(pet, function(){                          <-- Save doc
      var ret = memdb.first({ name: 'Tobi' });           <-- Invoke callback with first doc
      assert(ret == pet);                                <-- Assert document saved properly
      done();                                            <-- Tell Mocha you're done with this test case
    });
  });
});
```

This same rule applies to all of the hooks. For example, the `beforeEach()` hook to clear the database could add a callback, and Mocha could wait until it's called in order to move on. If `done()` is invoked with an error as the first argument, then Mocha will report the error and mark the hook or test case as a failure:

```
beforeEach(function(done){
  memdb.clear(done);
})
```

For more about Mocha, check out its full online documentation: http://visionmedia .github.com/mocha. Mocha also works for client-side JavaScript like nodeunit.

> **Mocha's use of nonparallel testing**
>
> Mocha executes tests one after another rather than in parallel, which makes test suites execute more slowly but makes writing tests easier. But Mocha won't let any test run for an inordinately long time. Mocha, by default, will only allow any given test to run for 2,000 milliseconds before failing it. If you have tests that take longer, you can run Mocha with the `--timeout` command-line option and then specify a larger number.
>
> For most testing, running tests serially is fine. If you find this problematic, there are other frameworks that execute in parallel, like Vows, covered in the next section.

10.1.4 Vows

The tests you can write using the Vows unit-testing framework are more structured than those of many other frameworks, with the structure intended to make the tests easy to read and maintain.

Vows uses its own BDD-flavored terminology to define test structure. In the realm of Vows, a test suite contains one or more *batches*. A batch can be thought of as a group of related *contexts*, or conceptual areas of concern that you want to test. The batches and contexts run in parallel. A context may contain a number of things: a *topic*, one or more *vows*, and/or one or more related contexts (inner contexts also run in parallel). A *topic* is testing logic that's related to a context. A *vow* is a test of the result of a topic. Figure 10.4 visually represents how Vows structures tests.

Vows, like nodeunit and Mocha, is geared toward automated application testing. The difference is primarily in flavor and parallelism, with Vows tests requiring a specific structure and terminology. In this section, we'll run through an example application test and explain how you can use a Vows test to run multiple tests at the same time.

Typically, you'd install Vows globally to give you access to the `vows` command-line test-running tool. Enter the following command to install Vows:

```
$ npm install -g vows
```

TESTING APPLICATION LOGIC WITH VOWS

You can trigger testing in Vows either by running a script containing test logic or by using the `vows` command-line test runner. The following example of a standalone test script (which can be run like any other Node script) uses one of the tests of the to-do application's core logic.

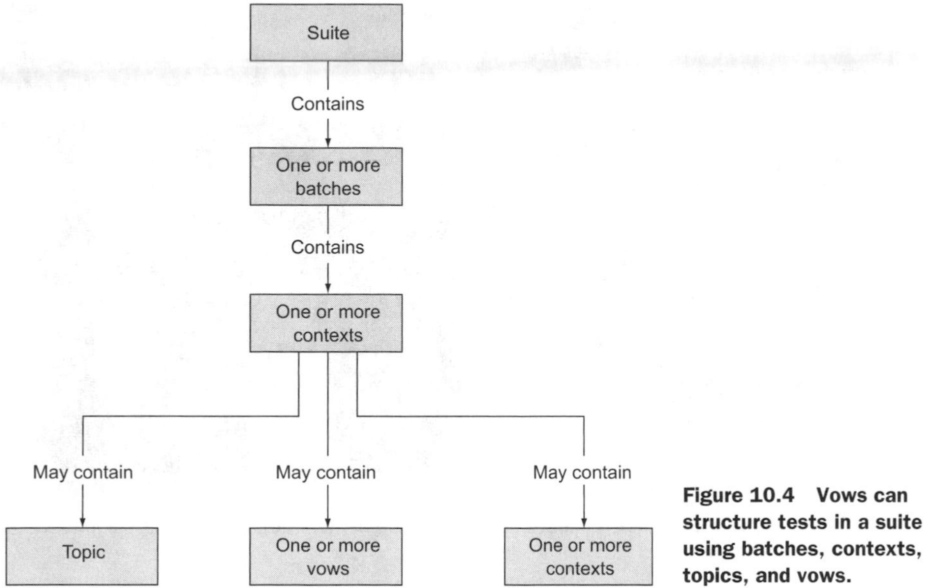

Figure 10.4 Vows can structure tests in a suite using batches, contexts, topics, and vows.

Listing 10.14 creates a batch. Within the batch, you define a context. Within the context, you define a topic and a vow. Note how the code makes use of the callback to deal with asynchronous logic in the topic. If a topic isn't asynchronous, a value can be returned rather than being sent via a callback.

Listing 10.14 Using Vows to test the to-do application

```
var vows = require('vows')
var assert = require('assert')
var Todo = require('./todo');

vows.describe('Todo').addBatch({                      <-- A batch
  'when adding an item': {                                      <-- A context
    topic: function () {                             <-- A topic
      var todo = new Todo();
      todo.add('Feed my cat');
      return todo;
    },
    'it should exist in my todos': function(er, todo) {          <-- A vow
       assert.equal(todo.getCount(), 1);
    }
  }
}).run();
```

If you want to include the previous code listing in a folder of tests, where it could be run with the Vows test runner, you'd change the last line to the following:

```
...
}).export(module);
```

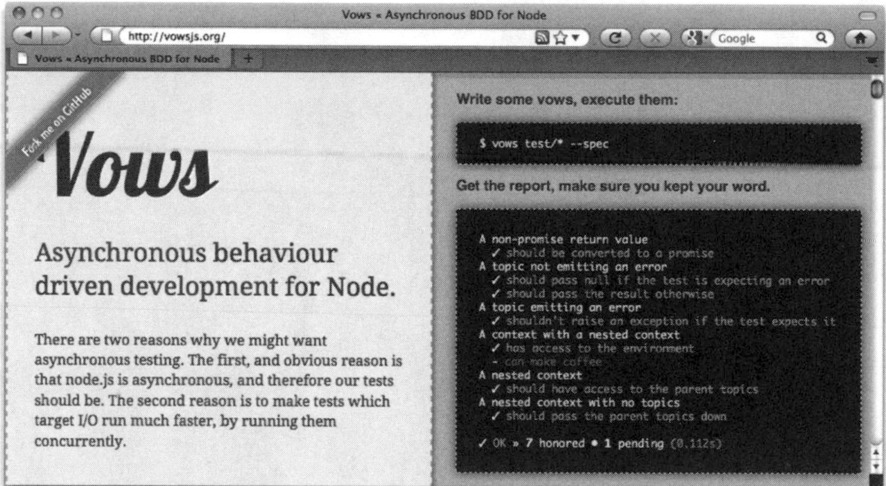

Figure 10.5 Vows combines full-featured BDD testing capabilities with features such as macros and flow control.

To run all tests in a folder named *test*, enter the following command:

```
$ vows test/*
```

For more about Vows, check out the project's online documentation (http://vowsjs.org/), as shown in figure 10.5.

Vows offers a comprehensive testing solution, but you might not like the test structure it imposes, as Vows requires the use of batches, contexts, topics, and vows. Or you might like the features of a competing testing framework or be familiar with another framework and see no need to learn Vows. If this sounds like you, should.js might be a good alternative to explore. Rather than being yet another testing framework, should.js offers a BDD-flavored alternative to using Node's assert module.

10.1.5 Should.js

Should.js is an assertion library that can help make your tests easier to read by allowing you to express assertions in a BDD-like style. It's designed to be used in conjunction with other testing frameworks, which lets you continue to use your own preferred framework. In this section, you'll learn how to write assertions with should.js and, as an example, you'll write a test for a custom module.

Should.js is easy to use with other frameworks because it augments `Object.prototype` with a single property: `should`. This allows you to write expressive assertions such as `user.role.should.equal("admin")`, or `users.should.include("rick")`.

TESTING MODULE FUNCTIONALITY USING SHOULD.JS

Let's say you're writing a Node command-line tip calculator that you want to use to figure out who should pay what amount when you split a bill with friends. You'd like to write tests for your calculation logic in a way that's easily understood by your nonprogrammer friends, because then they won't think you're cheating them.

To set up your tip calculator application, enter the following commands, which will set up a folder for the application and install should.js for testing:

```
$ mkdir -p tips/test
$ cd tips
$ touch index.js
$ touch test/tips.js
```

Now you can install should.js by running the following command:

```
$ npm install should
```

Next, edit the index.js file, which will contain the logic defining the application's core functionality. Specifically, the tip calculator logic includes four helper functions:

- `addPercentageToEach`—Increases each number in an array by a given percentage
- `sum`—Calculates the sum of each element in an array
- `percentFormat`—Formats a percentage for display
- `dollarFormat`—Formats a dollar value for display

Add this logic by populating index.js with the contents of the following listing.

Listing 10.15 Logic for calculating tips when splitting a bill

```
exports.addPercentageToEach = function(prices, percentage) {    <- Add percentage to array elements
  return prices.map(function(total) {
    total = parseFloat(total);
    return total + (total * percentage);
  });
}

exports.sum = function(prices) {    <- Calculate sum of array elements
  return prices.reduce(function(currentSum, currentValue) {
    return parseFloat(currentSum) + parseFloat(currentValue);
  })
}

exports.percentFormat = function(percentage) {    <- Format percentage for display
  return parseFloat(percentage) * 100 + '%';
}

exports.dollarFormat = function(number) {    <- Format dollar value for display
  return '$' + parseFloat(number).toFixed(2);
}
```

Now edit the test script in test/tips.js, as shown in listing 10.16. The script loads the tip logic module, defines a tax and tip percentage and the bill items to test, tests the addition of a percentage to each array element, and tests the bill total.

Listing 10.16 Logic that calculates tips when splitting a bill

```
var tips = require('..');                                  <-- Use tip logic module
var should = require('should');

var tax = 0.12;                                  <-- Define tax and tip rates
var tip = 0.15;
var prices = [10, 20];                                <-- Define bill items to test
var pricesWithTipAndTax = tips.addPercentageToEach(prices, tip + tax);

pricesWithTipAndTax[0].should.equal(12.7);          <-- Test tax and tip addition
pricesWithTipAndTax[1].should.equal(25.4);

var totalAmount = tips.sum(pricesWithTipAndTax).toFixed(2);
totalAmount.should.equal('38.10');                       <-- Test bill totaling

var totalAmountAsCurrency = tips.dollarFormat(totalAmount);
totalAmountAsCurrency.should.equal('$38.10');

var tipAsPercent = tips.percentFormat(tip);
tipAsPercent.should.equal('15%');
```

Run the script using the following command. If all is well, the script should generate no output, because no assertions have been thrown, and your friends will be reassured of your honesty:

```
$ node test/tips.js
```

Should.js supports many types of assertions—everything from assertions that use regular expressions to assertions that check object properties—allowing comprehensive testing of data and objects generated by your application. The project's GitHub page (http://github.com/visionmedia/should.js) provides comprehensive documentation of should.js's functionality.

Now that we've looked at tools designed for unit testing, let's move on to an altogether different style of testing: acceptance testing.

10.2 Acceptance testing

Acceptance testing, also called *functional testing*, tests outcomes, not logic. After you've created a suite of unit tests for your project, acceptance testing will provide an additional level of protection against bugs that unit testing might not detect.

Acceptance testing is similar, conceptually, to testing by end users who follow a list of things to test. But being automated makes acceptance testing fast, and it doesn't require human labor.

Acceptance testing also deals with complications created by client-side JavaScript behavior. If there's a serious problem created by client-side JavaScript, server-side unit testing won't catch it, but thorough acceptance testing will. For example, your application may make use of client-side JavaScript form validation. Acceptance testing will ensure that your validation logic works, rejecting and accepting input appropriately. Or, for another example, you may have Ajax-driven administration functionality—such as the ability to browse content to select featured content for a website's front page—that should only be available to authenticated users. To deal with this, you could write a test to ensure that the Ajax request produces expected results when the user logs in, and write another test to make sure that those who aren't authenticated can't access this data.

In this section, you'll learn how to use two acceptance-testing frameworks: Tobi and Soda. Soda provides the benefit of harnessing real browsers for acceptance testing, whereas Tobi, which we'll look at first, is easier to learn and to get up and running on.

10.2.1 Tobi

Tobi (https://github.com/LearnBoost/tobi) is an easy-to-use, acceptance-testing framework that emulates the browser and takes advantage of should.js, offering access to its assertion capabilities. The framework uses two third-party modules, jsdom and htmlparser, to simulate a web browser, allowing access to a virtual DOM.

Tobi enables you to painlessly write tests that will log into your web application, if need be, and send web requests that emulate someone using your application. If Tobi returns unexpected results, your test can then alert you to the problem.

Because Tobi must emulate a user's activities and check the results of web requests, it must often manipulate or examine DOM elements. In the world of client-side JavaScript development, web developers often use the jQuery library (http://jquery.com) when they need to interact with the DOM. Developers can also use jQuery on the server side, and Tobi's use of jQuery minimizes the amount of learning required to create tests with it.

In this section, we'll talk about how you can use Tobi to test any running web application, including non-Node applications, over the network. We'll also show you how to use Tobi to test a web application created with Express, even if the Express-based web application isn't running.

TESTING WEB APPLICATIONS WITH TOBI

If you'd like to create tests using Tobi, first create a directory for them (or use an existing application directory), and then change to the directory in the command line and enter the following to install Tobi:

```
$ npm install tobi
```

Listing 10.17 is an example of using Tobi to test web application functionality of a website—in this case running the to-do application we tested in chapter 5. The test attempts to create a to-do item, and then looks for it on the response page. If you run the script using Node and no exceptions are thrown, the test passed.

The script creates a simulated browser, uses it to perform an HTTP `GET` request for the main page with the entry form, fills in the form's fields, and submits the form. The script then checks the contents of a table cell for the text "Floss the Cat." If the table cell contains the text, the test passes.

Listing 10.17 Testing a web application via HTTP

```
var tobi = require('tobi');
var browser = tobi.createBrowser(3000, '127.0.0.1');          <— Create browser

browser.get('/', function(res, $){                             <— Get to-do form
  $('form')
    .fill({ description: 'Floss the cat' })                    <— Fill in form
    .submit(function(res, $) {                                 <— Submit data
      $('td:nth-child(3)').text().should.equal('Floss the cat');
    });
});
```

You can test the previous application without even running it. The following Tobi test shows how you'd do this:

```
var tobi = require('tobi');
var app = require('./app');
var browser = tobi.createBrowser(app);

browser.get('/about', function(res, $){
  res.should.have.status(200);
  $('div').should.have.one('h1', 'About');
  app.close();
});
```

Tobi doesn't include a test runner, but you can use it with unit-testing frameworks such as Mocha or nodeunit.

10.2.2 Soda

Soda (https://github.com/LearnBoost/soda) takes a different approach to acceptance testing. Whereas other Node acceptance-testing frameworks simulate browsers, Soda remotely controls real browsers. Soda, as shown in figure 10.6, does this by sending instructions to the Selenium Server (also known as Selenium RC), or the Sauce Labs on-demand testing service.

Selenium Server will open browsers on the machine on which it's installed, whereas Sauce Cloud will open virtual ones on a server somewhere on the internet.

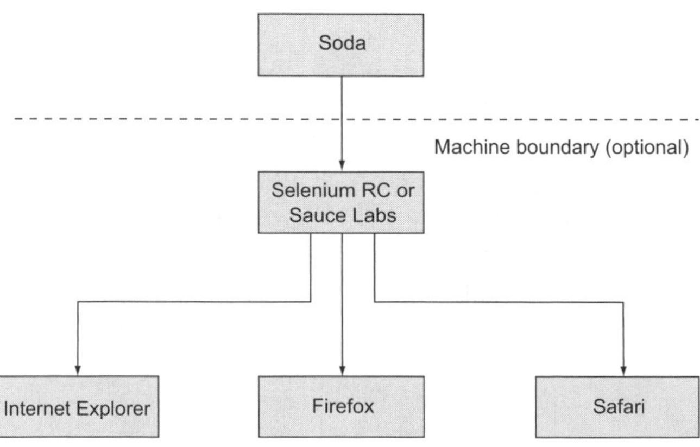

Figure 10.6 Soda is an acceptance-testing framework that allows real browsers to be remotely controlled. Whether using Selenium RC or the Sauce Labs service, Soda provides an API that allows Node to perform direct testing that takes into account the realities of different browser implementations.

Selenium Server and Sauce Labs, rather than Soda, do the talking to the browsers, but they relay any requested info back to Soda. If you want to do a number of tests in parallel and not tax your own hardware, consider using Sauce Labs.

In this section, you'll learn how to install Soda and the Selenium Server, how to test applications with Soda and Selenium, and how to test applications with Soda and Sauce Labs.

INSTALLING SODA AND THE SELENIUM SERVER

To do testing with Soda, you need to install the `soda` npm package and the Selenium Server (if you're not using Sauce Labs). Enter the following to install Soda:

```
$ npm install soda
```

Selenium Server requires Java to run. If Java isn't installed, please consult the official Java download page for instructions specific to your operating system (www.java.com/en/download/).

Installing Selenium Server is fairly straightforward. All you have to do is download a recent .jar file from the Selenium "Downloads" page (http://seleniumhq.org/download/). Once you've downloaded the file, you can run the server with the following command (although the filename will likely contain a different version number):

```
java -jar selenium-server-standalone-2.6.0.jar
```

TESTING WEB APPLICATIONS WITH SODA AND SELENIUM

Once you have the server running, you can include the following code in a script to set up for running tests. In the call to `createClient`, the `host` and `port` settings indicate the host and port used to connect to the Selenium Server. By default, these should be 127.0.0.1 and 4444, respectively. The `url` in the call to `createClient` specifies the base URL that you should open in the browser for testing, and the `browser` value specifies the browser to be used for testing:

```
var soda = require('soda')
var assert = require('assert');

var browser = soda.createClient({
  host: '127.0.0.1',
  port: 4444,
  url: 'http://www.reddit.com',
  browser: 'firefox'
});
```

In order to get feedback on what your testing script is doing, you may want to include the following code. This code prints each Selenium command as it's attempted:

```
browser.on('command', function(cmd, args){
  console.log(cmd, args.join(', '));
});
```

Next in your test script should be the tests themselves. The following listing is an example test that attempts to log a user into Reddit and fails if the text "logout" isn't present on the resulting page. Commands like `clickAndWait` are documented on the Selenium website (http://release.seleniumhq.org/selenium-core/1.0.1/reference.html).

Listing 10.18 A Soda test allows commands to control the actions of a browser.

```
browser
  .chain                                    <- Enable method chaining
  .session()                                <- Start Selenium session
  .open('/')                                <- Open URL
  .type('user', 'mcantelon')                <- Enter text into form field
  .type('passwd', 'mahsecret')
  .clickAndWait('//button[@type="submit"]') <- Click button and wait
  .assertTextPresent('logout')              <- Make sure text exists
  .testComplete()                           <- Mark test as complete
  .end(function(err){                       <- End Selenium session
    if (err) throw err;
    console.log('Done!');
  });
```

TESTING WEB APPLICATIONS WITH SODA AND SAUCE LABS

If you go the Sauce Labs route, sign up for the service at the Sauce Labs website (https://saucelabs.com) and change the code in your test script that returns `browser` to something like what you see in the following listing.

Listing 10.19 Using Soda to control a Sauce Labs browser

```
var browser = soda.createSauceClient({
  'url': 'http://www.reddit.com/',
  'username': 'yourusername',             <- Sauce Labs user name
  'access-key': 'youraccesskey',          <- Sauce Labs API key
  'os': 'Windows 2003',                   <- Desired operating system
  'browser': 'firefox',                   <- Desired browser type
  'browser-version': '3.6',               <- Desired browser version
  'name': 'This is an example test',
  'max-duration': 300                     <- Make test fail if it takes too long
  });
```

And that's it. You've now learned the fundamentals of a powerful testing method that can complement your unit tests and make your applications much more resistant to accidentally created bugs.

10.3 Summary

By incorporating automated testing into your development, you greatly decrease the odds of bugs creeping into your codebase, and you can develop with greater confidence.

If you're new to unit testing, Mocha and nodeunit are excellent frameworks to start with: they're easy to learn, flexible, and can work with should.js if you want to run

BDD-style assertions. If you like the BDD approach and are seeking a system for structuring tests and controlling flow, Vows may also be a good choice.

In the realm of acceptance testing, Tobi is a great place to start. Tobi is easy to set up and use, and if you're familiar with jQuery you'll be up and running quickly. If your needs require acceptance testing in order to take into account browser discrepancies, Soda may be worth running, but testing is slower and you must learn the Selenium API.

Now that you've got a handle on how automated testing can be conducted in Node, let's take a deeper dive into Node web application templating by looking at some template engines that will help boost your web development productivity and enjoyment.

11 Web application templating

This chapter covers

- How templating helps keep applications organized
- Creating templates using Embedded JavaScript
- Learning minimalist templating with Hogan
- Using Jade to create templates

In chapters 8 and 9, you learned some templating basics to use with the Express framework in order to create views. In this chapter, you'll focus exclusively on templating, learning how to use three popular template engines and how to use templating to keep any web application's code clean by separating logic from presentation markup.

If you're familiar with templating and the model-view-controller (MVC) pattern, you can skim through to section 11.2, where you'll start learning about the template engines we'll detail in this chapter, which include Embedded JavaScript, Hogan, and Jade. If you're not familiar with templating, keep reading—we'll explore it conceptually in the next few sections.

11.1 Using templating to keep code clean

You can use the model-view-controller (MVC) pattern to develop conventional web applications in Node as well as with nearly every other web technology. One of the key concepts in MVC is the separation of logic, data, and presentation. In MVC web applications, the user will typically request a resource from the server, which will cause the *controller* to request application data from the *model* and then pass the data to the *view*, which will finally format the data for the end user. This view portion of the MVC pattern is often implemented using one of various templating languages. When an application uses templating, the view will relay selected values, returned by the model, to a *template engine*, and specify what template file should define how to display the provided values.

Figure 11.1 shows how templating logic fits into the overall architecture of an MVC application.

Template files typically contain placeholders for application values as well as HTML, CSS, and sometimes small bits of client-side JavaScript to do things like display third-party widgets, such as Facebook's Like button, or to trigger interface behavior, such as hiding or revealing parts of the page. As template files focus on presentation rather than logic, front-end developers and server-side developers can work on them, which can help with a project's division of labor.

In this section, we'll render HTML with, and without, a template to show you the difference. But first, let's start with an example of templating in action.

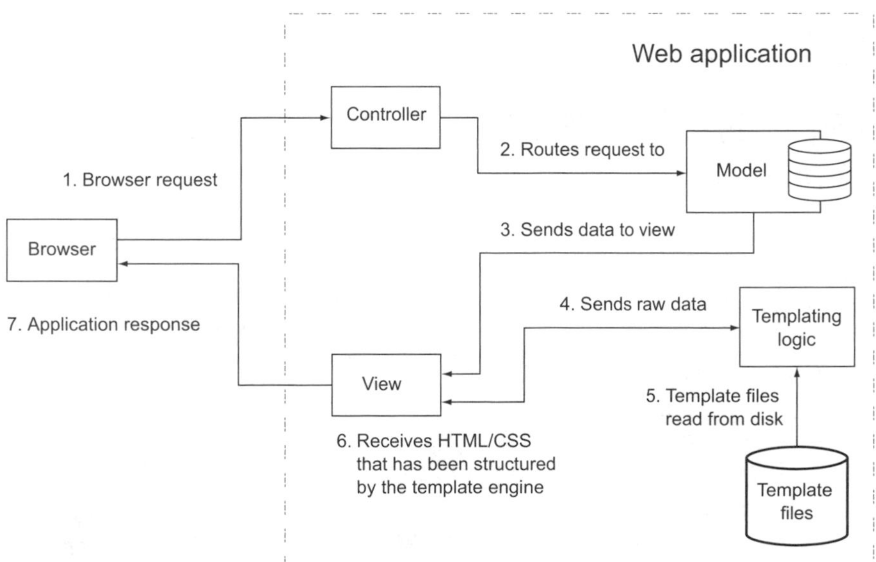

Figure 11.1 The flow of an MVC application and its interaction with the template layer

11.1.1 Templating in action

As a quick illustration of how you can apply templating, let's look at the problem of elegantly outputting HTML from a simple blogging application. Each blog entry will have a title, date of entry, and body text. The blog will look similar to what's shown in figure 11.2, in a web browser.

Blog entries will be read from a text file formatted like the following snippet from entries.txt. The --- in the following listing indicates where one entry stops and another begins.

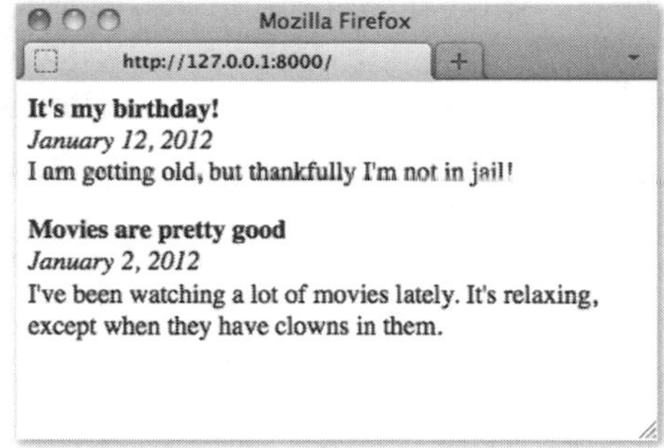

Figure 11.2 Example blog application browser output

Listing 11.1 Blog entries text file

```
title: It's my birthday!
date: January 12, 2012
I am getting old, but thankfully I'm not in jail!
---
title: Movies are pretty good
date: January 2, 2012
I've been watching a lot of movies lately. It's relaxing,
except when they have clowns in them.
```

The blog application code in blog.js will start by requiring necessary modules and reading in the blog entries, as shown in the following listing.

Listing 11.2 Blog entry file-parsing logic for a simple blogging application

```
var fs = require('fs');
var http = require('http');

function getEntries() {                          <- Function to read and parse blog entry text
  var entries = [];
  var entriesRaw = fs.readFileSync('./
     entries.txt', 'utf8');                      <- Read blog entry data from file

  entriesRaw = entriesRaw.split("---");          <- Parse text into individual blog entries

  entriesRaw.map(function(entryRaw) {
    var entry = {};
    var lines = entryRaw.split("\n");            <- Parse entry text into individual lines

    lines.map(function(line) {                   <- Parse lines into entry properties
      if (line.indexOf('title: ') === 0) {
        entry.title = line.replace('title: ', '');
      }
      else if (line.indexOf('date: ') === 0) {
        entry.date = line.replace('date: ', '');
      }
      else {
```

```
        entry.body = entry.body || '';
        entry.body += line;
      }
    });

    entries.push(entry);
  });

  return entries;
}

var entries = getEntries();
console.log(entries);
```

The following code, when added to the blog application, defines an HTTP server. When the server receives an HTTP request, it'll return a page containing all blog entries. This page is rendered using a function called `blogPage`, which we'll define next:

```
var server = http.createServer(function(req, res) {
  var output = blogPage(entries);

  res.writeHead(200, {'Content-Type': 'text/html'});
  res.end(output);
});

server.listen(8000);
```

Now you need to define the `blogPage` function, which renders the blog entries into a page of HTML that can be sent to the user's browser. You'll implement this by trying two approaches:

- Rendering HTML without a template
- Rendering HTML using a template

Let's look at rendering without a template first.

RENDERING HTML WITHOUT A TEMPLATE

The blog application could output the HTML directly, but including the HTML with the application logic would result in clutter. In the following listing, the `blogPage` function illustrates a nontemplated approach to displaying blog entries.

Listing 11.3 Template engines separate presentation details from application logic.

```
function blogPage(entries) {
    var output = '<html>'                 <- Too much HTML interspersed with logic
               + '<head>'
               + '<style type="text/css">'
               + '.entry_title { font-weight: bold; }'
               + '.entry_date { font-style: italic; }'
               + '.entry_body { margin-bottom: 1em; }'
               + '</style>'
               + '</head>'

               + '<body>';
```

```
    entries.map(function(entry) {
      output += '<div class="entry_title">' + entry.title + "</div>\n"
              + '<div class="entry_date">' + entry.date + "</div>\n"
              + '<div class="entry_body">' + entry.body + "</div>\n";
    });

    output += '</body></html>';

    return output;
  }
```

Note that all of this presentation-related content, CSS definitions, and HTML adds many lines to the application.

RENDERING HTML USING A TEMPLATE

Rendering HTML using templating allows you to remove the HTML from the application logic, cleaning up the code considerably.

To try out the demos in this section, you'll need to install the Embedded JavaScript (EJS) module into your application directory. You can do this by entering the following on the command line:

```
npm install ejs
```

The following code loads a template from a file and then defines a new version of the `blogPage` function, this time using the EJS template engine, which we'll show you how to use in section 11.2:

```
var ejs = require('ejs');
var template = fs.readFileSync('./template/blog_page.ejs', 'utf8');

  function blogPage(entries) {
    var values = {entries: entries};
    return ejs.render(template, {locals: values});
  }
```

The EJS template file contains HTML markup (keeping it out of the application logic) and placeholders that indicate where data passed to the template engine should be put. The EJS template file that shows the blog entries would contain the HTML and placeholders shown in the following listing.

Listing 11.4 An EJS template for displaying blog entries

```
<html>
  <head>
    <style type="text/css">
      .entry_title { font-weight: bold; }
      .entry_date { font-style: italic; }
      .entry_body { margin-bottom: 1em; }
    </style>
  </head>

  <body>
    <% entries.map(function(entry) { %>          // Placeholder that loops through blog entries
      <div class="entry_title"><%= entry.title %></div>     // Placeholders for bits of data in each entry
      <div class="entry_date"><%= entry.date %></div>
```

```
      <div class="entry_body"><%= entry.body %></div>
    <% }); %>
  </body>
</html>
```

Community-contributed Node modules also provide template engines, and a wide variety of them exist. If you consider HTML and/or CSS inelegant, because HTML requires closing tags and CSS requires opening and closing braces, take a closer look at template engines. They allow template files to use special "languages" (such as the Jade language, which we'll cover later in this chapter) that provide a shorthand way of specifying HTML, CSS, or both.

These template engines can make your templates cleaner, but you may not want to take the time to learn an alternative way of specifying HTML and CSS. Ultimately, what you decide to use comes down to a matter of personal preference.

In the rest of this chapter, you'll learn how to incorporate templating in your Node applications through the lens of three popular template engines:

- The Embedded JavaScript (EJS) engine
- The minimalist Hogan engine
- The Jade template engine

Each of these engines allows you to write HTML in an alternative way. Let's start with EJS.

11.2 Templating with Embedded JavaScript

Embedded JavaScript (https://github.com/visionmedia/ejs) takes a fairly straightforward approach to templating, and it will be familiar territory for folks who've used template engines in other languages, such as JSP (Java), Smarty (PHP), ERB (Ruby), and so on. EJS allows you to embed EJS *tags* as placeholders for data within HTML. EJS also lets you execute raw JavaScript logic in your templates for tasks such as conditional branching and iteration, much like PHP does.

In this section, you'll learn how to do the following:

- Create EJS templates
- Use EJS filters to provide commonly needed, presentation-related functionality, such as text manipulation, sorting, and iteration
- Integrate EJS with your Node applications
- Use EJS for client-side applications

Let's dive deeper into the world of EJS templating.

11.2.1 Creating a template

In the world of templating, the data sent to the template engine for rendering is sometimes called the *context*. The following is a bare-bones example of Node using EJS to render a simple template using a context:

```
var ejs = require('ejs');
var template = '<%= message %>';
var context = {message: 'Hello template!'};

console.log(ejs.render(template, {locals: context}));
```

Note the use of locals in the second argument sent to render. The second argument can include rendering options as well as context data, which means the use of locals ensures that individual bits of context data aren't interpreted as EJS options. But it's possible in most cases to pass the context itself as the second option, as the following render call illustrates:

```
console.log(ejs.render(template, context));
```

If you pass a context to EJS directly as the second argument to render, make sure you don't name context values using any of the following terms: cache, client, close, compileDebug, debug, filename, open, or scope. These values are reserved to allow the changing of template engine settings.

CHARACTER ESCAPING

When rendering, EJS escapes any special characters in context values, replacing them with HTML entity codes. This is intended to prevent cross-site scripting (XSS) attacks, in which malicious web application users attempt to submit JavaScript as data in the hopes that, when displayed, it'll execute in some other user's browser. The following code shows EJS's escaping at work:

```
var ejs = require('ejs');
var template = '<%= message %>';
var context = {message: "<script>alert('XSS attack!');</script>"};

console.log(ejs.render(template, context));
```

The previous code will display the following output:

```
&lt;script&gt;alert('XSS attack!');&lt;/script&gt;
```

If you trust the data being used in your template and don't want to escape a context value in an EJS template, you can use <%- instead of <%= in your template tag, as the following code demonstrates:

```
var ejs = require('ejs');
var template = '<%- message %>';
var context = {
  message: "<script>alert('Trusted JavaScript!');</script>"
};

console.log(ejs.render(template, context));
```

Note that if you don't like the characters used by EJS to specify tags, you can customize them, like so:

```
var ejs = require('ejs');

ejs.open = '{{:'
ejs.close = '}}:'
```

```
var template = '{{= message }}';
var context = {message: 'Hello template!'};

console.log(ejs.render(template, context));
```

Now that you know the basics of EJS, let's look at some things you can do with it that make managing the presentation of data easier.

11.2.2 Manipulating template data using EJS filters

EJS provides support for *filters*—a feature that allows you to easily do lightweight data transformations. To indicate that you're using a filter, you add a colon (`:`) to the opening characters of your EJS tag. For example:

- `<%=:` would be used for escaped EJS output using a filter.
- `<%-:` would be used for unescaped output using a filter.

Filters can also be *chained*, meaning you can put multiple filters in a single EJS tag and display the cumulative effect of all filters (similar to the "pipe" concept on *UNIX systems). In the next few sections, we'll run through a number of filters that are useful in common scenarios.

FILTERS THAT HANDLE SELECTION

EJS filters are put into EJS tags. To give you an example of the usefulness of filters, imagine an application that allows users to let people know what movies they've watched. One bit of important information might be the most recent movie they've watched. The EJS tag in the template in the following example displays the last movie in an array of movies by using a `last` filter to display only the last item in an array:

```
var ejs = require('ejs');
var template = '<%=: movies | last %>';
var context = {'movies': [
  'Bambi',
  'Babe: Pig in the City',
  'Enter the Void'
]};

console.log(ejs.render(template, context));
```

Note that `first` is also a valid filter. If you want to get a specific item from a list, you could use the `get` filter. The EJS tag `<%=: movies | get:1 %>` will display the second item in the `movies` array (with item 0 being the first item). You can also use the `get` filter to show properties if the context value is an object rather than an array.

FILTERS FOR CASE MANIPULATION

EJS filters can also be used to change case. The EJS tag in the following template includes a filter that will capitalize the first letter in a context value, in this case changing the displayed value from "bob" to "Bob":

```
var ejs = require('ejs');
var template = '<%=: name | capitalize %>';
var context = {name: 'bob'};

console.log(ejs.render(template, context));
```

If you want to display a context value entirely in uppercase, you could use the `upcase` filter. Conversely, using the `downcase` filter will display the value in lowercase.

FILTERS FOR TEXT MANIPULATION

Text can be sliced and diced by EJS filters. You can truncate text, append or prepend to text, and even replace parts of your text.

Truncating text to a certain character count allows you to prevent long strings of text from causing problems with HTML layouts. The following code, for example, will truncate the title text to 20 characters, displaying "The Hills are Alive":

```
var ejs = require('ejs');
var template = '<%=: title | truncate:20 %>';
var context = {title: 'The Hills are Alive With the Sound of Critters'};

console.log(ejs.render(template, context));
```

If you want to truncate text to a certain number of words, an EJS filter supports that, too. In the previous example you could replace the EJS tag with `<%=: title | truncate_words:2 %>` to truncate the context value to two words. The output would then be "The Hills."

The `replace` filter uses `String.prototype.replace(pattern)` behind the scenes, so it accepts either a string or a regexp. The following code shows an example of automatically abbreviating a word using an EJS filter:

```
var ejs = require('ejs');
var template = "<%=: weight | replace:'kilogram','kg' %>";
var context = {weight: '40 kilogram'};

console.log(ejs.render(template, context));
```

You can append text by adding a filter like `append:'some text'`. Similarly, you can prepend text using a filter like `prepend:'some text'`.

FILTERS THAT DO SORTING

EJS filters can also sort. Returning to the previously cited movie title example, you could use EJS filters to sort the movies by title and display the first item in alphabetical order, as illustrated by figure 11.3.

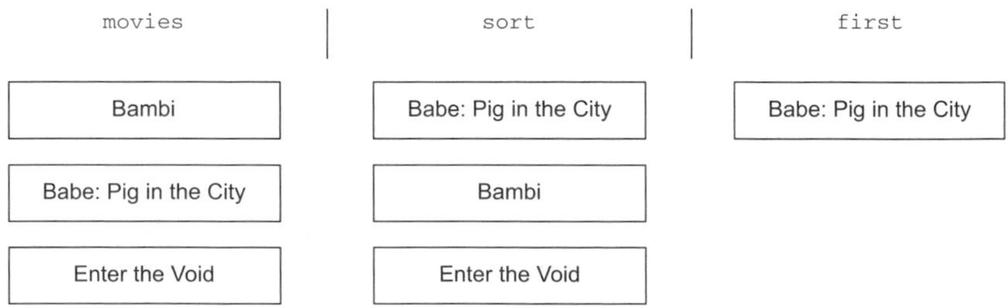

Figure 11.3 Visualizing the use of EJS filters to process arrays of text

The following code implements this:

```
var ejs = require('ejs');
var template = '<%=: movies | sort | first %>';
var context = {'movies': [
  'Bambi',
  'Babe: Pig in the City',
  'Enter the Void'
]};

console.log(ejs.render(template, context));
```

If you want to sort an array composed of objects, but you'd like to sort by comparing object properties, you can do so using filters:

```
var ejs = require('ejs');
var template = "<%=: movies | sort_by:'name' | first | get:'name' %>";
var context = {'movies': [
  {name: 'Babe: Pig in the City'},
  {name: 'Bambi'},
  {name: 'Enter the Void'}
]};

console.log(ejs.render(template, context));
```

Note the use of `get:'name'` at the end of the filter chain. You use that because the sort returns an object, and you need to select which property of the object to display.

THE MAP FILTER

The EJS `map` filter allows you to specify the property of an object that you want subsequent filters to operate on. In the previous example, you could use the filter chain using `map`. As an alternative to having to specify the property using the `sort_by` filter and then having to specify the property to display using the `get` filter, you would use the `map` filter to create an array from object properties. The resulting EJS would be `<%=: movies | map:'name' | sort | first %>`.

CREATING CUSTOM FILTERS

Although EJS comes with filters for most common needs, you may want something beyond what EJS offers. If you want a filter that could, for example, round to an arbitrary decimal place, you'll find there's no built-in filter to do this. Luckily, with EJS it's easy to add your own custom filters, as the following listing shows.

Listing 11.5 Defining your own custom EJS filters

```
var ejs = require('ejs');
var template = '<%=: price * 1.145 | round:2 %>';
var context = {price: 21};

ejs.filters.round = function(number, decimalPlaces) {
number = isNaN(number) ? 0 : number;
  decimalPlaces = !decimalPlaces ? 0 : decimalPlaces;

  var multiple = Math.pow(10, decimalPlaces);
```

Define a function on ejs.filters object

First argument is input value, context, or previous filter result

```
  return Math.round(number * multiple) / multiple;
};

console.log(ejs.render(template, context));
```

As you can see, filters in EJS provide a great way to lessen the amount of logic you need in order to prepare data for display. Rather than doing these transformations to your data manually before rendering the template, EJS provides nice built-in mechanisms that do it for you.

11.2.3 Integrating EJS into your application

Because it's awkward to store templates in files along with application code, and doing so clutters up your code, we'll show you how to use Node's filesystem API to read them from separate files.

Move to a working directory and create a file named *app.js* containing the code in the following listing.

Listing 11.6 Storing template code in files

```
var ejs = require('ejs');
var fs = require('fs');
var http = require('http');
var filename = './template/students.ejs';      // Note location of template file

var students = [                                // Data to pass to template engine
  {name: 'Rick LaRue', age: 23},
  {name: 'Sarah Cathands', age: 25},
  {name: 'Bob Dobbs', age: 37}
];

var server = http.createServer(function(req, res) {     // Create HTTP server
  if (req.url == '/') {
    fs.readFile(filename, function(err, data) {         // Read template from file
      var template = data.toString();
      var context = {students: students};
      var output = ejs.render(template, context);       // Render template
      res.setHeader('Content-type', 'text/html');
      res.end(output);                                  // Send HTTP response
    });
  } else {
    res.statusCode = 404;
    res.end('Not found');
  }
});

server.listen(8000);
```

Next, create a child directory called *template*. You'll keep your templates in this directory. Create a file named *students.ejs* in the template directory, so the structure of your application should look like figure 11.4

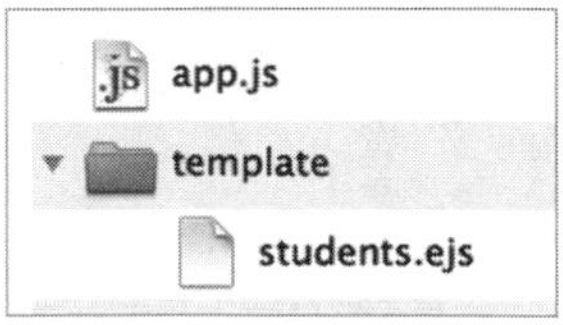

Enter the code in the following listing into students.ejs.

app.js
template
students.ejs

Figure 11.4 Structure of our EJS application

Listing 11.7 EJS template that renders an array of students

```
<% if (students.length) { %>
  <ul>
    <% students.forEach(function(student) { %>
      <li><%= student.name %> (<%= student.age %>)</li>
    <% }) %>
  </ul>
<% } %>
```

CACHING EJS TEMPLATES

EJS supports optional, in-memory caching of template functions. What this means is that EJS, after parsing your template file once, will store the function that's created by the parsing. Rendering a cached template will be faster because the parsing step can be skipped.

If you're doing initial development of a Node web application, and you want to see any changes you make to your template files reflected immediately, you won't want to enable caching. But if you're deploying an application to production, enabling caching is a quick, easy win. Caching is conditionally enabled via the `NODE_ENV` environment variable.

To try out caching, change the call to EJS's `render` function in the previous example to the following:

```
var cache = process.env.NODE_ENV === 'production';
var output = ejs.render(
  template,
  {students: students, cache: cache, filename: filename}
);
```

Note that the `filename` option doesn't necessarily have to be a file—you can use a unique value that identifies whichever template you're rendering.

Now that you've learned how to integrate EJS with your Node applications, let's look at how EJS can be used in a different way: in web browsers.

11.2.4 Using EJS for client-side applications

We've shown you an example that uses EJS with Node; now let's take a quick look at using EJS in the browser. To use EJS on the client side, you'll first want to download the EJS engine to your working directory, as shown by the following commands:

```
cd /your/working/directory
curl https://raw.github.com/visionmedia/ejs/master/ejs.js -o ejs.js
```

Once you download the ejs.js file, you can use EJS in your client-side code. The following listing shows a simple client-side application of EJS.

Listing 11.8 Using EJS to add templating capabilities to the client side

```
<html>
  <head>
  <title>EJS example</title>
```

```
    <script src="ejs.js"></script>
    <script
    ➥src="http://ajax.googleapis.com/ajax/libs/jquery/1.8/jquery.js">
    </script>
  </head>
  <body>

    <div id='output'></div>

    <script>
      var template = "<%= message %>";
      var context = {message: 'Hello template!'};

      $(document).ready(function() {
        $('#output').html(
          ejs.render(template, context)
        );
      });
    </script>
  </body>
</html>
```

Include jQuery library for DOM manipulation

Placeholder for rendered template output

Template to use to render content

Data to use with template

Wait until browser loads page

Render template to div with ID "output"

You've now learned how to use a fully featured Node template engine, so it's time to look at the Hogan template engine, which deliberately limits the functionality available to templating code.

11.3 Using the Mustache templating language with Hogan

Hogan.js (https://github.com/twitter/hogan.js) is a template engine that was created by Twitter for its templating needs. Hogan is an implementation of the popular Mustache (http://mustache.github.com/) template language standard, which was created by GitHub's Chris Wanstrath.

Mustache takes a minimalist approach to templating. Unlike EJS, the Mustache standard deliberately doesn't include conditional logic, nor any built-in content-filtering capabilities other than escaping content to prevent XSS attacks. Mustache advocates that template code should be kept as simple as possible.

In this section you'll learn

- How to create and implement Mustache templates in your application
- The different template tags available in the Mustache standard
- How to organize your templates using "partials"
- How to fine-tune Hogan with your own delimiters and other options

Let's look at the alternative approach Hogan provides for templating.

11.3.1 Creating a template

To use Hogan in an application, or to try out the demos in this section, you'll need to install Hogan in your application directory. You can do this by entering the following command on the command line:

```
npm install hogan.js
```

The following is a bare-bones example of Node using Hogan to render a simple template using a context. Running it will output the text "Hello template!"

```
var hogan = require('hogan.js');
var template = '{{message}}';
var context = {message: 'Hello template!'};

var template = hogan.compile(template);
console.log(template.render(context));
```

Now that you know how to process Mustache templates with Hogan, let's look at what tags Mustache supports.

11.3.2 Mustache tags

Mustache tags are conceptually similar to EJS's tags. Mustache tags serve as placeholders for variable values, indicate where iteration is needed, and allow you to augment Mustache's functionality and add comments to your templates.

DISPLAYING SIMPLE VALUES

To display a context value in a Mustache template, include the name of the value in double braces. Braces, in the Mustache community, are known as "mustaches." If you want to display the value for context item `name`, for example, you'd use the Hogan tag `{{name}}`.

Like most template engines, Hogan escapes content by default to prevent XSS attacks. But to display an unescaped value in Hogan, you can either add a third mustache or prepend the name of the context item with an ampersand. Using the previous `name` example, you could display the context value unescaped by either using the `{{{name}}}` or `{{&name}}` tag formats.

If you want to add a comment in a Mustache template, you can use this format: `{{! This is a comment }}`.

SECTIONS: ITERATING THROUGH MULTIPLE VALUES

Although Hogan doesn't allow the inclusion of logic in templates, it does include an elegant way to iterate through multiple values in a context item using Mustache *sections.*

The following context, for example, contains an item with an array of values:

```
var context = {
  students: [
    { name: 'Jane Narwhal', age: 21 },
    { name: 'Rick LaRue', age: 26 }
  ]
};
```

If you want to create a template that will display each student in a separate HTML paragraph, with output similar to the following, it would be a straightforward task using a Hogan template:

```
<p>Name: Jane Narwhal, Age: 21 years old</p>
<p>Name: Rick LaRue, Age: 26 years old</p>
```

The following template would produce the desired HTML:

```
{{#students}}
  <p>Name: {{name}}, Age: {{age}} years old</p>
{{/students}}
```

INVERTED SECTIONS: DEFAULT HTML WHEN VALUES DON'T EXIST

What if the value of the students item in the context data wasn't an array? If the value was a single object, for example, the template would display it. But sections won't display if the corresponding item's value is undefined or false, or is an empty array.

If you want your template to output a message indicating that values don't exist for a section, Hogan supports what Mustache calls *inverted sections*. The following template code, if added to the previous student display template, would display a message when no student data exists in the context:

```
{{^students}}
  <p>No students found.</p>
{{/students}}
```

SECTION LAMBDAS: CUSTOM FUNCTIONALITY IN SECTION BLOCKS

In order to allow developers to augment Mustache's functionality, the Mustache standard lets you define section tags that process template content through a function call, rather than iterating through arrays. This is called a *section lambda*.

As an example use of a section lambda, listing 11.9 shows how you'd use one to add Markdown support when rendering a template. Note that the example uses the github-flavored-markdown module, which you'll have to install by entering `npm install github-flavored-markdown` on your command line.

In the following listing, the `**Name**` in the template gets rendered to `<strong>Name</strong>` when passing through the Markdown parser called by the section lambda logic.

Listing 11.9 Using a lambda in Hogan

```
var hogan = require('hogan.js');
var md = require('github-flavored-markdown');    <- Require Markdown parser

var template = '{{#markdown}}'                   <- Mustache template
             + '**Name**: {{name}}'                 also contains
             + '{{/markdown}}';                     Markdown formatting

var context = {
  name:     'Rick LaRue',
  markdown: function() {
    return function(text) {
      return md.parse(text);                     <- Template context includes a
    };                                              section lambda to parse
  }                                                 Markdown in the template
};

var template = hogan.compile(template);
console.log(template.render(context));
```

Section lambdas allow you to easily implement things like caching and translation mechanisms into your templates.

PARTIALS: REUSING TEMPLATES WITHIN OTHER TEMPLATES

When writing templates, you want to avoid unnecessarily repeating the same code in multiple templates. One way to avoid this is to create *partials*. Partials are templates used as building blocks that are included in other templates. Another use of partials is to break up complicated templates into simpler templates.

The following listing, for example, uses a partial to separate the template code used to display student data from the main template.

Listing 11.10 The use of partials in Hogan

```
var hogan = require('hogan.js');

var studentTemplate = '<p>Name: {{name}}, '            // Template code used for partial
                    + 'Age: {{age}} years old</p>';
var mainTemplate = '{{#students}}'                     // Main template code
                 + '{{>student}}'
                 + '{{/students}}';

var context = {
  students: [{
     name: 'Jane Narwhal',
     age: 21
  },{
     name: 'Rick LaRue',
     age: 26
  }]
};
                                                       // Compiling the main and partial templates
var template = hogan.compile(mainTemplate);
var partial = hogan.compile(studentTemplate);

var html = template.render(context, {student: partial});   // Rendering the main template and partial
console.log(html);
```

11.3.3 Fine-tuning Hogan

Hogan is fairly simple to use—once you've learned its vocabulary of tags, you should be off and running. You may need to tweak only a couple of things as you use it.

If you don't like Mustache-style braces, you can change the delimiters Hogan uses by passing the `compile` method an option to override them. The following example shows compiling in Hogan using EJS-style delimiters:

```
hogan.compile(text, {delimiters: '<% %>'});
```

If you'd like to use section tags that don't begin with the # character after the opening mustaches, you can do that with another `compile` method option: `sectionTags`. You might, for example, want to use a different tag format for section tags in which lambdas are employed. The following listing alters the earlier example in listing 11.9 to use an underscore prefix to differentiate the markdown section tag from subsequent section tags that iterate rather than employ lambdas.

Listing 11.11 Using custom section tags in Hogan

```
var hogan = require('hogan.js');
var md = require('github-flavored-markdown');      <-- Require Markdown parser

var template = '{{_markdown}}'                     <-- Custom tag used in template
             + '**Name**: {{name}}'
             + '{{/markdown}}';

var context = {
  name:     'Rick LaRue',
  _markdown: function(text) {                      <-- Lambda for custom tag
    return md.parse(text);
  }
};

var template = hogan.compile(
  template,
  {sectionTags: [{o: '_markdown', c: 'markdown'}]}   <-- Custom opening and closing tags defined
);
console.log(template.render(context));
```

When using Hogan, you won't have to change any options to enable caching. Caching is built into the compile function and is enabled by default.

Now that you've learned two fairly straightforward Node template engines, let's look at the Jade template engine, which approaches the problem of dealing with presentation markup differently than EJS and Hogan.

11.4 Templating with Jade

Jade (http://jade-lang.com) offers an alternative way to specify HTML. The key difference between Jade and the majority of other templating systems is the use of meaningful whitespace.

When creating a template in Jade, you use indentation to indicate HTML tag nesting. HTML tags also don't have to be explicitly closed, which eliminates the problem of accidentally closing tags prematurely, or not at all. Using indentation also results in templates that are less visually dense and easier to maintain.

For a quick example of this at work, let's look at how you'd represent this snippet of HTML:

```
<html>
  <head>
    <title>Welcome</title>
  </head>
  <body>
    <div id="main" class="content">
      <strong>"Hello world!"</strong>
    </div>
  </body>
</html>
```

This HTML could be represented using the following Jade template:

```
html
  head
    title Welcome
  body
    div.content#main
      strong "Hello world!"
```

Jade, like EJS, allows you to embed JavaScript, and you can use it on the server or client side. But Jade offers additional features, such as support for template inheritance and mixins. Mixins allow you to define easily reusable mini-templates to represent the HTML used for commonly occurring visual elements, such as item lists and boxes. Mixins are very similar in concept to the Hogan.js partials, which you learned about in the previous section. Template inheritance makes it easy to organize the Jade templates needed to render a single HTML page into multiple files. You'll learn about these features in detail later in this section.

To install Jade in a Node application directory, enter the following on the command line:

```
npm install jade
```

Installing Jade with the `-g` global flag is also useful because it gives you access to a `jade` command-line tool that allows you to quickly render a template to HTML. The following command-line use would result in the template/sidebar.jade file being rendered to sidebar.html in the template directory. The Jade command-line tool gives you an easy way to experiment with Jade syntax:

```
jade template/sidebar.jade
```

In this section you'll learn

- Jade basics, such as specifying class names, attributes, and block expansion
- How to add logic to your Jade templates using built-in keywords
- How to organize your templates using inheritance, blocks, and mixins

To get started, let's look at the basics of Jade usage and syntax.

11.4.1 Jade basics

Jade uses the same tag names as HTML, but it lets you lose the opening and closing < and > characters and instead uses indentation to express tag nesting.

A tag can have one or more CSS classes associated with it by adding `.<classname>`. A `div` element with the `content` and `sidebar` classes applied to it would be represented like this:

```
div.content.sidebar
```

CSS IDs are assigned by adding `#<ID>` to the tag. You'd add a CSS ID of `featured_content` to the previous example using the following Jade representation:

```
div.content.sidebar#featured_content
```

> **div tag shorthand**
>
> Because the `div` tag is commonly used in HTML, Jade offers a shorthand way of specifying it. The following example will render to the same HTML as the previous example:
>
> ```
> .content.sidebar#featured_content
> ```

Now that you know how to specify HTML tags and their CSS classes and IDs, let's look at how to specify HTML tag attributes.

SPECIFYING TAG ATTRIBUTES

You can specify tag attributes by enclosing the attributes in parentheses, separating the specification of each attribute from the next with a comma. You can specify a hyperlink that'll open in a different tab by using the following Jade representation:

```
a(href='http://nodejs.org', target='_blank')
```

As the specification of tag attributes can lead to long lines of Jade, the template engine provides you with some flexibility. The following Jade is valid and equivalent to the previous example:

```
a(href='http://nodejs.org',
  target='_blank')
```

You can also specify attributes that don't require a value. The next Jade example shows the specification of an HTML form that includes a `select` element with an option preselected:

```
strong Select your favorite food:
form
  select
    option(value='Cheese') Cheese
    option(value='Tofu', selected) Tofu
```

SPECIFYING TAG CONTENT

In the previous code snippet, you also saw examples of tag content: "Select your favorite food:" after the `strong` tag; "Cheese" after the first `option` tag; and "Tofu" after the second `option` tag.

This is the normal way to specify tag content in Jade, but it's not the only way. Although this style is great for short bits of content, it can result in Jade templates with overly long lines if a tag's content is lengthy. Luckily, as the following example shows, Jade allows you to specify tag content using the | character:

```
textarea
  | This is some default text
  | that the user should be
  | provided with.
```

If the HTML tag, such as the `style` and `script` tags, only ever accepts text (meaning it doesn't allow nested HTML elements), then the | characters can be left out entirely, as the following example shows:

```
style
  h1 {
    font-size: 6em;
    color: #9DFF0C;
  }
```

Having two separate ways to express long tag content and short tag content helps you keep your Jade templates looking elegant. Jade also supports an alternative way to express nesting, called *block expansion*.

KEEPING IT ORGANIZED WITH BLOCK EXPANSION

Jade normally expresses nesting through indentation, but sometimes indentation can lead to excess whitespace.

For example, here's a Jade template that uses indentation to define a simple list of links:

```
ul
  li
    a(href='http://nodejs.org/') Node.js homepage
  li
    a(href='http://npmjs.org/') NPM homepage
  li
    a(href='http://nodebits.org/') Nodebits blog
```

A more compact way to express the previous example is by using a Jade block expansion. With block expansion, you add a colon after your tag to indicate nesting. The following code generates the same output as the previous listing, but in four lines instead of seven:

```
ul
  li: a(href='http://nodejs.org/') Node.js homepage
  li: a(href='http://npmjs.org/') NPM homepage
  li: a(href='http://nodebits.org/') Nodebits blog
```

Now that you've had a good look at how to represent markup using Jade, let's look at how you can integrate Jade with your web application.

INCORPORATING DATA IN JADE TEMPLATES

Data is relayed to the Jade engine in the same basic way as in EJS. The template is first compiled into a function that's then called with a context in order to render the HTML output. The following is an example of this:

```
var jade = require('jade');
var template = 'strong #{message}';
var context = {message: 'Hello template!'};

var fn = jade.compile(template);
console.log(fn(context));
```

In the previous example, the `#{message}` in the template specified a placeholder to be replaced by a context value.

Context values can also be used to supply values for attributes. The next example would render `<a href="http://google.com"></a>`:

```
var jade = require('jade');
var template = 'a(href = url)';
var context = {url: 'http://google.com'};

var fn = jade.compile(template);
console.log(fn(context));
```

Now that you've learned how HTML is represented using Jade, and how you can provide Jade templates with application data, let's look at how you can incorporate logic in Jade.

11.4.2 Logic in Jade templates

Once you supply Jade templates with application data, you need logic to deal with that data. Jade allows you to directly embed lines of JavaScript code into your templates, which is how you define logic in your templates. Code like `if` statements, `for` loops, and `var` declarations are common. Before we dive into the details, here's an example Jade template rendering a contact list to give you a practical feel for how you might use Jade logic in an application:

```
h3.contacts-header My Contacts

if contacts.length
  each contact in contacts
    - var fullName = contact.firstName + ' ' + contact.lastName
    .contact-box
      p fullName
      if contact.isEditable
        p: a(href='/edit/+contact.id) Edit Record
      p
        case contact.status
          when 'Active'
            strong User is active in the system
          when 'Inactive'
            em User is inactive
          when 'Pending'
            | User has a pending invitation
else
  p You currently do not have any contacts
```

Let's first look at the different ways Jade handles output when embedding JavaScript code.

USING JAVASCRIPT IN JADE TEMPLATES

Prefixing a line of JavaScript logic with `-` will execute the JavaScript without including any value returned from the code in the template's output. Prefixing JavaScript logic with `=` will include a value returned from the code, escaped to prevent XSS attacks. But if your JavaScript generates code that shouldn't be escaped, you can prefix it with `!=`. Table 11.1 summarizes these prefixes.

Table 11.1 Prefixes used to embed JavaScript in Jade

Prefix	Output
=	Escaped output (for untrusted or unpredictable values, XSS-safe)
!=	Output without escaping (for trusted or predictable values)
-	No output

Jade includes a number of commonly used conditional and iterative statements that can be written without prefixes: `if`, `else if`, `else`, `case`, `when`, `default`, `until`, `while`, `each`, and `unless`.

Jade also allows you to define variables. The following shows two ways to assign values that are equivalent in Jade:

```
- var count = 0
count = 0
```

The unprefixed statements have no output, just like the - prefix discussed previously.

ITERATING THROUGH OBJECTS AND ARRAYS

Values passed in a context are accessible to JavaScript in Jade. In the next example, we'll read a Jade template from a file and pass the Jade template a context containing a couple of messages that we intend to display in an array:

```
var jade = require('jade');
var fs = require('fs');
var template = fs.readFileSync('./template.jade');
var context = { messages: [
  'You have logged in successfully.',
  'Welcome back!'
]};

var fn = jade.compile(template);
console.log(fn(context));
```

The Jade template would contain the following:

```
- messages.forEach(function(message) {
  p= message
- })
```

The final HTML output would look like this:

```
<p>You have logged in successfully.</p><p>Welcome back!</p>
```

Jade also supports a non-JavaScript form of iteration: the `each` statement. `each` statements allow you to cycle through arrays and object properties with ease.

The following is equivalent to the previous example, but using `each` instead:

```
each message in messages
  p= message
```

You can cycle through object properties using a slight variation, like this:

```
each value, key in post
  div
    strong #{key}
    p value
```

CONDITIONALLY RENDERING TEMPLATE CODE

Sometimes templates need to make decisions about how data is displayed depending on the value of the data. The next example illustrates a conditional in which, roughly half the time, the script tag is outputted as HTML:

```
- var n = Math.round(Math.random() * 1) + 1
- if (n == 1) {
  script
    alert('You win!');
- }
```

Conditionals can also be written in Jade using a cleaner, alternative form:

```
- var n = Math.round(Math.random() * 1) + 1
  if n == 1
    script
      alert('You win!');
```

If you're writing a negated conditional, such as `if (n != 1)`, you could use Jade's `unless` keyword:

```
- var n = Math.round(Math.random() * 1) + 1
  unless n == 1
    script
      alert('You win!');
```

USING CASE STATEMENTS IN JADE

Jade also supports a non-JavaScript form of conditional similar to a `switch`: the `case` statement. `case` statements allow you to specify an outcome based on a number of template scenarios.

The following example template shows how the `case` statement can be used to display results from the search of a blog in three different ways. If the search finds nothing, a message is shown indicating that. If a single blog post is found, it's displayed in detail. If multiple blog posts are found, an `each` statement is used to iterate through the posts, displaying their titles:

```
case results.length
  when 0
    p No results found.
  when 1
    p= results[0].content
  default
    each result in results
      p= result.title
```

11.4.3 Organizing Jade templates

With your templates defined, you next need to know how to organize them. As with application logic, you don't want to make your template files overly large. A single template file should correspond to a conceptual building block: a page, a sidebar, or blog post content, for example.

In this section, you'll learn a few mechanisms that allow different template files to work together to render content:

- Structuring multiple templates with template inheritance
- Implementing layouts using block prepending/appending
- Template including
- Reusing template logic with mixins

Let's begin by looking at template inheritance in Jade.

STRUCTURING MULTIPLE TEMPLATES WITH TEMPLATE INHERITANCE

Template inheritance is one means of structuring multiple templates. The concept treats templates, conceptually, like classes in the object-oriented programming paradigm. One template can extend another, which can in turn extend another. You can use as many levels of inheritance as makes sense.

As a simple example, let's look at using template inheritance to provide a basic HTML wrapper that you can use to wrap page content. In a working directory, create a folder called *template* in which you'll put the example's Jade file. For a page template, you'll create a file called *layout.jade* containing the following Jade:

```
html
  head
    block title
  body
    block content
```

The layout.jade template contains the bare-bones definition of an HTML page as well as two *blocks*. Blocks are used in template inheritance to define where a descendant template can provide content. In layout.jade there's a `title` block, allowing a descendent template to set the title, and a `content` block, allowing a descendent template to set what is to be displayed on the page.

Next, in your working directory's template directory, create a file named *page.jade*. This template file will populate the `title` and `content` blocks:

```
extends layout

block title
  title Messages

block content
  each message in messages
    p= message
```

Finally, add the logic in the following listing (a modification of an earlier example in this section), which will display the template results, showing inheritance in action.

Listing 11.12 Template inheritance in action

```
var jade = require('jade');
var fs = require('fs');
var templateFile = './template/page.jade';
var iterTemplate = fs.readFileSync(templateFile);
var context = {messages: [
  'You have logged in successfully.',
  'Welcome back!'
]};

var iterFn = jade.compile(
  iterTemplate,
  {filename: templateFile}
);

console.log(iterFn(context));
```

Now let's look at another template inheritance feature: block prepending and appending.

IMPLEMENTING LAYOUTS USING BLOCK PREPENDING/APPENDING

In the previous example, the blocks in layout.jade contained no content, which made setting the content in the page.jade template straightforward. But if a block in an inherited template *does* contain content, this content can be built upon, rather than replaced, by descendent templates using block prepending and appending. This allows you to define common content and add to it, rather than replace it.

The following layout.jade template contains an additional block, `scripts`, which contains content—a `script` tag that'll load the jQuery JavaScript library:

```
html
  head
    block title
    block scripts
      script(src='//ajax.googleapis.com/ajax/libs/jquery/1.8/jquery.js')
  body
    block content
```

If you want the page.jade template to additionally load the jQuery UI library, you could do this by using the template in the following listing.

Listing 11.13 Using `block append` to load an additional JavaScript file

```
extends layout                                  <- This template extends layout template
baseUrl = "http://ajax.googleapis.com/ajax/libs/jqueryui/1.8/"

block title
  title Messages

block style                                     <- Define style block
```

```
  link(rel="stylesheet", href= baseUrl+"themes/flick/jquery-ui.css")

block append scripts                                   ◁ Append this scripts block to
  script(src= baseUrl+"jquery-ui.js")                    the one defined in layout

block content
  count = 0
  each message in messages
    - count = count + 1
    script
      $(function() {
        $("#message_#{count}").dialog({
          height: 140,
          modal: true
        });
      });
    != '<div id="message_' + count + '">' + message + '</div>'
```

But template inheritance isn't the only way to integrate multiple templates. You also can use the `include` Jade command.

TEMPLATE INCLUDING

Another tool for organizing templates is Jade's `include` command. This command incorporates the contents of another template. If you add the line `include footer` to the layout.jade template from the earlier example, you'll end up with the following template:

```
html
  head
    block title
    block style
    block scripts
      script(src='//ajax.googleapis.com/ajax/libs/jquery/1.8/jquery.js')
  body
    block content
    include footer
```

This template would include the contents of a template named *footer.jade* in the rendered output of layout.jade, as illustrated in figure 11.5.

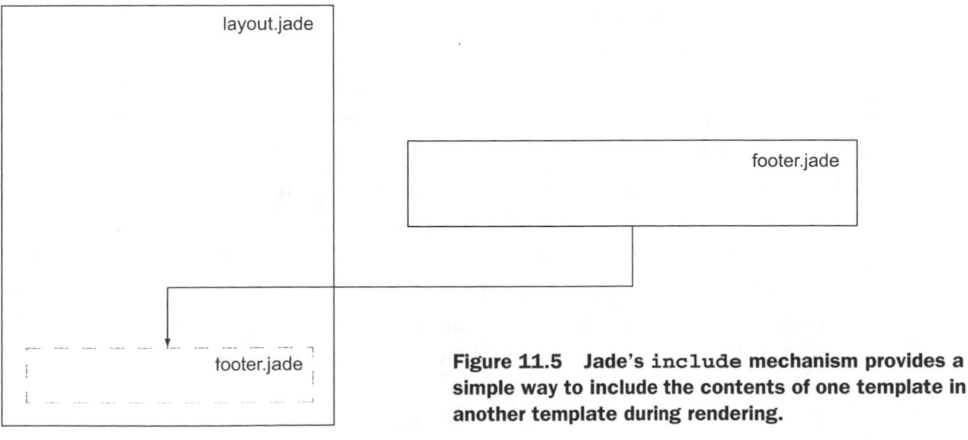

Figure 11.5 Jade's `include` mechanism provides a simple way to include the contents of one template in another template during rendering.

This could be used, for example, to add information about the site, or design elements, to layout.jade. You can also include non-Jade files by specifying the file extension (for example, `include twitter_widget.html`).

REUSING TEMPLATE LOGIC WITH MIXINS

Although Jade's `include` command is useful for bringing in previously created chunks of code, it's not ideal for creating a library of reusable functionality that you can share between pages and applications. For this, Jade provides the `mixin` command, which lets you define reusable Jade snippets.

A Jade mixin is analogous to a JavaScript function. A mixin can, like a function, take arguments, and these arguments can be used to generate Jade code.

Let's say, for example, your application handles a data structure similar to the following:

```
var students = [
  {name: 'Rick LaRue', age: 23},
  {name: 'Sarah Cathands', age: 25},
  {name: 'Bob Dobbs', age: 37}
];
```

If you want to define a way to output an HTML list derived from a given property of each object, you could define a mixin like the following one to accomplish this:

```
mixin list_object_property(objects, property)
  ul
    each object in objects
      li= object[property]
```

You could then use the mixin to display the data using this line of Jade:

```
mixin list_object_property(students, 'name')
```

By using template inheritance, `include` statements, and mixins, you can easily reuse presentation markup and can prevent your template files from becoming larger than they need to be.

11.5 Summary

Now that you've learned how three popular HTML template engines work, you can use the technique of templating to keep your application logic and presentation organized. The Node community has created many template engines, which means that if there's something you don't like about the three you've tried in this chapter, you can check out other engines: https://npmjs.org/browse/keyword/template.

The Handlebars.js template engine (https://github.com/wycats/handlebars.js/), for example, extends the Mustache templating language, adding additional features such as conditional tags and globally available lambdas. Dustjs (https://github.com/akdubya/dustjs) prioritizes performance and features such as streaming. For a list of Node template engines, check out the consolidate.js project (https://github.com/visionmedia/consolidate.js), which provides an API that abstracts the use of template engines, making it easy to use multiple engines in your applications. But if the idea of having to learn any kind of template language at all seems distasteful, an engine called Plates (https://github.com/flatiron/plates) allows you to stick to HTML, using its engine's logic to map application data to CSS IDs and classes within your markup.

If you find Jade's way of dealing with the separation of presentation and application logic appealing, you might also want to look at Stylus (https://github.com/LearnBoost/stylus), a project that takes a similar approach to dealing with the creation of CSS.

You now have the final piece you need to create professional web applications. In the next chapter, we'll look at deployment: how to make your application available to the rest of the world.

Part 3

Going further with Node

In the last part of the book, you'll learn how to use Node for things other than traditional web applications and how to add real-time components to web applications using Socket.io. You'll also learn how Node can be used to create non-HTTP TCP/IP servers and even command-line tools.

In addition to these new uses, you'll learn how the Node community ecosystem works, where you can go to get help, and how you can contribute your own creations back to the Node community at large via the Node Package Manager repository.

12 Deploying Node applications and maintaining uptime

This chapter covers

- Choosing where to host your Node application
- Deploying a typical application
- Maintaining uptime and maximizing performance

Developing a web application is one thing, but putting it into production is another. For every web platform, there are tips and tricks that increase stability and maximize performance, and Node is no different.

When you're faced with deploying a web application, you'll find yourself considering where to host it. You'll want to consider how to monitor your application and keep it running. You may also wonder what you can do to make it as fast as possible. In this chapter, you'll get an overview of how to address these concerns for your Node web application.

To start, let's look at where you might choose to host your application.

12.1 Hosting Node applications

Most web application developers are familiar with PHP-based applications. When an Apache server with PHP support gets an HTTP request, it'll map the path portion of the requested URL to a specific file, and PHP will execute the contents of the file. This functionality makes it easy to deploy PHP applications: you upload PHP files to a certain location of the filesystem, and they become accessible via web browsers. In addition to being easy to deploy, PHP applications can also be hosted cheaply, because servers are often shared between a number of users.

Deploying Node applications using Node-specific cloud-hosting services offered by companies like Joyent, Heroku, Nodejitsu, VMware, and Microsoft is no more difficult. Node-specific cloud-hosting services are worth looking into if you want to avoid the trouble of administering your own server or want to benefit from Node-specific diagnostics, such as Joyent SmartOS's ability to measure which logic in a Node application performs slowest. The Cloud9 website, itself built using Node.js, even offers a browser-based integrated development environment (IDE) in which you can clone projects from GitHub, work on them via the browser, and then deploy them to a number of Node-specific cloud hosting services, listed in table 12.1.

Table 12.1 Node-specific cloud-hosting and IDE services

Name	Website
Heroku	www.heroku.com/
Nodejitsu	www.nodejitsu.com/
VMware's Cloud Foundry	www.cloudfoundry.com/
Microsoft Azure SDK for Node.js	www.windowsazure.com/en-us/develop/nodejs/
Cloud9 IDE	http://c9.io/

An alternative to Node-specific cloud hosting is running your own server. Linux is a popular choice for Node servers and offers more flexibility than Node-specific cloud hosting because you can easily install any related applications you need, such as database servers. Node-specific cloud-hosting services typically offer a limited selection of related applications.

Linux server administration is its own realm of expertise, however. If you choose to handle your own deployment, you'll need to read up on your chosen Linux variant to be sure you're familiar with setup and maintenance procedures.

> **VIRTUALBOX** If you're new to server administration, you can experiment by running software like VirtualBox (www.virtualbox.org/), which allows you to run a virtual Linux computer on your workstation, no matter what operating system your workstation runs.

If you're familiar with the various server options, you may want to skim through this chapter until you get to section 12.2, which is where we'll start to talk about the basics of deployment. First, let's talk about the options available to you:

- Dedicated servers
- Virtual private servers
- General-purpose cloud servers

Let's tackle some of the options you have when choosing to host your own Node applications.

12.1.1 Dedicated and virtual private servers

Your server may either be a physical one, commonly known as a *dedicated* server, or a virtual one. Virtual servers run inside physical servers and are assigned a share of the physical server's RAM, processing power, and disk space. Virtual servers emulate physical servers and you can administer them in the same way. More than one virtual server can run inside a physical server.

Dedicated servers are usually more expensive than virtual servers and often require more setup time because components may have to be ordered, assembled, and configured. Virtual private servers (VPSs), on the other hand, can be set up quickly because they're created inside preexisting physical servers.

VPSs are a good hosting solution for web applications if you don't anticipate quick growth in usage. VPSs are cheap and can easily be allocated additional resources, when needed, such as disk space and RAM. The technology is established, and many companies, such as Linode (www.linode.com/) and Prgmr (http://prgmr.com/xen/) make it easy to get up and running.

VPSs, like dedicated servers, can't usually be created on demand. Nor can they handle quick growth in usage, because that requires the ability to quickly add more servers without relying on human intervention. To handle such requirements, you'll need to use cloud hosting.

12.1.2 Cloud hosting

Cloud servers are similar to VPSs in that they're virtual emulations of dedicated servers. But they have an advantage over dedicated servers and VPSs in that their management can be fully automated. Cloud servers can be created, stopped, started, and destroyed using a remote interface or API.

Why would you need this? Let's say you've founded a company that has Node-based corporate intranet software. You'd like clients to be able to sign up for your service and, shortly after signing up, receive access to their own server running your software. You could hire technical staff to set up and deploy servers for these clients around the clock, but unless you maintained your own data center, they'd still have to coordinate with dedicated or VPS server providers to provide the needed resources in a timely manner. By using cloud servers, you could have a management server send instructions via an API to your cloud hosting provider to give you access to new servers as needed. This level of automation enables you to deliver services to the customer quickly and without human intervention. Figure 12.1 illustrates how you can use cloud hosting to automate the creation and destruction of an application's servers.

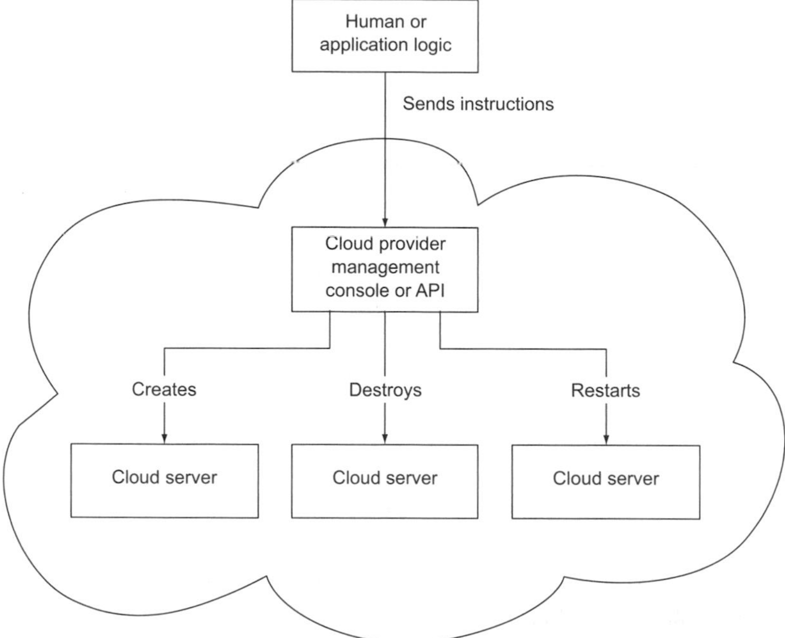

Figure 12.1 Creating, starting, stopping, and destroying cloud servers can be fully automated.

The downside to using cloud servers is that they tend to be more expensive than VPSs and can require some knowledge specific to the cloud platform.

Amazon Web Services

The oldest and most popular cloud platform is Amazon Web Services (AWS; http://aws.amazon.com/). AWS consists of a range of different hosting-related services, like email delivery, content-delivery networks, and lots more. Amazon's Elastic Compute Cloud (EC2), one of AWS's central services, allows you to create servers in the cloud whenever you need them.

EC2 virtual servers are called *instances*, and they can be managed using either the command line or a web-based control console, shown in figure 12.2. As command-line use of AWS takes some time to get used to, the web-based console is recommended for first-time users.

Luckily, because AWS is ubiquitous, it's easy to get help online and find related tutorials, such as Amazon's "Getting Started with Amazon EC2 Linux Instances" (http://mng.bz/cw8n).

Rackspace Cloud

A more basic, easier-to-use cloud platform is Rackspace Cloud (www.rackspace.com/cloud/). This gentler learning curve may be appealing, but Rackspace Cloud offers a smaller range of cloud-related products and functionality than does AWS, and it has a

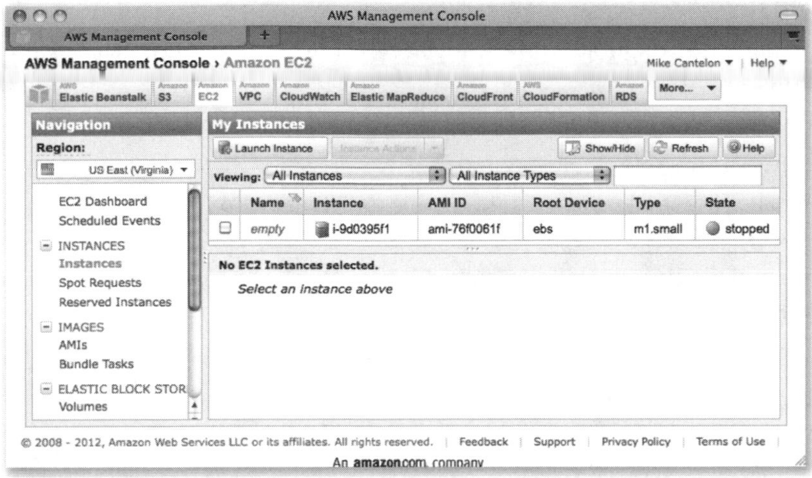

Figure 12.2 The AWS web console provides an easier way to manage Amazon cloud servers for new users than the command line.

somewhat clunkier web interface. Rackspace Cloud servers can be managed using a web interface, or with community-created command-line tools.

Table 12.2 summarizes the hosting options we've talked about in this section.

Table 12.2 Summary of hosting options

Suitable traffic growth	Hosting option	Relative cost
Slow	Dedicated	$$
Linear	Virtual private server	$
Unpredictable	Cloud	$$$

Now that you've had an overview of where you can host your Node applications, let's look at exactly how you'd get your Node application running on a server.

12.2 Deployment basics

Suppose you've created a web application that you want to show off, or maybe you've created a commercial application and need to test it before putting it into full production. You'll likely start with a simple deployment, and then do some work later to maximize uptime and performance. In this section, we'll walk you through a simple, temporary Git deployment, as well as how you can keep the application up and running with Forever. Temporary deploys don't persist beyond reboots, but they have the advantage of being quick to set up.

12.2.1 Deploying from a Git repository

Let's quickly go through a basic deployment using a Git repository to give you a feel for the fundamental steps.

Deployment is most commonly done by following these steps:

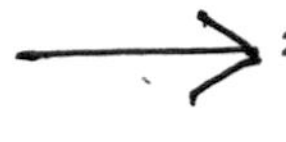

1. Connect to a server using SSH.
2. Install Node and version control tools (such as Git or Subversion) on the server if needed.
3. Download application files, including Node scripts, images, and CSS stylesheets, from a version control repository to the server.
4. Start the application.

Here's an example of an application starting after downloading the application files using Git:

```
git clone https://github.com/Marak/hellonode.git
cd hellonode
node server.js
```

Like PHP, Node doesn't run as a background task. Because of this, the basic deployment we outlined would require keeping the SSH connection open. As soon as the SSH connection closes, the application will terminate. Luckily, it's fairly easy to keep your application running using a simple tool.

AUTOMATING DEPLOYMENT You can automate deployment of your Node application in a number of ways. One is to use a tool like Fleet (https://github.com/substack/fleet), which allows you to deploy to one or more servers using `git push`. A more traditional approach is to use Capistrano, as detailed in the "Deploying node.js applications with Capistrano" post on Evan Tahler's Bricolage blog (http://mng.bz/3K9H).

12.2.2 Keeping Node running

Let's say you've created a personal blog using the Cloud9 Nog blogging application (https://github.com/c9/nog), and you want to deploy it, making sure that it stays running even if you disconnect from SSH.

The most popular tool in the Node community for dealing with this is Nodejitsu's Forever (https://github.com/nodejitsu/forever). It keeps your application running after you disconnect from SSH and, additionally, restarts it if it crashes. Figure 12.3 shows, conceptually, how Forever works.

You can install Forever globally using the `sudo` command.

THE SUDO COMMAND Often when installing an npm module *globally* (with the `-g` flag), you'll need to prefix the `npm` command with the `sudo` command (www.sudo.ws/) in order to run npm with superuser privileges. The first time you use the `sudo` command, you'll be prompted to enter your password. Then the command specified after it will be run.

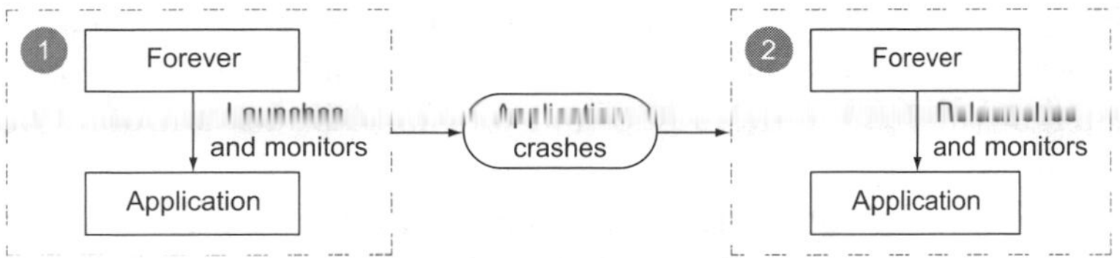

1 The Forever application launches your server application and monitors it for any potential crashes.

2 When the application crashes, Forever takes action and relaunches the application.

Figure 12.3 The Forever tool helps you keep your application running, even if it crashes.

If you're following along, install it now using this command:

```
sudo npm install -g forever
```

Once you've installed Forever, you can use it to start your blog and keep it running with the following command:

```
forever start server.js
```

If you want to stop your blog for some reason, you can use Forever's `stop` command:

```
forever stop server.js
```

When using Forever, you can get a list of what applications the tool is managing by using its `list` command:

```
forever list
```

Another useful capability of Forever is that it can optionally restart your application when any source files have changed. This frees you from having to manually restart each time you add a feature or fix a bug.

To start Forever in this mode, use the `-w` flag:

```
forever -w start server.js
```

Although Forever is an extremely useful tool for deploying applications, you may want to use something more full-featured for long-term deploys. In the next section, we'll look at some industrial-strength monitoring solutions and see how to maximize application performance.

12.3 Maximizing uptime and performance

Once a Node application is release-worthy, you'll want to make sure it starts and stops when the server starts and stops, and that it automatically restarts when the server crashes. It's easy to forget to stop an application before a reboot or to forget to restart an application afterward.

You'll also want to make sure you're taking steps to maximize performance. For example, it makes sense when you're running your application on a server with a quad-core CPU to not use only a single core. If you're using only a single core and your web application's traffic increases significantly, a single core may not have the processing capability to handle the traffic, and your web application won't be able to consistently respond.

In addition to using all CPU cores, you'll want to avoid using Node to host static files for high-volume production sites. Node is geared toward interactive applications, such as web applications and TCP/IP protocols, and it can't serve static files as efficiently as software optimized to do only that. For serving static files you'll want to use technologies like Nginx (http://nginx.org/en/), which specializes in serving static files. Alternatively, you could upload all your static files to a content delivery network (CDN), like Amazon S3 (http://aws.amazon.com/s3/), and reference those files in your application.

In this section, we'll cover some server uptime and performance tips:

- Using Upstart to keep your application up and running through restarts and crashes
- Using Node's cluster API to utilize multicore processors
- Serving Node application static files using Nginx

Let's start by looking at a very powerful and easy-to-use tool for maintaining uptime: Upstart.

12.3.1 Maintaining uptime with Upstart

Let's say you're happy with an application and want to market it to the world. You want to make dead sure that if you restart a server, you don't then forget to restart your application. You also want to make sure that if your application crashes, it's not only automatically restarted, but the crash is logged and you're notified, which allows you to diagnose any underlying issues.

Upstart (http://upstart.ubuntu.com) is a project that provides an elegant way to manage the starting and stopping of any Linux application, including Node applications. Modern versions of Ubuntu and CentOS support the use of Upstart.

You can install Upstart on Ubuntu, if it's not already installed, with this command:

```
sudo apt-get install upstart
```

You can install Upstart on CentOS, if it's not already installed, with this command:

```
sudo yum install upstart
```

Once you've installed Upstart, you'll need to add an Upstart configuration file for each of your applications. These files are created in the /etc/init directory and are named something like my_application_name.conf. The configuration files do not need to be marked as executable.

The following will create an empty Upstart configuration file for this chapter's example application:

```
sudo touch /etc/init/hellonode.conf
```

Now add the contents of the following listing to your config file. This setup will run the application when the server starts up and stop it upon shutdown. The exec section is what gets executed by Upstart.

Listing 12.1 A typical Upstart configuration file

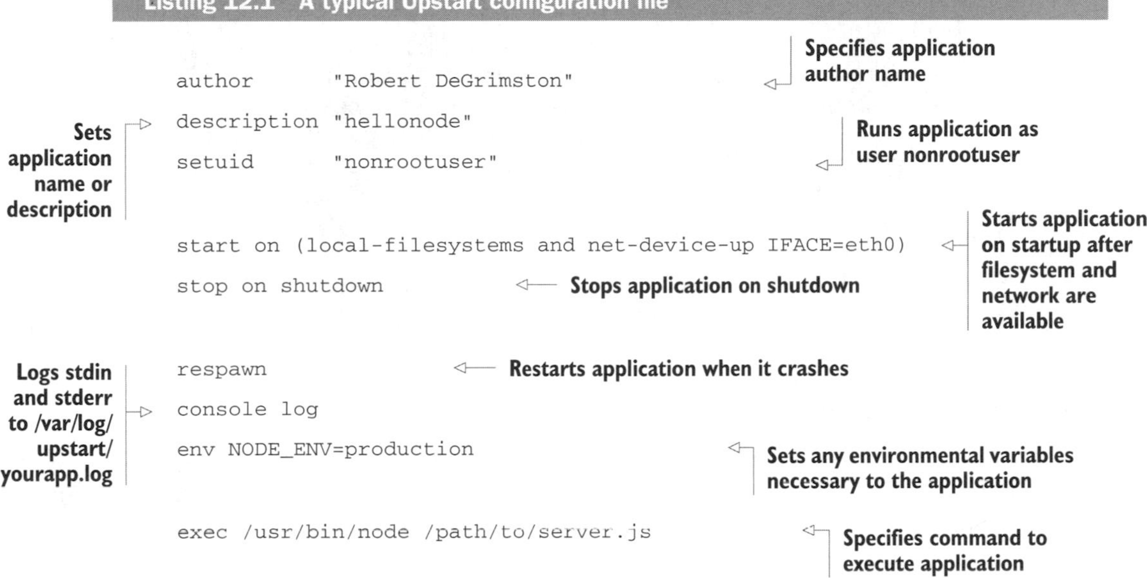

author "Robert DeGrimston"
Specifies application author name
Sets application name or description
description "hellonode"
setuid "nonrootuser"
Runs application as user nonrootuser
start on (local-filesystems and net-device-up IFACE=eth0)
Starts application on startup after filesystem and network are available
stop on shutdown
Stops application on shutdown
Logs stdin and stderr to /var/log/upstart/yourapp.log
respawn
Restarts application when it crashes
console log
env NODE_ENV=production
Sets any environmental variables necessary to the application
exec /usr/bin/node /path/to/server.js
Specifies command to execute application

This configuration will keep your process up and running after the server restarts and even after it crashes unexpectedly. All the application-generated output will be sent to /var/log/upstart/hellonode.log, and Upstart will manage the log rotation for you.

Now that you've created an Upstart configuration file, you can start your application using the following command:

```
sudo service hellonode
```

If your application was started successfully, you'll see a line like this:

```
hellonode start/running, process 6770
```

Upstart is highly configurable. Check out the online cookbook (http://upstart.ubuntu.com/cookbook/) for all the available options.

Upstart and respawning

When the `respawn` option is used, Upstart will by default continually reload your application on crashes *unless* the application is restarted 10 times within 5 seconds. You can change this limit using the `respawn limit COUNT INTERVAL` option, where `COUNT` is the number of times within the `INTERVAL`, which is specified in seconds. For example, you'd set a limit of 20 times in 5 seconds like this:

```
respawn
respawn limit 20 5
```

(continued)
If your application is reloaded 10 times within 5 seconds (the default limit), typically there's something wrong in the code or configuration, and it will never start successfully. Upstart won't try to restart after reaching the limit in order to save resources for other processes.

It's a good idea to do health checks outside of Upstart that provide alerts to the development team through email or some other means of quick communication. A health check, for a web application, can simply involve hitting the website and seeing if you get a valid response. You could roll your own methods or use tools such as Monit (http://mmonit.com/monit/) or Zabbix (www.zabbix.com/) for this.

Now that you know how to keep your application running regardless of crashes and server reboots, the next logical concern is performance. Node's cluster API can help with this.

12.3.2 The cluster API: taking advantage of multiple cores

Most modern computer CPUs have multiple cores, but a Node process uses only one of them when running. If you were hosting a Node application on a server and wanted to maximize the server's usage, you could manually start multiple instances of your application on different TCP/IP ports and use a load balancer to distribute web traffic to these different instances, but that's laborious to set up.

To make it easier to use multiple cores for a single application, the cluster API was added to Node. This API makes it easy for your application to simultaneously run multiple "workers" on different cores that each do the same thing and respond to the same TCP/IP port. Figure 12.4 shows how an application's processing would be organized using the cluster API on a four-core processor.

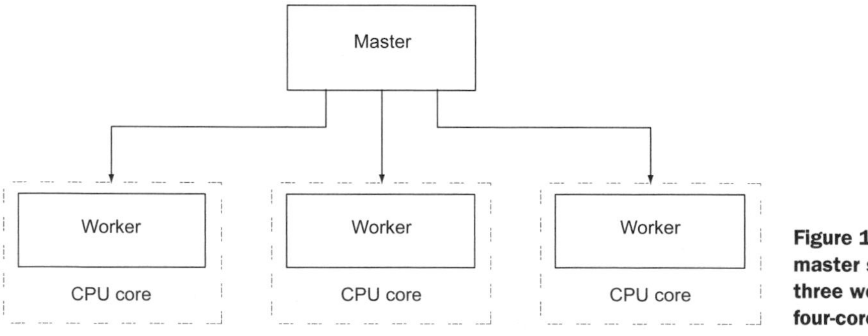

Figure 12.4 A master spawning three workers on a four-core processor

The following listing automatically spawns a master process and a worker for each additional core.

Listing 12.2 A demonstration of Node's cluster API

```
var cluster = require('cluster');
var http = require('http');
var numCPUs = require('os').cpus().length;        <-- Determine number of cores server has

if (cluster.isMaster) {
  for (var i = 0; i < numCPUs; i++) {       <-- Create a fork for each core
    cluster.fork();
  }

  cluster.on('exit', function(worker, code, signal) {
    console.log('Worker ' + worker.process.pid + ' died.');
  });
} else {
  http.Server(function(req, res) {          <-- Define work to be done by each worker
    res.writeHead(200);
    res.end('I am a worker running in process ' + process.pid);
  }).listen(8000);
}
```

Because masters and workers run in separate operating system processes, which is necessary if they're to run on separate cores, they can't share state through global variables. But the cluster API does provide a means for the master and workers to communicate.

The following listing shows an example in which messages are passed between the master and the workers. A count of all requests is kept by the master, and whenever a worker reports handling a request, it's relayed to each worker.

Listing 12.3 A demonstration of Node's cluster API

```
var cluster = require('cluster');
var http = require('http');
var numCPUs = require('os').cpus().length;
var workers = {};
var requests = 0;

if (cluster.isMaster) {
  for (var i = 0; i < numCPUs; i++) {
    workers[i] = cluster.fork();

    (function (i) {
      workers[i].on('message', function(message) {     <-- Listen for messages from worker
        if (message.cmd == 'incrementRequestTotal') {
          requests++;                                   <-- Increase request total
          for (var j = 0; j < numCPUs; j++) {
            workers[j].send({                           <-- Send new request total to each worker
              cmd:      'updateOfRequestTotal',
              requests: requests
            });
          }
```

```
        }
      });
    })(i);
    }

    cluster.on('exit', function(worker, code, signal) {
      console.log('Worker ' + worker.process.pid + ' died.');
    });
  } else {
    process.on('message', function(message) {
      if (message.cmd == 'updateOfRequestTotal') {
        requests = message.requests;
      }
    });

    http.Server(function(req, res) {
      res.writeHead(200);
      res.end('Worker in process ' + process.pid
        + ' says cluster has responded to ' + requests
        + ' requests.');
      process.send({cmd: 'incrementRequestTotal'});
    }).listen(8000);
  }
```

Use closure to preserve the value of worker

Listen for messages from master

Update request count using master's message

Let master know request total should increase

Using Node's cluster API is a simple way of creating applications that take advantage of modern hardware.

12.3.3 Hosting static files and proxying

Although Node is an effective solution for serving dynamic web content, it's not the most efficient way to serve static files such as images, CSS stylesheets, or client-side JavaScript. Serving static files over HTTP is a specific task for which specific software projects are optimized, because they've focused primarily on this task for many years.

Fortunately Nginx (http://nginx.org/en/), an open source web server optimized for serving static files, is easy to set up alongside Node to serve those files. In a typical Nginx/Node configuration, Nginx initially handles each web request, relaying requests that aren't for static files back to Node. This configuration is illustrated in figure 12.5.

The configuration in the following listing, which would be put in the Nginx configuration file's `http` section, implements this setup. The configuration file is conventionally stored in a Linux server's `/etc` directory at /etc/nginx/nginx.conf.

Listing 12.4 A configuration file that uses Nginx to proxy Node.js and serve static files

```
http {

  upstream my_node_app {
    server 127.0.0.1:8000;
   }

  server {

    listen 80;
    server_name localhost domain.com;
```

IP and port of Node application

Port on which proxy will receive requests

```
      access_log /var/log/nginx/my_node_app.log;

      location ~ /static/ {
        root /home/node/my_node_app;
        if (!-f $request_filename) {
          return 404;
        }
      }

      location / {
        proxy_pass http://my_node_app;
        proxy_redirect off;

        proxy_set_header X-Real-IP $remote_addr;
        proxy_set_header X-Forwarded-For $proxy_add_x_forwarded_for;
        proxy_set_header Host $http_host;
        proxy_set_header X-NginX-Proxy true;
      }
    }
}
```

Handles file requests for URL paths starting with /static/

Defines URL path the proxy will respond to

By using Nginx to handle your static web assets, you'll ensure that Node is dedicated to doing what it's best at.

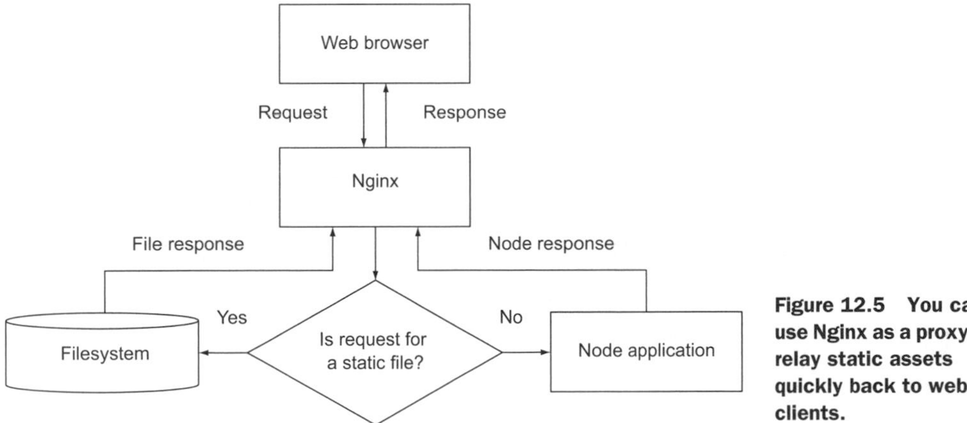

Figure 12.5 You can use Nginx as a proxy to relay static assets quickly back to web clients.

12.4 Summary

In this chapter, we've introduced a number of Node hosting options, including Node-specific hosting, dedicated hosting, virtual private server hosting, and cloud hosting. Each option suits different use cases.

Once you're ready to deploy a Node application to a limited audience, you can get up and running quickly by using the Forever tool to supervise your application. For long-term deployment, you may want to automate your application's starts and stops using Upstart.

To get the most of your server resources, you can take advantage of Node's cluster API to run application instances simultaneously on multiple cores. If your web application needs to serve static assets such as images and PDF documents, you may also want to run the Nginx server and proxy your Node application through it.

Now that you have a good handle on the ins and outs of Node web applications, it's a good time to look at all the other things Node can do. In the next chapter, we'll look at Node's other uses: everything from building command-line tools to scraping data from websites.

13 Beyond web servers

This chapter covers

- Using Socket.IO for real-time cross-browser communication
- Implementing TCP/IP networking
- Using Node's APIs to interact with the operating system
- Developing and working with command-line tools

Node's asynchronous nature enables you to perform I/O-intensive tasks that might be difficult or inefficient in a synchronous environment. We've mostly covered HTTP applications in this book, but what about other kinds of applications? What else is Node useful for?

The truth is that Node is tailored not only for HTTP, but for all kinds of general-purpose I/O. This means you can build practically any type of application using Node, such as command-line programs, system administration scripts, and real-time web applications.

In this chapter, you'll learn how to create real-time web servers that go beyond the traditional HTTP server model. You'll also learn about some of Node's other APIs that you can use to create other kinds of applications, like TCP servers or command-line programs.

We'll start by looking at Socket.IO, which enables real-time communication between browsers and the server.

13.1 Socket.IO

Socket.IO (http://socket.io) is arguably the best-known module in the Node community. People who are interested in creating real-time web applications, but have never heard of Node, usually hear about Socket.IO sooner or later, which then brings them to Node itself. Socket.IO allows you to write real-time web applications using a bidirectional communication channel between the server and client.

At its simplest, Socket.IO has an API very similar to the WebSocket API (http://www .websocket.org), but has built-in fallbacks for older browsers where such features did not yet exist. Socket.IO also provides convenient APIs for broadcasting, volatile messages, and a lot more. These features have made Socket.IO very popular for web-based browser games, chat apps, and streaming applications.

HTTP is a stateless protocol, meaning that the client is only able to make single, short-lived requests to the server, and the server has no real notion of connected or disconnected users. This limitation prompted the standardization of the WebSocket protocol, which specifies a way for browsers to maintain a full-duplex connection to the server, allowing both ends to send and receive data simultaneously. WebSocket APIs allow for a whole new breed of web applications utilizing real-time communication between the client and server.

The problem with the WebSocket protocol is that it's not yet finalized, and although some browsers have begun shipping with WebSocket, there are still a lot of older versions out there, especially of Internet Explorer. Socket.IO solves this problem by utilizing WebSocket when it's available in the browser, and falling back to other browser-specific tricks to simulate the behavior that WebSocket provides, even in older browsers.

In this section, you'll build two sample applications using Socket.IO:

- A minimal Socket.IO application that pushes the server's time to connected clients
- A Socket.IO application that triggers page refreshes when CSS files are edited

After you build the example apps, we'll show you a few more ways you can use Socket.IO by briefly revisiting the upload-progress example from chapter 4. Let's start with the basics.

13.1.1 Creating a minimal Socket.IO application

Let's say you want to build a quick little web application that constantly updates the browser in real time with the server's UTC time. An app like this would be useful to identify differences between the client's and server's clocks. Now try to think of how you could build this application using the http module or the frameworks you've learned about so far. Although it's possible to get something working using a trick like long-polling, Socket.IO provides a cleaner interface for accomplishing this. Implementing this app with Socket.IO is about as simple as you can get.

To build it, you can start by installing Socket.IO using npm:

```
npm install socket.io
```

The following listing shows the server-side code, so save this file for now and you can try it out when you have the client-side code as well.

Listing 13.1 A Socket.IO server that updates its clients with the time

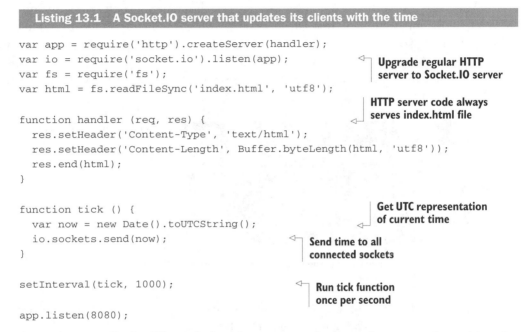

```
var app = require('http').createServer(handler);
var io = require('socket.io').listen(app);
var fs = require('fs');
var html = fs.readFileSync('index.html', 'utf8');

function handler (req, res) {
  res.setHeader('Content-Type', 'text/html');
  res.setHeader('Content-Length', Buffer.byteLength(html, 'utf8'));
  res.end(html);
}

function tick () {
  var now = new Date().toUTCString();
  io.sockets.send(now);
}

setInterval(tick, 1000);

app.listen(8080);
```

Upgrade regular HTTP server to Socket.IO server

HTTP server code always serves index.html file

Get UTC representation of current time

Send time to all connected sockets

Run tick function once per second

As you can see, Socket.IO minimizes the amount of extra code you need to add to the base HTTP server. It only took two lines of code involving the `io` variable (which is the variable for your Socket.IO server instance) to enable real-time messages between your server and clients. In this clock server example, you invoke the `tick()` function once per second to notify all the connected clients of the server's time.

The server code first reads the index.html file into memory, and you need to implement that now. The following listing shows the client side of this application.

Listing 13.2 A Socket.IO client that displays the server's broadcasted time

```
<!DOCTYPE html>
<html>
  <head>
    <script type="text/javascript" src="/socket.io/socket.io.js">
    </script>
    <script type="text/javascript">
      var socket = io.connect();
      socket.on('message', function (time) {
        document.getElementById('time').innerHTML = time;
```

Connect to Socket.IO server

When message event is received, server has sent the time

Update time span element with server time

```
      });
    </script>
  </head>
  <body>Current server time is: <b><span id="time"></span></b>
  </body>
</html>
```

TRYING IT OUT

You're now ready to run the server. Fire it up with `node clock-server.js` and you'll see the response "info - socket.io started." This means that Socket.IO is set up and ready to receive connections, so open up your browser to the URL http://localhost:8080/. With any luck, you'll be greeted by something that looks like figure 13.1. The time will be updated every second from the message received by the server. Go ahead and open another browser at the same time to the same URL, and you'll see the values change together in sync.

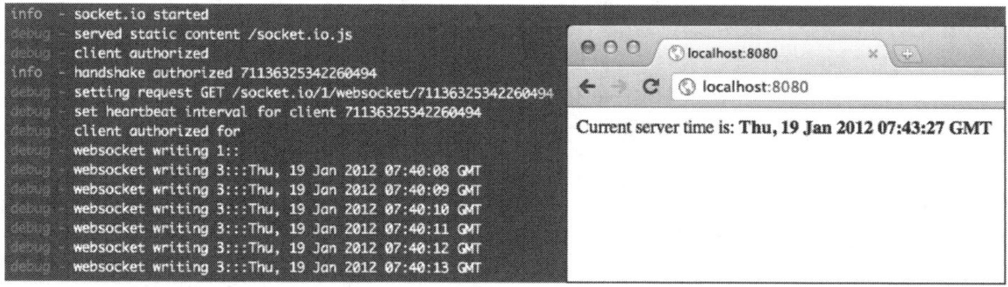

Figure 13.1 The clock server running in a terminal window with a client in a browser connected to the server

Just like that, you have real-time communication between the client and server with just a few lines of code, thanks to Socket.IO.

> **OTHER KINDS OF MESSAGING WITH SOCKET.IO** Sending a message to all the connected sockets is only one way that Socket.IO enables you to interact with connected users. You can also send messages to individual sockets, broadcast to all sockets except one, send volatile (optional) messages, and a lot more. Be sure to check out Socket.IO's documentation for more information (http://socket.io/#how-to-use).

Now that you have an idea of the simple things that are possible with Socket.IO, let's take a look at another example of how server-sent events can be beneficial to developers.

13.1.2 Using Socket.IO to trigger page and CSS reloads

Let's quickly take a look at the typical workflow for web page designers:

1. Open the web page in multiple browsers.
2. Look for styling on the page that needs adjusting.
3. Make changes to one or more stylesheets.

4 Manually reload *all* the web browsers.
5 Go back to step 2.

One step you could automate is step 4, where the designer needs to manually go into each web browser and click the Refresh button. This is especially time-consuming when the designer needs to test different browsers on different computers and various mobile devices.

But what if you could eliminate this manual refresh step completely? Imagine that when you save the stylesheet in your text editor, *all* the web browsers that have that page open automatically reload the changes in the CSS sheet. This would be a huge time-saver for devs and designers alike, and Socket.IO matched with Node's `fs.watchFile` and `fs.watch` functions make it possible in just a few lines of code.

We'll use `fs.watchFile()` in this example instead of the newer `fs.watch()` because we're assured this code will work the same on all platforms, but we'll cover the behavior of `fs.watch()` in depth later.

> **FS.WATCHFILE() VS. FS.WATCH()** Node.js provides two APIs for watching files: `fs.watchFile()` (http://mng.bz/v6dA) is rather expensive resource-wise, but it's more reliable and works cross-platform. `fs.watch()` (http://mng.bz/5KSC) is highly optimized for each platform, but it has behavioral differences on certain platforms. We'll go over these functions in greater detail in section 13.3.2.

In this example, we'll combine the Express framework with Socket.IO. They work together seamlessly, just like the regular `http.Server` in the previous example.

First, let's look at the server code in its entirety. Save the following code as watch-server.js if you're interested in running this example at the end.

Listing 13.3 Express/Socket.IO server that triggers events on file change

```
var fs = require('fs');
var url = require('url');
var http = require('http');
var path = require('path');
var express = require('express');
var app = express();
var server = http.createServer(app);
var io = require('socket.io').listen(server);
var root = __dirname;

app.use(function (req, res, next) {
  req.on('static', function () {
    var file = url.parse(req.url).pathname;
    var mode = 'stylesheet';
    if (file[file.length - 1] == '/') {
      file += 'index.html';
      mode = 'reload';
    }
```

Create Express app server

Wrap HTTP server to create Socket.IO instance

Use middleware to begin watching files returned by static middleware

Register static event emitted by static() middleware component

```
    createWatcher(file, mode);          <-- Determine filename served
  });                                       and call createWatcher()
  next();
});
                                        Set up server as basic
app.use(express.static(root));      <-- static file server

var watchers = {};                      <-- Keep list of active files
                                            being watched
function createWatcher (file, event) {
  var absolute = path.join(root, file);

  if (watchers[absolute]) {
    return;
  }
                                                    Begin watching file
  fs.watchFile(absolute, function (curr, prev) {  <-- for any change
    if (curr.mtime !== prev.mtime) {              <-- Check if mtime (last
      io.sockets.emit(event, file);                   modified time) changed;
    }                                                 if so, fire Socket.IO event
  });

  watchers[absolute] = true;            <-- Mark file as
}                                           being watched

server.listen(8080);
```

At this point you have a fully functional static file server that's prepared to fire `reload` and `stylesheet` events across the wire to the client using Socket.IO.

Now let's take a look at the basic client-side code. Save this as index.html so that it gets served at the root path when you fire up the server next.

Listing 13.4 Client-side code to reload stylesheets after receiving server events

```
<!DOCTYPE html>
<html>
  <head>
    <title>Socket.IO dynamically reloading CSS stylesheets</title>
    <link rel="stylesheet" type="text/css" href="/header.css" />
    <link rel="stylesheet" type="text/css" href="/styles.css" />
    <script type="text/javascript" src="/socket.io/socket.io.js">
    </script>
    <script type="text/javascript">
      window.onload = function () {
        var socket = io.connect();              <-- Connect to server

        socket.on('reload', function () {       <-- Receive reload
          window.location.reload();                 event from server
        });

        socket.on('stylesheet', function (sheet) {              <-- Receive
          var link = document.createElement('link');                stylesheet
          var head = document.getElementsByTagName('head')[0];      event from
          link.setAttribute('rel', 'stylesheet');                   server
          link.setAttribute('type', 'text/css');
          link.setAttribute('href', sheet);
          head.appendChild(link);
        });
```

```
    }
  </script>
</head>
<body>
  <h1>This is our Awesome Webpage!</h1>
  <div id="body">
    <p>If this file (<code>index.html</code>) is edited, then the
    server will send a message to the browser using Socket.IO telling
    it to refresh the page.</p>

    <p>If either of the stylesheets (<code>header.css</code> or
    <code>styles.css</code>) are edited, then the server will send a
    message to the browser using Socket.IO telling it to dynamically
    reload the CSS, without refreshing the page.</p>
  </div>
  <div id="event-log"></div>
</body>
</html>
```

TRYING IT OUT

Before this will work, you'll need to create a couple of CSS files, header.css and styles.css, because the index.html file loads those two stylesheets when it loads.

Now that you have the server code, the index.html file, and the CSS stylesheets that the browser will use, you can try it out. Fire up the server:

```
$ node watch-server.js
```

Once the server has started, open your web browser to http://localhost:8080 and you'll see the simple HTML page being served and rendered. Now try altering one of the CSS files (perhaps tweak the background color of the `body` tag), and you'll see the stylesheet reload in the browser right in front of your eyes, without even reloading the page itself. Try opening the page in multiple browsers at once.

In this example, `reload` and `stylesheet` are custom events that you have defined in the application; they're not part of Socket.IO's API. This demonstrates how the `socket` object acts like a bidirectional `EventEmitter`, which you can use to emit events that Socket.IO will transfer across the wire for you.

13.1.3 Other uses of Socket.IO

As you know, HTTP was never originally intended for any kind of real-time communication. But with advances in browser technologies, like WebSocket, and with modules like Socket.IO, this limitation has been lifted, opening a big door for all kinds of new applications that were never before possible in the web browser.

Back in chapter 4 we said that Socket.IO would be great for relaying upload progress events back to the browser for the user to see. Using a custom `progress` event would work well:

```
form.on('progress', function(bytesReceived, bytesExpected) {    <-- Updated from example in section 4.4.3
  var percent = Math.floor(bytesReceived / bytesExpected * 100);

  socket.emit('progress', { percent: percent });    <-- Relay uploaded percentage using Socket.IO
 });
```

For this relaying to work, you'll need to get access to the `socket` instance that matches the browser uploading the file. That's beyond the scope of this book, but there are resources on the internet that can help you figure that out. (For starters, take a look at

Daniel Baulig's "socket.io and Express: tying it all together" article on his *blinzeln* blog: www.danielbaulig.de/socket-ioexpress.)

Socket.IO is game changing. As mentioned earlier, developers interested in real-time web applications often hear about Socket.IO before knowing about Node.js—a testament to how influential and important Socket.IO is. It's consistently gaining traction in web gaming communities and being used for more creative games and applications than one could have thought possible. It's also a very popular pick for use in applications written in Node.js competitions, like Node Knockout (http://nodeknockout.com). What awesome thing will you write with it?

13.2 TCP/IP networking in depth

Node is well suited for networking applications, because those typically involve a lot of I/O. Besides the HTTP servers you've learned much about already, Node supports any type of TCP-based networking. Node is a good platform for writing an email server, file server, or proxy server, for example, and it can also be used as a client for these kinds of services. Node provides a few tools to aid in writing high quality and performant I/O applications, and you'll learn about them in this section.

Some networking protocols require values to be read at the byte level—chars, ints, floats, and other data types involving binary data. But JavaScript doesn't include any native binary data types to work with. The closest you can get is crazy hacks with strings. Node picks up the slack by implementing its own `Buffer` data type, which acts as a piece of fixed-length binary data, making it possible to access the low-level bytes needed to implement other protocols.

In this section you'll learn about the following topics:

- Working with buffers and binary data
- Creating a TCP server
- Creating a TCP client

Let's first take a deeper look at how Node deals with binary data.

13.2.1 Working with buffers and binary data

The `Buffer` is a special data type that Node provides for developers. It acts as a slab of raw binary data with a fixed length. Buffers can be thought of as the equivalent of the `malloc()` C function or the `new` keyword in C++. Buffers are very fast and light objects, and they're used throughout Node's core APIs. For example, they're returned in `data` events by all `Stream` classes by default.

Node exposes the `Buffer` constructor globally, encouraging you to use it as an extension of the regular JavaScript data types. From a programming point of view, you can think of buffers as similar to arrays, except they're not resizable and can only contain the numbers 0 through 255 as values. This makes them ideal for storing binary data of, well, anything. Because buffers work with raw bytes, you can use them to implement any low-level protocol that you desire.

TEXT DATA VS. BINARY DATA

Say you wanted to store the number 121234869 in memory using a `Buffer`. By default, Node assumes that you want to work with text-based data in buffers, so when you pass the string `"121234869"` to the `Buffer` constructor function, a new `Buffer` object will be allocated with the string value written to it:

```
var b = new Buffer("121234869");

console.log(b.length);
9
console.log(b);
<Buffer 31 32 31 32 33 34 38 36 39>
```

In this case, it would return a 9-byte `Buffer`. This is because the string was written to the `Buffer` using the default human-readable text-based encoding (UTF-8), where the string is represented with 1 byte per character.

Node also includes helper functions for reading and writing binary (machine-readable) integer data. These are needed for implementing machine protocols that send raw data types (like ints, floats, doubles, and so on) over the wire. Because you want to store a number value in this example, it's possible to be more efficient by utilizing the helper function `writeInt32LE()` to write the number 121234869 as a machine-readable binary integer (assuming a little-endian processor) into a 4-byte `Buffer`.

There are other variations of the `Buffer` helper functions, as well:

- `writeInt16LE()` for smaller integer values
- `writeUInt32LE()` for unsigned values
- `writeInt32BE()` for big-endian values

There are lots more, so be sure to check the `Buffer` API documentation page (http://nodejs.org/docs/latest/api/buffer.html) if you're interested in them all.

In the following code snippet, the number is written using the `writeInt32LE` binary helper function:

```
var b = new Buffer(4);
b.writeInt32LE(121234869, 0);

console.log(b.length);
4
console.log(b);
<Buffer b5 e5 39 07>
```

By storing the value as a binary integer instead of a text string in memory, the data size is decreased by half, from 9 bytes down to 4. Figure 13.2 shows the breakdown of these two buffers and essentially illustrates the difference between human-readable (text) protocols and machine-readable (binary) protocols.

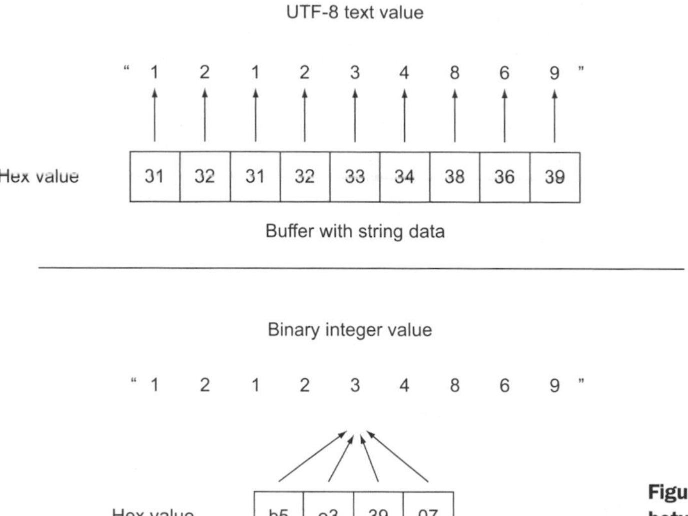

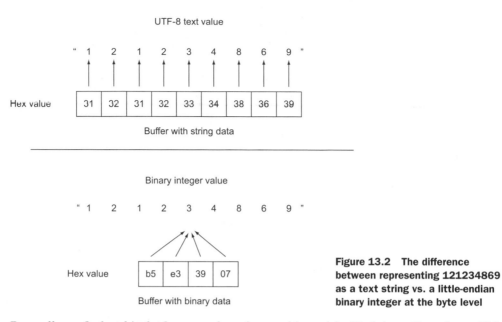

Figure 13.2 The difference between representing 121234869 as a text string vs. a little-endian binary integer at the byte level

Regardless of what kind of protocol you're working with, Node's `Buffer` class will be able to handle the proper representation.

BYTE ENDIANNESS The term *endianness* refers to the order of the bytes within a multibyte sequence. When bytes are in *little-endian* order, the least significant byte (LSB) is stored first, and the byte sequence is read from right to left. Conversely, *big-endian* order is when the first byte stored is the most significant byte (MSB) and the byte sequence is read from left to right. Node.js offers equivalent helper functions for both little-endian and big-endian data types.

Now it's time to put these `Buffer` objects to use by creating a TCP server and interacting with it.

13.2.2 Creating a TCP server

Node's core API sticks to being low-level, exposing only the bare essentials for modules to build on. Node's http module is a good example of this, building on top of the net module to implement the HTTP protocol. Other protocols, like SMTP for email or FTP for file transfer, need to be implemented on top of the net module as well, because Node's core API doesn't implement any other higher-level protocols.

WRITING DATA

The net module offers a raw TCP/IP socket interface for your applications to use. The API for creating a TCP server is very similar to creating an HTTP server: you call `net.createServer()` and give it a callback function that will be invoked upon each connection. The main difference in creating a TCP server is that the callback function only takes one argument (usually named `socket`), which is the `Socket` object, as opposed to the `req` and `res` arguments used when creating an HTTP server.

THE SOCKET CLASS The `Socket` class is used by both the client and server aspects of the net module in Node. It's a `Stream` subclass that's both `readable` and `writable` (bidirectional). That is, it emits `data` events when input data has been read from the socket, and it has `write()` and `end()` functions for sending output data.

Let's quickly look at a bare-bones `net.Server` that waits for connections and then invokes a callback function. In this case, the logic inside the callback function simply writes "Hello World!" to the socket and closes the connection cleanly:

```
var net = require('net');

net.createServer(function (socket) {
  socket.write('Hello World!\r\n');
  socket.end();
}).listen(1337);
console.log('listening on port 1337');
```

Fire up the server for some testing:

```
$ node server.js
listening on port 1337
```

If you were to try to connect to the server in a web browser, it wouldn't work because this server doesn't speak HTTP, only raw TCP. In order to connect to this server and see the message, you need to connect with a proper TCP client, like `netcat(1)`:

```
$ netcat localhost 1337
Hello World!
```

Great! Now let's try using `telnet(1)`:

```
$ telnet localhost 1337
Trying 127.0.0.1...
Connected to localhost.
Escape character is '^]'.
Hello World!
Connection closed by foreign host.
```

`telnet` is usually meant to be run in an interactive mode, so it prints out its own stuff as well, but the "Hello World!" message does get printed right before the connection is closed, just as expected.

As you can see, writing data to the socket is easy. You just use `write()` calls and a final `end()` call. This API intentionally matches the API for HTTP `res` objects when writing a response to the client.

READING DATA

It's common for servers to follow the request-response paradigm, where the client connects and immediately sends a request of some sort. The server reads the request and processes a response of some sort to write back to the socket. This is exactly how the HTTP protocol works, as well as the majority of other networking protocols in the wild, so it's important to know how to read data in addition to writing it.

Fortunately, if you remember how to read a request body from an HTTP `req` object, reading from a TCP socket should be a piece of cake. Complying with the readable `Stream` interface, all you have to do is listen for `data` events containing the input data that was read from the socket:

```
socket.on('data', function (data) {
  console.log('got "data"', data);
});
```

By default, there's no encoding set on the `socket`, so the `data` argument will be a `Buffer` instance. Usually, this is exactly how you want it (that's why it's the default), but when it's more convenient, you can call the `setEncoding()` function to have the `data` argument be the decoded strings instead of buffers. You also listen for the `end` event so you know when the client has closed their end of the socket and won't be sending any more data:

```
socket.on('end', function () {
  console.log('socket has ended');
});
```

You can easily write a quick TCP client that looks up the version string of the given SSH server by simply waiting for the first `data` event:

```
var net = require('net');

var socket = net.connect({ host: process.argv[2], port: 22 });
socket.setEncoding('utf8');

socket.once('data', function (chunk) {
  console.log('SSH server version: %j', chunk.trim());
  socket.end();
});
```

Now try it out. Note that this oversimplified example assumes that the entire version string will come in one chunk. Most of the time this works just fine, but a proper program would buffer the input until a `\n` char was found. Let's check what the github.com SSH server uses:

```
$ node client.js github.com
SSH server version: "SSH-2.0-OpenSSH_5.5p1 Debian-6+squeeze1+github8"
```

CONNECTING TWO STREAMS WITH SOCKET.PIPE()

Using `pipe()` (http://mng.bz/tuyo) in conjunction with either the readable or writable portions of a `Socket` object is also a good idea. In fact, if you wanted to write a basic TCP server that echoed everything that was sent to it back to the client, you could do that with a single line of code in your callback function:

```
socket.pipe(socket);
```

This example shows that it only takes one line of code to implement the IETF Echo Protocol (http://tools.ietf.org/rfc/rfc862.txt), but more importantly it demonstrates that you can `pipe()` both *to* and *from* the `socket` object. Of course, you would usually do this with more meaningful stream instances, like a filesystem or gzip stream.

HANDLING UNCLEAN DISCONNECTIONS

The last thing that should be said about TCP servers is that you need to anticipate clients that disconnect but don't cleanly close the socket. In the case of `netcat(1)`, this would happen when you press Ctrl-C to kill the process, rather than pressing Ctrl-D to cleanly close the connection. To detect this situation, you listen for the `close` event:

```
socket.on('close', function () {
  console.log('client disconnected');
});
```

If you have cleanup to do after a socket disconnects, you should do it from the `close` event, not the `end` event, because `end` won't fire if the connection isn't closed cleanly.

PUTTING IT ALL TOGETHER

Let's take all these events and create a simple echo server that logs stuff to the terminal when the various events occur. The server is shown in the following listing.

Listing 13.5 A simple TCP server that echoes any data it receives back to the client

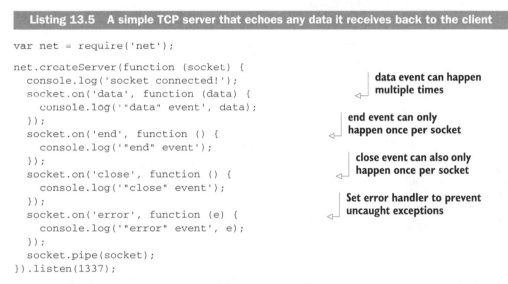

```
var net = require('net');

net.createServer(function (socket) {
  console.log('socket connected!');
  socket.on('data', function (data) {
    console.log('"data" event', data);
  });
  socket.on('end', function () {
    console.log('"end" event');
  });
  socket.on('close', function () {
    console.log('"close" event');
  });
  socket.on('error', function (e) {
    console.log('"error" event', e);
  });
  socket.pipe(socket);
}).listen(1337);
```

- data event can happen multiple times
- end event can only happen once per socket
- close event can also only happen once per socket
- Set error handler to prevent uncaught exceptions

Fire up the server and connect to it with `netcat` or `telnet` and play around with it a bit. You should see the `console.log()` calls for the events being printed to the server's stdout as you mash around on the keyboard in the client app.

Now that you can build low-level TCP servers in Node, you're probably wondering how to write a client program in Node to interact with these servers. Let's do that now.

13.2.3 Creating a TCP client

Node isn't only about server software; creating client networking programs is just as useful and just as easy in Node.

The key to creating raw connections to TCP servers is the `net.connect()` function; it accepts an options argument with `host` and `port` values and returns a `socket` instance. The `socket` returned from `net.connect()` starts off disconnected from the server, so you'll usually want to listen for the `connect` event before doing any work with the socket:

```
var net = require('net');

var socket = net.connect({ port: 1337, host: 'localhost' });
socket.on('connect', function () {
  // begin writing your "request"
  socket.write('HELO local.domain.name\r\n');
  ...
});
```

Once the `socket` instance is connected to the server, it behaves just like the `socket` instances you get inside a `net.Server` callback function.

Let's demonstrate by writing a basic replica of the `netcat(1)` command, as shown in the following listing. Basically, the program connects to the specified remote server and pipes stdin from the program to the socket, and then pipes the socket's response to the program's stdout.

Listing 13.6 A basic replica of the `netcat(1)` command implemented using Node

```
var net = require('net');
var host = process.argv[2];
var port = Number(process.argv[3]);

var socket = net.connect(port, host);

socket.on('connect', function () {
  process.stdin.pipe(socket);
  socket.pipe(process.stdout);
  process.stdin.resume();
});

socket.on('end', function () {
  process.stdin.pause();
});
```

- Parse host and port from command-line arguments
- Create socket instance and begin connecting to server
- Handle connect event when a connection to server is established
- Pipe process's stdin to socket
- Pipe socket's data to process's stdout
- Call resume() on stdin to begin reading data
- Pause stdin when end event happens

You can use this client to connect to the TCP server examples you wrote before. Or if you're a Star Wars fan, try invoking this netcat replica script with the following arguments for a special Easter egg:

```
$ node netcat.js towel.blinkenlights.nl 23
```

Sit back and enjoy the output shown in figure 13.3. You deserve a break.

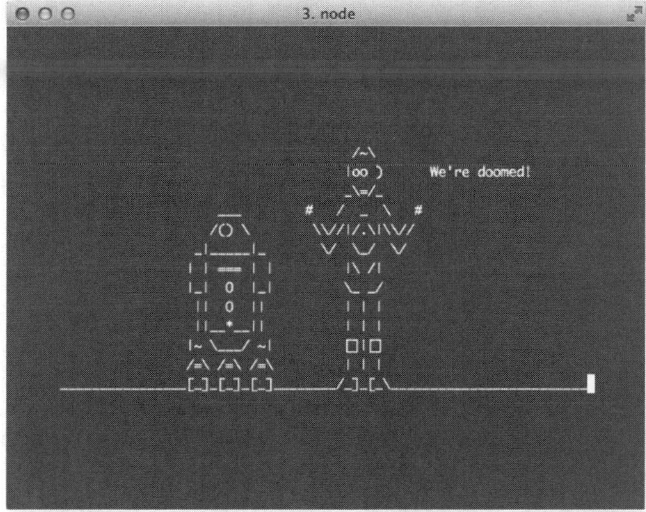

Figure 13.3 Connecting to the ASCII Star Wars server with the netcat.js script

That's all it takes to write low-level TCP servers and clients using Node.js. The net module provides a simple, yet comprehensive, API, and the `Socket` class follows both the readable and writable `Stream` interfaces, as you would expect. Essentially, the net module is a showcase of the core fundamentals of Node.

Let's switch gears once again and look at Node's core APIs that allow you to interact with the process's environment and query information about the runtime and operating system.

13.3 Tools for interacting with the operating system

Often you'll find yourself wanting to interact with the environment that Node is running in. This might involve checking environment variables to enable debug-mode logging, implementing a Linux joystick driver using the low-level fs functions to interact with /dev/js0 (the device file for a game joystick), or launching an external child process like `php` to compile a legacy PHP script.

All these kinds of actions require you to use some of the Node core APIs, and we'll cover some of these modules in this section:

- *The global* `process` *object*—Contains information about the current process, such as the arguments given to it and the environment variables that are currently set
- *The fs module*—Contains the high-level `ReadStream` and `WriteStream` classes that you're familiar with by now, but also houses low-level functions that we'll look at
- *The* `child_process` *module*—Contains both low-level and high-level interfaces for spawning child processes, as well as a special way to spawn `node` instances with a two-way message-passing channel

The `process` object is one of those APIs that a large majority of programs will interact with, so let's start with that.

13.3.1 The process global singleton

Every Node process has a single global `process` object that every module shares access to. Useful information about the process and the context it's running in can be found in this object. For example, the arguments that were invoked with Node to run the current script can be accessed with `process.argv`, and you can get or set the environment variables using the `process.env` object. But the most interesting feature of the `process` object is that it's an `EventEmitter` instance, which emits very special events, such as `exit` and `uncaughtException`.

The `process` object has lots of bells and whistles, and some of the APIs not discussed in this section will be covered later in the chapter. In this section, we'll focus on the following:

- Using `process.env` to get and set environment variables
- Listening for special events emitted by `process`, such as `exit` and `uncaughtException`
- Listening for signal events emitted by `process`, like `SIGUSR2` and `SIGKILL`

USING PROCESS.ENV TO GET AND SET ENVIRONMENT VARIABLES

Environment variables are great for altering the way your program or module will work. For example, you can use these variables to configure your server, specifying which port to listen on. Or the operating system can set the `TMPDIR` variable to specify where your programs should output temporary files that can be cleaned up later.

> **ENVIRONMENT VARIABLES?** In case you're not already familiar with environment variables, they're a set of key/value pairs that any process can use to affect the way it will behave. For example, all operating systems use the `PATH` environment variable as a list of file paths to search when looking up a program's location by name (with `ls` being resolved to /bin/ls).

Suppose you wanted to enable debug-mode logging while developing or debugging your module, but not during regular use, because that would be annoying for consumers of your module. A great way to do this is with environment variables. You could look up what the `DEBUG` variable is set to by checking `process.env.DEBUG`, as shown in the next listing.

Listing 13.7 Define a debug function based on a `DEBUG` environment variable

```
var debug;
if (process.env.DEBUG) {
  debug = function (data) {
    console.error(data);
  };
} else {
  debug = function () {};
}
```

- Set debug function based on process.env.DEBUG
- When DEBUG is set, debug function will log the argument to stderr
- When DEBUG isn't set, debug function is empty and does nothing

```
debug('this is a debug call');

console.log('Hello World!');

debug('this another debug call');
```

Call debug function in various places throughout the code

If you try running this script regularly (without the `process.env.DEBUG` environment variable set), you'll see that calls to `debug` do nothing, because the empty function is being called:

```
$ node debug-mode.js
Hello World!
```

To test out debug mode, you need to set the `process.env.DEBUG` environment variable. The simplest way to do this when launching a Node instance is to prepend the command with `DEBUG=1`. When in debug mode, calls to the `debug` function will then be printed to the console as well as to the regular output. This is a nice way to get diagnostic reporting to stderr when debugging a problem in your code:

```
$ DEBUG=1 node debug-mode.js
this is a debug call
Hello World!
this is another debug call
```

The debug community module by T.J. Holowaychuk (https://github.com/visionmedia/debug) encapsulates precisely this functionality with some additional features. If you like the debugging technique presented here, you should definitely check it out.

SPECIAL EVENTS EMITTED BY PROCESS

Normally there are two special events that get emitted by the `process` object:

- `exit` gets emitted right before the process exits.
- `uncaughtException` gets emitted any time an unhandled error is thrown.

The `exit` event is essential for any application that needs to do something right before the program exits, like clean up an object or print a final message to the console. One important thing to note is that the `exit` event gets fired after the event loop has already stopped, so you won't have the opportunity to start any asynchronous tasks during the `exit` event. The exit code is passed as the first argument, and it's `0` on a successful exit.

Let's write a script that listens on the `exit` event to print an "Exiting..." message:

```
process.on('exit', function (code) {
  console.log('Exiting...');
});
```

The other special event emitted by `process` is the `uncaughtException` event. In the perfect program, there will never be any uncaught exceptions, but in the real world, it's better to be safe than sorry. The only argument given to the `uncaughtException` event is the uncaught `Error` object.

When there are no listeners for "error" events, any uncaught errors will crash the process (this is the default behavior for most applications), but when there's at least one listener, it's up to that listener to decide what to do with the error. Node won't exit automatically, though it is considered mandatory to do so in your own callback. The Node.js documentation explicitly warns that any use of this event should contain a `process.exit()` call within the callback; otherwise you'll leave the application in an undefined state, which is bad.

Let's listen for `uncaughtException` and then throw an uncaught error to see it in action:

```
process.on('uncaughtException', function (err) {
  console.error('got uncaught exception:', err.message);
  process.exit(1);
});

throw new Error('an uncaught exception');
```

Now when an unexpected error happens, you're able to catch the error and do any necessary cleanup before you exit the process.

CATCHING SIGNALS SENT TO THE PROCESS

UNIX has the concept of *signals*, which are a basic form of interprocess communication (IPC). These signals are very primitive, allowing for only a fixed set of names to be used and no arguments to be passed.

Node has default behaviors for a few signals, which we'll go over now:

- `SIGINT`—Sent by your shell when you press Ctrl-C. Node's default behavior is to kill the process, but this can be overridden with a single listener for `SIGINT` on `process`.
- `SIGUSR1`—When this signal is received, Node will enter its built-in debugger.
- `SIGWINCH`—Sent by your shell when the terminal is resized. Node resets `process.stdout.rows` and `process.stdout.columns` and emits a `resize` event when this is received.

Those are the three signals that Node handles by default, but you can also listen for any of these signals and invoke a callback function by listening for the signal on the `process` object.

Say you've written a server, but when you press Ctrl-C to kill the server, it's an unclean shutdown, and any pending connections are dropped. The solution to this is to catch the `SIGINT` signal and stop the server from accepting connections, letting any existing connections complete before the process completes. This is done by listening for `process.on('SIGINT', ...)`. The name of the event emitted is the same as the signal name:

```
process.on('SIGINT', function () {
  console.log('Got Ctrl-C!');
  server.close();
});
```

Now when you press Ctrl-C on your keyboard, the `SIGINT` signal will be sent to the Node process from your shell, which will invoke the registered callback instead of killing the process. Because the default behavior of most applications is to exit the process, it's usually a good idea to do the same in your own `SIGINT` handler, after any necessary shutdown actions happen. In this case, stopping a server from accepting connections will do the trick. This also works on Windows, despite its lack of proper signals, because Node handles the equivalent Windows actions and simulates artificial signals in Node.

You can apply this same technique to catch any of the UNIX signals that get sent to your Node process. These signals are listed in the Wikipedia article on UNIX signals: http://wikipedia.org/wiki/Unix_signal#POSIX_signals. Unfortunately, signals don't generally work on Windows, except for the few simulated signals: `SIGINT`, `SIGBREAK`, `SIGHUP`, and `SIGWINCH`.

13.3.2 Using the filesystem module

The fs module provides functions for interacting with the filesystem of the computer that Node is running on. Most of the functions are one-to-one mappings of their C function counterparts, but there are also higher-level abstractions like the `fs.readFile()`, `fs.writeFile()`, `fs.ReadStream`, and `fs.WriteStream` classes, which build on top of `open()`, `read()`, `write()`, and `close()`.

Nearly all of the low-level functions are identical in use to their C counterparts. In fact, most of the Node documentation refers you to the equivalent `man` page explaining the matching C function. You can easily identify these low-level functions because they'll always have a synchronous counterpart. For example, `fs.stat()` and `fs.statSync()` are the low-level bindings to the `stat(2)` C function.

> **SYNCHRONOUS FUNCTIONS IN NODE.JS** As you already know, Node's API is mostly asynchronous functions that never block the event loop, so why bother including synchronous versions of these filesystem functions? The answer is that Node's own `require()` function is synchronous, and it's implemented using the `fs` module functions, so synchronous counterparts were necessary. Nevertheless, in Node, synchronous functions should *only* be used during startup, or when your module is initially loaded, and *never* after that.

Let's take a look at some examples of interacting with the filesystem.

MOVING A FILE

A seemingly simple, yet very common, task when interacting with the filesystem is moving a file from one directory to another. On UNIX platforms you use the `mv` command for this, and on Windows it's the `move` command. Doing the same thing in Node should be similarly simple, right?

Well, if you browse through the fs module in the REPL or in the documentation (http://nodejs.org/api/fs.html), you'll notice that there's no `fs.move()` function.

But there is an fs.rename() function, which is the same thing, if you think about it. Perfect!

But not so fast there. fs.rename() maps directly to the rename(2) C function, and one gotcha with this function is that it doesn't work across physical devices (like two hard drives). That means the following code wouldn't work properly and would throw an EXDEV error:

```
fs.rename('C:\\hello.txt', 'D:\\hello.txt', function (err) {
  // err.code === 'EXDEV'
});
```

What do you do now? Well, you can still create new files on D:\ and read files from C:\, so copying the file over will work. With this knowledge, you can create an optimized move() function that calls the very fast fs.rename() when possible and copies the file from one device to another when necessary, using fs.ReadStream and fs.WriteStream. One such implementation is shown in the following listing.

Listing 13.8 A move() function that renames, if possible, or falls back to copying

```
var fs = require('fs');

module.exports = function move (oldPath, newPath, callback) {
  fs.rename(oldPath, newPath, function (err) {       <- Call fs.rename() and hope it works
    if (err) {
      if (err.code === 'EXDEV') {     <- Fall back to copy technique if EXDEV error
        copy();
      } else {
        callback(err);            <- Fail and report to caller if any other kind of error
      }
      return;
    }
    callback();                   <- If fs.rename() worked, you're done
  });

  function copy () {
    var readStream = fs.createReadStream(oldPath);      <- Reads original file and pipes it to the destination path
    var writeStream = fs.createWriteStream(newPath);
    readStream.on('error', callback);
    writeStream.on('error', callback);
    readStream.on('close', function () {
      fs.unlink(oldPath, callback);     <- Unlink (delete) original file once copy is done
    });
    readStream.pipe(writeStream);
  }
}
```

You can test this module directly in the node REPL if you like:

```
$ node
> var move = require('./copy')
> move('copy.js', 'copy.js.bak', function (err) { if (err) throw err })
```

Note that this copy function only works with files, not directories. To make it work for directories, you'd have to first check if the given path was a directory, and if it was you'd call fs.readdir() and fs.mkdir() as necessary. You can implement that on your own.

> **FS MODULE ERROR CODES** The fs module returns standard UNIX names for the filesystem error codes (www.gnu.org/software/libc/manual/html_node/Error-Codes.html), so some familiarity with those names is required. These names get normalized by libuv even on Windows, so that your application only needs to check for one error code at a time. According to the GNU documentation page, an EXDEV error happens when "an attempt to make an improper link across file systems was detected."

WATCHING A DIRECTORY OR FILE FOR CHANGES

fs.watchFile() has been around since the early days. It's expensive on some platforms because it uses polling to see if the file has changed. That is, it stat()s the file, waits a short period of time, and then stat()s again in a continuous loop, invoking the watcher function any time the file has changed.

Suppose you're writing a module that logs changes from the system log file. To do this, you'd want a callback function to be invoked any time the global system.log file is modified:

```
var fs = require('fs');

fs.watchFile('/var/log/system.log', function (curr, prev) {
  if (curr.mtime.getTime() !== prev.mtime.getTime()) {
    console.log('"system.log" has been modified');
  }
});
```

The curr and prev variables are the current and previous fs.Stat objects, which should have different timestamps for one of the file times attached. In this example, the mtime values are being compared, because you only want to be notified when the file is modified, not when it's accessed.

fs.watch() was introduced in the Node v0.6 release. As we mentioned earlier, it's more optimized than fs.watchFile() because it uses the platform's native file change notification API for watching files. Because of this, the function is also capable of watching for changes to any file in a directory. In practice, fs.watch() is less reliable than fs.watchFile() because of differences between the various platforms' underlying file-watching mechanisms. For example, the filename parameter doesn't get reported on OS X when watching a directory, and it's up to Apple to change that in a future release of OS X. Node's documentation keeps a list of these caveats at http://nodejs.org/api/fs.html#fs_caveats.

USING COMMUNITY MODULES: FSTREAM AND FILED

As you've seen, the fs module, like all of Node's core APIs, is strictly low-level. That means there's plenty of room to innovate and create awesome abstractions on top of it. Node's active collection of modules is growing on npm every day, and as you might guess, there are some quality ones that extend the fs module.

For example, the fstream module by Isaac Schlueter (https://github.com/isaacs/fstream) is one of the core pieces of npm itself. This module is interesting because it began life as a part of npm and then got extracted because its general-purpose functionality was useful to many kinds of command-line applications and sysadmin scripts. One of the awesome features that sets fstream apart is its seamless handling of permissions and symbolic links, which are maintained by default when copying files and directories.

By using fstream, you can perform the equivalent of `cp -rp sourceDir destDir` (copying a directory and its contents recursively, and transferring over ownership and permissions) by simply piping a `Reader` instance to a `Writer` instance. In the following example, we also utilize fstream's filter feature to conditionally exclude files based on a callback function:

```
fstream
  .Reader("path/to/dir")
  .pipe(fstream.Writer({ path: "path/to/other/dir", filter: isValid )

// checks the file that is about to be written and
// returns whether or not it should be copied over
function isValid () {
  // ignore temp files from text editors like TextMate
  return this.path[this.path.length - 1] !== '~';
}
```

The filed module by Mikeal Rogers (https://github.com/mikeal/filed) is another influential module, mostly because it was written by the same author as the highly popular request module. These modules made popular a new kind of flow control over `Stream` instances: listening for the `pipe` event, and acting differently based on what is being piped to it (or what it is being piped to).

To demonstrate the power of this approach, take a look at how filed turns a regular HTTP server into a full-featured static file server with just one line of code:

```
http.createServer(function (req, res) {
  req.pipe(filed('path/to/static/files')).pipe(res);
});
```

This code takes care of sending `Content-Length` with the proper caching headers. In the case where the browser already has the file cached, filed will respond to the HTTP request with a 304 Not Modified code, skipping the steps of opening and reading the file from the disk process. These are the kinds of optimizations that acting on the `pipe` event make possible, because the `filed` instance has access to both the `req` and `res` objects of the HTTP request.

We've demonstrated two examples of good community modules that extend the base fs module to do awesome things or expose beautiful APIs, but there are many more. The `npm search` command is a good way to find published modules for a given task. Say you wanted to find another module that simplifies copying files from one destination to another: executing `npm search copy` could bring up some useful results. When you find a published module that looks interesting, you can execute `npm info` module-name to get information about the module, such as its description, home page, and published versions. Just remember that for any given task, it's likely that someone has attempted to solve the problem with an npm module, so always check there before writing something from scratch.

13.3.3 Spawning external processes

Node provides the child_process module to create child subprocesses from within a Node server or script. There are two APIs for this: a high-level one, `exec()`, and a low-level one, `spawn()`. Either one may be appropriate, depending on your needs. There's also a special way to create child processes of Node itself, with a special IPC channel built in, called `fork()`. All of these functions are meant for different use cases:

- `cp.exec()`—A high-level API for spawning commands and buffering the result in a callback
- `cp.spawn()`—A low-level API for spawning single commands into a `ChildProcess` object
- `cp.fork()`—A special way to spawn additional Node processes with a built-in IPC channel

We'll look at each of these in turn.

PROS AND CONS TO CHILD PROCESSES There are benefits and drawbacks to using child processes. One obvious downside is that the program being executed needs to be installed on the user's machine, making it a dependency of your application. The alternative would be to use JavaScript to do whatever the child process did. A good example of this is `npm`, which originally used the system `tar` command when extracting Node packages. This caused problems because there were conflicts relating to incompatible versions of `tar`, and it's very rare for a Windows computer to have `tar` installed. These factors led to node-tar (https://github.com/isaacs/node-tar) being written entirely in JavaScript, not using any child processes.

On the flip side, using external applications allows a developer to tap into a wealth of applications written in other languages. For example, gm (http://aheckmann.github.com/gm/) is a module that utilizes the powerful GraphicsMagick and ImageMagick libraries to perform all sorts of image manipulation and conversions within a Node application.

BUFFERING COMMAND RESULTS USING CP.EXEC()

The high-level API, `cp.exec()`, is useful for when you want to invoke a command, and you only care about the final result, not about accessing the data from a child's stdio streams as they come. This API allows you to enter full sequences of commands, including multiple processes piped to one another.

One good use case for the `exec()` API is when you're accepting user commands to be executed. Say you're writing an IRC bot, and you'd like to execute commands when the user enters something beginning with a period (`.`). For example, if a user typed

.ls as their IRC message, the bot would execute ls and print the output back to the IRC room. As shown in the following listing, you need to set the timeout option, so that any never-ending processes are automatically killed after a certain period of time.

Listing 13.9 Using cp.exec() to run user-entered commands through the IRC bot

```
var cp = require('child_process');

room.on('message', function (user, message) {
  if (message[0] === '.') {
    var command = message.substring(1);
    cp.exec(command, { timeout: 15000 },
      function (err, stdout, stderr) {
        if (err) {
          room.say(
            'Error executing command "' + command + '": ' + err.message
          );
          room.say(stderr);
        } else {
          room.say('Command completed: ' + command);
          room.say(stdout);
        }
      }
    );
  }
});
```

room object represents connection to an IRC room (from some theoretical IRC module)

message event is emitted for each IRC message sent to room

Check if message content begins with a period

Spawn child process and have Node buffer result in a callback, timing out after 15 seconds

There are some good modules already in the npm registry that implement the IRC protocol, so if you'd like to write an IRC bot for real, you should definitely use one of the existing modules (both irc and irc-js in the npm registry are popular).

For times when you need to buffer a command's output, but you'd like Node to automatically escape the arguments for you, there's the execFile() function. This function takes four arguments, rather than three, and you pass the executable you want to run, along with an array of arguments to invoke the executable with. This is useful when you have to incrementally build up the arguments that the child process is going to use:

```
cp.execFile('ls', [ '-l', process.cwd() ],
            function (err, stdout, stderr) {
  if (err) throw err;
  console.error(stdout);
});
```

SPAWNING COMMANDS WITH A STREAM INTERFACE USING CP.SPAWN()

The low-level API for spawning child processes in Node is cp.spawn(). This function differs from cp.exec() because it returns a ChildProcess object that you can interact with. Rather than giving cp.spawn() a single callback function when the process completes, cp.spawn() lets you interact with each stdio stream of the child process individually.

The most basic use of cp.spawn() looks like this:

```
var child = cp.spawn('ls', [ '-l' ]);

// stdout is a regular Stream instance, which emits 'data',
// 'end', etc.
child.stdout.pipe(fs.createWriteStream('ls-result.txt'));

child.on('exit', function (code, signal) {
  // emitted when the child process exits
});
```

The first argument is the program you want to execute. This can be a single program name, which will be looked up in the current `PATH`, or it can be an absolute path to a program. The second argument is an array of string arguments to invoke the process with. In the default case, a `ChildProcess` object contains three built-in `Stream` instances that your script is meant to interact with:

- `child.stdin` is the *writable* `Stream` that represents the child's stdin.
- `child.stdout` is the *readable* `Stream` that represents the child's stdout.
- `child.stderr` is the *readable* `Stream` that represents the child's stderr.

You can do whatever you want with these streams, such as piping them to a file or socket or some other kind of writable stream. You can even completely ignore them if you like.

The other interesting event that happens on `ChildProcess` objects is the `exit` event, which is fired when the process has exited and the associated stream objects have all ended.

One good example module that abstracts the use of `cp.spawn()` into helpful functionality is node-cgi (https://github.com/TooTallNate/node-cgi), which allows you to reuse legacy Common Gateway Interface (CGI) scripts in your Node HTTP servers. CGI was really just a standard for responding to HTTP requests by invoking CGI scripts as child processes of an HTTP server with special environment variables describing the request. For example, you could write a CGI script that uses `sh` as the CGI interface:

```
#!/bin/sh
echo "Status: 200"
echo "Content-Type: text/plain"
echo
echo "Hello $QUERY_STRING"
```

If you were to name that file hello.cgi (don't forget to `chmod +x hello.cgi` to make it executable), you could easily invoke it as the response logic for HTTP requests in your HTTP server with a single line of code:

```
var http = require('http');
var cgi = require('cgi');

var server = http.createServer( cgi('hello.cgi') );
server.listen(3000);
```

With this server set up, when an HTTP request hits the server, node-cgi would handle the request by doing two things:

- Spawning the hello.cgi script as a new child process using `cp.spawn()`
- Passing the new process contextual information about the current HTTP request using a custom set of environment variables

The hello.cgi script uses one of the CGI-specific environment variables, `QUERY_STRING`, which contains the query-string portion of the request URL. The script uses this in the response, which gets written to the script's stdout. If you were to fire up this example server and send an HTTP request to it using `curl`, you'd see something like this:

```
$ curl http://localhost:3000/?nathan
Hello nathan
```

There are a lot of very good use cases for child processes in Node, and node-cgi is one example. As you get your server or application to do what it needs to do, you'll find that you inevitably have to utilize them at some point.

DISTRIBUTING THE WORKLOAD USING CP.FORK()

The last API offered by the child_process module is a specialized way of spawning additional Node processes, but with a special IPC channel built in. Since you're always spawning Node itself, the first argument passed to `cp.fork()` is a path to a Node.js module to execute.

Like `cp.spawn()`, `cp.fork()` returns a `ChildProcess` object. The major difference is the API added by the IPC channel: the child process now has a `child.send(message)` function, and the script being invoked by `fork()` can listen for `process.on('message')` events.

Suppose you want to write a Node HTTP server that calculates the Fibonacci sequence. You might try naively writing the server all in one shot, as shown in the next listing.

Listing 13.10 A non-optimal implementation of a Fibonacci HTTP server in Node.js

```
var http = require('http');

function fib (n) {                          // Calculates the Fibonacci number
  if (n < 2) {
    return 1;
  } else {
    return fib(n - 2) + fib(n - 1);
  }
}

var server = http.createServer(function (req, res) {
  var num = parseInt(req.url.substring(1), 10);
  res.writeHead(200);
  res.end(fib(num) + "\n");
});
server.listen(8000);
```

If you fire up the server with `node fibonacci-naive.js` and send an HTTP request to http://localhost:8000, the server will work as expected, but calculating the Fibonacci sequence for a given number is an expensive, CPU-bound computation. While your Node server's single thread is grinding away at calculating the result, no additional HTTP requests can be served. Additionally, you're only utilizing one CPU core here, and you likely have others that are sitting there doing nothing. This is bad.

A better solution is to fork Node processes during each HTTP request and have the child process do the expensive calculation and report back. `cp.fork()` offers a clean interface for doing this.

This solution involves two files:

- fibonacci-server.js will be the server.
- fibonacci-calc.js does the calculation.

First, here's the server:

```
var http = require('http');
var cp = require('child_process');

var server = http.createServer(function(req, res) {
  var child = cp.fork(__filename, [ req.url.substring(1) ]);
  child.on('message', function(m) {
    res.end(m.result + '\n');
  });
});
server.listen(8000);
```

The server uses `cp.fork()` to place the Fibonacci calculation logic in a separate Node process, which will report back to the parent process using `process.send()`, as shown in the following fibonacci-calc.js script:

```
function fib(n) {
  if (n < 2) {
    return 1;
  } else {
    return fib(n - 2) + fib(n - 1);
  }
}

var input = parseInt(process.argv[2], 10);
process.send({ result: fib(input) });
```

You can start the server with `node fibonacci-server.js` and, again, send an HTTP request to http://localhost:8000.

This is a great example of how dividing up the various components that make up your application into multiple processes can be a great benefit to you. `cp.fork()` provides `child.send()` and `child.on('message')` to send messages to and receive messages from the child. Within the child process itself, you have `process.send()` and `process.on('message')` to send messages to and receive messages from the parent. Use them!

Let's switch gears once more and look at developing command-line tools in Node.

13.4 Developing command-line tools

Another task commonly fulfilled by Node scripts is building command-line tools. By now, you should be familiar with the largest command-line tool written in Node: the Node Package Manager, a.k.a. npm. As a package manager, it does a lot of filesystem operations and spawning of child processes, and all of this is done using Node and its asynchronous APIs. This enables npm to install packages in parallel, rather than serially, making the overall process faster. And if a command-line tool *that* complicated can be written in Node, then anything can.

Most command-line programs have common process-related needs, like parsing command-line arguments, reading from stdin, and writing to stdout and stderr. In this section, you'll learn about the common requirements for writing a full command-line program, including the following:

- Parsing command-line arguments
- Working with stdin and stdout streams
- Adding pretty colors to the output using ansi.js

To get started on building awesome command-line programs, you need to be able to read the arguments the user invoked your program with. We'll take a look at that first.

13.4.1 Parsing command-line arguments

Parsing arguments is an easy and straightforward process. Node provides you with the `process.argv` property, which is an array of strings, which are the arguments that were used when Node was invoked. The first entry of the array is the Node executable, and the second entry is the name of your script. Parsing and acting on these arguments simply requires iterating through the array entries and inspecting each argument.

To demonstrate, let's write a quick script called args.js that prints out the result of `process.argv`. Most of the time you won't care about the first two entries, so you can `slice()` them off before processing:

```
var args = process.argv.slice(2);
console.log(args);
```

When you invoke this script standalone, you'll get an empty array because no additional arguments were passed in:

```
$ node args.js
[]
```

But when you pass along "hello" and "world" as arguments, the array contains string values as you'd expect:

```
$ node args.js hello world
[ 'hello', 'world' ]
```

As with any terminal application, you can use quotes around arguments that have spaces in them to combine them into a single argument. This is not a feature of Node, but rather of the shell that you're using (likely bash on a UNIX platform or cmd.exe on Windows):

```
$ node args.js "tobi is a ferret"
[ 'tobi is a ferret' ]
```

By UNIX convention, every command-line program should respond to the -h and --help flags by printing out usage instructions and then exiting. The following listing shows an example of using Array#forEach() to iterate through the arguments and parse them in the callback, printing out the usage instructions when the expected flag is encountered.

Listing 13.11 Parsing process.argv using Array#forEach() and a switch block

```
var args = process.argv.slice(2);

args.forEach(function (arg) {
  switch (arg) {
    case '-h':
    case '--help':
      printHelp();
      break;
  }
});

function printHelp () {
  console.log('   usage:');
  console.log(' $ AwesomeProgram <options> <file-to-awesomeify>');
  console.log('   example:');
  console.log(' $ AwesomeProgram --make-awesome not-yet.awesome');
  process.exit(0);
}
```

Slice off first two entries, which you're not interested in

Iterate through arguments, looking for -h or --help

Add additional flags/ switches here as necessary

Print out helpful message, and then quit

You can easily extend that switch block to parse additional switches. Community modules like commander.js, nopt, optimist, and nomnom (to name a few) all solve this problem in their own ways, so don't feel that using a switch block is the only way to parse the arguments. Like so many things in programming, there's no single correct way to do it.

Another task that every command-line program will need to deal with is reading input from stdin and writing structured data to stdout. Let's take a look at how this is done in Node.

13.4.2 Working with stdin and stdout

It's common for UNIX programs to be small, self-contained, and focused on a single task. These programs are then combined by using pipes, feeding the results of one process to the next, until the end of the command chain. For example, using standard UNIX commands to retrieve the list of unique authors from any given Git repository, you could combine the git log, sort, and uniq commands like this:

```
$ git log --format='%aN' | sort | uniq
```

```
Mike Cantelon
Nathan Rajlich
TJ Holowaychuk
```

These commands run in parallel, feeding the output of the first process to the next, continuing on until the end. To adhere to this piping idiom, Node provides two `Stream` objects for your command-line program to work with:

- `process.stdin`—A `ReadStream` to read input data from
- `process.stdout`—A `WriteStream` to write output data to

These objects act like the familiar stream interfaces that you've already learned about.

WRITING OUTPUT DATA WITH PROCESS.STDOUT

You've been using the `process.stdout` writable stream implicitly every time you've called `console.log()`. Internally, the `console.log()` function calls `process.stdout.write()` after formatting the input arguments. But the `console` functions are more for debugging and inspecting objects. When you need to write structured data to stdout, you can call `process.stdout.write()` directly.

Say your program connects to an HTTP URL and writes the response to stdout. `Stream#pipe()` works well in this context, as shown here:

```
var http = require('http');
var url = require('url');

var target = url.parse(process.argv[2]);
var req = http.get(target, function (res) {
  res.pipe(process.stdout);
});
```

Voilà! An absolutely minimal `curl` replica in only seven lines of code. Not too bad, huh? Next up let's cover `process.stdin`.

READING INPUT DATA WITH PROCESS.STDIN

Before you can read from stdin, you must call `process.stdin.resume()` to indicate that your script is interested in data from stdin. After that, stdin acts like any other readable stream, emitting `data` events as data is received from the output of another process, or as the user enters keystrokes into the terminal window.

The following listing shows a command-line program that prompts the user for their age before deciding whether to continue executing.

Listing 13.12 An age-restricted program that prompts the user for their age

```
var requiredAge = 18;                                   <- Set age limit

process.stdout.write('Please enter your age: ');        <- Specify question for user to answer

process.stdin.setEncoding('utf8');                      <- Set up stdin to emit UTF-8 strings instead of buffers

process.stdin.on('data', function (data) {
  var age = parseInt(data, 10);                         <- Parse data into a number
  if (isNaN(age)) {                                     <- If user didn't enter a valid number, print a message saying so
```

```
    console.log('%s is not a valid number!', data);
  } else if (age < requiredAge) {
    console.log('You must be at least %d to enter, ' +
                'come back in %d years',
                requiredAge, requiredAge - age);
  } else {
    enterTheSecretDungeon();
  }
  process.stdin.pause();
});

process.stdin.resume();

function enterTheSecretDungeon () {
    console.log('Welcome to The Program :)');
}
```

If user's given age is less than 18, print a message saying to come back in a few years

If previous conditions are met, continue executing

Waits for a single data event before closing stdin

Call resume() to start reading because process.stdin begins in a paused state

DIAGNOSTIC LOGGING WITH PROCESS.STDERR

There's also a `process.stderr` writable stream in every Node process, which acts exactly like the `process.stdout` stream, except that it writes to stderr instead. Because stderr is usually reserved for debugging, and not for sending structured data and piping, you'll generally use `console.error()` instead of accessing `process.stderr` directly.

Now that you're familiar with the built-in stdio streams in Node, which is crucial knowledge for building any command-line program, let's move on to something a bit more colorful (pun intended).

13.4.3 Adding colored output

Lots of command-line tools use colored text to make things easier to distinguish on the screen. Node itself does this in its REPL, as does npm for its various logging levels. It's a nice bonus feature that any command-line program can easily benefit from, and adding colored output to your programs is rather easy, especially with the support of community modules.

CREATING AND WRITING ANSI ESCAPE CODES

Colors on the terminal are produced by ANSI *escape codes* (the ANSI name comes from the American National Standards Institute). These escape codes are simple text sequences written to the stdout that have special meanings to the terminal—they can change the text color, change the position of the cursor, make a beep sound, and more.

Let's start simply. To print the word "hello" in the color green in your script, a single `console.log()` call is all it takes:

```
console.log('\033[32mhello\033[39m');
```

If you look closely, you can see the word "hello" in the middle of the string with some weird-looking characters on either side. This may look confusing at first, but it's rather simple. Figure 13.4 breaks up the green "hello" string into its three distinct pieces.

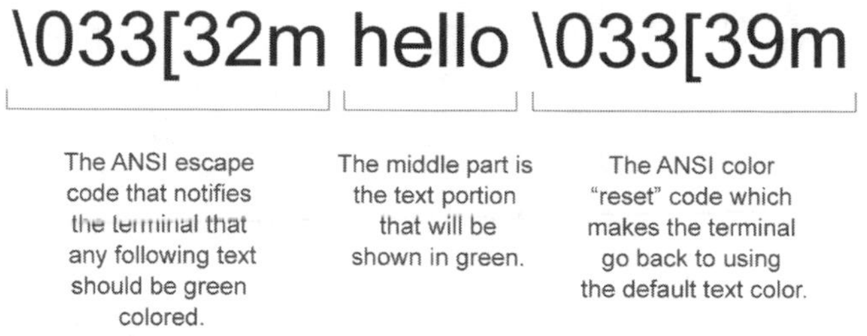

\033[32m hello \033[39m

The ANSI escape code that notifies the terminal that any following text should be green colored.

The middle part is the text portion that will be shown in green.

The ANSI color "reset" code which makes the terminal go back to using the default text color.

Figure 13.4 Outputting "hello" in green text using ANSI escape codes

There are a lot of escape codes that terminals recognize, and most developers have better things to do with their time than memorize them all. Thankfully, the Node community comes to the rescue again with multiple modules, such as colors.js, cli-color, and ansi.js, that make using colors in your programs easy and fun.

ANSI ESCAPE CODES ON WINDOWS Technically, Windows and its command prompt (cmd.exe) don't support ANSI escape codes. Fortunately for us, Node interprets the escape codes on Windows when your scripts write them to stdout, and then calls the appropriate Windows functions to produce the same results. This is interesting to know, but not something you'll have to think about while writing your Node applications.

FORMATTING FOREGROUND COLORS USING ANSI.JS

Let's take a look at ansi.js (https://github.com/TooTallNate/ansi.js), which you can install with `npm install ansi`. This module is nice because it's a very thin layer on top of the raw ANSI codes, which gives you greater flexibility compared to the other color modules (they only work with a single string at a time). In ansi.js, you set the *modes* (like "bold") of the stream, and they're persistent until cleared by one of the `reset()` calls. As an added bonus, ansi.js is the first module to support 256 color terminals, and it can convert CSS color codes (such as `#FF0000`) into ANSI color codes.

The ansi.js module works with the concept of a *cursor*, which is really just a wrapper around a writable stream instance with lots of convenience functions for writing ANSI codes to the stream, all of which support chaining. To print the word "hello" in green text again, using ansi.js syntax, you would write this:

```
var ansi = require('ansi');
var cursor = ansi(process.stdout);

cursor
  .fg.green()
  .write('Hello')
  .fg.reset()
  .write('\n');
```

You can see here that to use ansi.js you first have to create a `cursor` instance from a writable stream. Because you're interested in coloring your program's output, you pass `process.stdout` as the writable stream that the `cursor` will use. Once you have the `cursor`, you can invoke any of the methods it provides to alter the way that the text output will be rendered to the terminal. In this case, the result is equivalent to the `console.log()` call from before:

- `cursor.fg.green()` sets the foreground color to green
- `cursor.write('Hello')` writes the text "Hello" to the terminal in green
- `cursor.fg.reset()` resets the foreground color back to the default
- `cursor.write('\n')` finishes up with a newline

Programmatically adjusting the output using the `cursor` provides a clean interface for changing colors.

FORMATTING BACKGROUND COLORS USING ANSI.JS

The ansi.js module also supports background colors. To set the background color instead of the foreground color, replace the `fg` portion of the call with `bg`. For example, to set a red background color, you'd call `cursor.bg.red()`.

Let's wrap up with a quick program that prints this book's title information to the terminal in colors, as shown in figure 13.5.

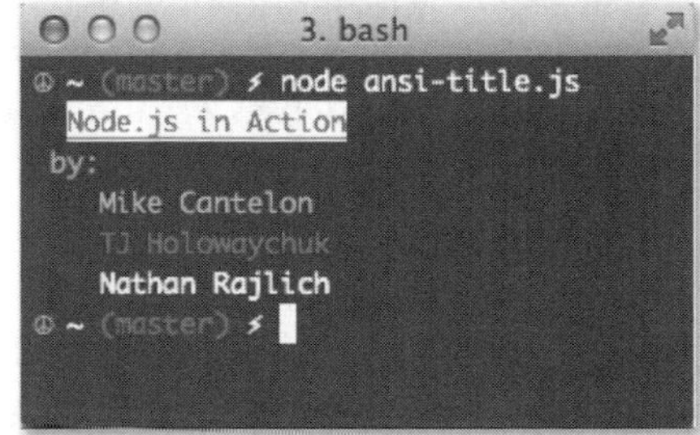

Figure 13.5 The result of ansi-title.js script printing out the name of this book and the authors in different colors

The code to output fancy colors like these is verbose, but very straightforward, because each function call maps directly to the corresponding escape code being written to the stream. The code shown in the following listing consists of two lines of initialization followed by one really long chain of function calls that end up writing color codes and strings to `process.stdout`.

Listing 13.13 A simple program that prints this book's title and authors in pretty colors

```
var ansi = require('ansi');
var cursor = ansi(process.stdout);

cursor
  .reset()
  .write('  ')
  .bold()
  .underline()
  .bg.white()
  .fg.black()
  .write('Node.js in Action')
  .fg.reset()
  .bg.reset()
  .resetUnderline()
  .resetBold()
  .write('  \n')
  .fg.green()
  .write(' by:\n')
  .fg.cyan()
```

```
.write('    Mike Cantelon\n')
.fg.magenta()
.write('    TJ Holowaychuk\n')
.fg.yellow()
.write('    Nathan Rajlich\n')
.reset()
```

Color codes are only one of the key features of ansi.js. We haven't touched on the cursor-positioning codes, how to make a beep sound, or how to hide and show the cursor. You can consult the ansi.js documentation and examples to see how that works.

13.5 Summary

Node is primarily designed for I/O-related tasks, such as creating HTTP servers. But as you've learned throughout this chapter, Node is well suited for a large variety of different tasks, such as creating a command-line interface to your application server, a client program that connects to the ASCII Star Wars server, a program that fetches and displays statistics from stock market servers—the possibilities are only limited by your imagination. Take a look at npm or node-gyp for a couple of complicated examples of command-line programs written using Node. They're great examples to learn from.

In this chapter, we talked about a couple of community modules that could aid in the development of your next application. In the next chapter, we'll focus on how you can find these awesome modules in the Node community, and how you can contribute modules you've developed back to the community for feedback and improvements. The social interaction is the exciting stuff!

14 The Node ecosystem

This chapter covers

- Finding online help with Node
- Collaborating on Node development using GitHub
- Publishing your work using the Node Package Manager

To get the most out of Node development, you need to know where to go for help and how to share your contributions with the rest of the community.

As in most open source communities, the development of Node and related projects happens via online collaboration. Many developers work together to submit and review code, document projects, and report bugs. When developers are ready to release a new version of Node, it's published on the official Node website. When a release-worthy third-party module has been created, it can be published to the npm repository to make it easy for others to install. Online resources provide the support you need to work with Node and related projects.

Figure 14.1 illustrates how you can use online resources for Node-related development, distribution, and support.

You'll likely need support before you need to collaborate, so let's first look at where you can go online to get help when you need it.

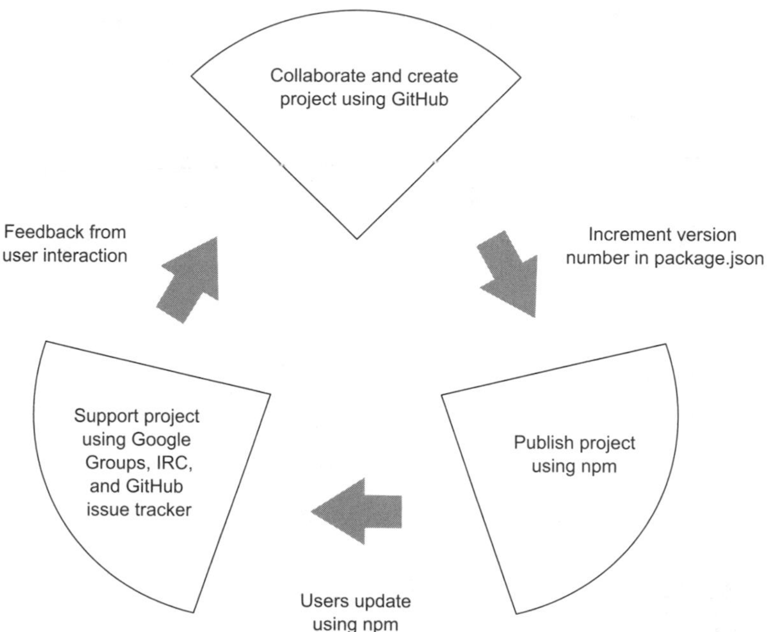

Figure 14.1 Node-related projects are created online collaboratively, often via the GitHub website. They're then published to npm, and documentation and support are provided via online resources.

14.1 Online resources for Node developers

As the Node world is an ever-changing one, you'll find the most up-to-date references online. At your disposal are numerous websites, online discussion groups, and chat rooms where you can find the information you need.

14.1.1 Node and module references

Table 14.1 lists a number of Node-related online references and resources. The most useful websites for referencing the Node APIs and learning about available third-party modules are the Node.js and npm homepages, respectively.

Table 14.1 Useful Node.js references

Resource	URL
Node.js homepage	http://nodejs.org/
Node.js up-to-date core documentation	http://nodejs.org/api/
Node.js blog	http://blog.nodejs.org/
Node.js job board	http://jobs.nodejs.org/
Node Package Manager (npm) homepage	http://npmjs.org/

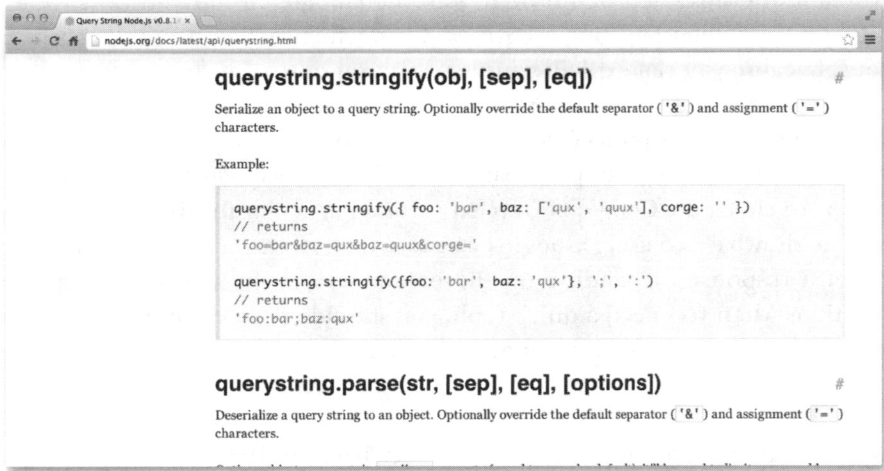

Figure 14.2 In addition to providing links to useful Node-related resources, nodejs.org offers authoritative API documentation for every released version of Node

When you attempt to implement something using Node, or any of its built-in modules, the Node homepage is an invaluable resource. The site (shown in figure 14.2) documents the entirety of the Node framework, including each of its APIs. You'll always find documentation for the most recent version of Node on the site. The official blog also documents the latest Node advances and shares important community news. There's even a job board.

When you're shopping for third-party functionality, the npm repository search page is the place to go. It lets you use keywords to search through the thousands of modules available in npm. If you find a module that you'd like to check out, click on the module's name to bring up its detail page, where you'll find links to the module's project homepage, if any, and useful information such as what other npm packages depend on the module, the module's dependencies, which versions of Node the module is compatible with, and license information.

Nevertheless, these websites may not answer all your questions about how to use Node or other third-party modules. Let's look at some other great places to ask for help online.

14.1.2 Google Groups

Google Groups have been set up for Node and some other popular third-party modules, including npm, Express, node-mongodb-native, and Mongoose.

Google Groups are useful for tough or in-depth questions. For example, if you were having trouble figuring out how to delete MongoDB documents using the node-mongodb-native module, you could go to the node-mongodb-native Google Group (https://groups.google.com/forum/?fromgroups#!forum/node-mongodb-native) and search it to see if anyone else had the same problem. If no one has dealt with your problem, the next step would be to join the Google Group and post your question. You can write lengthy Google Groups posts, which is helpful for complicated questions, because you can explain your issue thoroughly.

There's no central list that includes all Node-related Google Groups. You may find them mentioned in project documentation, but generally you'll have to search the web. You could, for example, search Google for "*nameofsomemodule* node.js google group" to check if a Google Group exists for a particular third-party module.

The drawback to using Google Groups is that often you have to wait hours or days to get a response, depending on the parameters of the Google Group. For simple questions when you need a quick reply, you should consider entering an internet chat room, where you can often get a quick answer.

14.1.3 IRC

Internet Relay Chat (IRC) was created way back in 1988, and while some think it archaic, it's still alive and active—and it's the best online way to get answers to quick questions about open source software. IRC rooms are called *channels*, and they exist for Node and various third-party modules. You won't find a list of Node-related IRC channels anywhere, but third-party modules that have a corresponding IRC channel will sometimes mention it in their documentation.

To get your question answered on IRC, connect to an IRC network (http://chatzilla.hacksrus.com/faq/#connect), change to the appropriate channel, and send your question to the channel. Out of respect to the folks in the channel, it's good to do some research beforehand to make sure your question can't be solved with a quick web search.

If you're new to IRC, the easiest way to get connected is using a web-based client. Freenode, the IRC network on which most Node-related IRC channels exists, has a web client available at http://webchat.freenode.net/. To join a channel, enter the appropriate name into the connection form. You don't need to register, and you can enter any nickname you want. (If someone is already using the name you choose, the underscore character (_) will be appended to the end of your nickname to differentiate you.)

Once you click Connect, you'll end up in a channel with any other users in the room listed on the right in a sidebar.

14.1.4 GitHub issues

If a project's development occurs on GitHub, another place to look for problems and solutions is the project's GitHub issue queue. To get to the issue queue, navigate to the project's main GitHub page and click the Issues tab. You can use the search field to look for issues related to your problem. An example issue queue is shown in figure 14.3.

If you're unable to find an issue that addresses your problem, and you think your problem may be due to a bug in the project's code, you can click the New Issue button on the issues page to describe the bug. Once you've created an issue, the project maintainers will be able to reply on that issue page and either address the issue or ask questions to get a better idea of your problem.

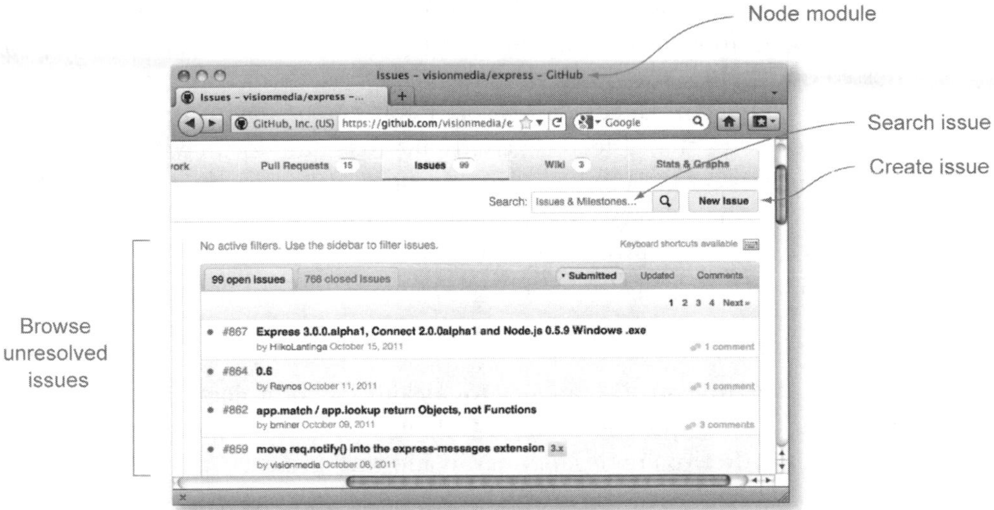

Figure 14.3 For projects hosted on GitHub, the issue queue can be helpful if you think you've identified a problem in the project's code.

> **ISSUE TRACKER IS NOT A SUPPORT FORUM** Depending on the project, it may not be considered appropriate for you to open general support questions on the project's GitHub issue tracker. This is usually the case if the project has set up another means for users to get general support, like a Google Group. It's a good idea to check the project's README file to see if it has a preference regarding general support or questions.

Now that you know where to go to file issues online for projects, we'll talk about GitHub's nonsupport role—it's the website through which most Node development collaboration takes place.

14.2 GitHub

GitHub is the center of gravity for much of the open source world, and it's critical for Node developers. The GitHub service provides hosting for Git, a powerful version control system (VCS), and includes a web interface that allows you to easily browse Git repositories. Open source projects can use GitHub for free.

> **GIT** The Git VCS has become a favorite among open source projects. It's a distributed version control system (DVCS), which, unlike Subversion and many other VCSs, you can use without a network connection to a server. Git was released in 2005, inspired by a proprietary VCS called BitKeeper. The publisher of BitKeeper had granted the Linux kernel development team free use of the software, but revoked it when suspicion arose that members of the team were attempting to figure out BitKeeper's inner workings. Linus Torvalds, the creator of Linux, decided to create an alternative VCS with similar functionality, and, within months, Git was being used by the Linux kernel development team.

In addition to Git hosting, GitHub provides projects with issue tracking, wiki, and web page hosting functionality. Because most Node projects in the npm repository are hosted on GitHub, knowing how to use GitHub is helpful for getting the most out of Node development. GitHub gives you a convenient way to browse code, check for unresolved bugs, and, if need be, contribute fixes and documentation.

Another use of GitHub is to *watch* a project. Watching a project provides you with notification of any changes to the project. The number of people watching a project is often used to gauge a project's overall popularity.

GitHub may be powerful, but how do you use it? Let's delve into that next.

14.2.1 Getting started on GitHub

When you've come up with an idea for a Node-based project or a third-party module, you'll want to set up an account on GitHub, if you haven't already, for easy access to Git hosting. After you're set up, you can add your projects, which you'll learn to do in the next section.

Because GitHub requires use of Git, you'll want to configure it before continuing to GitHub. Thankfully, GitHub offers help pages for Mac, Windows, and Linux to help you properly get set up (https://help.github.com/articles/set-up-git). Once you've configured Git, you'll need to get set up on GitHub by registering on its website and providing a Secure Shell (SSH) public key. You need the SSH key to keep your interactions with GitHub secure.

You'll learn the details of each of these steps in the next section. Note that you only have to do these steps once, not every time you add a project to GitHub.

GIT CONFIGURATION AND GITHUB REGISTRATION

To use GitHub, you need to configure your Git tool. You need to provide it with your name and email address using the following two commands:

```
git config --global user.name "Bob Dobbs"
git config --global user.email subgenius@example.com
```

Next, register on the GitHub website. Go to the sign-up page (https://github.com/signup/free), fill it in, and click Create an Account.

PROVIDING GITHUB WITH AN SSH PUBLIC KEY

Once you're registered, you'll need to provide GitHub with an SSH public key (https://help.github.com/articles/generating-ssh-keys). You'll use this key to authenticate your Git transactions. Follow these steps:

1. Visit https://github.com/settings/ssh in your browser.
2. Click Add SSH Key.

At this point, what you need to do varies depending on your operating system. GitHub will detect your operating system and show the relevant instructions.

14.2.2 Adding a project to GitHub

Once you're set up on GitHub, you can add a project to your account and begin pushing commits to it.

To do so, you first create a GitHub repository for your project, which we'll go over shortly. After that, you create a Git repository on your local workstation, which is where you do your work before pushing it to the GitHub repository. Figure 14.4 outlines this process.

You can also view your project files using GitHub's web interface.

CREATING A GITHUB REPOSITORY

Creating a repository on GitHub involves the following steps:

1. Log in to github.com in your web browser.
2. Visit https://github.com/new.
3. Fill out the resulting form, describing your repository, and click Create Repository.
4. GitHub creates an empty Git repository and issues a queue for your project.
5. GitHub will present the steps you need to take to use Git to push your code to GitHub.

It's helpful to understand what each of these steps does, so we'll run through an example and demonstrate the bare essentials of using Git.

SETTING UP AN EMPTY GIT REPOSITORY

To add an example project to GitHub, you'll first need to create an example Node module. For this example, we'll create a module containing some URL-shortening logic and call it node-elf.

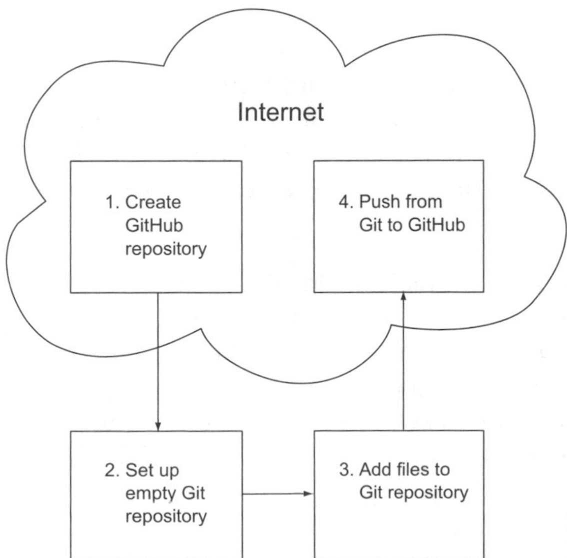

Figure 14.4 The steps in adding a Node project to GitHub

First, create a temporary directory for your project using the following commands:

```
mkdir -p ~/tmp/node-elf
cd ~/tmp/node-elf
```

To use this directory as a Git repository, enter the following command (which will create a directory called .git that contains repository metadata):

```
git init
```

ADDING FILES TO A GIT REPOSITORY

Now that you've set up an empty repository, you'll want to add some files. For this example, we'll add a file containing URL-shortening logic. Save the following listing's content in a file called index.js in this directory.

Listing 14.1 A Node module for URL shortening

```
exports.initPathData = function(pathData) {
  pathData = (pathData) ? pathData : {};
  pathData.count = (pathData.count) ? pathData.count : 0;
  pathData.map   = (pathData.map) ? pathData.map : {};
}

exports.shorten = function(pathData, path) {
  exports.initPathData(pathData);
  pathData.count++;
  pathData.map[pathData.count] = path;
  return pathData.count.toString(36);
}

exports.expand = function(pathData, shortened) {
  exports.initPathData(pathData);
  var pathIndex = parseInt(shortened, 36);
  return pathData.map[pathIndex];
}
```

Initialization function is called implicitly by shorten() and expand()

Accepts a "path" string and returns a shortened URL mapping to it

Accepts a previously shortened URL and returns the expanded URL

Next, let Git know that you want this file in your repository. The git add command works differently than other version control systems. Instead of adding files to your repository, the add command adds files to Git's *staging area*. The staging area can be thought of as a checklist where you indicate newly added files, or files that you've changed and that you'd like to be included in the next revision of your repository:

```
git add index.js
```

Git now knows that it should track this file. You could add other files to the staging area if you want to, but for now you only need to add this one file.

To let Git know you'd like to make a new revision in the repository, including the changed files you've selected in the staging area, use the commit command. As in other VCSs, the commit command can take a -m command-line flag to indicate a message describing the changes in the new revision:

```
git commit -m "Added URL shortening functionality."
```

The version of the repository on your workstation now contains a new revision. To view a list of repository changes, enter the following command:

```
git log
```

Pushing from Git to GitHub

At this point, if your workstation was suddenly struck by lightning, you'd lose all your work. To safeguard against unexpected events, and to get the full benefits of GitHub's web interface, you'll want to send changes you've made in your local Git repository to your GitHub account. But before doing this, you've got to let Git know where it should send changes to. To do this, you need to add a Git remote repository. These are referred to as *remotes.*

The following line shows how you add a GitHub remote to your repository. Replace `username` with your username, and note that `node-elf.git` indicates the name of the project:

```
git remote add origin git@github.com:username/node-elf.git
```

Now that you've added a remote, you can send your changes to GitHub. In Git terminology, sending changes is called a repository *push.* In the following command, you tell Git to push your work to the *origin* remote defined in the previous command. Every Git repository can have one or more branches, which are, conceptually, separate working areas in the repository. You want to push your work into the *master* branch:

```
git push -u origin master
```

In the push command, the `-u` option tells Git that this remote is the *upstream* remote and branch. The upstream remote is the default remote used.

After doing your first push with the `-u` option, you'll be able to do future pushes by using the following command, which is easier to remember:

```
git push
```

If you go to GitHub and refresh your repository page, you should now see your file.

Creating a module and hosting it on GitHub is a quick and dirty way to be able to reuse it. For example, if you want to use your sample module in a project, you could enter the commands in the following example:

```
mkdir ~/tmp/my_project/node_modules
cd ~/tmp/my_project/node_modules
git clone https://github.com/mcantelon/node-elf.git elf
cd ..
```

The `require('elf')` command would then provide access to the module. Note that when cloning the repository, you use the last command-line argument to name the directory into which you're cloning.

You now know how to add projects to GitHub, including how to create a repository on GitHub, how to create and add files to a Git repository on your workstation, and how to push your workstation repository to GitHub. You'll find many excellent resources online to help you go further. If you're looking for comprehensive instruction on how to use Git, Scott Chacon, one of the founders of GitHub, has written a thorough book called *Pro Git* that you can purchase or read free online (http://progit.org/). If a hands-on approach is more your style, the official Git site's documentation page lists a number of tutorials that will get you up and running (http://git-scm.com/documentation).

14.2.3 Collaborating using GitHub

Now that you know how to create a GitHub repository from scratch, let's look at how you can use GitHub to collaborate with others.

Suppose you're using a third-party module and you run into a bug. You may be able to examine the module's source code and figure out a way to fix it, and you could email the author of the code, describing your fix and attaching files containing your fixes. But this would require the author to do some tedious work. The author would have to compare your files to the latest code and incorporate the fixes from your files. But if the author was using GitHub, you could *clone* the author's project repository, make some changes, and then inform the author via GitHub of the bug fix. GitHub would then show the author, on a web page, the differences between your code and the version you duplicated, and, if the bug fix is acceptable, combine the fixes with the latest code via a single mouse click.

In GitHub parlance, duplicating a repository is known as *forking*. Forking a project allows you to do anything you want to your copy with no danger to the original repository. You don't need the permission of the original author to fork: anyone can fork any project and submit their contributions back to the original project. The original author may not approve your contribution, but even then you still have your own fixed version, which you can continue to maintain and enhance independently. If your fork were to grow in popularity, others might well fork your fork, and offer contributions of their own.

Once you've made changes to a fork, you can submit these changes to the original author with a *pull request*, which is a message asking a repository author to *pull* changes. *Pulling*, in Git parlance, means importing work from a fork and combining the work with your own. Figure 14.5 illustrates a GitHub collaboration scenario.

Now, let's walk through an example of forking a GitHub repository for the purpose of collaboration. This process is shown in figure 14.6.

Forking starts the collaboration process by duplicating the repository on GitHub to your own account (known as forking) (A). You then clone the forked repository to your workstation (B), make changes to it, commit the changes (C), push your work back to GitHub (D), and send a pull request to the owner of the original repository asking them to consider your changes (E). If they want to include your changes in their repository, they'll approve your pull request.

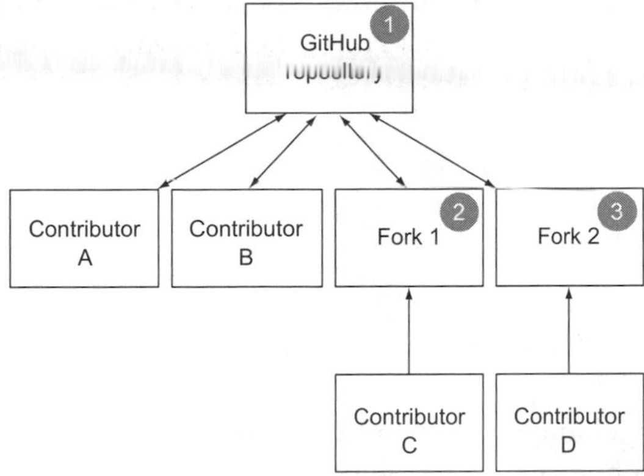

1. A GitHub repository is created by Contributor A. Contributor A gets a friend, Contributor B, involved to help with the project.

2. Contributor C decides he'd like to add a feature to the project and creates Fork 1. When the original repository is updated, contributors to the fork can "pull" changes, updating their fork's code. Contributor C has tried to get Contributors A and B to accept his feature, but they'd rather not because they have a different vision for the project, so Contributor C's features are only ever available on his fork.

3. Contributor D finds a bug in the web framework, and decides she wants to spend some time fixing it, so she creates Fork 2. Contributor D's bug fixes are accepted by Contributors A and B, however, and she submits "pull request" to the original repository, which results in her code getting "pulled" into the original repository after being reviewed by Contributors A and B.

Figure 14.5 A typical GitHub development scenario

Let's say you want to fork the `node-elf` repository you created earlier in this chapter and add code that exports the module's version. This would allow anyone using the module to ensure that they're using the right version.

First, log into GitHub and navigate to the repository's main page: https://github.com/mcantelon/node-elf. On the repository page, click the Fork button to duplicate the repository. The resulting page will be similar to the original repository page, with something like "forked from mcantelon/node-elf" displayed under the repository name.

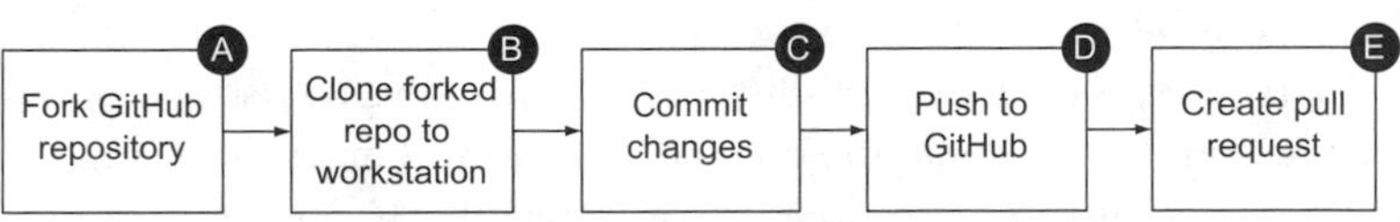

Figure 14.6 The process of collaborating on GitHub via forking

After forking, your next steps are to clone the repository to your workstation, make your changes, and push the changes to GitHub. The following commands will do this for the node-elf repository:

```
mkdir -p ~/tmp/forktest
cd ~/tmp/forktest
git clone git@github.com:chickentown/node-elf.git
cd node-elf
echo "exports.version = '0.0.2';" >> index.js
git add index.js
git commit -m "Added specification of module version."
git push origin master
```

Once you've pushed your changes, click Pull Request on your fork's repository page, and enter the subject and body of a message describing your changes. Click Send Pull Request. Figure 14.7 shows a screenshot containing typical content.

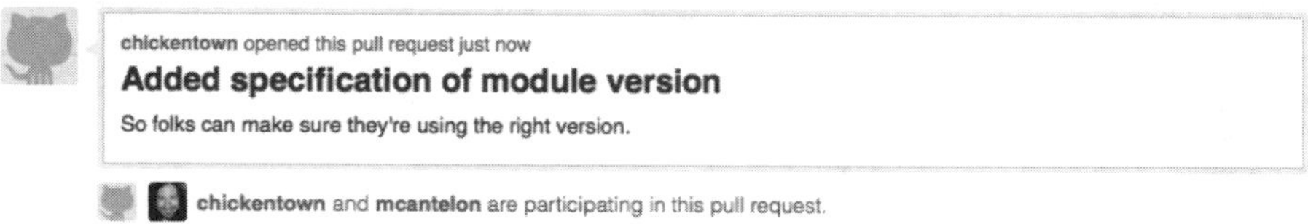

Figure 14.7 The details of a GitHub pull request

The pull request is then added to the issue queue of the original repository. The owner of the original repository can then, after reviewing your changes, incorporate them by clicking Merge Pull Request, entering a commit message, and clicking Confirm Merge. This automatically closes the issue.

Once you've collaborated with someone and have created a great module, the next step is getting it out into the world. The best way to do so is to add it to the npm repository.

14.3 Contributing to the npm repository

Suppose you've worked on the URL-shortening module for some time, and you think it would be useful to other Node users. To publicize it, you could post on Node-related Google Groups, describing its functionality. But you'd be limited in the number of Node users you'd reach, and as people start using your module, you wouldn't have a way to let them know about updates to the module.

To solve the problems of discoverability and providing updates, you can publish to npm. With npm, you can easily define a project's dependencies, allowing them to be automatically installed at the same time as your module. If you've created a module designed to store comments about content (such as blog posts), you could include a module handling MongoDB storage of comment data as a dependency. Or a module that provides a command-line tool might have a helper module for parsing command-line arguments as a dependency.

Up to this point in the book, you've used npm to install everything from testing frameworks to database drivers, but you haven't yet published anything. In the next sections, we'll show you the steps involved in publishing your own work on npm:

1. Preparing a package
2. Writing a package specification
3. Testing a package
4. Publishing a package

We'll start with preparing the package.

14.3.1 Preparing a package

Any Node module you want to share with the world should be accompanied by related resources, such as documentation, examples, tests, and related command-line utilities. The module should come with a README file that provides enough information to get users started quickly.

The package directory should be organized using subdirectories. Table 14.2 lists conventional subdirectories—bin, docs, example, lib, and test—and what you'd use each of them for.

Table 14.2 Conventional subdirectories in a Node project

Directory	Use
bin	Command-line scripts
docs	Documentation
example	Examples of application use
lib	Core application functionality
test	Test scripts and related resources

Once you've organized your package, you'll want to prepare it for publishing to npm by writing a package specification.

14.3.2 Writing a package specification

When you publish a package to npm, you need to include a machine-readable package specification file. This JSON file is called package.json, and it includes information about your module, such as its name, description, version, dependencies, and other characteristics. Nodejitsu has a handy website that shows a sample package.json file and explains what each part of the sample file is for when you hover your mouse over it (http://package.json.nodejitsu.com/).

In a package.json file, only the name and version are mandatory. Other characteristics are optional, but some, if defined, can make your module more useful. By defining a `bin` characteristic, for example, you can let npm know which files in your package are meant to be command-line tools, and npm will make them globally available.

A sample specification might look like this:

```
{
    "name": "elf"
  , "version": "0.0.1"
  , "description": "Toy URL shortener"
  , "author": "Mike Cantelon <mcantelon@example.com>"
  , "main": "index"
  , "engines": { "node": "0.4.x" }
}
```

For comprehensive documentation on available package.json options, enter the following command:

```
npm help json
```

Because generating JSON by hand is only slightly more fun than hand-coding XML, let's look at some tools that make it easier. One such tool, ngen, is an npm package that, when installed, adds a command-line tool called ngen. After asking a number of questions, ngen will generate a package.json file. It'll also generate a number of other files that are normally included in npm packages, such as a Readme.md file.

You can install ngen with the following command:

```
npm install -g ngen
```

After ngen is installed, you'll have a global `ngen` command that, when run in your project root directory, will ask you questions about your project and generate a package.json file, as well as some other files commonly used when writing Node packages. Some files that you don't need may be generated, and you can delete them. Generated files include a .gitignore file that specifies a number of files and directories that shouldn't normally be added to the Git repository of a project that will be published to npm. Also, an .npmignore file is generated, which serves a similar function, letting npm know what files can be ignored when publishing the package to npm.

Here's a sample output of running the ngen command:

```
Project name: elf
Enter your name: Mike Cantelon
Enter your email: mcantelon@gmail.com
Project description: URL shortening library

create : /Users/mike/programming/js/shorten/node_modules/.gitignore
create : /Users/mike/programming/js/shorten/node_modules/.npmignore
create : /Users/mike/programming/js/shorten/node_modules/History.md
create : /Users/mike/programming/js/shorten/node_modules/index.js
...
```

Generating a package.json file is the hardest part of publishing to npm. Once you've completed this step, you're ready to publish your module.

14.3.3 Testing and publishing a package

Publishing a module to npm involves three steps, which we'll go over in this section:

1. Test the installation of your package locally.
2. Add an npm user, if you haven't already.
3. Publish the package to npm.

TESTING PACKAGE INSTALLATION

To test a package locally, use npm's `link` command from the root directory of your module. This command makes your package globally available on your workstation, where Node can use it like a package conventionally installed by npm.

```
sudo npm link
```

Now that your project is linked globally, you can install it in a separate test directory by using the `link` command followed by the name of the package:

```
npm link elf
```

When you've installed the package, do a quick test of requiring the module by executing the `require` function in the Node REPL, as shown in the following code. In the results, you should see the variables or functions that your module provides:

```
node
> require('elf');
{ version: '0.0.1',
  initPathData: [Function],
  shorten: [Function],
  expand: [Function] }
```

If your package passed the test and you've finished developing it, use npm's `unlink` command from the root directory of your module:

```
sudo npm unlink
```

Your module will now no longer be globally available on your workstation, but later, once you've completed publishing your module to npm, you'll be able to install it normally using the `install` command.

Having tested your npm package, the next step is to create an npm publishing account, if you haven't previously set one up.

ADDING AN NPM USER

Enter the following to create your own npm publishing account:

```
npm adduser
```

You'll be prompted for a username, an email address, and a password. If your account is successfully added, you won't see an error message.

PUBLISHING TO NPM

The next step is to publish. Enter the following to publish your package to npm:

```
npm publish
```

You may see the warning, "Sending authorization over an insecure channel," but if you don't see additional errors, your module was published successfully. You can verify that your publish was successful by using npm's `view` command:

```
npm view elf description
```

If you'd like to include one or more private repositories as npm package dependencies, you can. Perhaps you have a module of useful helper functions you'd like to use, but not release publicly on npm.

To add a private dependency, where you'd normally put the dependency module's name, you can put any name that's different from the other dependency names. Where you'd normally put the version, you put a Git repository URL. In the following example, an excerpt from a package.json file, the last dependency is a private repository:

```
"dependencies" : {
  "optimist" : ">=0.1.3",
  "iniparser" : ">=1.0.1",
  "mingy": ">=0.1.2",
  "elf": "git://github.com/mcantelon/node-elf.git"
},
```

Note that any private modules should also include package.json files. To make sure you don't accidentally publish one of these modules, set the `private` property in its package.json file to `true`:

```
"private": true,
```

Now you're equipped to set up, test, and publish your own modules to the npm repository.

14.4 Summary

As with most successful open source projects, Node has an active online community, which means you'll find plenty of available online resources as well as quick answers to your questions using online references, Google Groups, IRC, or GitHub issue queues.

In addition to being a place where projects keep track of bugs, GitHub also provides Git hosting and the ability to browse Git repository code using a web browser. Using GitHub, other developers can easily fork your open source code if they want to contribute bug fixes, add features, or take a project in a new direction. You can also easily submit changes made to a fork back to the original repository.

Once a Node project has reached the stage where it's worth sharing with the world, you can submit it to the Node Package Manager repository. Inclusion in npm makes your project easier for others to find, and if your project is a module, inclusion in npm means your module will be easy to install.

You know how to get the help you need, collaborate online, and share your work. Node is what it is because of the active and involved community that surrounds it. You're encouraged to get active and be a part of the Node community!

appendix A Installing Node and community add-ons

Node is easy to install on most operating systems. Node can either be installed using conventional application installers or by using the command line. Command-line installation is easy on OS X and Linux, but it's not recommended for Windows.

To help you get started, the following sections detail the Node installation on OS X, Windows, and Linux operating systems. The last section in this appendix explains how you can use the Node Package Manager (npm) to find and install useful add-ons.

A.1 OS X setup

Installing Node on OS X is quite straightforward. The official installer (http://nodejs.org/#download), shown in figure A.1, provides an easy way to install a precompiled version of Node and npm.

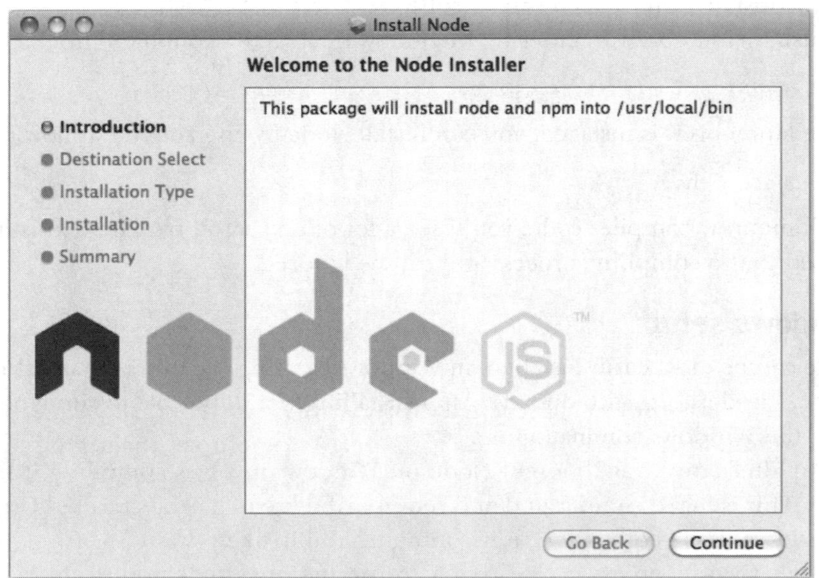

Figure A.1 The official Node installer for OS X

If you'd rather install from source, you can either use a tool called Homebrew (http://mxcl.github.com/homebrew/), which automates installation from source, or you can manually install from source. Installing Node from source on OS X, however, requires you to have Xcode developer tools installed.

> **XCODE** If you don't have Xcode installed, you can download Xcode from Apple's website (http://developer.apple.com/downloads/). You'll have to register with Apple as a developer, which is free, to access the download page. The full Xcode installation is a large download (approximately 4 GB), so as an alternative Apple also offers Command Line Tools for Xcode, which is available for download on the same web page and gives you the minimal functionality needed to compile Node and other open source software projects.
>
> To quickly check if you have Xcode, you can start the Terminal application and run the command `xcodebuild`. If you have Xcode installed, you should get an error indicating that your current directory "does not contain an Xcode project."

Either method requires entering OS X's command-line interface by running the Terminal application that is usually found in the Utilities folder in the main Applications folder.

If you're compiling from source, see section A.4 for the necessary steps.

A.1.1 Installation with Homebrew

An easy way to install Node on OS X is by using Homebrew, an application for managing the installation of open source software.

Install Homebrew by entering the following into the command line:

```
ruby -e "$(curl -fsSkL raw.github.com/mxcl/homebrew/go)"
```

Once Homebrew is installed, you can install Node by entering the following:

```
brew install node
```

As Homebrew compiles code, you'll see a lot of text scroll by. The text is information related to the compiling process and can be ignored.

A.2 Windows setup

Node can be most easily installed on Windows by using the official standalone installer (http://nodejs.org/#download). After installing, you'll be able to run Node and npm from the Windows command line.

An alternative way to install Node on Windows involves compiling it from source code. This is more complicated and requires the use of a project called Cygwin, which provides a Unix-compatible environment. You'll likely want to avoid using Node through Cygwin unless you're trying to use modules that won't otherwise work on Windows or need to be compiled, such as some database driver modules.

To install Cygwin, navigate to the Cygwin installer download link in your web browser (http://cygwin.com/install.html) and download setup.exe. Double-click

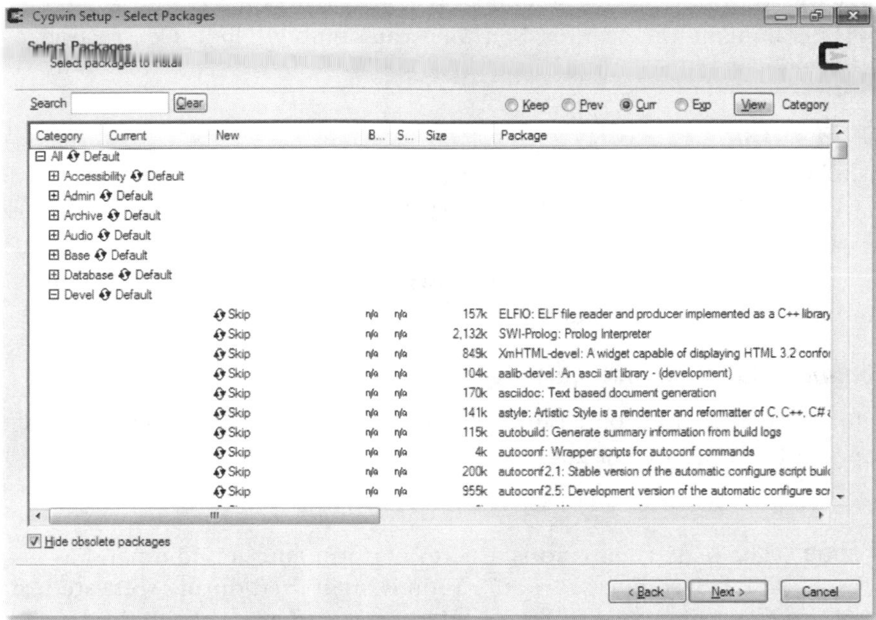

Figure A.2 Cygwin's package selector allows you to select open source software that will be installed on your system.

setup.exe to start installation, and then click Next repeatedly to select the default options until you reach the Choose a Download Site step. Select any of the download sites from the list, and click Next. If you see a warning about Cygwin being a major release, click OK to continue.

You should now see Cygwin's package selector, as shown in figure A.2.

You'll use this selector to pick the software functionality you'd like installed in your Unix-like environment (see table A.1 for a list of Node development–related packages to install).

Once you've selected the packages, click Next.

You'll then see a list of packages that the ones you've selected depend on. You need to install those as well, so click Next again to accept them. Cygwin will now download the packages you need. Once the download has completed, click Finish.

Table A.1 Cygwin packages needed to run Node

Category	Package
devel	gcc4-g++
devel	git
devel	make
devel	openssl-devel
devel	pkg-config
devel	zlib-devel
net	inetutils
python	python
web	wget

Start Cygwin by clicking the desktop icon or Start menu item. You'll be presented with a command-line prompt. You then can compile Node (see section A.4 for the necessary steps).

A.3 Linux setup

Installing Node on Linux is usually painless. We'll run through installations from source code on two popular Linux distributions: Ubuntu and CentOS. Node is also available through package managers on a number of distributions, and there are other installation instructions on GitHub: https://github.com/joyent/node/wiki/Installing-Node.js-via-package-manager.

A.3.1 Ubuntu installation prerequisites

Before installing Node on Ubuntu, you'll need to install prerequisite packages. This is done on Ubuntu 11.04 or later using a single command:

```
sudo apt-get install build-essential libssl-dev
```

> **SUDO** The `sudo` command is used to perform another command as "superuser" (also referred to as "root"). Sudo is often used during software installation because files need to be placed in protected areas of the filesystem, and the superuser can access any file on the system regardless of file permissions.

A.3.2 CentOS installation prerequisites

Before installing Node on CentOS, you'll need to install prerequisite packages. This is done on CentOS 5 using the following commands:

```
sudo yum groupinstall 'Development Tools'
sudo yum install openssl-devel
```

Now that you've installed the prerequisites, you can move on to compiling Node.

A.4 Compiling Node

Compiling Node involves the same steps on all operating systems.

On the command line, you first enter the following command to create a temporary folder into which you'll download the Node source code:

```
mkdir tmp
```

Next, you navigate into the directory created in the previous step:

```
cd tmp
```

You now enter the following command:

```
curl -O http://nodejs.org/dist/node-latest.tar.gz
```

Next, you'll see text indicating the download progress. Once progress reaches 100 percent, you're returned to the command prompt. Enter the following command to decompress the file you received:

```
tar zxvf node-latest.tar.gz
```

You should then see a lot of output scroll past, and you'll be returned to the command prompt. At the prompt, enter the following command to list the files in the current folder, which should include the name of the directory you just decompressed:

```
ls
```

Next, enter the following command to move into this directory:

```
cd node-v*
```

You're now in the directory containing Node's source code. Enter the following command to run a configuration script that will prepare the right installation for your specific system:

```
./configure
```

Next, enter the following command to compile Node:

```
make
```

Node normally takes a little while to compile, so be patient and expect to see a lot of text scroll by. The text is information related to the compiling process and can be ignored.

> **A CYGWIN QUIRK** If you're running Cygwin on Windows 7 or Vista, you may run into errors during this step. These are due to an issue with Cygwin rather than an issue with Node. To address them, exit the Cygwin shell, and then run the ash.exe command-line application (located in the Cygwin directory; usually c:\cygwin\bin\ash.exe). On the ash command line, enter `/bin/rebaseall -v`. When this completes, restart your computer. This should fix your Cygwin issues.

At this point, you're almost done. Once text stops scrolling and you again see the command prompt, you can enter the final command in the installation process:

```
sudo make install
```

When that's finished, enter the following command to run Node and have it display its version number, verifying that it has been successfully installed:

```
node -v
```

You should now have Node on your machine!

A.5 Using the Node Package Manager

With Node installed, you'll be able to use built-in modules that provide you with APIs to perform networking tasks, interact with the filesystem, and do other things commonly needed in applications. Node's built-in modules are referred to collectively as the Node *core*. While Node's core encompasses a lot of useful functionality, you'll likely want to use community-created functionality as well. Figure A.3 shows, conceptually, the relationship between the Node core and add-on modules.

Depending on what language you've been working in, you may or may not be familiar with the idea of community repositories of add-on functionality. These repositories are akin to libraries of useful application building blocks that can help you do things that the language itself doesn't easily allow out of the box. These repositories are usually modular: rather than fetching the entire library all at once, you can usually fetch just the add-ons you need.

The Node community has its own tool for managing community add-ons: the Node Package Manager (npm). In this section, you'll learn how to use npm to find community add-ons, view add-on documentation, and explore the source code of add-ons.

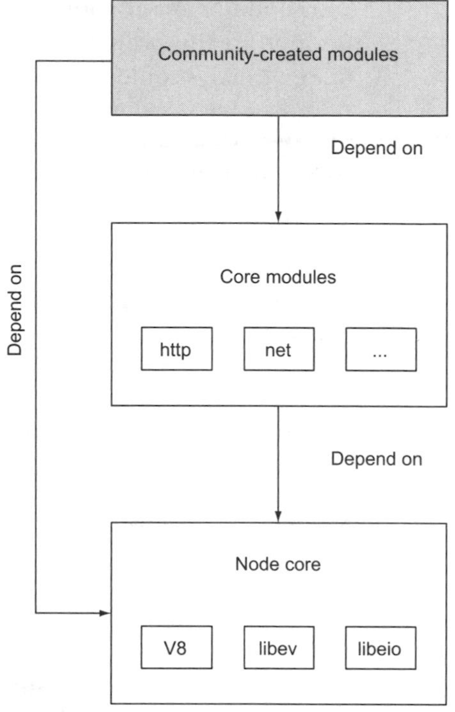

Figure A.3 The Node stack is composed of globally available functionality, core modules, and community-created modules.

npm is missing on my system

If you've installed Node, then npm is likely already installed. You can test it by running `npm` on the command line and seeing if the command is found. If not, you can install npm by doing the following:

```
cd /tmp
git clone git://github.com/isaacs/npm.git
cd npm
sudo make install
```

Once you've installed npm, enter the following on a command line to verify that npm is working (by asking it to output its version number):

```
npm -v
```

If npm has installed correctly, you should see a number similar to the following:

```
1.0.3
```

If you run into problems installing npm, the best thing to do is to visit the npm project on GitHub (http://github.com/isaacs/npm), where the latest installation instructions can be found.

A.5.1 Searching for packages

The npm command-line tool provides convenient access to community add-ons. These add-on modules are referred to as *packages* and are stored in an online repository. For users of PHP, Ruby, and Perl, npm is analogous to PEAR, Gem, and CPAN, respectively.

The npm tool is extremely convenient. With npm you can download and install a package using a single command. You can also easily search for packages, view package documentation, explore a package's source code, and publish your own packages so they can be shared with the Node community.

You can use npm's `search` command to find packages available in its repository. For example, if you wanted to search for an XML generator, you could simply enter this command:

```
npm search xml generator
```

The first time npm does a search, there's a long pause as it downloads repository information. Subsequent searches, however, are quick.

As an alternative to command-line searching, the npm project also maintains a web search interface to the repository: http://search.npmjs.org/. This website, shown in figure A.4, also provides statistics on how many packages exist, which packages are the most depended on by others, and which packages have recently been updated.

The npm web search interface also lets you browse individual packages, showing useful data such as the package dependencies and the online location of a project's version control repository.

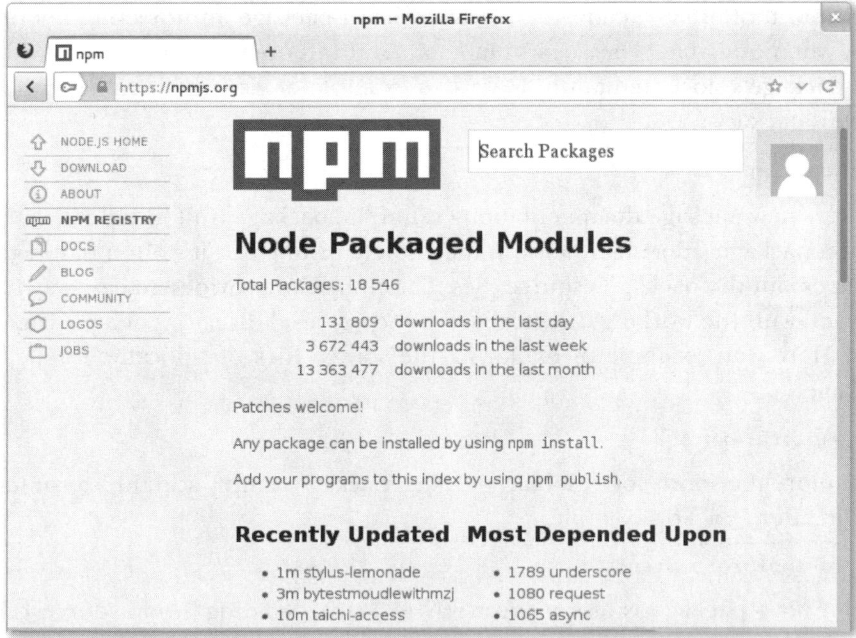

Figure A.4 The npm search website provides useful statistics on module popularity.

A.5.2 Installing packages

Once you've found packages you'd like to install, there are two main ways of doing so using npm: locally and globally.

Locally installing a package puts the downloaded module into a folder called node_modules in the current working directory. If this folder doesn't exist, npm will create it.

Here's an example of installing the express package locally:

```
npm install express
```

Globally installing a package puts the downloaded module into the /usr/local directory on non-Windows operating systems, a directory traditionally used by Unix to store user-installed applications. In Windows, the Appdata\Roaming\npm subdirectory of your user directory is where globally installed npm modules are put.

Here's an example of installing the express package globally:

```
npm install -g express
```

If you don't have sufficient file permissions when installing globally, you may have to prefix your command with `sudo`. For example,

```
sudo npm install -g express
```

After you've installed a package, the next step is figuring out how it works. Luckily, npm makes this easy.

A.5.3 Exploring documentation and package code

The npm tool offers a convenient way to view a package author's online documentation, when available. The `docs` npm command will open a web browser with a specified package's documentation. Here's an example of viewing documentation for the express package:

```
npm docs express
```

You can view package documentation even if the package isn't installed.

If a package's documentation is incomplete or unclear, it's often handy to be able to check out the package's source files. The npm tool provides an easy way to spawn a subshell with the working directory set to the top-level directory of a package's source files. Here's an example of exploring the source files of a locally installed express package:

```
npm explore express
```

To explore the source of a globally installed package, simply add the `-g` command-line option after `npm`. For example:

```
npm -g explore express
```

Exploring a package is also a great way to learn. Reading Node source code often introduces you to unfamiliar programming techniques and ways of organizing code.

appendix B
Debugging Node

During development, and especially while learning a new language or framework, debugging tools and techniques can be helpful. In this appendix, you'll learn a number of ways to figure out exactly what's going on with your Node application code.

B.1 Analyzing code with JSHint

Syntax- and scope-related errors are a common pitfall of development. The first line of defense, when attempting to determine the root of an application problem, is to look at the code. If you look at the source code, however, and don't immediately see a problem, another thing worth doing is running a utility to check your source code for problems.

JSHint is one such utility. It can alert you to show-stopping errors, such as functions called in code that aren't defined anywhere, as well as to stylistic concerns, such as not heeding the JavaScript convention of capitalizing class constructors. Even if you never run JSHint, reading over the types of errors it looks for will alert you to possible coding pitfalls.

JSHint is a project based on JSLint, a JavaScript source code analysis tool that has been around for a decade. JSLint, however, is not very configurable, and that's where JSHint comes in.

JSLint is, in the opinion of many, overly strict in terms of enforcing stylistic recommendations. JSHint, conversely, allows you to tell it what you want it to check for and what you want it to ignore. Semicolons, for example, are technically required by JavaScript interpreters, but most interpreters use automated semicolon insertion (ASI) to insert them where they're missing. Because of this, some developers omit them in their source code to lessen visual noise, and their code runs without issue. Whereas JSLint would complain that a lack of semicolons is an error, JSHint can be configured to ignore this "error" and check for show-stopping issues.

Installing JSHint makes available a command-line tool called `jshint` that checks source code. JSHint should be installed globally using npm by executing this command:

```
npm install -g jshint
```

Once you've installed JSHint, you can check JavaScript files by simply entering something like the following example:

```
jshint my_app.js
```

You'll most likely want to create a configuration file for JSHint that indicates what you want it to check. One way to do so is to copy the default configuration file, available on GitHub (https://github.com/jshint/node-jshint/blob/master/.jshintrc), to your workstation and modify it.

If you name your version of the config file .jshintrc and include it in your application directory, or in any parent directory of your application directory, JSHint will automatically find and use it.

Alternatively, you can run JSHint using the config flag to specify a configuration file location. The following example shows JSHint being told to use a configuration file with a nonstandard filename:

```
jshint my_app.js --config /home/mike/jshint.json
```

For details about each specific configuration option, check out the JSHint website: http://www.jshint.com/docs/#options.

B.2 Outputting debugging information

If your code appears to be legitimate, but your application is still behaving unexpectedly, you may want to add debugging output to get a better sense of what's going on under the hood.

B.2.1 Debugging with the console module

The console module is a built-in Node module that provides functionality useful for console output and debugging.

OUTPUTTING APPLICATION STATUS INFORMATION

The `console.log` function is used to output application status information to standard output; `console.info` is another name for the same function. Arguments can be provided, `printf()`-style (http://en.wikipedia.org/wiki/Printf):

```
console.log('Counter: %d', counter);
```

For outputting warnings and errors, the `console.warn` and `console.error` functions operate similarly. The only difference is that instead of printing to standard output, they print to standard error. This enables you to, if desired, redirect warnings and errors to a log file, as the following example shows:

```
node server.js 2> error.log
```

The `console.dir` function will output an object's contents. The next example output shows what this looks like:

```
{ name: 'Paul Robeson',
  interests: [ 'football', 'politics', 'music', 'acting' ] }
```

OUTPUTTING TIMING INFORMATION

The console module includes two functions that, when used together, allow you to time the execution of parts of your code. More than one thing can be timed simultaneously.

To start timing, add the following line to your code at the point you'd like timing to start:

```
console.time('myComponent');
```

To end timing, returning the time elapsed since timing started, add this line to your code at the point where timing should stop:

```
console.timeEnd('myComponent');
```

The preceding line will display the elapsed time.

OUTPUTTING STACK TRACES

A stack trace provides you with information about what functions executed before a certain point in application logic. When Node encounters an error during application execution, for example, it outputs a stack trace to provide information about what led, in the application's logic, to the error.

At any point during your application, you can output a stack trace, without causing your application to stop, by executing `console.trace()`.

This will produce output similar to the following example stack trace:

```
Trace:
    at lastFunction (/Users/mike/tmp/app.js:12:11)
    at secondFunction (/Users/mike/tmp/app.js:8:3)
    at firstFunction (/Users/mike/tmp/app.js:4:3)
    at Object.<anonymous> (/Users/mike/tmp/app.js:15:3)
    ...
```

Note that stack traces display execution in reverse chronological order.

B.2.2 *Using the debug module to manage debugging output*

Debugging output is useful, but if you're not actively troubleshooting an issue, it can end up being visual noise. Ideally you could switch debugging output on or off.

One way to toggle debugging output is to use an environmental variable. T.J. Holowaychuk's debug module provides a handy tool for this, allowing you to manage debugging output using the `DEBUG` environmental variable. Chapter 13 details the use of the debug module.

B.3 *Node's built-in debugger*

For debugging needs beyond adding simple debugging output, Node comes with a built-in command-line debugger. The debugger is invoked by starting your application using the `debug` keyword, like this:

```
node debug server.js
```

```
2. Shell
$ node debug server.js
< debugger listening on port 5858
connecting... ok
break in server.js:1
  1 var http = require('http');
  2
  3 http.createServer(function (req, res) {
debug> 
```

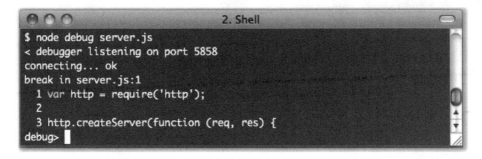

Figure B.1 Starting the built-in Node debugger

When running a Node application this way, you'll be shown the first few lines of your application and presented with a debugger prompt, as shown in figure B.1.

The "break in server.js:1" line means that the debugger has stopped before executing the first line.

B.3.1 Debugger navigation

At the debugger prompt, you can control the execution of your application. You could enter `next` (or just `n`) to execute the next line; alternatively, you could enter `cont` (or just `c`) to have it execute until interrupted.

The debugger can be interrupted by the termination of the application or by what are called *breakpoints*. Breakpoints are points where you want the debugger to stop execution so you can examine application state.

One way to add a breakpoint is by adding a line to your application where you want to put the breakpoint. This line should contain the statement `debugger;`, as listing B.1 shows. The `debugger;` line won't do anything while running Node normally, so you can leave it and there will be no ill effects.

Listing B.1 Adding a breakpoint programmatically

```
var http = require('http');

function handleRequest(req, res) {
  res.writeHead(200, {'Content-Type': 'text/plain'});
  res.end('Hello World\n');
}

http.createServer(function (req, res) {
  debugger;                                  // Adds a breakpoint to code
  handleRequest(req, res);
}).listen(1337, '127.0.0.1');

console.log('Server running at http://127.0.0.1:1337/');
```

If you run listing B.1 in debug mode, it'll first break at line 1. If you then enter `cont` into the debugger, it'll proceed to create the HTTP server, awaiting a connection. If you create a connection by visiting http://127.0.0.1:1337 with a browser, you'll see that it breaks at the `debugger;` line.

Enter next to continue to the next line of code. The current line will now be a function call to handleRequest. If you again enter next to continue to the next line, the debugger won't descend into each line of handleRequest. But if you enter step, the debugger will descend into the handleRequest function, allowing you to troubleshoot any issues with this particular function. If you change your mind about wanting to debug handleRequest, you can enter out (or o) to step out of the function.

Breakpoints can be set from within the debugger in addition to being specified in source code. To put a breakpoint in the current line in the debugger, enter setBreakpoint() (or sb()) into the debugger. It's possible to set a breakpoint at a specific line (sb(line)) or when a specific function is being executed (sb('fn()')).

When you want to unset a breakpoint, there's the clearBreakpoint() function (cb()). This function takes the same arguments as the setBreakpoint() function, only it does the inverse.

B.3.2 Examining and manipulating state in the debugger

If you want to keep an eye on particular values in the application, you can add what are called *watchers*. Watchers inform you of the value of a variable as you navigate through code.

For example, when debugging the code in listing B.1, you could enter watch ("req.headers['user-agent']") and, for each step, you'd see what type of browser made the request. To see a list of watchers, you'd enter the watchers command. To remove a watcher, you'd use the unwatch command; unwatch("req.headers['user-agent']"), for example.

If at any point during debugging, you want to be able to fully examine, or manipulate, the state, you can use the repl command to enter a Read-Eval-Print-Loop (REPL). This allows you to enter any JavaScript expression and have it evaluate. To exit the REPL and return to the debugger, press Ctrl-C.

Once you're done debugging, you can exit the debugger by pressing Ctrl-C twice, by pressing Ctrl-D, or by entering the .exit command.

These are the basics of debugger use. For more information on what can be done with the debugger, visit the official Node page: http://nodejs.org/api/debugger.html.

B.4 Node Inspector

Node Inspector is an alternative to Node's built-in debugger. It uses a WebKit-based browser such as Chrome or Safari, rather than the command line, as an interface.

B.4.1 Starting Node Inspector

Before you begin debugging, Node Inspector should be installed globally with the following npm command. After installation, the node-inspector command will be available on your system:

```
npm install -g node-inspector
```

To debug a Node application, start it using the --debug-brk command-line option:

```
node --debug-brk server.js
```

Using the --debug-brk option causes the debugging to insert a breakpoint before the first line of your application. If this isn't desired, you can use the --debug option instead.

Once your application is running, start Node Inspector:

```
node-inspector
```

Node Inspector is interesting because it uses the same code as WebKit's Web Inspector, but plugged into Node's JavaScript engine instead, so web developers should feel right at home using it.

Once Node Inspector is running, navigate to http://127.0.0.1:8080/debug?port=5858 in your WebKit browser, and you should see the Node Inspector. If you ran Node Inspector using the --debug-brk option, it will immediately show the first script in your application, as in figure B.2. If you used the --debug option, you'll have to use the script selector, indicated by the script name "step.js" in figure B.2, to select the script you'd like to debug.

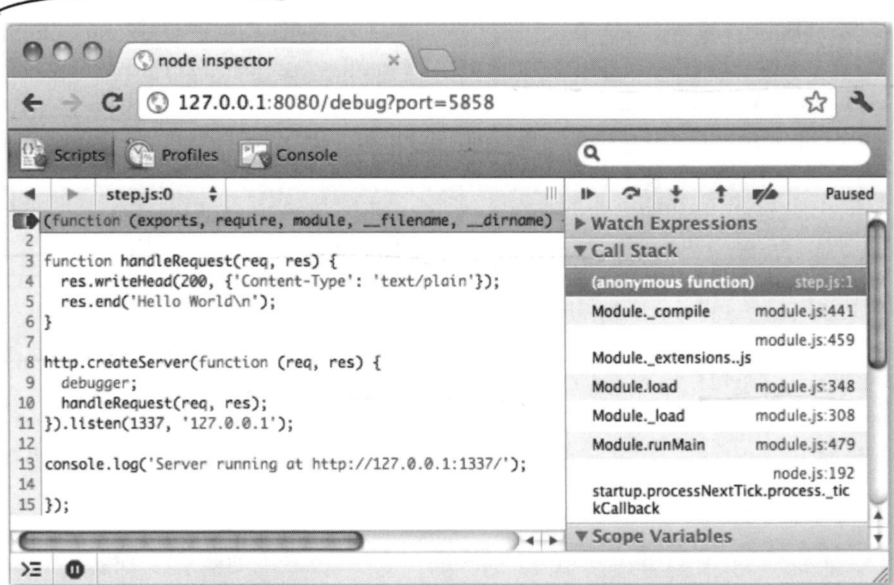

Figure B.2 The Node Inspector

A red arrow is shown to the left of the line of code that will execute next.

B.4.2 Node Inspector navigation

To step to the next function call in your application, click the button that looks like a small circle with an arrow arcing over it. Node Inspector, like the command-line Node debugger, allows you to step into functions as well. When the red arrow is to the left of a function call, you can descend into the function by clicking the small circle with an arrow pointing down at it. To step out of the function, click the small circle with an arrow pointing up. If you're using Node core or community modules, the debugger will switch to script files for these modules as you step through your application. Don't be alarmed: it will at some point return to your application's code.

To add breakpoints while running Node Inspector, click the line number to the left of any line of a script. If you'd like to clear all breakpoints, click the button to the right of the step-out button (arrow pointing up).

Node Inspector also has the interesting feature of allowing you to change code as your application runs. If you'd like to change a line of code, simply double-click on it, edit it, and then click out of the line.

B.4.3 Browsing state in Node Inspector

As you debug your application, you can inspect state using the collapsible panes under the buttons that allow you to navigate in the debugger, as shown in figure B.3. These allow you to inspect the call stack and variables in the scope of code currently being executed. Variables can be manipulated by double-clicking on them and changing their values. You can also, as with Node's built-in command-line debugger, add watch expressions that will display as you step through your application.

For more details about how to get the most out of Node Inspector, visit its GitHub project page: https://github.com/dannycoates/node-inspector/.

WHEN IN DOUBT, REFRESH If you run into any odd behavior while using Node Inspector, refreshing the browser may help. If that doesn't work, try restarting both your Node application and Node Inspector.

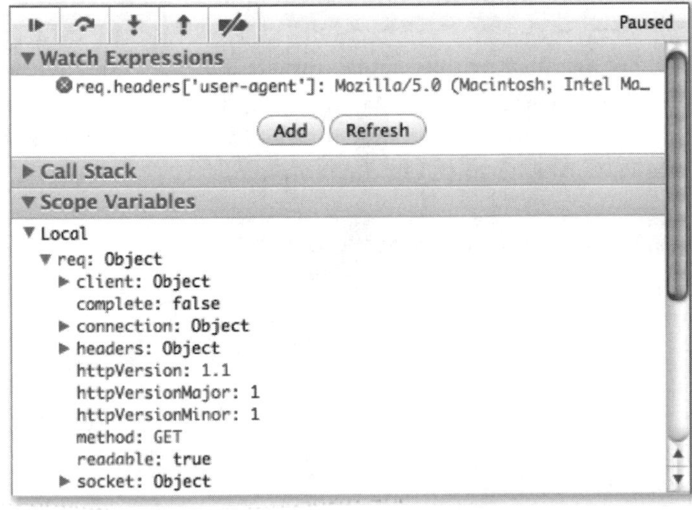

Figure B.3 Browsing application state using Node Inspector

appendix C Extending and configuring Express

Express does a lot right out of the box, but extending Express and tweaking its configuration can simplify development and allow it to do more.

C.1 Extending Express

Let's start by looking at how to extend Express. In this section, you'll learn how to

- Create your own template engines
- Take advantage of community-created template engines
- Improve your applications using modules that extend Express

C.1.1 Registering template engines

Engines may provide Express support out of the box by exporting an `__express` method. But not every engine will provide this, or you may want to write your own engines. Express facilitates this by providing the `app.engine()` method. In this section, we'll take a look at writing a small markdown template engine with variable substitution for dynamic content.

The `app.engine()` method *maps* a file extension to a callback function so that Express knows how to use it. In the following listing, the .md extension is passed so that render calls such as `res.render('myview.md')` will use the callback function to render the file. This abstraction enables practically any template engine to be used within the framework. In this custom template engine, braces are used around local variables to allow for dynamic input—for example, `{name}` will output the value of `name` wherever it's found in the template.

Listing C.1 Handling the .md extension

```
var express = require('express');
var http = require('http');
var md = require('github-flavored-markdown').parse;    <- Require a markdown implementation
var fs = require('fs');

var app = express();
```

```
app.engine('md', function(path, options, fn){            <-- Map this callback to .md files
  fs.readFile(path, 'utf8', function(err, str){          <-- Read file contents as a string
    if (err) return fn(err);                             <-- Delegate errors to Express
    try {
      var html = md(str);                                <-- Convert string of markdown to HTML
      html = html.replace(/\{([^}]+)\}/g, function(_, name){   <-- Perform brace substitutions
        return options[name] || '';                      <-- Default the value to '' (empty string)
      });
      fn(null, html);                                    <-- Pass rendered HTML to Express
    } catch (err) {
      fn(err);                                           <-- Catch any errors thrown
    }
  });
});
```

The template engine in listing C.1 will allow you to write dynamic markdown views. For example, if you want to greet a user with markdown, it might look like this:

```
# {name}

Greetings {name}! Nice to have you check out our application {appName}.
```

C.1.2 Templates with consolidate.js

The consolidate.js project was created exclusively for Express 3.x, and it provides a single unified API for many of Node's template engines. This means Express 3.x allows you to use more than 14 different template engines out of the box, or if you're working on a library that uses templates, you can take advantage of the wide selection of engines provided by consolidate.js.

For example, Swig is a Django-inspired template engine. It uses tags embedded within HTML to define logic, as shown here:

```
<ul>
  {% for pet in pets %}
    <li>{{ pet.name }}</li>
  {% endfor %}
</ul>
```

Depending on the template engine and your editor's syntax-highlighting support, you'll probably be tempted to have HTML-style engines use the .html extension rather than an extension based on the engine name, such as .swig. You can do this with the Express `app.engine()` method. Once called, when Express renders a .html file, it will use Swig:

```
var cons = require('consolidate');
app.engine('html', cons.swig);
```

The EJS template engine would also likely be mapped to .html because it also uses embedded tags:

```
<ul>
  <% pets.forEach(function(pet){ %>
    <li><%= pet.name %></li>
  <% }) %>
</ul>
```

Some template engines use an entirely different syntax, and it doesn't make sense to map them to .html files. Jade is a good example of this, sporting its own declarative language. Jade could be mapped with the following call:

```
var cons = require('consolidate');
app.engine('jade', cons.jade);
```

For details and a list of supported template engines, visit the consolidate.js project repository at https://github.com/visionmedia/consolidate.js.

C.1.3 Express extensions and frameworks

You might be wondering what options are available for developers who use more structured frameworks, like Ruby on Rails. Express has several options for those situations.

The Express community has developed several higher-level frameworks built on top of Express to provide directory structure, as well as high-level, opinionated features, such as Rails-style controllers. In addition to these frameworks, Express also sports a variety of plugins to extend its functionality.

EXPRESS-EXPOSE

The express-expose plugin can be used to expose server-side JavaScript objects to the client side. For example, if you wanted to expose the JSON representation of the authenticated user, you might invoke `res.expose()` to provide the `express.user` object to your client-side code:

```
res.expose(req.user, 'express.user');
```

EXPRESS-RESOURCE

Another great plugin is express-resource, a resourceful routing plugin used for structured routing.

Routing can be accomplished in many ways, but it boils down to a request method and path, which is what Express provides out of the box. Higher-level concepts can be built on top.

The following example shows how you might define actions for showing, creating, and updating a user resource in a declarative fashion. First, here's what you'd add in app.js:

```
app.resource('user', require('./controllers/user'));
```

And here's what the controller module ./controllers/user.js would look like.

Listing C.2 The user.js resource file

```
exports.new = function(req, res){
  res.send('new user');
};

exports.create = function(req, res){
  res.send('create user');
};

exports.show = function(req, res){
  res.send('show user ' + req.params.user);
};
```

For a full list of plugins, template engines, and frameworks, visit the Express wiki at https://github.com/visionmedia/express/wiki.

C.2 Advanced configuration

In the previous chapter, you learned how to configure Express using the `app.configure()` function, and we covered a number of configuration options. In this section, you'll learn about additional configuration options that you can use to change default behavior and unlock additional functionality.

Table C.1 lists Express configuration options we didn't discuss in chapter 8.

Table C.1 Built-in Express settings

`default engine`	Default template engine used
`views`	View lookup path
`json replacer`	Response JSON manipulation function
`json spaces`	Amount of spaces used to format JSON responses
`jsonp callback`	Support JSONP with `res.json()` and `res.send()`
`trust proxy`	Trust reverse proxy
`view cache`	Cache template engine functions

The `views` configuration option is fairly straightforward and is used to designate where view templates live. When you create an application skeleton on the command line using the `express` command, the `views` configuration option is automatically set to the application's views subdirectory.

Now let's look at a more involved configuration option: `json_replacer`.

C.2.1 Manipulating JSON responses

Suppose you have the `user` object set up with private properties such as an object's `_id`. By default, a call to the `res.send(user)` method would respond with JSON such as `{"_id":123,"name":"Tobi"}`. The `json replacer` is a setting that takes a function that Express will pass to `JSON.stringify()` during `res.send()` and `res.json()` calls.

The standalone Express application in the following listing illustrates how you could use this function to omit properties starting with `"_"` for any JSON response. In this example, the response is now `{"name":"Tobi"}`.

Listing C.3 Using `json_replacer` to control and modify JSON data

```
var express = require('express');
var app = express();

app.set('json replacer', function(key, value){
  if ('_' == key[0]) return;
  return value;
});

var user = { _id: 123, name: 'Tobi' };

app.get('/user', function(req, res){
  res.send(user);
});

app.listen(3000);
```

Note that individual objects, or object prototypes, can implement the `.toJSON()` method. This method is used by `JSON.stringify()` when converting an object to a JSON string. This is a great alternative to the `json_replacer` callback if your manipulations don't apply to every object.

Now that you've learned how to control what data is exposed during JSON output, let's look at how you can fine-tune JSON formatting.

C.2.2 JSON response formatting

The `json spaces` configuration setting affects `JSON.stringify()` calls in Express. This setting indicates the number of spaces to use when formatting JSON as a string.

By default, this method will return compressed JSON, such as `{"name":"Tobi","age":2,"species":"ferret"}`. Compressed JSON is ideal for a production environment, as it reduces the response size. But during development, uncompressed output is much easier to read.

The `json spaces` setting is automatically set to 0 in production; it's set to 2 in development, which produces the following output:

```
{
  "name": "Tobi",
  "age": 2,
  "species": "ferret"
}
```

C.2.3 Trusting reverse proxy header fields

By default, Express internals won't trust reverse proxy header fields in any environment. Reverse proxies are out of scope for this book, but if your application is running behind a reverse proxy, such as Nginx, HAProxy, or Varnish, you'll want to enable `trust proxy` so that Express knows these fields are safe to check.

index

Numerics

A

D

J

K

L

O

P

Q

R

T

U

V

W

RELATED MANNING TITLES

Single Page Web Applications
JavaScript end-to-end
by Michael S. Mikowski and Josh C. Powell

ISBN: 978-1-617290-75-6
432 pages, $44.99
September 2013

Secrets of the JavaScript Ninja
by John Resig and Bear Bibeault

ISBN: 978-1-933988-69-6
392 pages, $39.99
December 2012

Third-Party JavaScript
by Ben Vinegar and Anton Kovalyov

ISBN: 978-1-617290-54-1
288 pages, $44.99
March 2013

jQuery in Action, Second Edition
by Bear Bibeault and Yehuda Katz

ISBN: 978-1-935182-32-0
488 pages, $44.99
June 2010

For ordering information go to www.manning.com